Construction Safety Law, Management, and Technology

CONSTRUCTION SAFETY LAW, MANAGEMENT, AND TECHNOLOGY

HONG KONG EXPERIENCE

LEE Hung-kwong
李鴻光

香港城市大學出版社
City University of Hong Kong Press

ISBN: 978-962-937-432-7

Published by
City University of Hong Kong Press
Tat Chee Avenue
Kowloon, Hong Kong
Website: www.cityu.edu.hk/upress
E-mail: upress@cityu.edu.hk

Printed in Hong Kong

I dedicate this book to my parents

Table of Contents

PART III: EXAMPLES AND APPLICATION IN HONG KONG

PART IV: PRACTITIONER ASSESSMENT TOOLS

List of Tables

List of Figures

List of Acronyms and Abbreviations

ACGIH	American Conference of Governmental Industrial Hygienists
AG	Attorney-General
ALR	accident loss ratio
AOI	accident occurrence index
ASLI	automatic safe load indicator
BS EN	British Standards, European Standards
CEDD	Civil Engineering and Development Department
CICTA	Construction Industry Council Training Academy
CIRIA	Construction Industries Research and Information Association
CONIAC	Construction Industry Advisory Committee
CoP	Code of Practice
CRM	Ccrew Resource Management
CS(S)Rs	Construction Sites (Safety) Regulations
EC	European Declaration of Conformity
EDLoA	equivalent day loss of an accident
EHSRs	Essential Health and Safety Requirements
ETA	event tree analysis
FAC	first aid treatment case
FIUO	Factories and Industrial Undertakings Ordinance
FIURs	Factories and Industrial Undertakings Regulations

FIU(LA&LG)Rs	Factories and Industrial Undertakings (Lifting Appliances and Lifting Gear) Regulations
FIU(SM)R	Factories and Industrial Undertakings (Safety Management) Regulation
FIU(SO&SS)Rs	Factories and Industrial undertakings (Safety Officers and Safety Supervisors) Regulations
FTA	fault tree analysis
GFTs	general failure types
GN	Guidance Notes
HASAW Act	United Kingdom Health and Safety at Work etc. Act
HAZOP	Hazard and Operability study
HK	Hong Kong (also HKSAR)
HM	His/Her Majesty
HRA	health risk assessment
HSE	Health, Safety, and Environment (also SHE or EHS)
IEC	International Electrotechnical Commission
IN	Improvement Notice
IS	industrial safety
ISAS	Independent Safety Audit Scheme
ISO	International Standards Organisation
ISRS	International Safety Rating System
KCTL	Kwai Chung Town Lot
LML	load moment limiter
LN	Legal Notice
LPG	liquefied petroleum gas
LTIC	lost-time injury case
MBMSS	metal-bamboo matrix system scaffolding
MCB	magnetic circuit breaker
MORT	management oversight risk tree
MSDS	material safety data sheet
MTC	medical treatment case
MTR	Mass Transit Railway
OHS	occupational health and safety (also OSH)
OHSAS	Occupational Health and Safety Assessment Series
OSHC	Occupational Safety and Health Council
OSHO	Occupational Safety and Health Ordinance
PE	polyethylene

PIC	permanent bodily injury case
PP	polypropylene
PPE	personal protection equipment
PRC	People's Republic of China
RCCB	residual current circuit breaker
RCI	rated capacity indicator
RCL	rated capacity limiter
RMAA	Repair, Maintenance, Alteration, and Addition (Safety Accreditation)
SAR	Special Administrative Region
SIR	safety investment ratio
SN	Suspension Notice
STEP	Sequentially timed event plotting
SWL	safe working load
TEDL	total equivalent day loss
TLV	threshold limit value
TSI	total safety investment
UK	United Kingdom
UKHSC	United Kingdom Health and Safety Commission
UKHSE	United Kingdom Health and Safety Executive
US	United States
WLL	working load limit

Foreword

I have known Mr LEE Hung-kwong for a long time, since the 1980s when he was a senior civil servant with the Labour Department. He is not only an expert in construction safety but has developed a passion for the subject. He is always willing to share his knowledge and experience with young people and fellow safety practitioners. The Hong Kong Institute of Construction is much indebted to him for his contributions as one of the longest serving part-time lecturers on construction safety.

This book, *Construction Safety Law, Management, and Technology: Hong Kong Experience*, is Mr LEE's third publication on construction safety. It provides a comprehensive overview on the status of construction safety in Hong Kong, with special reference to three accident-prone construction operations, namely tower cranes, mobile cranes, and bamboo scaffolding.

The book is an excellent source of information for study and research on the subject. The Hong Kong construction industry will greatly benefit from the author's indulgence.

CHAN Ka-kui, GBS, JP
Past Chairman of the Construction Industry Council,
2016–2022

Foreword

It is an honour to be invited to write a foreword for LEE Hung-kwong on his new book, *Construction Safety Law, Management, and Technology: Hong Kong Experience*. I am delighted to know that Mr LEE has taken the initiative to write a book for students and practitioners who are working to become safety professionals in the Hong Kong Construction Industry. This industry plays an important role in Hong Kong's economic development. In recent years, we have made massive improvements in construction safety, decreasing the accident incident rate per 1,000 employees from 54.9 in 2009 to 29 in 2019. These figures show that everyone plays a significant role in the effective implementation of safety measures on construction sites.

This book is well organised and is the first to cover three interrelated topics: law, management, and technology. It includes a wide range of both practical and theoretical information. The practical portion includes highly relevant issues experienced by practitioners and captures a unique experience. I find the book incredibly impressive. When I first read it, especially Chapter 10 about bamboo scaffolding, it evoked memories of when I was the Chairman of the Occupational Safety and Health Council (OSHC). OSHC worked together with the Labour Department, insurance sector, trade associations, and labour unions to launch the OSH Star Enterprise Pilot Scheme on Repair, Maintenance, Alteration, and Addition (RMAA) Safety Accreditation. Its aim is to help RMAA enterprises and practitioners to raise their safety awareness through stringent assessment criteria and practical safety training courses, thus lowering the number of accidents in the industry.

I want to take this opportunity to congratulate Mr LEE on his publication and I look forward to seeing more of his work get published.

Ir Wong Tin Cheung, BBS, JP
Vice Chairman of Yau Lee Holdings Limited
Past Chairman of Occupational Safety and Health Council (2011–2017)

Foreword

I am delighted to write this Foreword for LEE Hung-kwong (李鴻光), who is a civil engineer-turned-safety expert. Mr Lee graduated with a degree in Civil Engineering from the Loughborough University of Technology in 1979. Since graduation, he has taken a special interest in construction safety, serving both the public and private sectors.

Since 1985, Mr Lee has served as a key figure in part-time courses at the former Construction Industry Training Authority in Hong Kong. He has been lecturing on the current Construction Industry Council's Construction Safety Officers Course and Safety Auditors Training Course as well as other safety training courses organised by various Hong Kong universities. Through his conscious efforts, he has developed a number of useful training materials on construction safety. The present book, written by Mr Lee, *Construction Safety Law, Management, and Technology: Hong Kong Experience*, can be trusted to be instructive and revealing and is long overdue.

I strongly recommend this book to students who are pursuing a career in construction safety and to different personnel who are conscious of the need to improve safety in construction works.

Professor Tam Chi-ming
FCIOB, FHKIE, FHKICM
Head of Division of Building Science & Technology
City University of Hong Kong

Foreword

I met LEE Hung-kwong as a safety expert in a tower crane defence case in 2007. Since then, I have worked with him to provide safety-related opinions on multiple cases related to safety in construction activities.

Mr LEE has served as a factory inspector in the Hong Kong Labour Department and in the private sector for over 45 years. His working experience has equipped him with the knowledge that enables him to offer valuable safety advice in all the cases I have worked on, much of which has resulted in favourable judgments for my clients.

Mr LEE has quoted my criticism of section 13(1) of the Factories and Industrial Undertakings Ordinance, Chapter 59, in Chapter 5 of this book. I hope that such criticism will one day be settled fairly and justly to the purity of law or to all or any of those involved.

I note that Mr LEE has included his observations, lessons learned, and remarks in cases that are relevant to the construction industry. Some cases quoted were cases that I was involved and am familiar with.

Notably, the law chapters and references in this book are not addressed to lawyers, and I would recommend this book, and these law chapters, in particular to students studying to be safety officers, practising safety officers, site engineers, and construction managers as well as those charged with legal safety duties and responsibilities in construction work.

The importance of the rule of law as applied to safety and health in construction activities is vital to secure a clear understanding of the safety law and its requirements and hence improvement of safety performance in construction work.

Toby R.W. Jenkyn-Jones
Barrister-at-law
South China Chambers, Hong Kong
(The late Mr Toby Jenkyn-Jones saw this foreword in draft form but sadly passed away on 11 September 2018)

Foreword

I have offered myself to write this foreword to my long-standing friend and alumnus LEE Hung-kwong. We first met in the 1970s in the regular dinner meetings held on the first Friday of every month of the Hong Kong branch guild of Loughborough University. Mr LEE was a Loughborough graduate in Civil Engineering in 1979. I was a graduate of Chemical Engineering in 1963.

Professionally, he has been the occupational safety adviser for my thermo-flask business which, since 1940, has been engaged in the manufacturing of products from metals, plastics, glass, etc. We converted our factory building en-block into the first hotel in Kowloon Bay in 2015. It was opened in 2017. Prior to that, we had to relocate the whole manufactory plant to other suitable premises in Kowloon. Throughout these processes, Mr LEE kept an eye on these complicated projects, and his competent occupational health and safety advice was invaluable to their successful completion safely and without undue delay.

As an engineering colleague, I congratulate him on this book, mainly on his vast, deep, and long experiences in occupational health and safety, both as a practitioner and lecturer. Such selfless endeavours will greatly benefit those who are associated with the safety profession. I would urge them to utilise his knowledge wisely and promote safety in the construction industry and make construction sites a safe place to work.

I cannot end this foreword without mentioning our treasured branch guild and some anecdotes from its decades of existence. In the 1970s, when

Lord Pilkington, our Chancellor at that time and the inventor-owner of the famous Pilkington Float Glass Works of St. Helen, Lancashire, visited us with Lady Pilkington, our late alumnus Eric KO Fook-kou entertained them and all guild members at their family penthouse at the Tak Shing Building in Central. In his speech, Lord Pilkington dropped a word of encouragement. He said: "I don't care what you boys do so long as it keeps you together and going." He was referring to some of us who were playing the monthly game of Blackjack. And at that time there were rarely female graduates. Perhaps his comments are why the guild's monthly affair has continued up to today. Seriously speaking, the guild owes more to our collected spirit and desire to see each other. The late Professor David Johns (the Dean of Engineering Faculty of Loughborough University since the 1970s, the Foundation Director of the City Polytechnic of Hong Kong in 1983, and overseer of the design and construction of the now City University of Hong Kong campus) had been very supportive of the Loughborough Alumni group in Hong Kong. In early 1990s, he returned to the United Kingdom for professional advancement but every year he would re-visit Hong Kong. He would try to make sure that his trip could allow him to join us on the first Friday of the month for his favourite game of Bridge with three or four senior boys. A couple of years ago, the present Vice Chancellor, Professor Robert Allison, visited us and threw a dinner party. We were pleasantly surprised to have seven tables of 12 persons each. Apart from six staff members from the University, others were graduates mainly living in Hong Kong including many expatriates working locally. On that occasion, nearly a third of the participants were ladies; what a change!

I take this opportunity to congratulate LEE Hung-kwong on the publication of his third book in the construction safety field. We are both happy and greatly benefited from our higher education at Loughborough.

Philip Leung
Managing Director of Wei Yit Vacuum Flask Manufactory Limited
Owner of Camlux Hotel, Kowloon Bay, Hong Kong

Foreword

LEE Hung-kwong is a Loughborough alumnus of the Hong Kong Branch. He graduated from Loughborough University in 1979. I met Mr LEE when he was appointed as a part-time lecturer in safety subjects at the Hong Kong Polytechnic University in the 1980s. Mr LEE also participated in my research studies in an accident costing in the construction industry.

The accident costing method Mr LEE describes in Chapter 11 "Accident Economics" in this new book is related to the research study I carried out with him previously. The costing model in this chapter looks at accidents in financial terms—for example, how accidents can cost a company and what should be the optimum safety investment to prevent an accident. The study concluded that about 1% of the contract value should be invested in safety, though the government generously recommends 2% (probably a guess without basis). Looking forward, I would like to recommend the existing 2%, which is currently devoted to safety, be split into 1% on safety and 1% on quality and environment.

This textbook, to my knowledge, is one of the first attempts to cover three topics in construction safety: law, management, and technology. It is certainly beneficial to both students and practitioners who are concerned with safety-at-work in Hong Kong. I would particularly recommend this book to students taking construction safety courses and those taking building construction or civil engineering courses. In the future, they will have the roles and responsibilities to manage safety on construction activities.

Congratulations to Mr LEE!

Dr TANG Siu-lam
BSc (University of Hong Kong),
MSc (National University of Singapore),
PhD (Loughborough, United Kingdom), FICE

Foreword

The last 50 years have witnessed a boom in the Hong Kong construction industry with the completion of numerous and varied mega projects. However, they were not achieved without paying a price. In the 1980s and 1990s, the accident figures were high, with a peak of over 300 cases per 1,000 workers. With this in their minds and hearts, the Government and stakeholders have taken pains to transform the safety approach from prescriptive to regulatory, effectively minimising the accident rate to 30 per 1,000 workers. Compared with other developed cities, there is still ample room for the industry to improve.

The effort to help lower the accident rate is multi-fold, and a lot can be learned from the focal aspects of operations, technology, and management. To equip oneself as a good safety practitioner and to enhance the performance of the whole construction company, there is a common and pressing problem in finding highly relevant writings on the precious experience gained over decades by the industry in Hong Kong.

LEE Hung-kwong, currently an Adjunct Associate Professor at The University of Hong Kong, has over 45 years of splendid experience in construction safety. During his early years, he worked in the Labour Department, enforcing the regulations being properly observed on construction sites. Later, he was appointed as a safety consultant of a large international firm. For the last two decades or more, he has been working as an independent consultant to advise contractors in accident prevention as well as firms that are involved in legal disputes in construction safety.

In this book, LEE Hung-kwong not only presents his enriched experience in audits and legal proceedings but shares his unique insights in enhancing safety in construction. Well covered are the reasons behind and the preventive measures of those accidents typically found and frequently occurring in Hong Kong, including falling from height, the use of cranes, and the collapse of bamboo scaffolding. On the management side, various audits of safety management and legal cases are also narrated in detail. This book, besides recording the author's own work, vividly depicts the development in safety measures in the Hong Kong construction industry during the last half a century. Those who are currently involved in, and those who have a plan to join, the construction safety arena should find this reference book a very useful one.

Ir Dr S.W. Poon
Adjunct Professor,
Department of Real Estate and Construction
and Former Deputy Head, Department of Real Estate
and Construction, The University of Hong Kong
and Former Chairman of Safety Specialist Committee,
The Hong Kong Institution of Engineers

Foreword

The author of this book, LEE Hung-kwong, is renowned as an expert on safety in the construction industry. I have had the privilege to work with the author on numerous occasions when he had been engaged as an expert in both giving evidence in court and in writing opinions for litigation purposes.

The author brings to this book his considerable experience in this area of expertise. The book contains a mass of materials. He presents construction safety law, management, and technology in a way that is easily and clearly accessible to both specialist and lay readers. Specifically, this book is an exposition of the law of construction safety, discussing both its theory and practice, and meets the needs of students who undertake occupational safety and health courses at any level, department officers, registered safety officers, and legal practitioners in the area of construction safety law. In the first chapter of this book, the author gives an introduction to the history of construction safety in Hong Kong, followed by a discussion of the substance of construction safety law. It covers the major construction safety legislation and subsidiary regulations in Hong Kong, including a detailed analysis with full reference to case law. With the increasing number of prosecutions in construction safety cases, this is an essential read for anyone engaged in any way with the subject.

Last but not least, the effectiveness of construction safety law is never straightforward. Its enemies rely on ignorance and complacency. I hope this book will serve as an inspiration to all who are dedicated to the prevention and reduction of accidents on construction worksites.

Peter T.K. Wong

Barrister-at-law

Trinity Chambers, Hong Kong

Foreword

I met LEE Hung-kwong (李鴻光先生) in a workshop session about occupational safety in 2011. Our partnership and friendship started when we discovered Mr Lee's safety concept perfectly coincided with our company's motto — "people-oriented service to society" (以人為本、服務社會). Mr LEE has been contributing and devoting his time and effort to the construction safety in Hong Kong for the past few decades, and this book is his way of sharing his practical experience and knowledge with practitioners in the construction industry. It provides unique practical insight towards the safety management of the construction industry in Hong Kong with reference to different practical cases and related legal issues in construction safety. It provides a comprehensive analysis of the law, management, and technology which is vital to construction safety in Hong Kong as well as globally.

As the senior management of China Geo-Engineering Corporation (CGC), I deeply believe that inculcating a good safety culture is the best way of achieving "zero accidents" in construction work. Therefore, since the beginning of 2012, CGC has initiated a series of ongoing safety promotional campaigns, including Monthly "Co-workers' Caring Home Visit", Quarterly Sub-Contractors Safety Workshop Gatherings, and Annual Safety Fun Day. Throughout these activities, CGC is working to create a strong corporate safety culture and ensure that safety information is well disseminated from the top management to the frontline staff, the events' participants, their family members, and eventually to the entire community.

With Mr LEE's sustainable effort and support in promoting occupational safety, we are striving to collaborate and maintain a safe working environment, as well as disseminating the importance and methods of good occupational safety practices in the construction industry. This publication is an example of a helpful contribution in construction safety. It will be a good reference for safety practitioners. Mr LEE — Congratulations!

Ir LEE Chi-tong Tom (李志棠先生)
Director of China Geo-Engineering Corporation

Foreword

LEE Hung-kwong, the author of this book, has been providing safety consulting services to the Chevalier Construction Company for years. His expertise in occupational safety in construction work adds value to our safety management systems. Chevalier is a group of companies mainly engaged in building and engineering construction works. It was established in 1970. One of its associate companies, Lam Woo & Co. Ltd, has a history traceable back to the late nineteenth century in Hong Kong. Chevalier group has witnessed the changes in the building industry and has proudly committed to serving in construction for more than a century and beyond.

In this book, Mr LEE explains the evolution of safety-at-work in the construction industry over the past 70 years as well as the rationale for these changes and the enactment of related safety legislation. For example, Chapter 5 describes how managers in construction should respond to the general duties of both employers and employees. In particular, the safe system of work mandates comprehensive risk identification and assessment for construction activities. It creates the whole framework of effective and imaginative organization for safety. The chapter also highlights legal cases and the insight that can be gained from them.

The bamboo scaffolding chapter (Chapter 10) attracts my particular interest as it is unique in the construction world. The technique is inherited from Guangdong Province in China. By the turn of the twentieth century, there were three major trades in the local building market — namely, masonry, carpentry, and bamboo scaffolding. While masonry is fading from the industry and carpentry has experienced great changes due to mechanization and industrialization, bamboo scaffolding is still a common practice, which depends on traditional craftsmanship. This chapter allows readers to understand the trade practice in greater depth and how safety legislation promotes preserving its heritage.

I strongly recommend this book, not only to students pursuing construction safety courses but also to construction managers, who are accountable to regulatory authorities, for providing a healthy and safe working environment in construction work.

LAU Ho-kwong
Operations Director
Chevalier (Construction) Company Limited

Preface

The construction industry has been identified as one of the most dangerous industries in developing and developed economies, and the construction industry in the Hong Kong Special Administrative Region (SAR) is of no exception. It has for many years been responsible for the highest annual figures of both fatal and serious injury accidents. Such accident statistics are neither enviable nor acceptable.

This book on construction safety focuses on safety and health at building and civil engineering construction sites and deals with important topics under safety law, safety management, and safety technology. It is written for students taking occupational safety and health courses, for safety practitioners in the construction industry, and those concerned with promoting occupational safety and health on construction sites. The insights provided are the culmination of my 50 years as a health, safety, and environmental practitioner in both the government and private sectors of Hong Kong's construction industry. It also contains some of the lecturing topics I have delivered at various universities and training institutes over the years. It is my hope that the facts, examples, and opinions I have provided in the following pages will benefit all those charged with managing safety and health on construction sites.

HOW TO USE THIS BOOK

This book is designed to help students and safety practitioners access important information to help guide their decisions on construction sites. Each part and chapter has easy to digest introductions and summaries that were written to condense the other information presented in the main body of the chapter. Headings are used to break all of the information into easily identified sections. The end of each chapter concludes with a set of citations readers may wish to refer to for more information and a list of discussion questions. Notably, definitions and the details of legal cases are flagged using icons in the margin (a construction/traffic cone and a gavel, respectively) for easy identification.

Definitions

Legal cases

WHAT TO EXPECT

This book focuses on three interdependent disciplines: law, technology, and management. These encompass the essentials in "hard" and "soft" power in worksite accident prevention. The deliberate and innovative prioritisation of management and organisational techniques is emphasised.

■ Part I: An Introduction to Construction Safety

This introductory section provides some historical context and outlines the basic principles required to understand the rest of the book.

Chapter 1 gives a historical background of the administrative framework of safety, health, and welfare at work in Hong Kong. It highlights particular aspects of the field from the city's time as a British Colony (before 1997) up to its present status as an SAR of the People's Republic of China (PRC). Notably, worksite administration in Hong Kong has benefited from its relationship with the United Kingdom throughout history, beginning in the Industrial Revolution. Various terms and concepts essential to the field are also explained in this chapter.

Chapter 2 discusses the basic principles for managing safety and health at construction sites. These principles "bang the drum" in terms of being effective in improving and raising safety standards and preventing accidents. These principles should be applied in both the boardroom and the worksite. Leadership and commitment are priorities in the competitive construction industry. Safety and health at work is good for business. If applied successfully, these principles invoke good business management.

Chapter 3 highlights a list of applicable ordinances and subsidiary regulations that deal specifically with construction activities, including the Factories and Industrial Undertakings Ordinance, Chapter 59 (FIUO)—namely, section 4 (detailing the power of officers), section 6A (which covers general duties), section 7A (which covers the Code of Practice (CoP) on Safety Management), section 13 (detailing the liability of proprietors), section 18 (explaining the limits of what is considered reasonably practicable), the Construction Sites (Safety) Regulations, and applicable Factories and Industrial Undertakings Regulations (FIURs)—as well as the Occupational Safety and Health Ordinance (OSHO), Chapter 509 (sections 9 and 10).

Part II: The Legal Stance on Construction Safety

This section includes four chapters: one that provides a general overview of the legal enforcement and repercussions of applicable construction safety laws, and three others that detail particular legislation and the legal cases related to each. Notably, these legal discussions and case descriptions are meant to be a reference for students of occupational safety and health as well as safety practitioners, many of whom may or may not have studied law in depth. As these individuals have special responsibilities, including providing advice on legal compliance in construction work, a general understanding of these laws and their application is necessary. The author has acted as a safety expert in some of the cited cases for the prosecution or defence and provides apt reflection on each of them. Thus, while other reference texts should be referred to for more in-depth knowledge of the legal cases, these chapters can be used as a guide.

Chapter 4 provides a general discussion of legal hierarchy, enforcement, and repercussions for non-compliance with the legislation described in Chapter 3. It explains the underlying legal aspects of the

FIUO and OSHO, codes of practice, and guidance notes as well as improvement and suspension notices and the role of safety officers and experts during a prosecution. Another key aspect of this chapter is an explanation of "who is responsible" for worksite safety. Various sections of this chapter also include case examples and explanations. This chapter acts as an introduction to the following three chapters, which focus on breaches of particular legislation.

Chapter 5 focuses on breaches of the FIUO, Chapter 59, particularly those involving sections 6A and 13. It compares the general duties described in section 6A to those in the United Kingdom Health and Safety at Work etc. Act (HASAW Act). These general duties impose the concept of self-regulation and the safe system of work. Since their establishment, these legal requirements have accumulated the highest number of trialled cases at Magistrates' Courts, High Courts, and the Court of Final Appeal. This chapter also includes updated case laws and judicial decisions, which are summarised for reference and include the lessons learned. All the court judgments are described to raise the awareness of proprietors and contractors of the safe systems of work for construction activities. These judgments leave no doubt as to the legal safety requirements at construction sites.

Chapter 6 is dedicated to breaches in the Construction Sites (Safety) Regulations (CS(S)Rs), including a thorough assessment of Regulation 38, which is essential and one of the most widely known regulations. This regulation applies to workers who fall, accidentally or otherwise, and sustain bodily injuries while working at height or above ground. The number of court trials involving this regulation exceeds that of all other regulations. This is not altogether surprising as workers operating at height account for the largest number of fatalities on construction sites. Staircases, floor edges, temporary floor openings, lift shaft openings, void spaces at chutes, and external faces of buildings and structures under construction as well as the slopes and sudden drops surrounding the sites are the most dangerous areas. Equipment, such as suspended working platforms (gondolas), scaffolding (bamboo, metal, or mixed), ladders, mobile working platforms, makeshift platforms, etc., associated with a significant number of accidents is highlighted in the chapter along with notable safety requirements that can help prevent accidents.

These requirements are associated with cited cases. In this chapter, these cases are digested to help examine the lessons that safety practitioners, proprietors, or contractors should learn and benefit from. The chapter also includes some key definitions relevant to the construction industry as well as an explanation of "strict liability" and practical options for defence during prosecution.

Chapter 7 concerns the individual sets of FIURs that are applicable to construction activities. Descriptions and relevant legal cases are included for regulations specific for construction work, including those concerning safety officers and supervisors, lifting appliances and lifting gear, notification of occupational diseases, quarry safety, blasting by abrasives, woodworking machinery, confined spaces, abrasive wheels, work in compressed air, spraying of flammable liquids, cartridge-operated fixing tools, protection of eyes, electricity, asbestos, dangerous substances, noise at work, suspended working platforms, safety management, loadshifting machinery, and gas welding and flame cutting. Some have specific cases cited, while other sections (particularly those without any reported breaches) focus on what safety practitioners should know about that regulation to continue avoiding repercussions.

Part III: Examples and Application in Hong Kong

Moving past the legislative and legal sectors, this section uses the specific examples of tower cranes, mobile cranes, and bamboo scaffolding to exemplify safety measures practitioners and students should be aware of in the Hong Kong SAR.

Chapter 8 provides a description of tower cranes, including their basic mechanics, principles, and safe use. Tower cranes (of various brand and model) are indispensable on every construction site in Hong Kong, a place where high-rise buildings are constantly under construction to meet the incessant housing demands of the population. Any accident arising from the installation, alteration, or subsequent dismantling of a tower crane can be disastrous and often attracts significant media attention. Several general cases are described along with a more in-depth study of one particular example case. This chapter also highlights examples of real-life error-forcing conditions and how to mitigate such risks.

Chapter 9, like the previous chapter, deals with the mechanics and principles of another type of lifting appliance: mobile cranes. Mobile cranes are extensively used on construction sites across Hong Kong, and any accident involving a mobile crane is likely to draw as much attention as that involving a tower crane. Examples of such accidents are given, both in Hong Kong and overseas. Many of the factors contributing to mobile crane accidents are shared along with how safety can be enhanced. This includes a list of points to check during an accident investigation involving a mobile crane.

Chapter 10 is dedicated to bamboo scaffolding, a builder's heritage which is commonly seen on iconic buildings under construction. Unlike other parts of the world, Hong Kong has not banned the use of bamboo scaffolding. It is typically used for constructing temporary working platforms for buildings, building maintenance, sign-board installation, building decoration, and renovation work. Bamboo scaffolding has several advantages over metal scaffolding, many of which are related to its weight and flexibility. However, it can only be set up and dismantled by highly trained and skilled workers. The introduction of scaffolding that combines both bamboo and metal is an innovative approach for setting up temporary working platforms. These two materials offer synergies through their different characteristics. However, their safe use together may require a novel practical code of practice. This chapter details the structural basics of bamboo scaffolding along with safe use guidelines. Various accidents involving scaffolding are described.

Part IV: Practitioner Assessment Tools

This final section describes practitioner assessment tools related to accident economics and safety auditing.

Chapter 11 discusses accident economics as a cost-benefit approach to understanding the benefits of establishing effective safety management systems. Two accident costing methods are proposed in this chapter to aid construction managers who are concerned with the economic effects of site accidents. Both have been extensively researched regarding their application in the Hong Kong construction environment. Accident costing is an essential means to reinforce good safety management as sound business management.

Chapter 12 outlines two safety management system audit schemes. These schemes give site managers options to assess (or reassess) their safety and health management systems. Safety auditing is considered one of the most powerful tools to secure certainty and enhance safety on a worksite. The two audits schemes described in this chapter are suitable for construction companies that wish to not only comply with the requirements under the Factories and Industrial Undertakings (Safety Management) Regulation but desire continual improvement in their safety management systems. The role of an auditor, and thus the need to choose an auditor wisely, is described. They play an essential role in the auditing process as their judgement will be used to propose steps for improvement.

CLOSING WORDS AND ACKNOWLEDGEMENTS

Following a final summary of the text, a brief discussion about what I have gained personally from my experience, and my hopes regarding the future directions of the construction safety field in Hong Kong and globally, I have also included a list of additional references in the bibliography.

I am grateful to my former colleagues, L.M. Leung, Michael C.M. Leung, and the late Winky W.K. Chan as well as the late Toby R.W. Jenkyn-Jones (barrister-at-law) for their constructive comments and suggestions on the legal chapters. I also offer thanks to David M.C. Ho, K.C. Chan, Dr S.Y. Chan, C.W. Chan, Mandy S.W. Chan, Andreas Ganahl, Benjamin Ertl, Henry Lam, C.Y. Law, C.M. Chiu, Eric C.Y. Lee, and Kelvin Lo for their contributions. Finally, I am indebted to the City University of Hong Kong Press and in particular Abby Manthey, my editor, who has made an infinite editorial effort during the production of this book.

LEE Hung-kwong (李鴻光)
September 2022

PART I

AN INTRODUCTION TO CONSTRUCTION SAFETY

LEARNING OBJECTIVES

Part I provides an overview of the construction industry in Hong Kong, including a description of its historical and recent development as well as the principles of health, safety, and environment management and the relevant legislation. Upon completion of Part I, one should be able to:

1. Offer a historical account of the development of Hong Kong's safety-at-work procedures before and after the Second World War in general and for the construction industry in particular;
2. Describe the role of the government in the promotion of industrial safety;
3. Outline the legislation related to the construction industry;
4. Discuss the principles of health, safety, and environment management applicable to construction organisations; and
5. List applicable construction safety laws.

Understanding the history of the construction industry as well as the evolution of the relevant safety and health legislation is essential for all stakeholders in a construction project, including safety officers, contractors, company management, on-site workers, legislators, etc.

"Employment of women, young persons and children in certain industries"

– Factories and Workshops Ordinance (No. 18 of 1937)

"To amend the law relating to factories and industrial undertakings and to the employment of women, young persons and children therein"

– Factories and Industrial Undertakings Ordinance, Chapter 59 (1955)

1 The History of Construction Safety in Hong Kong

INTRODUCTION

This chapter outlines the history of safety and health at work with reference to its laws and its regulatory body in Hong Kong. It focuses on four phases: before 1945, after 1945, towards 1997, and after 1997. The roles of various driving forces underlying the implementation and subsequent amendments to these construction safety laws—namely, the regulatory body and safety practitioners—are also described.

THE HISTORY OF CONSTRUCTION SAFETY IN HONG KONG

Before 1945

Similar to the first United Kingdom Health and Morals of Apprentices Act in 1802 that was established to protect young children in textile mills, the first historical legislation concerning safety, health, and welfare in colonial Hong Kong focused on the protection of children in certain industries. This statute was the Industrial Employment of Children Ordinance of 1922 (No. 22 of 1922). Under this regulation, a "child" refers to a person under 15 years of age. A Protector and multiple Inspectors of juvenile workers were subsequently appointed to enforce these regulations. In the Ordinance, 11 regulations were prescribed including:

> No person shall employ any child under the age of 10 years in any factory.
>
> No person shall employ any child under the age of 12 years in carrying coal or building material or debris.
>
> No child shall be allowed to carry any weight which is unreasonably heavy having regard to the child's age and physical development, and no child whatever shall be allowed to carry load exceeding forty catties in weight.

These regulations were perhaps the first traceable introduction of legislation to protect children employed in the industrial environment of Hong Kong. Protection was extended to women and young persons in 1929 via the Industrial Employment of Women, Young Persons, and Children Amendment Ordinance. This Ordinance was later amended (No. 27 of 1932 and No. 30 of 1936) to provide further protection to workers.

In 1937, the Factories and Workshops Ordinance was enacted. The Protector, who was the Chairman of the Urban Council, or any person appointed by the Governor to be the Protector of Labour was responsible for the administration of this Ordinance. Inspectors, who enforced this Ordinance and its associated regulations, were known as Inspectors or Assistant Inspectors of Labour, Factories and Workshops. To further ensure that the employment of women, young persons, and children in industrial undertakings was regulated, factories and workshops had to be registered. Machinery guarding in factories was also required to be reported, and simple fire prevention, as well as means of escape from factories and workshops in tenement buildings, were stipulated.

Notably, the industrial activities in Hong Kong before the Second World War were limited, and the city was predominantly considered a trading port. This resulted in legislation being mainly confined to the conditions for and protection of children, women, and young persons engaged in employment.

After 1945

Things changed in Hong Kong after the Second World War. B.C.K. Hawkins was appointed the first Commissioner of Labour with the title of Labour Officer. According to the Labour Office Report, covering the period from 1 May 1946 to 31 March 1947, the office records containing information regarding industrial accidents up to that point had been destroyed during the war. Thus, tracking this information started anew. The registration of factories and workshops re-commenced in January 1946 under the new Labour Department. Of the three Europeans and six locals that made up the pre-war Inspectorate (all on secondment from the Health Inspectorate), only two Europeans and four locals were available and returned to their positions. By the end of March 1947, there were 978 factories and workshops in operation, and the estimated number of persons employed by them was 33,000 males and 18,700 females. A total of 5,065 inspections were carried out in that period.

The notable post-war rise in industrial development also led to an increase in industrial accidents and diseases worldwide. Hong Kong was no exception. The British Factory Inspectorate in the United Kingdom was undoubtedly asked to render assistance through the Home Office in London by various colonies of the British Empire where industries were developing. This continued association with the British Factory Inspectorate after the war is reflected in the Annual Department Report (1951–1952) written by the Commissioner of Labour, which specifies that "department training of the Inspectorate based on International Labour Organisation's publications, the United Kingdom Factories Act and pamphlets and other publications obtained by courtesy of Her Majesty's (HM) Chief Inspector of Factories in the United Kingdom, was continued". Similar writings were recorded in subsequent annual reports throughout the early 1950s.

While Hong Kong was reinstating its industrial regulations after the war, a large number of refugees with capital and technical know-how—principally in the textile manufacturing field—were also fleeing into the city from Mainland China. Moreover, as these industries were established, the Commonwealth Preference Tariff enabled Hong Kong to export textiles at competitive prices. In 1951, the international embargo on the export of strategic goods to Mainland China further enhanced the rapid growth of local industries. As industrial development continued, additional staff were required to enforce legislation and ensure safety. For example, in 1953, the Labour Department began to recruit new inspectors who were sent to the Sanitation Department for training. These qualified public health inspectors were then required to carry out health, safety, and welfare inspections at various industrial establishments.

The training syllabus used by the United Kingdom Royal Society of Health to educate public health inspectors included courses on a wide variety of topics, including elementary human anatomy and physiology, statutes and orders, water, air, ventilation and lighting, inspection and administration, collection and disposal of excreta and refuse, disposal of the dead, port sanitation, prevention of infectious diseases, health education, insect pests and other vermin, birth/death rate and rate of infant mortality, food and meat inspection, licensing of food establishments, etc. As industry began to flourish, the Factories and Workshops Ordinance was re-titled in 1955 as the Factories and Industrial Undertakings Ordinance (FIUO). One of the main reasons for this renaming was to reflect Hong Kong's willingness to meet its obligations under the International Labour Organisation Conventions. The FIUO was also updated to describe the scope of the legislation more accurately. It was modelled on the 1937 United Kingdom Factories Act with modifications that reflected local specifications. As a result, the title of the Inspectors was changed to "Labour Inspectors".

The updated FIUO was divided into an ordinance and regulations. The ordinance dealt with the appointment and power of the Inspectorate, the factory registration system, and the liabilities and penalties of factory proprietors. The regulations dealt specifically with the employment of children, women, and young persons (13 sections), reporting accidents and dangerous occurrences (2 sections), accident prevention (3 sections), prevention of and escape from fire (8 sections), and hygiene (8 sections). The FIUO generally recognised that to cope with the rapid growth of complex and diverse industries in the city, more technical knowledge was required for the public health inspectors. In 1956, HM Factory Inspector Arthur Quinn, who was also a barrister-at-law, was seconded from the United Kingdom Ministry of Labour and National Service and appointed as the Industrial Training and Safety Officer to train existing Labour Inspectors. Three major changes then followed. First, the practice of sending recruits to be qualified as public health inspectors was abandoned. Second, the need to send local inspectors to the United Kingdom for advanced technological training was realised. Third, the duties of Labour Inspectors relating to safety and health were refined. The Inspectors sent for the overseas course were given attachments with HM Factory Inspectors in industrial districts. The purpose of this was to provide trainees with practical insight into the standards of safety and health in British industries and the means the Inspectors used to attain them.

In subsequent years, to further enhance their expertise, Hong Kong Factory Inspectors were sent overseas for advanced safety courses with the British Safety Council and universities on industrial health, hygiene, and administration in addition to advanced safety training in Australia, New Zealand, and Canada. Senior members began to attend world congresses on the prevention of industrial accidents and diseases. In 1964, the then Labour Inspectorate was split into two separate classes: the Labour Inspectorate and the Factory Inspectorate. The Labour Inspectorate was responsible for enforcing regulations concerning the work hours of women and young persons as well as child employment in factories. The Factory Inspectorate was responsible for the enforcement of technical regulations concerning safety and health for all industrial workers. Thus, it was the Factory Inspectorate, with its title the same as their British counterpart, which looked after the safety and health of workers, and while it was 130 years after the first four inspectors were appointed in 1833 in Britain, the association of the Hong Kong Inspectorate with the British Inspectorate continued.

In the 1960s, HM Factory Inspector Frank Phillips arrived to take up the post of Industrial Safety Training Officer followed by the appointment of A.H. Carter to head the Industrial Safety Training Centre, which was established in 1967. In 1970, Mr R.K. Christy (a former HM Chief Factory Inspector) and Miss Anne Bettenson (a former HM Deputy Chief Factory Inspector of the United Kingdom Factory Inspectorate) made a brief visit to Hong Kong. During this time, newly recruited Assistant Factory Inspectors were sent to the Hong Kong Technical College for six months to study building technology, electrical engineering, mechanical engineering, and textile technology. In 1973, HM Factory Inspector Anthony Linehan* arrived and spent three years critically evaluating the Hong Kong industrial working environment and submitted a full report in 1976, titled "Report on the Industrial Undertaking Units of

* Anthony Linehan became Chief Factory Inspector, Health and Safety Executive, United Kingdom, in 1988.

the Labour Department and on Related Matters of Industrial Safety and Health". His report touched on areas of organisation and staffing of the Factory Inspectorate, including recruitment, training and examination, training of Inspectors after probation, the establishment of specialist support services, legislation, the industrial safety training centre, industrial health, non-government involvement in industrial safety and health, and accident notification and statistics. The report established the role the Factory Inspectorate would play in the years that followed.

During the three years Linehan was writing his report, various legislation was enacted. In 1973, for example, the Construction Sites (Safety) Regulations, which addressed the rising annual fatal and serious injury accidents on construction sites, were introduced. This set of regulations was brought into operation in May 1974. The FIUO regulations related to work in compressed air were enacted a year later in 1975 to deal with the introduction of compressed air for the construction of the first mass transit railway (MTR) tunnels in Hong Kong. In the meantime, in January 1975, the United Kingdom Health and Safety Executive (UKHSE) was formed, replacing the HM Factory Inspectorate. During this change, Audrey Pittom, then HM Deputy Chief Inspector of Factories and an active participant in the creation of the HSE, insisted that the title of the Health and Safety at Work etc. Act use the couplet "health and safety" as opposed to "safety and health". From this point on, the standard terms "occupational health and safety" (OHS) and "occupational safety and health" (OSH) have been used interchangeably and have the same meaning.

Following Linehan's 1976 report, John Wood, on secondment from the HM Factory Inspectorate/HSE, became the first office holder of the Chief Factory Inspector post in 1977. He served for about two years. In 1985, Stuart Nattrass, head of the Construction Industry Advisory Committee (CONIAC) of the UKHSE, visited the Hong Kong Factory Inspectorate and shared his experience. As the chairman of the CONIAC and a prominent figure in the construction safety industry in the United Kingdom, his views were exceedingly helpful in shaping regulation in the field. Further, in 1988, Brian Burke, a retired Health and Safety Executive Areas Director, also visited the Inspectorate for three months as Labour Adviser. Mr Burke produced another report for the Factory Inspectorate, titled "A Review of the Impact of Changing Circumstances on the Existing

Policies, Procedures, and Performance Standards of the Factory Inspectorate Division", moving the program forward and upward. Until 1978, the Factory Inspectorate, which administered the FIUO, called itself the Industrial Undertakings Unit. The formation of the Occupational Safety and Health Council (OSHC) in 1988 under a separate Ordinance was also the result of the implementation of the Linehan report.

From 1945 onward, safety and health at work were a primary focus as industrial activities increased in Hong Kong. In fact, in the 1970s and 1980s, following incessant publicity, the term "industrial safety," abbreviated IS, was widely recognised.

Towards 1997

With regard to safety on factory premises and on building and engineering construction sites, 1989 was a significant year for a number of reasons. The FIUO Amendment was enacted by the Hong Kong Legislative Council on 15 December 1989. This enactment was related to the rise in reported accidents that year, with the official safety record showing 26,399 construction accidents in total — 59 of which were fatal. Thus, the incidence rate was 374 per 1,000 workers in 1989. In other words, more than one in three construction workers was involved in a reportable accident that year. A reportable accident, defined under the Employees' Compensation Ordinance, Cap. 282, is an event leading to an employee being off duty from work for more than three days because of an injury sustained during their employment.

The events of 1989 brought safety legislation in Hong Kong into a new dimension. They also prompted the importation of the United Kingdom Health and Safety at Work etc. Act, 1974 (HASAW Act), which focuses on two types of industrial undertakings: factory premises and construction sites. The HASAW Act positively promotes safety and health at work. The key requirement is to develop a sound safety policy and the necessary organisation and arrangement for its implementation. It calls for a total commitment to safety and health at the top levels and the deliberate application of management and organisational skills.

During the introduction of the HASAW Act in Hong Kong, James D.G. Hammer, another former HM Chief Factory Inspector, visited the city in January 1990 and shared his views and experience with enforcing the Act in the United Kingdom. In the following years, additional insight was gained during visits by David Eves and Adrian Ellis who were senior members of the United Kingdom Health and Safety Commission (UKHSC) and the UKHSE. Notably, in addition to being a Deputy Director General in the UKHSE, Mr Eves was also the HM Chief Factory Inspector from 1985–1988 and 1992–2002.

Unfortunately, the HASAW Act did not bring any discernible improvement in safety on construction sites in Hong Kong. Indeed, in 1993, 12 people were killed by a free-falling passenger hoist on a construction site. This event caused all the stakeholders to re-examine safety administration. In July 1995, the Government published a territory-wide consultation paper reviewing industrial safety in Hong Kong that, among other things, recommended changes in industrial safety strategies ranging from enforcement to promoting safety management. One notable recommendation proposed was the establishment of a safety management system in each organisation that covers six main areas: company policy, safety plan, safety committee, safety audit or review, general safety training, and special safety training. To facilitate implementation by contractors, these six main areas of safety management were developed into 14 process elements in the FIU (Safety Management) Regulation.

After 1997

On 1 July 1997, Hong Kong returned to the People's Republic of China (PRC) as a Special Administrative Region (SAR), adopting the "One Country, Two Systems" policy. At the same time, LEE Kai-fat, an administrative officer, was posted as Deputy Commissioner to head the Occupational Safety and Health Branch in the Labour Department. Mr LEE was assigned the role of a change manager, an administrative position that was the first of its kind. Organisational changes then followed. For example, on 3 January 1998, the title of Factory Inspector was changed to Occupational Safety Officer after over 30 years of use. Further, enactment of the Occupational Safety and Health Ordinance (OSHO), Cap. 509, also brought workers in non-industrial sectors under the protection of the safety and health at work laws for the first time. This particular legislation covers occupational safety and health at work in practically all fields of economic activity, both industrial and non-industrial, and includes workers in offices, commercial premises, schools, hospitals, clinics, laboratories, and other workplaces. It prescribed standards for general working environments as well as specific workplace safety and health recommendations. The first regulation of the OSHO, for example, describes requirements for fire precautions, working environment, hygiene, first aid, and manual handling operations. The regulation came into operation on 1 January 1998, with the exception of the manual handling operations requirements that came into effect on 1 July 1998. These changes were again modelled from the British safety and health administration. Thus, historically speaking, construction safety in the region has been based on that of the United Kingdom from its simplest form to the total protection of the workforce in all sectors.

On 24 November 1999, the FIU (Safety Management) Regulation was passed by Hong Kong's Legislative Council. This set of regulations requires contractors or proprietors of construction sites, shipyards, factories, and other designated industrial undertakings (i.e., those involved in the generation and transmission of electricity, town gas, or liquefied petroleum gas as well as in the handling of containers) that have 100 or more workers as well as construction projects with contract values of HK$100 million or more to adopt the first 10 of the 14 process elements of the safety management system and to carry out safety audits. In contrast, construction sites and the abovementioned industrial undertakings employing 50 to 99 workers were only required to adopt the first 8 of the 14 process elements of the safety management system and to carry out safety reviews, which are less stringent than safety audits. The introduction of mandatory safety management systems in designated industrial undertakings through legislation is an important milestone in the safety and health laws in the Hong Kong SAR. Current legislation and regulations relevant to construction work are explained in Chapter 3.

THE DRIVING FORCES OF CONSTRUCTION SAFETY LEGISLATION

The regulatory body

Up to the early 1970s, the Factory Inspectorate of the Labour Department was only responsible for enforcing safety and health legislation for factories and workshops. In the mid-1970s, enforcement was extended to construction sites and work. Furthermore, after 1997, safety and health legislation was extended to non-industrial sectors, and in 2017, there were more than 400 officers responsible for inspecting factories and construction sites as well as other designated industrial undertakings and service establishments. They are deployed in various geographical divisions throughout the territory, with separate divisions looking after building and engineering construction activities.

Education

As the role of these inspectors has increased over time, the need for more technically trained inspectors has also increased. The minimum entry qualification for trainee inspectors in the 1960s was an Advanced Level pass in physics or chemistry, and the minimum age for entry was 21. However, in the late 1990s, some polytechnic diploma holders were recruited into the inspectorate even though the minimum entry qualification is a higher diploma in relevant subjects. Industrial experience, though preferred, was not essential.

The entry qualifications have gone largely unchanged since their establishment. With more university graduates coming into the job market, a reassessment of these entry qualifications is long overdue, and changes are required to keep abreast of the higher education levels of entrepreneurs and industrial workers. This includes limiting entry to those with at least a first-level degree in science or engineering, with preference going to those with post-graduate degrees. The Hong Kong SAR should reference the recruitment qualifications of developed countries, including the United Kingdom, Singapore, and Malaysia, to further refine their own policies.

Prosecutions

The regulatory body is responsible for bringing prosecutions against proprietors and operators who blatantly fail to comply with regulations. Transparency in the enforcement policy is essential, and the policy should be proportional, consistent, risk-based, and drive accountability. Unfortunately, the prosecution policy is not transparent, and breaches are often not prosecuted equally. This inequality is also notable in terms of case priority. While priority should be given to prosecuting high-risk breaches, the lack of transparency has led to minor infractions receiving unwarranted attention. As prosecution policies have not been publicly announced with regard to breaches of safety and health laws, the public is largely unaware of how breaches are treated. Outsider observations have, however, linked investigations of fatal accidents and serious bodily injuries with subsequent prosecutions if breaches of relevant regulations are detected or inferred. Indeed, prosecutions are often only conducted after serious accidents have occurred—a practice that should be exchanged for prosecuting breaches prior to an accident to enhance the credibility of the regulatory body. These prosecution cases are first heard and tried at Magistrates' Courts, while appeals are heard in Higher Courts. After 1997, a few cases were also brought up against several construction companies in the Court of Final Appeal. Successful convictions by the judiciary are periodically updated online.* Thus, prosecution by the regulatory body is seen as both a tool for improving safety and health and as a way of removing unfair competition from unscrupulous operators. Legal repercussions and specific cases affecting the construction field are discussed further in Chapters 4–7.

Safety practitioners

The regulatory body advocates that safety law is a minimum standard that organisations have to follow. However, some organisations view safety laws as excessive burdens to their business, and they are not willing to comply. This is opposed via regulations involving the compulsory employment of registered safety officers and safety supervisors in designated industries in the Hong Kong SAR. These safety personnel have a range of employment conditions, including part-time, full-time, and consultancy. Their engagement periods vary from a few months to a few years. The qualifications of these safety practitioners range from secondary school leavers to persons with a doctor of philosophy in safety.

Regardless of their employment conditions, period, or education, all safety practitioners in the Hong Kong SAR must be registered. There are a number of safety associations in the region, but there is one society in

* See the Labour Department website at: www.labour.gov.hk/eng/osh/content15.htm.

which members are registered according to strict regulations: the Society of Registered Safety Officers. This society was formed in 1990, and in 2021, had 546 registered members. Members are involved in advisory committees set up by the Labour Department as well as technical committees set up by the OSHC. Notably, the Society of Registered Safety Officers has organised the annual safe foreman awards with the Lighthouse Club (Hong Kong Branch) for more than 20 years.

While the regulatory body handles legislation and prosecution of safety law breaches, safety practitioners drive the day-to-day safety compliance on worksites, including performing assessments, making recommendations, and providing advice concerning legal compliance. In the FIU (Safety Officers and Safety Supervisors) Regulations, the law also requires registered safety officers to undertake continuing professional development, pushing them to stay up to date on recent regulatory changes and the evolving industrial environment. These practitioners are, therefore, one of the primary promoters of safety and health at work in the construction industry.

LOOKING FORWARD

How can safety practitioners effectively advise proprietors, educate workers, guide compliance, and promote safety and health in an ever-changing industrial environment? Sandra Dawson, an industrial sociologist, listed out the characteristics historically associated with professional groups. These characteristics are:

- clear attachment to a distinct body of knowledge;
- specific and lengthy training;
- restricted entrance and completion of prescribed courses;
- established and agreed code of ethics and standards of behaviour;
- provision of scarce resources and services to client groups; and
- strong involvement in evaluation, control, and promotion of the field.

As safety management groups adopt these characteristics, the status of the safety profession will enter into another era—Industry 4.0. In this new era, the internet and new forms of communication will mediate novel relationships to other practitioners and clients as well as enhance how the laws are understood and enforced locally and globally, ultimately helping safety practitioners perform their work better.

To enhance the role of safety practitioners, the construction industry needs to review their education and training programme as well as the accreditation process for safety practitioners. On the education front, for example, we need to introduce teaching subjects that are related to the complexity of the workforce in the construction industry, such as work psychology, work physiology, and behavioural science. We need to understand why the workforce behaves in certain ways and how they can be encouraged to behave safely. This is a task our universities and tertiary institutes will need to lead and promote.

Regarding training, we need to introduce a comprehensive instruction programme. Trainee safety practitioners need to seek attachments to senior practitioners to gain practical insight into how safety on worksites can be promoted and accidents can be prevented. A two-year training programme or attachment should be considered the minimum.

On the accreditation front, applicants for registration status under the law should preferably possess a relevant first degree in science or engineering. They should be able to communicate in both English and Chinese to help conduct their work in Hong Kong's bilingual environment. They should also produce evidence that they have undergone training in safety inspection, accident investigation, and site safety committee attendance and need to be able to deliver this information to management and workers at all levels in addition to managing people at work.

In Industry 4.0, technology will play a significant role. Safety practitioners need to be ready to plug into new technological equipment and play a leading role to help construction organisations utilise these new technologies to innovate and improve occupational safety and health in construction work.

Finally, safety practitioners need to be equally aware of changing environmental regulations in the safety and health field, particularly as some environmental issues (such as noise, indoor air quality, and hazardous substances) overlap with occupational safety and the health of workers. In fact, the safety departments of some private organisations have been re-titled as Health, Safety, and Environment (HSE) Departments and now oversee all matters related to all three sectors. This is largely a response to changing international attitudes towards environmentally friendly operations.

SUMMARY

Through the years of legislative development, various sets of regulations have been enacted (Table 1.1). Safety legislation has, in general, reflected the age of the workforce, the changing health challenges, and the evolving economic development in Hong Kong (shifting from a trade-centred city to an industrial manufacturing centre and then to a service-oriented and gig economy). The laws started with registration requirements and compliance with hardware provisions, and then expanded to include processes in the manufacturing industry. They have recently advanced into mandatory employment of safety professionals and the establishment of safety management systems that are necessary to improve safety and health performance. Although laws are not truly preventive as they always lag behind technological innovation and development, they are, nevertheless, regarded as an effective legal tool to improve safety. Moreover, laws are neither sufficiently flexible nor versatile to meet all kinds of employment or technological situations that may arise. It is reasonable to assume that the suitability and applicability of the existing legislation will need to be re-examined continuously to ensure that it still provides effective and efficient tools for the Hong Kong SAR to improve its safety and health performance as an international city.

Looking ahead, the successful safety practitioners of the future Industry 4.0 environment—who may serve in government, the private sector, or their own practices—will be university graduates or post-graduates (from various disciplines) that understand how to advise proprietors and contractors in the application of safety legislation. They will have broad safety, health, and environmental knowledge and excellent communication skills. These attributes will allow them to offer good advice and assist companies and organisations to continue their operations safely.

In conclusion, the field of construction safety has, from its inception, operated according to legislation that is continuously evolving. The

TABLE 1.1: Safety and health legislation in the Hong Kong SAR

Ordinances and Subsidiary Regulations	Year Enacted
Factories and Industrial Undertakings Ordinance, Chapter 59	**1955**
Factories and Industrial Undertakings Regulations	1955
FIU (Notification of Occupational Diseases) Regulations	1965
FIU (First Aid in Notifiable Workplaces) Regulations	1968
FIU (Blasting by Abrasives) Special Regulations	1969
Quarries (Safety) Regulations	1969
FIU (Woodworking Machinery) Regulations	1971
FIU (Electrolytic Chromium Process) Regulations	1972
Construction Sites (Safety) Regulations	1973
FIU (Lifting Appliances and Lifting Gear) Regulations	1974
FIU (Abrasive Wheels) Regulations	1975
FIU (Work in Compressed Air) Regulations	1975
FIU (Spraying of Flammable Liquids) Regulations	1976
FIU (Goods Lifts) Regulations	1976
FIU (Dry Batteries) Regulations	1976
FIU (Guarding and Operation of Machinery) Regulations	1976
FIU (Cartridge-operated Fixing Tools) Regulations	1977
FIU (Protection of Eyes) Regulations	1977
FIU (Cargo and Container Handling) Regulations	1978
FIU (Fire Precautions in Notifiable Workplaces) Regulations	1981
FIU (Electricity) Regulations	1982
FIU (Safety Officers and Safety Supervisors) Regulations	1986
FIU (Carcinogenic Substances) Regulations	1986
FIU (Dangerous Substances) Regulations	1988
FIU (Noise at Work) Regulation	1992
FIU (Suspended Working Platforms) Regulation	1994
FIU (Safety Management) Regulation	1999
FIU (Confined Spaces) Regulation*	1999
FIU (Loadshifting Machinery) Regulation	2000
FIU (Gas Welding & Flame Cutting) Regulation	2001
FIU (Asbestos) Regulation**	2014
Occupational Safety and Health Ordinance, Chapter 509	**1997**
Occupational Safety and Health Regulation	1997
Occupational Safety and Health (Display Screen Equipment) Regulation	2003

* Updated from the 1973 version of the regulation.

** Updated from the 1986 version of the regulation.

regulatory body and registered safety practitioners are the primary players in implementing and enforcing these laws. The goal is to keep workplaces safe. European countries have set a target of less than one workplace fatality per 100,000 employed persons per year on a sustained basis. This safety target embraces employed persons at all workplaces. In 2018, only four countries — Germany, the Netherlands, the United Kingdom, and Sweden — consistently achieved this target. Will the Hong Kong SAR be able to achieve a similar safety goal? What changes are required to mediate this in the construction industry? The following chapters evaluate the current principles, safety laws, and regulations as well as the repercussions for non-compliance. Ultimately, students and practitioners alike need to assess how to apply these theories in their work to help the Hong Kong SAR reach such challenging safety targets.

FURTHER READING

Booth, R.T., Hale, A.R., and Dawson, S. (1991) "Identifying and registering safety practitioners", *Safety Science*, Vol. 14, pp. 231–240.

European Union (EU) (June 2018) *Accidents at Work Statistics*.

Eves, D.C.T. (2018) *Two Steps Forward, One Step Back: A Brief History of the Origins, Development and Implementation of Health and Safety Law in the United Kingdom, 1802–2014*, available at: www.historyofosh,org.uk/brief/index.html, accessed 19 September 2021.

Kwok, A.K.Y. (ed) (2013) *The Qualification and Performance of Occupational Health and Safety Personnel: Ensuring Occupational Health and Safety for Workers. Venture Track Program Hong Kong*, Hong Kong Department of Civil and Environmental Engineering, The Hong Kong Polytechnic University.

Labour Department, Hong Kong SAR Government (1997) *The 50th Anniversary of the Labour Department 1946–1996*, Hong Kong: Government Printer.

United Kingdom Health and Safety Executive (1983) *Her Majesty's Inspectors of Factories 1833–1983: Essays to Commemorate 150 Years of Health and Safety Inspection*, London: HMSO.

DISCUSSION QUESTIONS

1. What challenges do you think future construction safety regulators will face? What changes do you think may be required regarding their future roles in the industry?

2. Considering the recent advances in computational, networking, and physical processes (and their integration) that characterise the 4th Industrial Revolution, what roles do you think these changes will play in construction safety? How will they likely affect the roles of safety and health professionals?
3. What improvements would you like to make in the accreditation standards for registered safety officers under the FIU (Safety Officers and Safety Supervisors) Regulations to deepen and broaden their professionalism?

"Our commitment is strengthened by an increasing understanding that improvement in health, safety, and environmental performance often enhances overall business efficiency and effectiveness"

– John Jennings
Former Chairman of the "Shell" Transport and Trading Company
and a Group Managing Director of the Royal Dutch/Shell Group

"The most reliable and effective protection for most workers is provided by the existence of many employers"

– Milton and Rose Friedman

2 Principles of Health, Safety, and Environment Management

INTRODUCTION

While there has been some improvement since the 1980s, building and engineering construction companies in Hong Kong continue to register fatalities and worksite accidents. Government accident statistics collected in compliance with the Employees' Compensation Ordinance, Cap. 282, show that from 2011 to 2019 there were about 30–40 bodily injury cases per 1,000 workers per year. The number of fatalities was about 0.286 per 1,000 workers per year. These statistics highlight a significant challenge for construction companies to reduce on-site injuries and fatalities — a challenge that must be addressed.

This chapter discusses principles for managing occupational safety and health. If applied correctly, these principles can markedly improve accident prevention in construction work. Furthermore, these principles can also be applied to environmental protection and sustainable development. Responsible organisations treat these matters under the banner of "health, safety, and environment" (abbreviated HSE, SHE, or EHS). These elements are typically blocked together because of overlapping subject matters and issues that can and should be dealt with together to be the most effective.

THE IMPORTANCE OF MANAGING HEALTH, SAFETY, AND ENVIRONMENTAL PERFORMANCE

There are obvious reasons why HSE performance should be important to management. These concepts are integral to business management, being closely inter-related with legal obligations, business performance, company branding, and financial matters. The word "safety" in this context is extended to include that of employees not directly involved with hazardous work activities and the public who may be endangered by a particular work activity.

Legal obligations

Employees' safety is a legal obligation and typically a contractual requirement in building and engineering construction projects. Under common law, it is the duty of an employer to ensure, so far as is reasonably practicable, a safe and healthy working environment for their employees. There are also various statutory laws covering HSE protection. Unfortunately, civil claim cases against employers' negligence (or that of other responsible parties) are increasing in the Hong Kong SAR, even when considered separately from criminal liabilities for non-compliance with safety laws. These civil claims fall within the purview of the Legal Aid Department.

Business performance

High safety standards should be an objective pursued by management in the same way and with as much vigour as other management objectives. Unfortunately, pursuing these objectives can be difficult as it may require management to overcome short- and long-term incompatibilities or goal conflicts amongst individuals, groups, and contractors. Safety and health laws should, therefore, be a starting point for managers, and compliance should not be regarded as the endpoint of safety and health management. Measuring HSE performance requires an assessment of the hazards inherent in work activities, which can then be eliminated or adequately controlled. Such measurement requires a careful quantitative and qualitative review of company compliance with pre-determined standards.

Authorities tasked with enforcing safety laws have the power to seek improvement, to stop or suspend work, and to prompt corrective actions to prevent hazards. In the Hong Kong SAR, contractors that have previous court convictions for deaths or serious bodily injuries suffered by workers or for breaches of environmental law may be suspended from bidding for government or public works contracts or held to more stringent assessment when they wish to undertake construction work. Disregarding safety regulations can, therefore, significantly affect business performance.

Company branding

An organisation's attitude towards safety also affects its brand and public image. Thus, preventing deaths and injuries can be considered a social and humanitarian concern. Stakeholders may also have an interest in these efforts. To provide a good, healthy, and hygienic working environment is one aspect of this; to protect employees from physical injuries or disease is another. Furthermore, occupational safety should not be confined to the workplace alone. More and more public concern is being directed to hazards that may affect the public, such as excessive lead content in potable water. These concerns are often related to environmental issues that industrial organisations must also address. Examples of local multi-fatality incidents that need to be avoided in the future include the Aberdeen Jumbo floating restaurant fire that occurred when it was under construction in October 1971, the Kwai Chung Cipel-Marco fur factory explosion-cum-fire in October 1986, the North Point passenger hoist incident in June 1993, the fire caused by welding work inside the bottom lift shaft of Garley commercial building on Nathan Road in November 1996, the Causeway Bay tower crane collapse in July 2007, and the multiple fatalities that occurred inside a lift shaft in the International Commerce Centre at Kowloon Station when it was under construction in September 2009. Major international disasters like the Flixborough chemical plant explosion in the United Kingdom (1974), the Sevesco chemical exposure disaster in Italy (1976), the liquefied petroleum gas (LPG) explosion in Mexico City (1984), the Bhopal gas leak tragedy in India (1984), the Chernobyl nuclear accident in what is now the Ukraine (1986), the Sandoz Warehouse chemical spill and fire in Switzerland (1986), the Piper Alpha oil platform explosion in the United Kingdom (1988), the Exxon Valdez oil spill in the Prince William Sound in the United States (1989), and the Fukushima Daiichi nuclear plant shut down in Japan (2011) are also memorable lessons for management. Even though these events occurred away from construction activities, they have still altered our understanding of workplace safety and the effect on company branding.

Financial burdens

The financial repercussions of worksite accidents offer another perspective. Injury to employees or the exposure and transmission of occupational diseases are regarded as a financial loss and often cost the business significant sums. For example, the events at the Three Mile Island nuclear plant in 1979 resulted in a US$1.3 billion loss. Further, the events at the Chernobyl nuclear plant, the Piper Alpha oil platform, and the Exxon Valdez oil spill resulted in losses of US$5.5 billion, US$3.0 billion, and US$20.0 billion, respectively. In the case of property damage, the loss is directly monetary. However, injury or disease also results in a loss of human resources, which can significantly affect the company's profit margin. In fact, a previous study by the United Kingdom Health and Safety Executive (UKHSE) revealed that successful companies usually manage their safety and health matters better than struggling companies. DuPont, for example, has been widely recognised as having one of the best industrial safety performances in the world. Its safety management techniques have been shown to be outstandingly effective over the long term. International chemical and energy companies like Dow Chemical and Shell also provide good examples of successful companies with top safety performance.

The prime objective of an enterprise is to grow and prosper, and safety should be considered an integral part of this objective. Any injury or ill-health at work and the damages (environmental or otherwise) arising from work activities should be regarded as losses. Ultimately, good safety performance is good business in that it reflects good overall management. Responsible organisations should be willing to periodically report their HSE performance openly as a way to maintain high standards.

GENERAL PRINCIPLES OF SAFETY MANAGEMENT

Various studies in the field of safety management have revealed effective and practical principles that successful companies typically follow. These include adopting a commitment to safety, establishing effective safety policies, viewing safety as a line responsibility, employing competent safety personnel, and following local and global safety standards and practices.

A commitment to safety

This is a key principle of safety management. It reveals management's attitude towards safety (and potential problems) and is critical to nurture an organisation's safety culture in the long run.

Ron Westrum, an American social scientist, identified three ways in which organisations habitually deal with safety problems. He classified organisational responses to hazards as denial, repair, or reform. Denial organisations will suppress whistle-blowers and encapsulate valid observations. Repair organisations will admit to and fix problems at the local level only. Reform organisations will admit to global problems and take widespread remedial action. Classification into one of these three groups predetermines the organisation's safety culture as pathological, calculative, and generative, respectively. Pathological organisations are ones whose safety measures are inadequate even under normal conditions. Safety is sacrificed in the pursuit of profit. Calculative organisations try to do their best using "by the book" methods. These are usually adequate under normal operating conditions but often fail under atypical or unforeseen circumstances. Generative organisations are characterised by their commitment to constant self-appraisal and reform. They set targets for themselves beyond ordinary expectations and fulfil them because they are willing to apply wide-ranging and often unconventional remedies. These organisations emphasise results rather than methods and value substance over form. On-site hazards tend to be quickly detected and eliminated because frontline personnel have permission to both identify issues and act to remedy them.

A commitment to safety calls for top management to demonstrate strong and visible leadership down the line. They should view work-related accidents as management failures. They should allocate sufficient resources to develop, operate, and maintain the management system and to achieve safety objectives. Managing safety in the workplace has to be seen as an essential part of a manager's daily responsibilities and should be included alongside other duties related to sales and marketing, production and work progress, cost control, profitability, and morale.

Management should "walk the talk" to demonstrate the level of safety they want to achieve. A non-exhaustive management priority list should include:

- establishing a high safety standard;
- taking a personal interest in workplace accident prevention;
- appointing competent safety staff;
- allocating sufficient funds to implement safety measures;
- participating in safety inspections;
- ensuring staff are competent as well as adequately trained and instructed; and
- keeping safety matters at the top of the agenda in management meetings.

This commitment must also be highly visible to be effective. To adhere to the items on this list, management will need to maintain a balance between conflicting business pressures. They will need to be innovative and self-questioning as well as willing to put forward new ideas about promoting safety and implementing up-to-date developments to avoid being left behind in the field.

In safety, management must be bold and lead the way with their commitment to safety. They must not gamble the business reputation or assets that may be exposed to unreasonable or unpredictable penalties.

Effective safety policies

The written promulgation of a company's safety policy by management is not just a legal requirement in the Hong Kong SAR but is a statement of intent. The policy should be signed by a top executive of the organisation as a demonstration of commitment and leadership. After all, the top personnel will ultimately be responsible for ensuring each employee's safety. For example, the safety policy of a project-based contract will need to be signed by the project manager.

In addition to its initial signing and dissemination, the policy should be regularly reviewed. If there are different nationalities employed by the company, then the policy should be written in a language that each can read and understand. It should also be distributed and available to all those concerned.

Safety policies may differ slightly depending on the worksite. However, an effective safety policy should be concise, easily understood, and available to every employee and the public. In addition to complying with basic legal requirements, a good safety policy should also incorporate the following philosophies:

- Accept that all bodily injuries can and should be prevented.
- Accident prevention at work is management's responsibility.
- Manage safety-at-work matters as any other critical business activity.
- Provide properly engineered facilities and safe working procedures.
- Train all employees to work safely.
- Require contractors to manage safety in line with the safety policy.
- Promote a culture in which those in the workforce share their commitment to safety.
- Implement a systematic approach to safety management designed to ensure compliance with the law.

Other applicable safety policies include no alcohol or drugs, no smoking, regular auditing, etc. An example safety policy from Gammon (Hong Kong) Limited is provided in Figure 2.1. The promulgation of a written safety policy is an essential safety management element, and an audit of its contents is required by law. Further details of various auditing schemes are provided in Chapter 12.

Safety as a line responsibility

The line manager or supervisor in an organisation is often the only person present at the worksite with the authority to implement safety policies and is, therefore, responsible for ensuring a safe working environment.

FIGURE 2.1: Example safety policy from Gammon (Hong Kong) Limited

Gammon

ZERO HARM
MAKE SAFETY PERSONAL

Policy on Health, Safety, Environment and Quality

We are committed to being a World Class organization, and to be the contractor of choice in Hong Kong, Macau, Singapore, China and Southeast Asia. We believe that Quality, Safety, Efficiency and Good Value are interrelated aspects of the excellent engineering upon which the Gammon business is based.

Over all business considerations, Safety will always take priority and nothing should compromise safety and our total commitment to Zero Harm.

We aim to work actively with Customers to provide added value, making best use of our abilities and resources to develop innovative solutions and manage risk such that delivery will be incident, accident and environmental occurrence free.

From the Executive Committee, Directors and our senior teams, the commitment to Health, Safety, Environment and Quality (HSEQ) will be highly visible, consistent and under regular review.

To underpin our philosophy and approach in HSEQ, we will set objectives (Bold Commitment, 25by25) and engage with the industry and stakeholders to challenge ourselves and the trade practices to continually "raise the bar" by improving standards for health, safety, environmental and quality performance.

We will adopt the four principles of:

Strong and Visible Leadership

- Leaders will be mindful of risks and informed as to how these are being addressed.
- They will maintain a fair and just culture that allows all of our stakeholders to engage in the delivery of this policy yet holds everyone accountable for their actions, the teams are resourced and competent to manage and mitigate risk.
- Leaders will adopt innovative thinking that promote culture for implementation and continual improvement of health, safety, environmental and quality performance.

Structured and Risk Based Approach

- In planning of operations, we will identify the specific risks, opportunities and consider life cycle stages relevant to each task and provide safe and healthy working conditions to achieve Zero Harm; prevent work-related injury, ill health, environmental occurrence and defects of products; improve outputs and to enhance quality, effectiveness, efficiency and preserve the environment.
- Practical and resilient methods will be developed to fully control these risks, otherwise work will not proceed. Method shall be reassessed where circumstances or operational controls change.
- We will adopt modern and innovative methods of construction in our Layers of Protection to eliminate and best manage occupational health and safety risks, quality defects and environmental impacts,

  - Design and Engineering
  - Plant and Equipment
  - Process
  - People

FIGURE 2.1: Continued

Effective Implementation and Supervision

- Frontline staff and managers are responsible for the implementation of agreed methods.
- Compliance with legislation, contractual requirements to which Gammon subscribes is a fundamental minimum requirement.
- The Gammon HSEQ Management System procedures, Golden Rules, Bold Commitments and Safety Standards define our minimum requirements including duties and responsibilities.
- We will maintain clean and tidy work fronts, clear access to all locations and effective emergency response process.
- Should any operation depart from the requirements of this policy, managers and supervisors must stop work and institute rectification and improvement measures.
- Senior managers will regularly monitor and support their staff to ensure that all operations are being conducted in accordance with this policy.

Engagement and Communication

We will:

- Monitor the needs of our business partners and be proactive in addressing their needs.
- Enhance customer satisfaction by providing a consistently high quality of services and products that satisfy applicable legal requirements; fulfill compliance obligations; meets and exceed customers' expectations.
- Engage frequently and proactively with local communities and the industry to find ways in which we can prevent pollution; protect ecosystems; use sustainable resource; mitigate climate change; minimize impacts and add value to the quality of life of those affected by our operations when we consider different life cycle stages.
- Ensure effective participation and consultation of employees, workers and workers' representatives in the HSEQ management system.
- Provide adequate and regular training and briefing to equip our workforce with the necessary safety, health and environmental awareness and competencies to meet work requirements.
- Seek continual improvement of HSEQ management system to enhance the performance through regular performance monitoring, System Assurance Validation (SAV), and by setting challenging Bold Commitments, objectives, targets and Gammon standards.

This policy, together with our management system, will be reviewed regularly and updated as appropriate to ensure continuing suitability and effectiveness.

This policy will be issued and explained to all staff through departmental briefings shall be displayed on company notice boards and will be available on our intranet.

Thomas HO, JP
Chief Executive
Gammon Construction Limited

February 2019

20190215

In construction work, project managers and site agents should regard safety as an integral part of their jobs and need to be concerned with maintaining high safety standards. These on-site project managers also typically chair the safety committee, acting as safety leaders in the organisation. Their safety performance should be regularly reviewed, and they should have an active interest in safety together with other business objectives. While other site safety personnel are often engaged to advise the line managers, the responsibilities related to enforcing safety standards cannot be delegated to other parties, legally or otherwise. Furthermore, sub-contractors working on the same site or project are required to operate according to the same requirements and provisions established by the main contractor's safety management system.

Competent safety personnel

By law, safety personnel must be registered to be employed in Hong Kong's construction industry and must comply with the requirements specified by the Factories and Industrial Undertakings Ordinance (FIUO)—namely, the FIU (Safety Officers and Safety Supervisors) Regulations. Safety officers operate at the intersection of law, technology, and industrial practicalities. These powerful forces create incompatibilities between theoretical ideals and the economic and technical realities as well as between the interests of developers, employers, sub-contractors, and employees. Safety officers need to effectively advise an organisation regarding legislative demands for safety and health requirements. They must also help establish policies that best suit the needs and circumstances of the organisation and help the company work with law and contract enforcement agencies. Their role is to advise, coordinate, and monitor. These roles are fair and establish reasonable expectations from the organisations they serve but are often not easy to meet and can be difficult to manage. A safety adviser must influence a number of people, both inside and outside the organisation. Inevitably, the role of a safety adviser involves taking a hard line with those who are ignorant, incompetent, or uncooperative with regard to safety, of which there will always be many.

The primary duties and responsibilities of safety personnel include:

- advising management on the implementation of a safety management system;

- guiding management during safety policy enactment and enforcement, audits, accident reporting, and investigation;
- providing technical safety information and experience to design engineers and other personnel;
- giving guidance on and participating in the preparation of instruction manuals, safety training courses, and worksite exercises;
- liaising with outside companies as well as industry, government, or non-government groups to develop consistent safety and health guidelines;
- coordinating appropriate safety performance monitoring and appraisal; and
- guiding management on the assessment of each contractor's safety performance.

The credibility of safety personnel rests on their ability to discharge the above duties and responsibilities with competence and due consideration of the constraints imposed by the law, technology, and financial pressures.

Local and global safety standards and practices

Safety management has two distinct aspects—hardware and software. The hardware aspect involves providing safe, sound, and suitable environments and equipment. While vital, technical excellence alone is not enough. Equally important is the ability of the workforce to display consistently safe and proper behaviour in carrying out various work tasks. The software aspect of safety covers the managerial organisation and the systems put in place to achieve high safety standards.

Notably, compliance with legal safety standards should not be considered the endpoint of safety practice but the starting point. In fact, safety standards should be set high, even above the legal requirements, whenever possible. Although the on-site work environment is difficult to control, particularly as the workforce and technology are constantly changing, setting standards higher than the legal restrictions can help companies to consistently adhere to these prescribed safety regulations.

In-house safety standards should:

- comply with the law as a starting point;
- be of a higher standard than is required by the law;

- require the use of environments and equipment of the highest safety standard and design (e.g., that follow global standards and specifications);
- be widely promulgated throughout an organisation;
- be understood by everyone within the organisation;
- be easy to comply with and abide by;
- be accepted by all;
- be adaptable to changes in the industry;
- be easily enforced; and
- be innovative.

MEASURING SAFETY PERFORMANCE

A common management principle is "what gets measured gets done." Simply, without measurement, there is no motivation to improve. This is why an organisation needs safety performance indicators. A common indicator of safety performance in the construction industry is the number of accidents per one thousand workers per year (abbreviated xx/1,000 workers/year). Another performance indicator is the number of accidents per hundred thousand man-hours worked (abbreviated xx/100,000 man-hours). However, these metrics cannot be relied upon to track safety performance in situations with an accident frequency of less than 10/1,000 workers/year or less than 1/100,000 man-hours, restricted by the law of diminishing return. They are also reactive indicators that record accidents after they have occurred. In contrast, examples of proactive performance indicators include the presence of:

- an accident prevention action plan;
- effective safety targets and objectives;
- multiple effective safety education and training courses;
- multiple external and independent safety audits and inspections;
- documented follow-up after audits and inspections;
- reduced insurance premiums and claims;
- short response time after an unsafe act audit; and
- measures to quickly identify potential incidents and implement precautions.

Some of these proactive performance indicators, including safety targets and objectives, safety education and training courses, and safety audits and inspections as well as the investigation of and response to accidents involving several of the metrics above, are discussed further in the next sections.

Safety targets and objectives

Safety targets should be quantified wherever possible. Examples of quantifiable safety targets are:

- application of digital techniques in safety inspections and audits;
- established comprehensive hazard identification plan and risk assessment databank for work activities;
- prohibited use of tower cranes, mobile cranes, or passenger hoists that have been used over a continuous ten-year period or have gone without proper preventive maintenance;
- provision and use of Y-type chinstraps in safety helmets;
- established pre-employment medical examination for workers doing high-risk tasks (e.g., tower crane operation, mobile crane operation, lorry-mounted crane operation, dump truck driving, and scaffolding work); and
- improved compliance with the law in terms of prosecutions, suspension or improvement notices (SNs or INs), and other documents issued by regulatory bodies.

These safety targets should also be linked to the long-term safety objectives of the company. Examples of these objectives include:

- being a leader in safety performance in the construction industry;
- promoting brand management based on safety-at-work measures;
- pre-employment and periodic medical examination for all construction workers; and
- employees are proud of their safety performance.

Safety targets and objectives should be reasonable, realistic, and achievable. Sub-contractors should also be consulted when setting such targets and objectives as their procedures, policies, and employees will also need to be aware of and comply with these targets.

Safety education and training courses

The primary objectives of safety training are to raise an individual's safety awareness and to improve an individual's safety know-how. In the construction industry, this is easier said than done. Workers who lack safety training often lack basic insight into their deficiencies and do not know what they are required to know. However, as safety training is mandated by law, frontline workers cannot be blamed for being insufficiently trained. Responsibility for this rests with management.

In the construction industry, skill level varies from highly skilled operators to general casual workers with minimum skill. In addition to skill, there are also gaps in age, culture, and experience between employees. Instilling safety awareness into such a diverse workforce is a challenging task for organisations, and implementing behavioural changes in workers to improve safety is exceedingly difficult. Not surprisingly, an employee's educational background can also significantly affect the effectiveness of safety training and how quickly they learn.

Safety training is, in principle, provided as part of the comprehensive on-the-job training offered by most companies. However, theoretical safety training is only a small part of the knowledge needed to act safely on a worksite. A psychological approach, for example, could also be an appropriate way to provide this knowledge. Indeed, psychologists suggest that unsafe behaviours can be broken down into the following five stages (using wearing a safety belt on the worksite as an example):

1. The *pre-contemplative stage*: the worker does not even consider wearing a safety belt or the consequences of breaking the safety rules concerning use.
2. The *contemplative stage*: the worker begins to believe it is a good idea to wear a safety belt but does not make a firm decision to adhere to this safety rule.
3. The *decision-making stage*: the worker firmly believes in the benefits of safety belt use and resolves to start wearing a safety belt on the worksite.

4. The *new habit stage*: the worker consistently implements their new-found decision to wear a safety belt on the worksite.
5. The *maintenance stage*: the worker successfully maintains their habit of wearing a safety belt on the worksite.

Psychological studies have also revealed that using fear in safety training via threats of accidents or similar techniques may not be as effective as illustrating the safe behaviour as a group norm, which the worker will feel social pressure to adopt. For example, industrial psychologists in the United States, the United Kingdom, and Japan, respectively, have shown the effective use of group norms in training sessions to reduce traffic accidents on roads by bus drivers and in shipyards. Such techniques can be used in construction worker training to raise their safety awareness and, ultimately, convince them to adopt safe behaviours.

Notably, knowledge of appropriate safety behaviour, whether as a theory or group norm, cannot necessarily be delivered by simply adding more training hours. Effective safety training is more a factor of quality than quantity. It is, therefore, important to monitor the quality of the training being delivered to the workforce. A company can do this via unsafe act (or safe act) auditing using behaviour-based observation. Safety training effectiveness is also apparent in the manifestation of deliberate changes in an employee's behaviour. Unfortunately, these changes are often frustratingly slow and challenging to implement consistently across a varied workforce. One step organisations can take to help aid their efforts is to ensure that frontline supervisors and managers are educated and trained to understand and discharge their roles, duties, and responsibilities in promoting worksite safety. Doing so will help mediate positive change in other employees by setting an example. While employee behaviour will not change overnight, continued reinforcement will help employees make safer decisions on the worksite.

Safety audits and inspections

There is a clear distinction between a safety inspection and a safety audit, although both are required by law. The FIUO—specifically the FIU (Safety Management) Regulation—defines a "safety audit" as an arrangement for (a) collecting, assessing, and verifying information on the efficiency, effectiveness, and reliability of a safety management system (including the elements specified in Schedule 4 of the regulation); and (b) considering improvements to the system (see Chapter 12 for examples of two audit schemes for construction activities). In contrast, a "safety inspection" is an on-site check carried out to assess particular items with a pre-established checklist. An inspection is widely considered to be less thorough than an audit, particularly as the latter is more likely to uncover the root cause of an irregularity in the work system or procedure. Notably, the human factors (i.e., the perceptual, mental, and physical capabilities of the employees and their interaction with their working environment) are mostly ignored in both types of assessment.

As construction organisations commonly use audits and reviews as business control instruments, a written policy and protocol should be established. External and independent audits are preferred as they can provide a more unbiased assessment than in-house auditors that are direct employees of the audited organisation. Only auditors that offer value-added recommendations should be engaged.

Furthermore, following both types of assessment, companies should follow-up with the recommendations made by the inspector, auditor, or reviewer. This not only highlights the organisation's drive for continual improvement but also acts as a preventive measure for possible accidents or infractions. Any substantial non-compliance should be brought to the attention of senior management.

Investigating and responding to accidents and incidents

The word "accident" has many implied meanings that can differ significantly depending on the context, be it general, legal, medical, scientific, or occupational. Section 3 of the Occupational Safety and Health Ordinance (OSHO), Cap. 509, indicates that from a legal perspective an "accident" includes any event that detrimentally affects the health of a person. In the context of occupational safety, most organisations have their own definition that expands upon this legal framework. For example, some organisations classify bodily injury cases under first-aid treatment cases (FACs), medical treatment cases (MTCs), lost-time injury cases (LTICs), permanent bodily injury cases (PICs), or fatalities. Thus, the word "accident" is rarely used in its classification or the administration of remedial action.

It is essential for management to view accidents or incidents as organisational failures. They must then use the situation as an opportunity to evaluate managerial weaknesses. To this end, executives should focus on discovering what failed in the safety management system that allowed the accident to occur. Other pertinent questions for preventing recurrence should be:

- What went wrong?
- Who was responsible?
- Who can prevent it from happening again?
- How can they prevent it from happening again?
- Who is responsible for carrying out the recommendations for preventing recurrence?
- When will remedial action be complete?
- How much will future accidents cost, in terms of money and other resources, versus how much it will cost to prevent them?

Management has a number of accident investigation and analysis techniques at their disposal to help answer these questions. Various analyses can also be used to address these questions pre-emptively.

Accident assessment techniques

Common assessment techniques include:

- *Sequentially Timed Event Plotting (STEP)*: This technique is based on the concept that an accident is a time-based process by which a perturbation transforms a dynamically stable activity into a series of unintended interacting changes or states that result in a harmful outcome.
- *Fault Tree Analysis (FTA)*: The FTA is a deductive and analytical technique that places the accident as the top event. This placement in the tree can also be used to highlight possible accident prevention measures. In its application, the FTA

designates logical gates, with a "must occur" event being represented by an "AND" gate and a "can occur" event being represented by an "OR" gate.

- *Management Oversight Risk Tree (MORT)*: This accident causation model was originally conceived and developed by W.G. (Bill) Johnson in 1970. The technique involves detailed investigations into the event, management, personnel, environment, and material that contributed to an accident. It enlists a series of questions under each investigative element. An FTA is used under this model.
- *TRIPOD Theory*: The TRIPOD theory was developed in the late 1980s by researchers at the University of Manchester in the United Kingdom and University of Leiden in the Netherlands for accident prevention at Shell, an international energy company. The theory consists of three "legs", hence the name. The "unsafe acts" leg concerns actions committed by workers that can be prevented by additional education and training that will enhance their safety awareness. The "accidents" leg focuses on events that happen despite preventive measures being in place, often resulting in the identification of relaxed or ineffective standards. Lessons in this leg are typically only learned after an accident has occurred. To proactively minimise workplace accidents, management should take early steps and respond immediately to accidents, which is the third leg. It includes 11 "General Failure Types (GFTs)": hardware, design, maintenance management, operating procedures, error-forcing conditions, housekeeping, incompatible goals, communication, organisation, training, and defence. These GFTs are the top-end contributing factors in accident prevention and provide a structured way to diagnose and learn from accidents. This theory embodies proactive accident prevention that is initiated by the top levels of the organisation. An example applying the TRIPOD theory can be found in Chapter 8.

For complex accident cases, outside safety consultants or specialists should be invited to investigate and provide technical knowledge or expertise that is not available in-house. Furthermore, all recommendations made after an accident investigation should be followed-up, and any lessons learned should be shared across all sites under the same management and, where appropriate, with other interested parties.

Potential incident analysis

Techniques for improving safety performance that focus on accident investigations are reactive. Establishing the immediate cause of an accident beyond all reasonable doubt is often more difficult than simply preventing it from happening in the first place. Another option is to implement the potential incident concept, similar to that adopted by the TRIPOD theory at Shell. Potential incidents are incidents that have not happened but would entail disastrous effects and heavily affect the company's business performance if they do occur. By definition, a potential incident is any hazardous scenario which (a) is a credible possibility, (b) is relevant to the construction activities being carried out, (c) may have foreseeable and quantifiable consequences, and (d) offers safety lessons that can be learned. Using this concept to assess potential incidents will fundamentally shift the company's safety culture and thinking from reactive to proactive. Therefore, companies should invest resources into potential incident identification as doing so is vital for accident prevention.

ENHANCING SAFETY PERFORMANCE

The ultimate goal of measuring safety performance is to identify areas the company can improve in order to enhance its safety performance. In addition to the weaknesses identified using the metrics outlined above, all construction companies should also take steps to enhance their ability to motivate, organise, and communicate as well as maintain their facilities and equipment.

Motivate, organise, and communicate

Research concerning workplace motivation has been carried out by Max Weber, Hertzberg, Henri Fayol, Elton Mayo, M.P. Follett, McGregor's X and Y, Rensis Likert, A.H. Maslow, and others. Thus, there is no lack of organisational theories for management to apply to their company. One notable example is the "Hawthorne effect" named after the Hawthorne factory complex of the Western Electric Company in the late 1920s. Although this example is not directly related to construction activities, it has profound safety implications, whereby workgroups can develop elaborate informal codes of practice that are understood and respected within the group but little known by those outside of it and not wholly compatible, or even in direct conflict with, company safety policies or rules. An example of the "Hawthorne effect" in the construction industry is the situations faced by bamboo scaffolding workers, formwork workers, and plasterers. These activities present conditions where the safety of the individual depends on the safe practices of the group as a whole.

To implement organisational changes and increase workplace motivation, management is required to communicate effectively with their workforce. Managing safety in a sizable construction or civil engineering project is often a problem with regard to safety communication. Hong Kong construction contractors fulfil their contractual obligations through an extensive system of sub-contracting. This contracting system requires the main contractor's direct labour force for the project to be small, typically less than one to eight percent of the total contract sum. The majority of the work is done through sub-contracting to firms with many workers. Multi-layer sub-contracting is a common feature, and sub-contractors hired by the main firm frequently further sub-contract their work to others. In this system, there can be multiple sub-sub-contractors and over 30 occupational tradesmen on a single worksite. Thus, it is not surprising that communication failures occur. Failure in safety communication between the main contractor and the sub-contractors or sub-sub-contractors falls into three categories: system failures, message failures, and reception failures.

System failures are indicative of issues in the "hardware" used to communicate safety policies. They occur when the necessary communication channels between the main contractor and sub-contractors or sub-sub-contractors do not exist. There may be safety committee meetings or a forum for communication amongst all sub-contractors, but representatives from the sub-sub-contractors may not be aware of or participate in these meetings.

Message failures occur when the necessary safety information is not transmitted downward to the sub-sub-contractors and their workforce. This type of failure occurs when the "hardware" of communication exists, but the information is not conveyed appropriately to the people that need it. A common cause of a message failure is uncertainty as to who is responsible for transmitting particular safety information and who is supposed to receive it.

Reception failures occur in situations where the safety communication channels exist and the safety information is transmitted, but the safety messages are misinterpreted by the recipient or are sent too late to be of any practical use. Effective prevention of system, message, and reception failures demands deliberate application of managerial and organisational skills. To better understand how to communicate with, organise, and motivate their employees more effectively, management can ask the following questions:

- Do employees see managers involved in safety activities, objective-setting, and monitoring?
- Do employees see management taking action and providing resources to support their stated policies and objectives?
- Do employees know they are accountable for their safety performance?
- Do employees know that blatant breaches of in-house safety rules will result in disciplinary action?
- Are appropriate and modern communication techniques used?

Maintain facilities and equipment

Safety principles should also be applied to the organisation's maintenance of existing facilities and equipment. Failure to check and update equipment can significantly contribute to both major and minor accidents. Many maintenance problems arise from the conflict between cost and safety. To resolve these conflicts and enhance safety performance, management must set specific maintenance objectives. For building sites, these objectives may involve the upkeep and assessment of various physical machines, including tower cranes, material hoists, passenger hoists, mobile cranes, derrick cranes, lorry-mounted cranes, mobile elevating working platforms, ladders, kung-fu stools, gondolas (temporary or permanent), concrete pump trucks, excavators, bobcats, forklift trucks, bench circular saws, bar-benders, electric generators, air receivers/compressors, chain blocks, oxy-acetylene gas cylinders, cartridge-operated fixing tools, abrasive grinding wheels or cutters, etc. It is, therefore, undesirable to use imported second-hand tools and machinery (or those with an untraceable source) without past maintenance records. Such machinery can have hidden defects or lack ergonomic considerations and may cause accidents or incidents in the future.

On civil engineering sites, the equipment used also includes excavating machines, such as tunnel boring machines, bulldozers, scrapers, drilling rigs (on land and at sea), graders and loader shovels, dredges, belt conveyors, road pavement construction machines, pre- and post-stressed equipment, and earth compactors. For compressed air tunnel work, a decompression chamber is also needed. Similar to the machinery listed above, the maintenance of these items is essential to ensure their safe and correct use.

The construction company should also select competent persons and examiners for testing, inspecting, and thoroughly examining all facilities and equipment. Management must consider the qualifications, working experience, and conversancy of these individuals prior to their employment. The assessments and the maintenance schedules for the facilities and equipment should be posted and easily accessed to ensure proper procedures are conducted judiciously.

SUMMARY

Organisations are required to balance various safety needs in their efforts to succeed. However, it is in their best interest to prioritise safety, and doing so will help them avoid legal repercussions, increase business performance, enhance the company brand, and decrease financial burdens. The principles of HSE management include a visible promise from leadership to adopt a commitment to safety, establish effective safety policies, view safety as a line responsibility, employ competent safety personnel, and follow the most up-to-date and innovative local and global legal safety standards and practices. Research has widely shown that there is no need to have an excessive number of principles, just the right and effective ones.

While the principles of HSE management may appear to be easily implemented, the ever-changing and dynamic workforce makes their application difficult. One essential aspect is measuring safety performance. This is largely done by establishing safety targets and objectives, providing safety education and training, conducting regular inspections and audits, and investigating and responding to accidents. Each of these metrics can be further enhanced by the company's commitment to motivating, organising, and communicating with their workforce as well as maintaining construction facilities and equipment. An organisation's safety culture says a lot about their business and relationship with their employees. Shifting to a more proactive approach is essential for accident prevention and decreased risk for both the employees and the company.

Taken together, if construction managers are able to act with unyielding commitment to these safety principles, assess and respond to subpar safety performance measures, and make the extra effort to enhance their relationship with their employees, then it is possible for the company to use their focus on safety to increase overall business performance and brand recognition.

FURTHER READING

Petersen, D. (1978) *Techniques of Safety Management*, McGraw Hill.

Reason, J. (1990) *Human Error*, Cambridge University Press.

Reason, J., and Parker, D. (1993) *Managing the Human Factor in Road Safety*, The Hague, Shell International Petroleum.

Reason, J., Shotton, R., Wagennar, W., Hudson, P., and Groeneweg, J. (January 1989) *Tripod: A Principled Basis for Safer Operations Prepared for Shell International.*

Report of the Commission of Inquiry (1972) *Fire on the "Jumbo": Floating Restaurant*, Hong Kong Government Printer.

Shell HSE Committee (1985) *Enhanced Safety Management.*

Shell HSE Committee (1994) *HSE Management System: Integrating HSE into the Business.*

Shell International Petroleum Company (November 1999) *Effective Proactive HSE Culture*.

United Kingdom Health and Safety Executive (1997) *Successful Health and Safety Management* (HSG65) (Second edition), HSE Books.

United Kingdom Health and Safety Executive (2005) *Investigating Accidents and Incidents: A Workbook for Employers, Unions, Safety Representatives and Safety Professionals* (HSG245).

Woo, K.H. (1997) *Final Report of the Inquiry into the Garley Building Fire on 20 November 1996*, Hong Kong, 26 August.

Yiu, N.S.N., and Chan, D.W.M. (2018) "In-depth investigation of safety management system in the Hong Kong construction industry: Literature review and research agenda", *International Advances on Mechanical and Civil Engineering*, Vol. 5, Issue 1, pp. 6–10.

DISCUSSION QUESTIONS

1. Why should construction contractors have to manage occupational safety and health on their worksites?
2. Discuss this statement: "The most reliable and effective protection for most workers is provided by the existence of many employers" (Milton and Rose Friedman).
3. What are the detailed arrangements and procedures necessary for producing effective action on the roles and functions of project managers, site agents, and foremen on worksites to promote safety?
4. What are the key occupational health risks that construction workers are facing in Hong Kong?

"Be you never so high, the Law is above you"

– Dr Thomas Fuller (1654–1734)

"Protection of workers' safety, health and welfare in factories and industrial undertakings"

– Factories and Industrial Undertakings Ordinance, Chapter 59

3 Applicable Construction Safety Laws in Hong Kong

INTRODUCTION

Safety and health legislation is an essential aspect of construction work. In Hong Kong, the Factories and Industrial Undertakings Ordinance (FIUO) and its 30 sets of subsidiary regulations are the primary documents referred to by safety practitioners and management in the construction field. The legislation contained in the FIUO aims to protect the safety and health of employees working in industrial settings, including factories, construction sites, cargo and container handling depots, mines, quarries, and catering establishments.

Before 1997, the FIUO and its subsidiary regulations only targeted employees working in the industrial sector. There was, therefore, a need to extend protection to employees working in non-industrial sectors, such as offices, schools, and department stores. The Occupational Safety and Health Ordinance (OSHO) was enacted in 1997 to ensure the safety and health of employees at work in both industrial and non-industrial sectors. Under this Ordinance, there are special provisions that effectively rectify serious breaches of safety legislation on construction sites established by both the FIUO and OSHO. This chapter briefly outlines these legislative documents and highlights those that are specific to the construction industry.

FACTORIES AND INDUSTRIAL UNDERTAKINGS ORDINANCE, CHAPTER 59

The FIUO, Cap. 59, can be traced back to 1955 when it was established as the primary safety ordinance in the growing industrial sector of the city. It administers safety, health, and welfare criteria for work in factories and other industrial undertakings. Before 1989, the safety legislation used in Hong Kong was mainly prescriptive, setting out specific requirements for hazardous processes and the use of specific machinery, such as lifting appliances and lifting gear. As the industrial sector expanded, there were always new processes and technology being developed, thus creating new hazards. The prevailing safety legislation was, in some cases, unable to handle these advances fast enough, and new legislation was sometimes irrelevant or out-of-date by the time it was enacted. To cope with this situation and to enhance industrial safety, the Hong Kong Government began to implement legal requirements framed in goal-setting terms that specify the objectives to be achieved rather than prescriptive recommendations. Therefore, industrial companies had a higher level of flexibility in the methods they used to achieve the objectives. Table 3.1 lists each section of the FIUO. The sections that are particularly important in the construction safety field are discussed below, including section 4, section 6A, section 7A, section 13, section 18, Construction Sites (Safety) Regulations (abbreviated CS(S)Rs), and specific Factories and Industrial Undertakings Regulations (abbreviated FIURs).

Section 4: Powers of officers

Section 4 of the FIUO lists the powers of occupational safety officers to enforce its subsidiary safety and health regulations. Their powers have been subsequently amended since 1965. In brief, occupational safety officers have the power to:

(a) enter, inspect, and examine any premises or place in which they know or have reasonable cause to believe that an industrial undertaking is being carried out;
(b) require the production of any register or other documents required to be kept under the FIUO;

TABLE 3.1: Outline of the Factories and Industrial Undertakings Ordinance

Section 1.	Short title
Section 2.	Interpretation
Section 3.	Certain functions to be exercised or performed by Commissioner personally
Section 4.	Powers of officers
Section 5.	(Repealed)
Section 6.	Employment not to be terminated, etc. by reason of fact that employee has given evidence in proceedings under Ordinance, etc.
Section 6A.	General duties of a proprietor
Section 6B.	General duties of persons employed
Section 6BA.	Proprietor of relevant industrial undertaking not to employ, etc. relevant person who does not have relevant certificate
Section 6C.	Meaning of at work (工作時)
Section 7.	Power of Commissioner to make regulations, etc.
Section 7A.	Codes of practice
Section 8.	Commissioner may amend the Schedules
Section 9.	Notification of workplaces
Section 9A.	Prohibition notices
Section 9B.	(Repealed)
Section 9C.	(Repealed)
Section 9D.	(Repealed)
Section 10.	Offences and penalties
Section 11.	(Repealed)
Section 11A.	(Repealed)
Section 11B.	(Repealed)
Section 11C.	(Repealed)
Section 12.	Continuing offences
Section 13.	Liability of proprietor
Section 14.	Liability of directors, partners, etc.
Section 14A.	Protection of public officers
Section 15.	Procedure
Section 16.	Presumptions
Section 17.	Prosecution of offences
Section 18.	Onus of proving limits of what is practicable, etc.
Section 19.	Civil liability
Schedule 1.	Dangerous Trades
Schedule 2.	Scheduled Trades
Schedule 3.	Specified Structures and Works
Schedule 4.	Specified Industrial Undertakings and Persons Employed at the Undertakings
Schedule 5.	Offences to be Prosecuted within 6 Months from Offence being Discovered by or Coming to Notice of Commissioner

(c) seize anything which may appear to be evidence of an offence against the FIUO or FIURs;
(d) take a declaration of truth statement from persons engaging in or related to matters involving occupational safety and health at the worksite; and
(e) require the posting of any legal or scheduled notices under the FIUO and FIURs.

Thus, the powers listed above and others in the section (see the FIUO for a full listing) provide occupational safety officers with the means to ensure compliance with ordinances and regulations related to that worksite.

Section 6A: General duties

The flexible, objective-focused FIUO also contains general duties for both employers and employees in addition to other more specific safety requirements that apply to all work activities and situations which may not be covered by existing legislation. This general duties provision (listed in section 6A) was modelled from section 2 of the United Kingdom Health and Safety at Work etc. Act (HASAW Act) of 1974 and appears as follows:

(1) It shall be the duty of every proprietor of an industrial undertaking to ensure, so far as is reasonably practicable, the health and safety at work of all persons employed at the industrial undertaking.
(2) Without prejudice to the generality of a proprietor's duty under subsection (1), the matters to which that duty extends include in particular:
   (a) the provision and maintenance of plant and systems of work that are, so far as is reasonably practicable, safe and without risks to health;
   (b) arrangements for ensuring, so far as is reasonably practicable, safety and absence of risks to health in connection with the use, handling, storage, and transport of articles and substances;
   (c) the provision of such information, instruction, training, and supervision as is necessary to ensure, so far as is

reasonably practicable, the health and safety at work of all persons employed at the industrial undertaking;

(d) the maintenance of any part of the industrial undertaking under the proprietor's control, so far as is reasonably practicable, in a condition that is safe and without risks to health and the provision and maintenance of means of access to and egress from it that are safe and without risks; and

(e) the provision and maintenance of a working environment for all persons employed at the industrial undertaking that is, so far as is reasonably practicable, safe, and without risks to health.

(3) Subject to subsection (4), a proprietor of an industrial undertaking who contravenes this section commits an offence and is liable to a fine of $500,000 (Amendment 40 of 1997, section 2).

(4) A proprietor of an industrial undertaking who contravenes this section wilfully and without reasonable excuse commits an offence and is liable to a fine of $500,000 and imprisonment for 6 months (Amendment 40 of 1997, section 2).

Compared with the HASAW Act, section 6A of the FIUO, Cap. 59 does not cover the roles of industrial designers, manufacturers, importers, or suppliers. For example, under the HASAW Act, designers and manufacturers are required to carry out or arrange to carry out any necessary research to eliminate or minimise any health or safety risks, as far as reasonably practicable, involved in the design and manufacturing processes. While these specifications are not explicitly made in the FIUO, Cap. 59, they should certainly be considered by companies and safety practitioners when assessing construction projects. Legal cases related to section 6A of the FIUO as well as relevant cases for section 2 of the HASAW Act are described in Chapter 5.

Section 7A: Codes of Practice

The FIUO also empowers the Commissioner for Labour to make and amend the safety regulations contained therein and to approve Codes of Practice (CoPs), many of which are applicable to the construction industry. These powers are explicitly stated in sections 7 and 7A of the FIUO, which were implemented via legal notice (LN) in 1993. In 2019, there were a total of 17 CoPs (Table 3.2). The application of these powers is further explained in Chapter 4 along with additional commentary concerning the legality and effectiveness of the CoPs.

Section 13: Liability of proprietors

Section 13 of the FIUO was introduced in 2003 and focuses on the legal responsibility of the proprietor(s). Its legal interpretation in the context of the construction industry is fully discussed in Chapter 5. It appears as follows:

> (1) Except as may be otherwise provided by regulations made under this Ordinance, the proprietor of every industrial undertaking in or in respect of which any offence against this Ordinance has been committed shall be guilty of a like offence, and shall be liable to the penalty prescribed for such offence.
> (2) It shall be no defence to a prosecution of the proprietor of an industrial undertaking for an offence against this Ordinance that the offence was committed without his knowledge or consent or that the actual offender has not been convicted of the offence.
> (3) Nothing in this section shall apply to an offence under section 6B or 6BA(15).

Section 13 has significant repercussions regarding prosecutions in the construction industry. Legal cases related to this section of the FIUO are described in Chapter 5.

Section 18: Onus of proving limits of what is practicable, etc.

Section 18 is a defence section for any defendant to prove the limits of what is practicable, as far as is reasonably practicable, all practical steps, adequate steps, or all reasonably practicable steps to do something to satisfy the duty or requirement. It appears as follows:

> (1) In a proceeding for an offence under a provision in this Ordinance consisting of a failure to comply with a duty or requirement to

TABLE 3.2: List of the current Codes of Practice

Code of Practice: Safety and Health at Work for Gas Welding and Flame Cutting
Code of Practice: Safety and Health at Work for Manual Electric Arc Welding
Code of Practice: Safety and Health at Work for Industrial Diving
Code of Practice: Safety and Health at Work with Asbestos
    Approved Method for Measuring Exposure to Asbestos in Air [GN 964]
Code of Practice for Bamboo Scaffolding Safety
Code of Practice on Mechanical Handling Safety in Container Yards
Code of Practice for Safe Use and Operation of Suspended Working Platforms
Code of Practice for Safety and Health at Work (Land-based Construction over water— Prevention of Fall)
Code of Practice for Safety and Health at Work in Confined Spaces
Code of Practice for Safety at Work (Lift and Escalator)
Code of Practice for Metal Scaffolding Safety
Code of Practice for Safe Use of Tower Cranes
Code of Practice for Safe Use of Mobile Cranes
Code of Practice on Safety Management
Code of Practice on Safe Use of Excavators
Code of Practice for Working with Display Screen Equipment
Code of Practice on Control of Air Impurities (Chemical Substances) in the Workplace

Note: Readers are advised to obtain updates of the Codes of Practice issued by the Labour Department.

do something so far as is necessary, where practicable, so far as is reasonably practicable, or so far as practicable or to take all reasonable steps, all practicable steps, adequate steps or all reasonably practicable steps to do something, the onus is on the accused to prove that it was not necessary, not practicable or not reasonably practicable to do more than was in fact done to satisfy the duty or requirement, or that he has taken all reasonable steps, or practicable steps or done the appropriate thing to satisfy the duty or requirement.

(2) In a proceeding for an offence under a provision in this Ordinance consisting of an exemption from compliance with a duty or requirement to do something where it is impracticable, not reasonably practicable, or rendered impracticable to comply with that duty or requirement, the onus is on the accused to prove that it was impracticable or not reasonably practicable to do more than was in fact done to comply with the duty or requirement.

(3) Subsections (1) and (2) do not apply where the offence is committed on or before the commencement (15 December 1989) of this section.

Construction companies have advanced this common law defence of "honest and reasonable belief" to defend the contractor in cases concerning safety duty and requirements. This section is not one that can be breached, per se, but its meaning with regard to proprietorship of the contractor(s) can be interpreted and applied to breaches of other sections of the FIUO.

The Construction Sites (Safety) Regulations

The CS(S)Rs listed in the FIUO were first passed in August 1973 (enforced in May 1974) to promote safety specifically in the construction industry. At their initial introduction to Hong Kong's Legislative Council, the Commissioner for Labour (then titled Commissioner of Labour) stated that "the intention of these special regulations is to introduce statutory safety requirements in the construction industry and to ensure the provision of certain measures designed to safeguard the health and improve the welfare of workers in the construction industry". After this initial introduction, the CS(S)Rs were subsequently amended in 1978, 1981, 1983, 1989, 1993, 1994, 1995, 1997, 1999, 2003, and 2008, but have remained unchanged since then. They establish applicable standards across all construction work, construction sites, and machinery, plants, tools, gear, and materials used to carry out the construction work. The CS(S)Rs include 12 Parts (Table 3.3).

Part I of the CS(S)Rs includes the interpretation of various terms and words used in the regulation, such as "competent examiner," "competent person," "construction site," "crane," "ladder," "lifting appliance," "scaffold," and "safe working load." This section also stipulates that all contractors on worksites are liable to prosecution for regulatory breaches, from the main contractor to the sub-sub-contractor and workers. It also empowers the Commissioner for Labour to grant exemptions to any requirements that they consider unnecessary or not reasonably practicable. For example, an exemption could be granted for the use of a

TABLE 3.3: Outline of the Construction Sites (Safety) Regulations as of 1 January 2008

Part I.	Preliminary
Part IA.	Employment of persons under 18 on construction sites
Part II.	Use of Hoists, etc.
Part III.	(Repealed)
Part IV.	Special Provisions as to Hoists
Part V.	Carrying of Persons and Securing of Loads on Hoists
Part VA.	Scaffolds, Working Platforms and Ladders, etc.
Part VI.	Excavations on Construction Sites
Part VII.	Miscellaneous Safety Requirements
Part VIII.	Notification of Construction Work
Part IX.	Health and Welfare
Part X.	Miscellaneous Provisions
First Schedule	Repealed in LN 285 of 1993
Second Schedule	Contents of first-aid boxes or cupboards
Third Schedule	Requirements with which certain safety equipment must comply

false car in a lift shaft to carry workers during building lifts installation. When an exemption is granted, a set of conditions are imposed on the contractors, and breaching these conditions will bring about automatic cancellation of the exemption. In practice, applications for exemption are rare, and few are granted.

Part IA restricts the employment of persons under 18 years of age on construction sites. If someone younger than 18 is employed anywhere on the site, then one of the following conditions must be met:

- the worker has been contracted and registered as an apprentice under the Apprenticeship Ordinance, Cap. 47;
- the worker has completed an apprenticeship and possesses a certificate of completion;
- the worker has taken an approved training course and possesses a certificate of completion; or
- the worker is undergoing supervised on-site training as part of an approved training course.

Part II deals with hoists. A "hoist" refers to a lifting machine, whether operated by mechanical or electrical power, with a carriage, platform, or cage, the movement of which is restricted by a guide or guides. By definition, this also includes the supports, well and enclosure, and the entire mechanical or electrical apparatus (if any) required in connection with the operation and safety of the hoist. However, this definition does not include a builder's lift or a tower working platform (see Part V). In addition to defining the term hoist, Part II also deals with the construction, maintenance, and inspection of said hoists. It includes information concerning the cabin requirements; construction of drums and pulleys, brakes, controls; and safety devices that should be used to mediate safe hoist operation. The training requirements for workers operating hoists or giving signals are also listed.

Notably, this part was extensively amended in LN 285 of 1993. Furthermore, upon the commencement of CS(S)Rs (Amendment) 2003 on 28 November 2003, the duties imposed on contractors responsible for a hoist were extended to any contractor who has direct control over any construction work which involves the use of a hoist.

Part III was repealed in LN 285 of 1993.

Part IV relates to special provisions for material hoists and was amended in LN 552 of 1995. It stipulates that all hoistways must be enclosed and that access gates must be closed when not in use. Every hoist must be equipped with a device to prevent the platform or cage from falling in the event of hoist rope failure. An overrunning device must also be provided. No hoist which is manufactured, substantially altered, or repaired after the commencement of these regulations may be used unless it has been examined and certified safe by a competent examiner within the previous six months. Part IV also indicates that the appointment of competent examiners rests with the hoist owner. The result of these tests and examinations of each hoist must also be recorded in certificated forms. The applicable safe working load of the hoist must be clearly and legibly marked on its platform or cage. Finally, this section specifies that the hoist shall not be used to carry any load greater than the applicable safe working load.

Part V prohibits a hoist from carrying people at any time and lists the requirements for loads to be safely secured on the hoist. Regarding the use of passenger hoists on worksites, two past accidents, in 1979 and 1993, influenced the information in this section. The first event involved the death of six workmen, while the second involved the death of 12. Both events were the result of improper management and control of passenger hoists by those responsible for their selection, installation, use, maintenance, and examination. Passenger hoists, also termed builders' lifts, are now dealt with under the Builder's Lifts and Tower Working Platforms (Safety) Ordinance, Cap. 470, which is administered by the Electrical and Mechanical Services Department.

Part VA was introduced in 1983 with 18 specific regulations concerning work performed at height. This section was added to replace the earlier regulation 45(c) and was last updated in LN 257 and LN 258 of 2003. It provides a greater degree of safety to persons working on construction sites from height-related incidents. These regulations include the safe use of scaffolds, working platforms, and ladders. Part VA also contains regulations from 38A to 38I, including the prohibition of boatswain's chair use under regulation 38G. Falling accounts for a large number of fatalities in construction work. Part VA stresses the required use of safety belts and harnesses. A schedule is also prescribed that specifies requirements for the width and covering of working platforms, gangways and runs, and working platforms as well as the height of toe-boards and guard-rails. Furthermore, multiple CoPs and Guidance Notes (GNs) related to the standards and specifications for safety nets, safety belts, and safety harnesses have been issued. These are described in more detail for scaffolding work in Chapter 10. The regulations included in Part VA are also reiterated in the CoP for Safety and Health at Work (Land-based Construction over Water—Prevention of Fall).

Part VI of the CS(S)Rs provides for the safety of people employed in excavations or earthworks. Common examples include the construction of trenches, caissons, tunnels, and slopes. These regulations indicate that suitable timber or other materials must be used to prevent the fall or dislodgement of earth or rock, and every part of an excavation or earthwork must be examined weekly by a competent person. Excavations, shafts, pits, or openings in the ground must be either securely covered or adequately fenced off, and stacking materials or placing plants or equipment near their edges (and thus endangering workers) is prohibited. As a general rule, excavation in loose soil conditions 1.2 metres (4 feet) deep or more should be timbered for safety. This section also indicates that attention should be paid to moving loads that may impose dynamic loads to the sides of excavations, which may in turn endanger those working inside the excavations. Moreover, in the event of an emergency, escape ladders or other adequate means are also required by this regulation, so far as practicable, to enable workers to reach positions of safety.

Part VII provides for certain miscellaneous measures to safeguard the safety and health of those employed in construction work. It stipulates measures for the prevention of dust and fume inhalation, eye protection, the fencing of machinery, the employment of trained and competent workmen to operate mechanical equipment, the safe use of electricity, protection against head injuries through the use of safety helmets, the protection from falling material, adequate workplace lighting, the prevention of injury by projecting nails or other objects, good housekeeping, the prevention of drowning, banning smoking, the maintenance of fire escapes and fire-fighting appliances, and sanitary conveniences.

Part VIII requires a contractor to notify the Commissioner for Labour in writing of certain information within seven days of the commencement of work, and likewise, within seven days of the date of work completion. Works of a minor nature (involving not more than 10 workmen) or short duration (less than six weeks) do not require notification. Also, the Commissioner for Labour can request (by written notice) information regarding any construction work.

Part IX is a provision for special first-aid facilities, including specifications for trained first-aid staff and the use of a first-aid box, stretchers, and splints. It also provides for certain welfare matters, such as the requirements for shelters and facilities for meals.

Part X deals with record keeping and contains penalty clauses that may be invoked in the event of any failure to comply with the CS(S)Rs. Every required form related to these regulations will be provided in a format approved by the Commissioner for Labour and published in the Government Gazette. The latest editions of these forms should be used.

Factories and Industrial Undertakings Regulations

This is the main set of regulations enacted under the FIUO. These regulations have been revised several times since their inception. Some sections of the regulations have themselves become new sets of subsidiary regulations. The most important sections of these regulations address the medical examination of a person employed to work underground, the reporting of accidents resulting in death or incapacitation, the reporting of dangerous occurrences, accident prevention, and hygiene.

Individual regulations applicable to construction work

Beyond the CS(S)Rs and the main set of FIURs, there are 28 additional sets of specific FIURs outlined in the FIUO, Cap. 59. Of these, 20 are particularly important for construction work. They list out certain general and specific safety requirements at construction sites. As the FIU (Safety Officers and Safety Supervisors) Regulations and the FIU (Lifting Appliances and Lifting Gear) Regulations play a key role in the field, they are discussed first and in detail.

Factories and Industrial Undertakings (Safety Officers and Safety Supervisors) Regulations

Abbreviated FIU(SO&SS)Rs, this set of regulations requires the compulsory employment of safety officers and safety supervisors by proprietors. Implementation of these regulations in 1986 made the construction industry the first in Hong Kong to be required by law to employ registered safety officers. The requirement for the shipbuilding and repair industry followed in 1995.

The FIU(SO&SS)Rs specify that the main contractor or specialist contractor must employ one registered safety officer on a full-time basis when the total number of persons employed on his construction site is 200 or more. This number was reduced to 100 following an amendment on 11 June 1995. A person who wishes to become a registered safety officer must apply to the Commissioner for Labour. Only registered safety officers are deemed to comply with this set of regulations. The responsibility of a safety officer is to assist the proprietor of a construction company to promote the safety and health of all workers. The registered safety officer is responsible for:

(a) advising the proprietor as to measures to be taken in the interest of the safety and health of persons employed in the industrial undertaking and, with the approval of the proprietor, implementing such measures;

(b) inspecting the industrial undertaking, or directing any person employed as a safety supervisor therein to inspect the industrial undertaking for the purpose of determining whether or not there is any machinery, plant, equipment, appliance, or process or any description of work carried on in the industrial undertaking which is of such a nature as to be liable to cause risk of bodily injury to any person employed in an industrial undertaking;

(c) reporting the findings of any inspection carried out under sub-paragraph (b) to the proprietor and recommending what measures, if any, ought to be taken as a result of that inspection;

(d) assisting in the supervision of any person employed as a safety supervisor in the industrial undertaking;

(e) advising the proprietor in the interest of the safety and health of persons employed in the industrial undertaking of any repairs or maintenance that ought to be carried out in respect of:

  (i) any premises comprising the industrial undertaking;

  (ii) any appliance, equipment, machinery, or plant in use in the industrial undertaking;

(f) investigating and reporting to the proprietor, or causing to be investigated and reported to the proprietor, the circumstances of any accident, or dangerous occurrence in the industrial undertaking and making recommendations to the proprietor to prevent similar accidents or dangerous occurrences;

(g) investigating and reporting to the proprietor, or causing to be investigated and reported to the proprietor, the circumstances of the suffering of any bodily injury by any person employed in the industrial undertaking and making recommendations to the proprietor to prevent similar suffering of any bodily injury;

(h) investigating and reporting to the proprietor every fatal accident in the industrial undertaking and making recommendations to the proprietor to prevent similar fatal accidents;

(i) receiving, discussing, and counter-signing every report submitted to him under regulation 17(1)(b)(iv) by a person employed as a safety supervisor;

(j) preparing and submitting to the proprietor a report as provided in regulation 15, paragraph (2) on or before the last day in every month; and

(k) advising the proprietor on the implementation of a safety management system in the industrial undertaking, including the duties listed below:
   (i) to assist in establishing, revising, and reviewing a safety and health policy of the industrial undertaking;
   (ii) to assist in organising a safety and health training programme;
   (iii) to assist in devising in-house safety rules and regulations;
   (iv) to assist in implementing safety and health plans, programmes, arrangements, and measures;
   (v) to assist in establishing a safety committee and implementing its recommendations;
   (vi) to assist in job hazard analysis, evaluation of potential hazards, and the identification of hazardous conditions and hazardous exposure; and
   (vii) to assist in conducting safety promotion, health assurance, and personal protection programmes.

The FIU(SO&SS)Rs also indicate that at least one safety supervisor is required if the number of workers on the construction site is 20 or more. This is one area where this set of regulations could be improved, and other thresholds should be set which would legally require additional safety supervisors; for example, one supervisor for 20–49 workers, two supervisors for 50–80 workers, etc. Unfortunately, this provision has not been proposed. It is important to note that safety supervisors need not be employed full-time in this role, but they must not be given other duties that could adversely affect their performance as safety supervisors. The responsibility of a safety supervisor is to assist the proprietor and the safety officer or officers in promoting worker safety and health. The main duties of a safety supervisor are specified as follows:

(a) to assist any person employed as a registered safety officer in the industrial undertaking in carrying out the duties of a registered safety officer under these regulations;

(b) to assist the proprietor responsible for the industrial undertaking in promoting the safety and health of persons employed therein including for that purpose:
   (i) advising the proprietor, or any person employed as a safety officer in the industrial undertaking, as to the observance by any person of the standards for the safety or protection of persons employed in the industrial undertaking;
   (ii) supervising the observance by any person of the standards for the safety or protection of persons employed in the industrial undertaking;
   (iii) promoting the safe carrying on of work in the industrial undertaking; and
   (iv) in the case where no person is employed as a safety officer in the industrial undertaking, preparing and submitting to the proprietor, or in the case where a person is employed as a safety officer in the industrial undertaking, to the safety officer, a report as provided in regulation 17, paragraph (2) on or before the last day in every week.

In 2002, regulations 7A and 7B of the FIU(SO&SS)Rs were amended. Under regulation 7B, once registered, a safety officer who wishes to renew their registration shall submit a renewal application to the Commissioner for Labour following the completion of a continuing professional development programme. This programme refers to a course, lecture, seminar, or other method of study that furthers their understanding of occupational safety and health in the field. A total of not less than 100 hours in such a programme must be accumulated by the safety officer within a four-year period before applying for registration renewal. Starting from 1 January 2023, at least one hour of these 100 or more hours must be completed in subjects related to professional ethics and integrity of registered safety officers.

Taken together, the objective of the FIU(SO&SS)Rs is to increase the quality and effectiveness of registered safety officers and supervisors rather than simply the quantity. The value added by a registered safety officer or safety supervisor is proportional to the work they do to increase their personal performance standards and development in the profession.

Safety practitioners should advocate for this practice in the construction industry and play a leading role in their education.

Factories and Industrial Undertakings (Lifting Appliances and Lifting Gear) Regulations

The FIU (Lifting Appliances and Lifting Gear) Regulations (abbreviated FIU(LA&LG)Rs) deal with the safe use of lifting appliances and lifting gear in construction work. Figure 3.1 shows examples of lifting gear frequently used on construction sites. This set of regulations (outlined in Table 3.4) was first enacted in 1974; however, its extension to construction sites was implemented in an amendment in June 1997. They specify the statutory duties of the owner of the lifting appliances and lifting gear to ensure safe use, with the terms "owner," "lifting appliance," and "lifting gear" being defined as follows:

> "Owner", in relation to any lifting appliance or lifting gear, includes the lessee or hirer thereof, and any overseer, foreman, agent or person in charge or having the control or management of the lifting appliance or lifting gear, and the contractor who has control over the way any construction work which involves the use of the lifting appliance or lifting gear is carried out and, in the case of a lifting appliance or lifting gear situated on or used in connection with work on a construction site, also includes the contractor responsible for the construction site (LN 285 of 1993; LN 260 of 2003).

> "Lifting appliance" comprises the crab, winch, teagle, pulley block, or gin wheel used for raising or lowering, crane, sheerlegs, excavator, pile driver, pile extractor, dragline, aerial ropeway, aerial cableway transporter or overhead runway, and any part of these components (LN 285 of 1993).

> "Lifting gear" includes the chain sling, rope sling, ring or similar gear, link, hook, plate clamp, shackle, swivel, and eyebolt.

This set of regulations mandates that the owner must have the lifting appliance and lifting gear periodically tested, examined, or inspected

FIGURE 3.1: Examples of different types of lifting gear

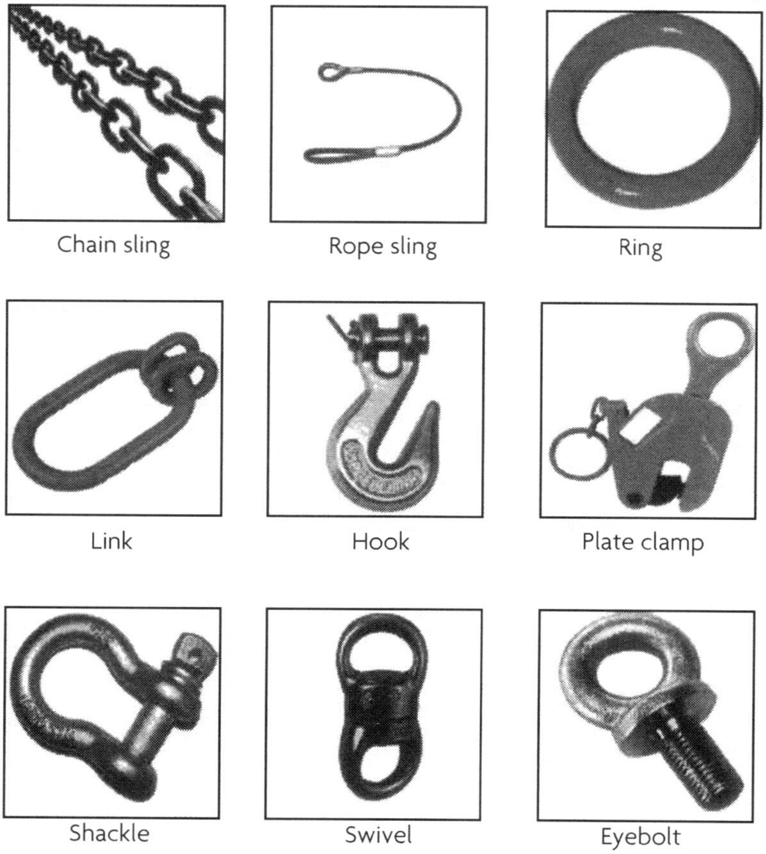

TABLE 3.4: Outline of the Factories and Industrial Undertakings (Lifting Appliances and Lifting Gear) Regulations

PART I: PRELIMINARY	
Regulation 1.	Citation
Regulation 2.	Application
Regulation 3.	Interpretation
PART II: LIFTING APPLIANCES	
Regulation 4.	Construction
Regulation 5.	Lifting appliances to be tested and examined prior to use
Regulation 6.	Repealed in LN 285 of 1993
Regulation 6A.	Report by competent examiner
Regulation 7.	Repealed in LN 285 of 1993

TABLE 3.4: Continued

Regulation 7A.	Periodical inspection by a competent person
Regulation 7B.	Automatic safe load indicator required
Regulation 7C.	Poles or beams supporting pulley blocks or gin wheels
Regulation 7D.	Stability of lifting appliances
Regulation 7E.	Anchoring and ballasting of cranes
Regulation 7F.	Stability of cranes secured by removable weights
Regulation 7G.	Use of cranes in bad weather
Regulation 7H.	Erection, dismantling or alteration of cranes to be under supervision of a competent person
Regulation 7I.	Multiple lifting appliances
Regulation 7J.	Load to be safely secured
Regulation 8.	Precautions to be taken where lifting appliance has travelling or slewing motion
Regulation 9.	Platforms for crane drivers and signallers
Regulation 10.	Cabins for drivers
Regulation 11.	Marking of safe working loads
Regulation 12.	Load not to exceed the safe working load
Regulation 12A.	Competent person to be in charge if load left suspended
Regulation 13.	Scotch and guy derrick cranes
Regulation 14.	Cranes with derricking jibs
Regulation 15.	Restriction on the use of cranes
Regulation 15A.	Operators of cranes and lifting appliances
Regulation 15B.	Operation
Regulation 15C.	Steam not to obscure workplace
Regulation 16.	Brakes, controls, safety devices, etc.
Regulation 17.	Drums and pulleys
PART III: CHAINS, ROPES AND LIFTING GEAR	
Regulation 18.	Construction, testing, examination and safe working load of chains, ropes and lifting gear
Regulation 18A.	Multiple slings
PART IIIA: MISCELLANEOUS	
Regulation 18B.	Carrying of persons by means of lifting appliances
Regulation 18C.	Keeping and displaying of certificates and reports
Regulation 18D.	Forms
PART IV: OFFENECES AND PENALTIES	
Regulation 19.	Offences by owners
Regulation 20.	Offences by persons employed
Regulation 21.	Offences by competent examiners
Regulation 22.	Offences by competent persons
Schedule 1.	Procedure for Testing and Examining Lifting Appliances and Lifting Gear
Schedule 2.	Repealed in LN 285 of 1993

by a competent examiner or a competent person. A certificate shall be obtained from the examiner in the approved form and must include a statement indicating that the lifting appliance is in safe working order. Regulation 7B of the FIU(LA&LG)Rs outlines the use of an automatic safe load indicator (ASLI) (described further in Chapter 7).

Factories and Industrial Undertakings (Notification of Occupational Diseases) Regulations

This set of regulations lists occupational diseases medical practitioners must report to the Commissioner for Labour when they are diagnosed or even just suspected. There is an Occupational Health Division in the Labour Department responsible for handling these reports and responses. For example, this list includes silicosis, which is a common occupational disease among construction workers in Hong Kong. Notably, workers confirmed to be affected by an occupational disease are entitled to compensation.

Quarries (Safety) Regulations

This set of statutory requirements is designed to ensure safety in quarrying operations. It lists the qualifications, duties, and responsibilities of an approved supervisor or deputy supervisor as well as the minimum safety measures required on quarry sites, including displaying warning notices, provisions for personal protective equipment, and provision of adequate first-aid equipment and personnel.

Factories and Industrial Undertakings (Blasting by Abrasives) Special Regulations

This set of special regulations allows the Commissioner for Labour to specify conditions to protect workers from developing silicosis or other occupational diseases arising from the blasting process. These regulations restrict the use of sand or free silica as an abrasive. The Commissioner for Labour may, however, permit (in writing) their use if certain precautionary measures have been taken, but this is rare.

Factories and Industrial Undertakings (Woodworking Machinery) Regulations

This set of regulations prescribes several statutory duties for the proprietor of establishments in which woodworking machinery is used. These include the provision of general safety measures for all machines, safeguarding, adequate lighting, good housekeeping, and sufficient space for safe operations. The modern designs of bench circular saws and other woodworking machinery, which include guards, make many of these regulations irrelevant.

Factories and Industrial Undertakings (Confined Spaces) Regulation

This regulation ensures the safety of employees working in a confined space. Confined spaces include pits, sewers, tanks, and silos where toxic gases may be present. The proprietor shall appoint a competent person to assess the working conditions in the confined space. This regulation also identifies safety measures to be taken before and during work. The proprietor or contractor shall also formulate and implement appropriate procedures to deal with any serious and imminent danger to workers inside a confined space. Only a certified worker who has received specific training and instruction is legally allowed to work in a confined space. This set of regulations was originally enacted in 1973 but was last amended in 1999. A related CoP (Safety and Health at Work in Confined Spaces) has also been issued.

Factories and Industrial Undertakings (Abrasive Wheels) Regulations

This set of regulations outlines the safety measures required for mounting and operating abrasive wheels. This includes marking the permissible speed in revolutions per minute of the wheel and the working speed of the spindle. Only competent persons, after training and gaining practical experience, can be appointed (in writing) by the proprietor. Notably, abrasive wheels for grinding have been largely replaced by more abrasive disc cutters on most construction sites.

Factories and Industrial Undertakings (Work in Compressed Air) Regulations

This set of regulations ensures that adequate precautions are taken to protect workers from sickness and ill-health arising from working in an environment with compressed air. These regulations were enacted in the 1970s during the construction of underground tunnels for the Mass Transit Railway (MTR), which was the first time compressed air was used for construction work in the city. It lays down the construction and design of the man-lock, decant lock, and medical lock. It also establishes the procedures for compression and decompression. The lock attendant is the party responsible for the compression and decompression of persons. Supervision by a medical practitioner is necessary for the person employed.

Factories and Industrial Undertakings (Spraying of Flammable Liquids) Regulations

The "spraying of flammable liquids" refers to the aerosolisation of a liquid with a flashpoint below 32 degrees Celsius or a mixture containing such liquid and its application to an article or structure with a pressurised spraying apparatus. This set of regulations is most commonly applied to the use of spray paint, but they also cover the spraying of thinners, varnishes, lacquers, sealing compounds, and petroleum-based adhesives. The regulations specify that the spraying process be carried out in a designated spraying room or area with efficient ventilation to remove any flammable vapour mist. The regulations go on to state that works may not use a source of ignition within six metres of any spraying area. Electrical appliances exposed to the flammable substance require specific construction, design, installation, and maintenance to prevent ignition.

Factories and Industrial Undertakings (Cartridge-operated Fixing Tools) Regulations

This set of regulations controls the use of cartridge-operated fixing tools on construction sites. It specifies that only approved tools can be used and outlines the required training and certification for the personnel working with these tools. These workers must not be under the age of 18.

Furthermore, the construction company must provide and maintain suitable personal protective equipment for every operator.

Factories and Industrial Undertakings (Protection of Eyes) Regulations

This set of regulations is adapted from the United Kingdom's Protection of Eyes Regulations of 1974 and similarly requires employers to provide suitable eye protection to workers engaging in certain industrial processes known to be particularly dangerous to the eyes. A total of 14 industrial activities requiring eyewear is listed in the Schedule of the regulations.

Factories and Industrial Undertakings (Electricity) Regulations

These regulations apply to all industrial undertakings that generate, transform, distribute, or use electricity. They specify the size and capacity of all apparatuses and conductors used. Further, they require companies to insulate all live conductors to prevent electrical incidents. There are also requirements pertaining to the construction and location of switchboards, switchboard apparatuses, and substations. It is the duty of the proprietor to provide and maintain insulation stands and screens or other protective equipment to protect against electrical hazards.

Factories and Industrial Undertakings (Asbestos) Regulation

This regulation imposes duties on those carrying out processes involving asbestos and aims to protect the health of workers employed in these processes. The regulation prohibits the use of blue asbestos (crocidolite), brown asbestos (amosite), or any substance containing either of these minerals. Some processes such as asbestos spraying, asbestos insulation, and the use of amphibole asbestos are prohibited. This regulation indicates that the proprietor must ensure that the nature and degree of exposure to asbestos are appropriately assessed and that all necessary precautionary measures have been implemented to prevent or reduce exposure. Such measures may include providing approved respiratory protection equipment and protective clothing as well as demarcating the zones where protective equipment is required. This regulation further explains that exposure of any worker to airborne asbestos must be monitored by an approved method. Young persons below 18 are not allowed to be employed in any process involving asbestos, and workers have to be medically examined before engaging in asbestos-related work processes as well as during and after project completion. A related CoP (Safety and Health at Work with Asbestos) has also been issued.

Factories and Industrial Undertakings (Dangerous Substances) Regulations

This piece of legislation applies to any dangerous substance that is present in any specified industrial undertaking (e.g., work in factories, quarries, mines, and construction sites). It specifies 231 chemical substances that legally require proper labelling, risk assessment, and precautionary safety measures. This substance list has not been updated or amended since its inception. The regulations also state that the proprietor shall provide information, training and instruction, and personal protective clothing to the employees using these substances.

Factories and Industrial Undertakings (Noise at Work) Regulation

This regulation stipulates the first, second, and peak action noise levels and the corresponding safety actions required to minimise the effect on employees and the public. In section 8 of these regulations, the proprietor must provide approved ear protectors and reduce employee exposure as much as reasonably practicable.

Factories and Industrial Undertakings (Suspended Working Platforms) Regulation

This regulation controls the safety of those who work on suspended working platforms (commonly called gondolas). It was enacted in June 1994. Gondolas are permanently or temporarily installed on building roofs during construction work. This regulation specifies that each worker must be equipped with a full-body harness and provided with an independent lifeline, which must be separately and securely anchored. Workers must be 18 years old or above and have completed a recognised training course. Gondolas must be inspected regularly by a competent examiner to obtain (and retain) a safety certificate before use. The safe working load and maximum number of passengers the gondola can carry must also be indicated, according to this regulation. A related CoP (Safe Use and Operation of Suspended Working Platform) has also been issued.

Factories and Industrial Undertakings (Safety Management) Regulation

The Hong Kong Government carried out a comprehensive safety review of the industrial sector in 1995. The review strongly focused on the construction industry. The government maintains that the primary party responsible for promoting safety and health in the workplace, and thus responsible for adhering to safety legislation, is the individual or group of individuals that decide to use certain industrial processes (and thus agree to monitor and minimise the risks associated with them) as well as the workers themselves. This regulation, established four years after the government's review, provides a framework for self-regulation with the aim of enhancing industrial safety standards. It includes both legislative and administrative objectives that can be achieved through a company system of safety management.

This particular regulation outlines, amongst other things, the requirements for contractors and proprietors employing a workforce of a certain size (50 to 99 or 100 and over) and for projects of a certain contract sum (HK$100 million or more) to carry out safety audits or safety reviews on their safety and health management systems. The safety auditors employed for this purpose must be registered by the Labour Department. While this regulation does not specify a particular audit scheme that must be adopted, it does list 14 safety management elements that the scheme must assess. These elements include safety policy; safety organization; safety training; in-house safety rules; inspection of hazardous conditions; personal protection equipment (PPE) programme; investigations of accidents or incidents; emergency preparedness and response; evaluation, selection, and control of sub-contractors; safety committees; job hazards analysis; promotional programme; accident control and elimination of hazards; and occupational health assurance. Two safety audit schemes fulfilling these regulatory requirements are described in Chapter 12. A related CoP (Safety Management) has also been issued.

Factories and Industrial Undertakings (Loadshifting Machinery) Regulation

This regulation was enacted by the Legislative Council in April 2000. Its purpose is to ensure that the loadshifting machines used in industrial undertakings are operated by licensed persons. Any loadshifting machines used on a construction site, including forklift trucks, bulldozers, loaders, excavators, trucks or lorries, compactors, dumpers, graders, locomotives, and scrapers, are within the ambit of this regulation. However, it does not apply to the operator of a truck or lorry who holds a valid driver's licence under the Road Traffic Ordinance, Cap. 374. A related CoP (Safe Use of Excavators) has also been issued.

Factories and Industrial Undertakings (Gas Welding and Flame Cutting) Regulation

This regulation was enacted by the Legislative Council in November 2001. It ensures that gas welding and flame cutting work is carried out by a person that is over 18 years of age and has taken and passed a recognised safety training course for these particular processes. A related CoP (Safety and Health at Work for Gas Welding and Flame Cutting) has also been issued.

Other regulations

While the individual regulations listed above are particularly relevant to the construction industry, there are also a number of additional regulations that safety practitioners may need to be familiar with depending on the specifications of their worksite or factory. This includes:

- Factories and Industrial Undertakings (Carcinogenic Substances) Regulations
- Factories and Industrial Undertakings (Cargo and Container Handling) Regulations

- Factories and Industrial Undertakings (Dry Batteries) Regulations
- Factories and Industrial Undertakings (Electrolytic Chromium Process) Regulations
- Factories and Industrial Undertakings (Fire Precautions in Notifiable Workplaces) Regulations
- Factories and Industrial Undertakings (First Aid in Notifiable Workplaces) Regulations
- Factories and Industrial Undertakings (Goods Lifts) Regulations
- Factories and Industrial Undertakings (Guarding and Operation of Machinery) Regulations

SECTIONS 9 AND 10 OF THE OCCUPATIONAL SAFETY AND HEALTH ORDINANCE, CHAPTER 509

The OSHO effectively extends the coverage of the FIUO to include the safety and health of employees in non-industrial sectors. Under the OSHO, the "employer" and the "occupier" of premises have some specific general duties, similar to those under section 6A of the FIUO. In this context, the "occupier" is defined as "a person who has any degree of control over the premises, or workplace… and, in particular, includes a person to whom subsection (5) or (6) applies". These subsections appear as follows:

> Subsection (5): A person who, under a lease or contract, has an obligation for: (a) the maintenance or repair of premises; or (b) the safety of, or the absence of risks to health arising from the condition or use of, any plant or substance located on the premises, is taken to be an occupier of the premises for the purposes of this Ordinance.
>
> Subsection (6): A person who, under a lease or contract, has an obligation to provide, maintain or repair a means of access to, or egress from, premises is taken to be an occupier of the premises for the purposes of this Ordinance.

In the construction industry, this definition includes the contractor(s) responsible for the worksite. The relevant provisions applicable are sections 9 and 10, which give the Commissioner for Labour the power to serve Improvement Notices (INs) and Suspension Notices (SNs). A description of INs and SNs and the consequences of non-compliance are provided in Chapter 4.

SUMMARY

This chapter lists the subsidiary safety regulations that safety practitioners need to be conversant in the construction industry. Many of these regulations were introduced in the late 1960s and 1970s and have had to be updated to stay relevant in the field. However, in an ever-changing technological environment, some of these regulations will still inevitably become outdated and, in some cases, invalid. For example, the new design for circular saw blades that includes automatic withdrawal has eliminated the need for the FIU (Woodworking Machinery) Regulations. Another example is the FIU (Blasting by Abrasives) Special Regulations, which is no longer relevant because abrasives do not contain free silica anymore. Keeping the list of occupational diseases under the FIU (Notification of Occupational Diseases) Regulations up to date is also challenging. As our understanding of workplace health has increased, it has become more and more obvious that work-related health complications can take time to manifest and may develop well after the worker has completed the work. Disease and ill-health can be caused by a number of worksite-related factors, including various chemical and toxic substances, biological agents, noise and vibration emanating from equipment, and in-situ radiation from building materials. These can be exacerbated by the worker's individual health, particularly if the worker has a pre-existing upper and lower limb disorder, performs manual handling at work, is an older worker, works excessively long hours, or is working in "Sick Building syndrome" conditions. Work stress caused by incompatible goals between workers, management, proprietors, safety officers, etc. is also a major factor, although this has not been studied in depth in the construction industry. These are only a few examples of regulations that have become outdated or require constant updating. When viewing these regulations together in the context of occupational health, it is natural to ask if additional health regulations should be established or refined to specifically target the construction industry.

In addition to possibly becoming outdated, the regulations covered in this chapter are also limited in certain respects. CoPs and GNs, in particular, are unduly restrictive in that they impose solutions rather than proactive, goal-setting objectives. They are also often expressed in a way that discourages alternatives and innovation, and compliance may take precedence over wider safety considerations. This prevents those in the field from implementing other simple and often more practical solutions.

Thus, as safety practitioners gain field experience it is important for them to convey their advice to proprietors in a manner that not only fulfils the requirement set by the regulations but also helps them consider proactive changes to their safety protocols. Their advice to companies is essential to help proprietors understand the laws and legal repercussions for non-compliance.

FURTHER READING

Clarke, J. (2016) *Redgrave's Health and Safety* (Ninth edition), LexisNexis.

Development Bureau, Hong Kong SAR Government (2018) *Construction Site Safety Manual, Chapter 2, March version.*

Health and Safety Authority, Ireland (2018) *Code of Practice for Access and Working Scaffolds.*

Labour Department, Hong Kong SAR (2017) *Concise Investigation Report for the Fatal Accident in Hong Kong-Zhuhai-Macao Bridge Project on 29 March 2017.*

Labour Department, Hong Kong SAR (n.d.) *Codes of Practices published by Labour Department made under section 7 of the Factories and Industrial Undertakings Ordinance, Chapter 59.*

DISCUSSION QUESTIONS

1. Is enacting and enforcing more safety regulations an effective way to promote safety in the construction industry in Hong Kong? What special sets of subsidiary regulations do you think should be passed by the Legislative Council to promote construction safety?
2. In the construction industry, employers and employees rarely discuss occupational health issues openly. How would you promote further discussion of this important topic?
3. What regulations apply to your current or future industry? Look up the most recent versions online and discuss any recent amendments.

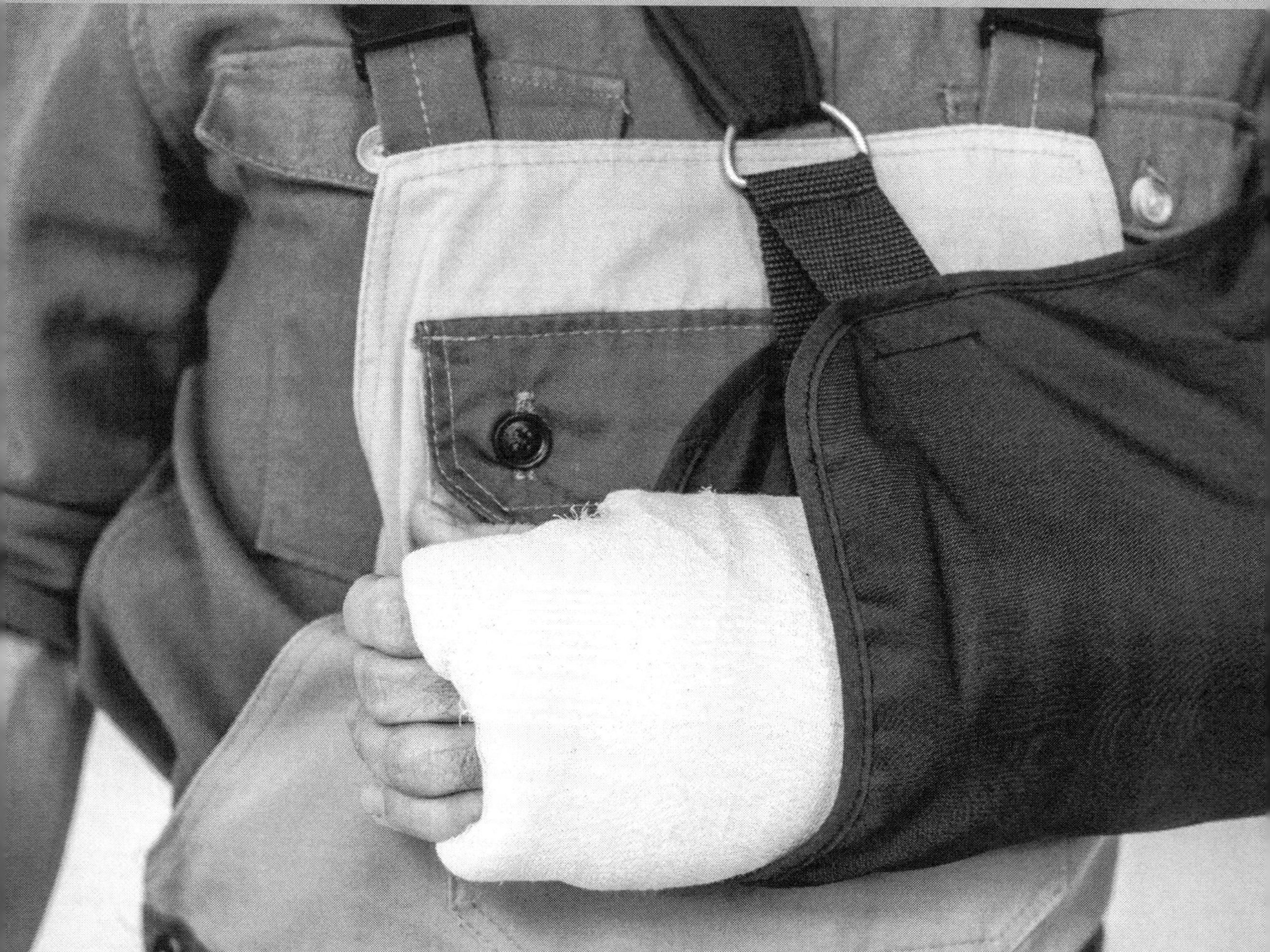

PART II

THE LEGAL STANCE ON CONSTRUCTION SAFETY

LEARNING OBJECTIVES

Part II provides an in-depth discussion of the legal regulations related to the construction industry, including a general explanation of enforcement and repercussions for breaches. Later chapters summarise legal cases involving specific regulatory breaches, with those involving safe systems of work and working at height being top legal concerns. Upon completion of Part II, one should be able to:

1. Outline the legal hierarchy and administration by regulatory bodies and the repercussions for breaches;
2. List the key players in legal proceedings;
3. Discuss the general duties requirements under section 6A of the Factories and Industrial Undertakings Ordinance, Chapter 59;
4. Discuss Regulation 38 of the Construction Sites (Safety) Regulations and the impact various court cases have had on the industry; and
5. Describe other construction-specific regulations and how legal authorities have dealt with breaches.

The case examples provided in these chapters are meant to aid stakeholders in pursuing safety on their worksites. They are provided in summary form and focus on the "lessons learned". They should not, however, be the sole reference when considering the law, and readers are encouraged to research the laws specific to their worksites and projects.

"The Factory Acts are there, not merely to protect the careful, the vigilant and the conscious workman, but human nature being what it is, the careless, the indolent, the inadvertent, the weary, and even perhaps in some cases, the disobedient"

– *Carr v Mercantile Produce Co. Ltd*
(1949) 2 KB 601, at 608

"No legislation, however, can protect a workman from his own perverted acts of stupidity. In my view, the deceased in this case made unsafe what was otherwise safe by his own act"

– Judge Duffy
The Queen v Hip Hing Construction Co. Ltd
(HCMA 440/1995)

4 Overview of Construction Safety Enforcement and Repercussions

INTRODUCTION

Legally, work carried out on a construction site is considered an industrial undertaking, which needs to comply with all relevant regulations and Codes of Practice (CoPs) applicable under the Factories and Industrial Undertakings Ordinance (FIUO), Cap. 59. This chapter discusses the regulatory hierarchy, enforcement, and repercussions for non-compliance in the construction field. These sections refer specifically to all relevant sets of Factories and Industrial Undertakings Regulations (FIURs) and sections 6A and 7A of the FIUO as well as the Occupational Safety and Health Ordinance (OSHO), Cap. 509 (sections 9 and 10), as outlined in Chapter 3.

LEGAL HIERARCHY AND POWER

The hierarchy of legal instruments issued by the Labour Department is layered as follows:

1. Ordinances (e.g., FIUO and OSHO);
2. Regulations (e.g., FIURs);

3. CoPs (e.g., section 7A of the FIUO); and
4. Guidance Notes (GNs) and pamphlets.

In Hong Kong, safety and health ordinances and regulations are enacted through the Legislative Council. The Commissioner for Labour is the individual responsible for initiating discussion and amendments to these legislative documents and has the power to issue CoPs and GNs. Notably, amendments to CoPs, GNs, and pamphlets are made and implemented much faster than changes to ordinances and regulations. However, the legal power of these documents varies.

ADMINISTRATIVE ENFORCEMENT OF ORDINANCES AND REGULATIONS

In Hong Kong, the authority responsible for enforcing safety and health legislation is vested in the Commissioner for Labour, who is the head of the Hong Kong Labour Department. In 1973, teams of occupational safety officers (previously known as Factory Inspectors) of the Labour Department were appointed by the Commissioner for Labour to act as enforcement officers. For example, the Construction Sites (Safety) Regulations (CS(S)Rs) are enforced by the Building and Engineering Construction Areas Offices of the Labour Department.

To enforce legislation, the officers will use the administrative instruments available to them. These include (a) issuing Improvement or Suspension Notices (INs or SNs) and (b) bringing prosecutions against offenders.

Improvement and Suspension Notices

The authority of the Commissioner to enforce legislation in both the industrial and non-industrial sectors is further specified in sections 9 and 10 of the OSHO. Section 9 gives the Commissioner for Labour the ability to serve an IN on an employer or an occupier of a worksite for breaches of the OSHO or FIUO. This responsibility is particularly important for circumstances in which it is likely that the breach will be continued or repeated. The IN requires the occupier to remedy the issue within a specified time (normally within 14 days from the issue date of the notice) and to refrain from repeating the problem. If the occupier fails to comply with the IN, they risk being fined HK$200,000 or imprisoned for 12 months. An example IN letter and template is shown in Figure 4.1.

Section 10 of the OSHO gives the Commissioner the right to enforce legislation via an SN. An SN is more severe than an IN, and the Commissioner will typically only use it when there is an imminent risk of death or serious bodily injury in connection with plant conditions or a particular activity (or the substances used for it) undertaken on the premises. An SN prohibits the occupier from using the plant or continuing the specified activity within the premises, often resulting in significant costs and financial losses for the company. After delivery to the occupier, the notice normally takes effect within 24 hours, at which point the work or activity in question is completely suspended. Non-compliance with an SN has severe consequences for the occupier, including (a) a fine of HK$500,000 and imprisonment for 12 months and (b) a further fine of HK$50,000 for each day (full or partial) during which the offender knowingly and intentionally continues the work specified in the SN. The potential risks associated with the suspended work or activity specified in the SN must be reduced or eliminated before the Commissioner will revoke the SN. An example SN letter and template are shown in Figure 4.2.

Past enforcement experience indicates that the normal enforcement actions (i.e., initiating prosecution) upon the discovery of serious breaches of safety legislation do not bring about prompt rectification of the unsafe conditions or activities, particularly as prosecution can be tedious and sometimes prolonged. Notably, the provisions outlined above allow Labour Department officers and the Commissioner to bypass the sometimes lengthy court procedures involved in prosecution (during which, in some cases, the proprietor may continue the work) and enforce immediate remedial action. The heavy sanctions of non-compliance with the IN or SN are often enough to mediate changes on the worksite or in the construction safety program of the proprietor, thus preventing incidents or accidents (or their recurrence) that could result in serious

FIGURE 4.1: Example Improvement Notice (IN)

Occupational Safety and Health Ordinance
Section 9

IMPROVEMENT NOTICE

Name:
Address:

Trading as*

I **HEREBY GIVE NOTICE** that I am of the opinion that at ______________

____

____________ you, as an [employer/ occupier of premises where a workplace is located], [are contravening/ have contravened in circumstances that make it likely that the contravention will be continued or repeated] the [Occupational Safety and Health Ordinance/ Factories and Industrial Undertakings Ordinance], namely______________________
____________in
that____
____
____
____
____.

By virtue of the power vested in me under section 9 of the Occupational Safety and Health Ordinance, I **HEREBY REQUIRE** you to [remedy the said contravention within __________ (days/ months)* i.e. on or before ________________ /refrain from continuing or repeating the said contravention].

Signature: (____________________)   Date: ____________
for Commissioner for Labour

[ ]: select as appropriate   Reference No. :__________
* : delete if appropriate

Notes: 1. Failure, without reasonable excuse, to comply with an improvement notice is a criminal offence and renders the offender liable to a fine of $200,000 and to imprisonment for 12 months under section 9(5) of the Occupational Safety and Health Ordinance.

2. The service of this notice does not relieve you of any legal liability for failing to comply with any statutory provisions referred to in the notice, or to perform any other statutory or common law duty resting on you.

3. Compliance with this notice would not be taken as an admission of the alleged contravention of the statutory provisions referred to in it.

FIGURE 4.2: Example Suspension Notice (SN)

Occupational Safety and Health Ordinance
Section 10

SUSPENSION NOTICE

Name:
Address:

Trading as*

I HEREBY GIVE you, as the [employer responsible for/ occupier of] premises where a workplace is located, namely ______________________________

____

______________ at ____

______________________________ ('the said premises'), NOTICE that I am of the opinion that because of [an activity undertaken on the said premises/ the condition or use of the said premises/ the condition or use of a plant located on the said premises/ the condition or use of a substance located on the said premises], namely ______________

____

______________________________ , there is an imminent risk of death or serious bodily injury , and that the matters which create, or are likely to create the said risk(s) are : __

____

____

By virtue of the power vested in me under section 10 of the Occupational Safety and Health Ordinance, I HEREBY DIRECT the said [activity not to be undertaken/ premises not to be used/ plant not to be used/ substance not to be used] while this notice remains in force.

This notice takes effect on [the date on which it is served/ ______________]

Signature: (______________________)
for Commissioner for Labour

Date: ______________

Reference No. : __________

[ ] : select as appropriate
* : delete as appropriate

bodily injury to workers. It is, therefore, common for the Labour Department to use these notices as a tool to prompt compliance with the safety legislation and enhance safety standards across the industry. However, while issuing INs or SNs to rectify unsafe and dangerous working conditions—a process used since 1997—is straightforward and simple, their effectiveness is unclear. Thus, until these methods can be shown to be effective or more appropriately used, enforcement of construction safety laws and regulations and long-term changes often require legal repercussions implemented via prosecution.

Prosecution

Prosecution statistics are published in the Annual Report of the Labour Department. Going through the prosecution statistics released in these reports, it becomes evident that officers will often prosecute breaches if they are confident they will be successful. This is often the case for simple and obvious breaches, such as working at height, fencing of dangerous places liable to cause falls or injury to workers, and utilising poor systems of work. Indeed, falls are considered to be the most hazardous incident in the construction industry. Many cases have been prosecuted involving falls on construction sites as well as other regulatory breaches. Amongst the wide-ranging requirements stipulated under the FIUO and its subsidiary regulations, it is interesting to analyse which regulations are the most commonly enforced by the occupational safety officers. These legal cases are discussed in more depth in Chapter 5 (breaches of section 6A of the FIUO), Chapter 6 (breaches of the CS(S)Rs), and Chapter 7 (breaches of other subsidiary FIURs).

The objectives of a prosecution are to:

- promote safety and health standards at work and deter non-compliance with the laws;
- impose penalties on those who fail to observe safety regulations thereby creating a level playing field for contractors by removing unfair competition from unscrupulous operators;
- demonstrate safety standards (and how they are monitored) in the industry to the community at large; and
- follow international practices, conventions, and recommendations.

At present, two categories of enforcing officers in the Labour Department can bring up prosecutions against offenders of the legislation in the FIUO, OSHO, and their subsidiary regulations—namely, occupational safety officers and occupational hygienists.

Occupational safety officers as "lay prosecutors"

The issuance of a prosecution summons must occur within six months of any breach detected, as mandated in the Limitation Ordinance, Cap. 347. An occupational safety officer can initiate a prosecution under the following circumstances:

- after accident investigations (fatal or otherwise) or dangerous occurrence investigations (scheduled in the FIUO) at worksites;
- during special tasks campaigns;
- after investigations of justifiable complaints lodged by workers or a third party via the telephone hotline established in the Labour Department or other means; and
- during routine site inspections.

It is generally felt that prosecutions after accidents, particularly accidents that arouse public interest, will greatly impact management. In almost all cases involving fatal accidents at construction sites, the employers or occupiers of the worksite have subsequently faced prosecution for breaches of safety regulations. There seems to be no exception to this.

Court records show that a substantial number of prosecutions are indeed taken up by occupational safety officers. In the case of simple and straightforward regulatory breaches, which do not require a substantial level of legal competence or legal training, the occupational safety officer will assume the role of prosecutor (i.e., "lay prosecutor") in the Magistrates' Courts. On the other hand, if the prosecution requires a high degree of legal competence and experience to prove breaches in complicated cases, then trained lawyers seconded from the Secretary for Justice in the Department of Justice will take up the prosecutorial duties in court.

As construction and engineering activities are complex and often complicated, it is important to examine the knowledge, technical competence, and specialist support services available to occupational safety officers when they seek to initiate a prosecution. Knowledge and technical competence are largely developed by the occupational safety officer through experience and training. They will need a broad understanding of the legislation and the local legal system. Occupational safety officers in the Labour Department have access to various specialists to can support their prosecutorial duties. These professionals are seconded from other government departments or appointed from tertiary educational institutions.

Occupational hygienists assist occupational safety officers in carrying out prosecutions for failing to observe occupational hygiene matters. Their expertise is primarily related to health and hygiene concerns such as exposure to harmful chemicals or substances, exposure to silica dust, exposure to noise, etc.

The role of safety experts

In legal proceedings related to occupational safety and health, safety experts are often engaged by both the prosecution and the defence to assist the court in making decisions on technical subjects of arguments or issues that are in dispute. The engagement of a safety expert, either general or specialist, arises from the need for additional information or insight concerning occupational safety and health that will be helpful to the court. Such engagement is, therefore, proactive. As a safety expert, the officer has to clearly explain to the court the rationale behind the charges and identify the legislation breached in the alleged offence. The expert's opinion is expressed in the form of a written report which should be sent to the opposing party (the defence or prosecution) before a legal proceeding. This will typically be challenged and scrutinised by the opposing counsel, who may have also appointed another safety expert with the opposite view. Other information about how a safety expert should express this opinion can be found in the Code of Conduct under Chapter 4A, Appendix D of the Rules of High Court. As an "expert witness", the safety expert will agree to be bound by and comply with these legal duties.

General safety experts

Before re-titling the post of Factory Inspector in the Labour Department, general safety experts engaged by the prosecution were Divisional Factory Inspectors who had experience and knowledge in the enforcement of safety laws and occupational safety. Upon re-titling, these experts are now assigned from a pool of senior occupational safety officers in the Labour Department. These general safety experts may have a diverse educational and training background, often working in other fields prior to joining the Labour Department. However, in general, desirable general safety experts should have a background in engineering and occupational safety and health, preferably at the post-graduate level. They should possess good communication skills, in both written and spoken English and Chinese. Practically, they need to be conversant with occupational safety and health laws and be aware of compliance (and non-compliance) activities. A general safety expert in the construction safety field should have experience with inspecting and auditing complex construction works, carrying out investigations of accidents or incidents, and serving as a witness in court, representing the prosecution or the defence. It is also preferable for the expert to have published works focused on occupational safety and health subjects.

Because of their experience with safety and health laws, they have long been accepted as general safety experts in courts. One issue still debated by safety practitioners is whether external safety experts should be appointed as witnesses for the prosecution or defence when a Labour Department officer is unavailable or unable to subjectively comment about the particular topic or event in question. It is the author's view that an external or intermediary pool of general safety experts from outside the Labour Department should be established to address this issue. Setting up this pool will add confidence and creditability to the decision-making process of the court and help to ensure fair prosecutions and convictions.

Specialist safety experts

In contrast to general safety experts, specialist safety experts should have deeper knowledge of topics within their respective fields. Specialist safety experts can also be consulted by both the prosecution and defence. This group of individuals includes occupational health doctors, mechanical engineers, electrical engineers, structural engineers, building surveyors, metallurgists, and skilled tradesmen (e.g., bamboo or metal scaffolders, electricians, etc.). For boilers or pressure vessels, a pressure surveyor will be engaged. When in-house specialist experts are not available, it may be necessary to engage experts from outside tertiary education institutions.

Example cases using testimony from safety experts as witnesses

While safety experts, general or specialist, do not decide cases, their opinions help provide a better understanding of the situation based upon their special skills, education, and experience. There are sometimes conflicts of opinions between the prosecution and the defence, and the court will then be left to decide which opinion it prefers. The prime function of a safety expert is to assist the court by giving a fair and honest opinion and not assisting their client to win the case despite being engaged and paid by the client. Indeed, for both general and specialist safety experts, courts tend to favour experts whose opinions are honest, reliable, knowledgeable, rational, and cogent. On the other hand, experts that have voiced speculative, biased, fanciful, superficial, partial, or impractical opinions are not favoured. The following cases explain examples when expert opinions influenced a court decision and, alternatively, when they were dismissed.

AG v Hsin Chong Construction (Asia) Limited (HCMA 708/1993)

In this case, a scaffolder with 20 years of experience in the bamboo scaffolding trade, who had compiled a book on bamboo scaffolding, was accepted as a trade expert.

HKSAR v Shun Tak Properties Limited (HCMA 1014/2006)/[2009] 3 HKLRD 299

Following a court ruling concerning a suspended working platform not being properly maintained under the FIU (Suspended Working Platforms) Regulation, an appeal was laid. Technical evidence from a mechanical expert was submitted by the defence as "fresh evidence" against the Magistrate's decision. The Court said that "a witness, expert or otherwise, should not comment on the findings of a Magistrate, let alone [state] that these findings are erroneous". The Court further advised that if the "fresh evidence"—in this case, a technical report prepared by an expert after the Magistrate's ruling—was relevant to the maintenance issue or any other issues, then the expert should have been called before the Magistrate had adjudicated upon the matter. The opinion was dismissed. This case stresses the need to engage experts in the initial trial and not thereafter.

HKSAR v China Geo-Engineering Corporation (TWS847/2012)

In this case, three experts were called upon by the defence to give opinions: a general safety expert, a landscape architect, and a geo-technical engineer. The Court held, amongst other things, that "weeding work" for unwanted grass growing on a stabilisation slope in the catchment areas of a reservoir under maintenance was not "construction work" under the law.

HKSAR v Penta-Ocean Construction Company Limited (ESS31076/2015)

The Magistrate agreed with the defence expert in this case that doing surface de-plastering work using a kung-fu stool was not "heavy-duty work". Kung-fu stools are traditional tools that have been used for many years for indoor plastering and de-plastering work in Hong Kong. In this case, the height of the kung-fu stool used was much lower than two metres, and the ceiling height of the worksite was only 2.8 metres. While noting that the kung-fu stool was not the best option, the Court held that it was not unsafe to use the stool for de-plastering under these circumstances, as explained by the safety expert. This case is also addressed in Chapter 5.

HKSAR v China State Construction Engineering (Hong Kong) Limited (KCS4705/2013)

The Magistrate hearing this case agreed with the defence expert that a worker would not fall through an un-glassed aluminium window frame inside a housing unit as the size of the un-glassed aluminium window frame was not large enough. The safety expert gave his opinion with the help of anthropometry in ergonomics. Anthropometry refers to the collection, analysis, and tabulation of numerical data concerning the physical body dimensions of workers. It branches into structural anthropometry and functional anthropometry.

HKSAR v Leighton Contractors (Asia) Limited (KTS17711/2017)

Application of ergonomics was also accepted in this case regarding the size of temporary floor openings on building sites and the risk to workers who could fall through and sustain bodily injuries. In this case, the Court held that based on the calculations of the safety expert, it was not possible for a worker wearing thicker warm clothing to fall through a temporary rectangular floor opening that was 410 mm × 460 mm in size.

HKSAR v The Jardine Engineering Corporation Limited (ESS3296/2017)

Here, the Court accepted the opinion of an electrician that inspection work could be carried out at floor level without riding on an A-shaped wooden ladder. The case was brought against an electrician seen doing his inspection work riding on such a ladder which was considered unsafe.

HKSAR v Penta-Ocean Construction Company Limited (STS5733/2016)

This was a case of the unsafe lifting of falsework frames in a teagle opening that caused bodily injury to a worker. A tower crane was used. The defence's safety expert expressed their opinion that the accused company had a well-practised safe system of lifting falsework frames and that the injury was caused by incompetent persons conducting unauthorised lifting. The two workers, including the injured, who engaged in the lifting process, did not possess certification of competency in rigging or signalling. This expert rationale was accepted by the Magistrate.

HKSAR v Leighton Contractors (Asia) Limited (HCMA 1029/2000)

In this case, the Court rejected the evidence of the general safety expert for the prosecution as his opinion was an expression of ideals and counsel of perfection arrived at in hindsight in an attempt to explain what, on the face of it, was inexplicable. In short, his opinion was that the worker fatality at the worksite would have been avoided if he had received safety instructions in writing. Similarly, in *HKSAR v Leighton Contractors (Asia) Limited* (HCMA 508/2015), the Court had to decide to accept or reject evidence of an expert by giving cogent reasons. The reason given for not accepting the opinion of the defence expert was that the Magistrate found the prosecution's expert's opinion was more credible and reliable on the alleged safe system of work.

HKSAR v Hong Dau Construction Company Limited and Others (HCMA 186/2017)/[2018] HKCFI 1462

During the legal proceedings of this case, statements by the general safety expert, such as "if the workers did so carefully", were found to be unacceptable. Such an attitude was viewed by the Court as being unproductive and obviously not conducive to the provision and maintenance of a safe system of work.

The Queen v Otis Elevator Co. (H.K.) Ltd (Criminal 1985 No. 931)

In this case, an appeal was allowed for failure to resolve the conflict of opinions expressed by two experts, a factory inspector for the prosecution and a defence safety expert. The background of the appeal was that the factory inspector was of the view that the bamboo scaffolding itself was an insufficient anchorage, rather than the incident being caused by the lack of independent safety belts or an independent anchorage. However, the expert admitted that he had never heard of an accident caused by the failure of bamboo scaffolding itself. The defence expert discussed the merits and demerits of independent lifelines, separate anchorages, and bamboo scaffolding. He found that there were advantages and disadvantages in each of the three methods of securing belts, adding that, in his experience, the practice of attaching a safety belt to bamboo scaffolding was a safe one and, in some circumstances, the best system. The Magistrate, unfortunately, made no effort to resolve the conflicts between the two experts. For this reason alone, the High Court allowed the appeal and the conviction quashed.

HKSAR v Paul Y. Construction and Engineering Co. Ltd and Paul Y. Plant Hire Co. Ltd (HCMA 161/2007)

During the proceedings, the Court accepted the opinions expressed by the specialist safety expert for the prosecution and rejected the opinions expressed by the defence safety expert. Both experts were professors in metallurgy. Their opinions were given concerning the material properties of the locking pins used in the mast sections of a tower crane. In this case, the locking pins, the failure of which led to the accident, were not supplied from the original manufacturer of the tower crane.

The Queen v Kai Tai Construction Engineering Company Limited (HCMA 1123/1995)/[1996] 1 HKC 645

In this case, Judge Duffy found that the safety expert who investigated the accident for the prosecution could not be an independent and impartial witness. In an earlier decision by Judge Duffy in *The Queen v Manfield Building Contractors Limited* (HCMA 499/1991), it was also similarly found that the expert for the prosecution in charge of the accident investigation could not be admissible. These two decisions were further refined in *The Queen v Chung Chen-hsin* (HCCC 397/1995), in which it was explained that expert opinions must be assessed based on their admissibility and the weight of admissible evidence.

THE LEGAL NATURE AND LIMITATIONS OF CODES OF PRACTICE

In addition to ordinances and regulations, CoPs also carry some legal power, but failure to comply is not considered a serious offence. However, non-compliance with a CoP could still be submitted to a court during a prosecution. This means that while a construction company or individual may not be prosecuted for not complying with a CoP, this non-compliance could be used if they are prosecuted for another crime. It is, therefore, important for proprietors, directors, managers, and safety officers responsible for safety on a construction site to be aware of all

CoPs as well as the more legally prosecutable ordinances and regulations. Section 7A of the FIUO empowers the Commissioner for Labour to make and approve CoPs.

Of particular note is the CoP on Safety Management. This CoP, like many others, is written as a methodical must-do checklist. It attempts to tell companies and individuals how to comply with the regulations but does not directly explain why. While seemingly counter-intuitive, effective safety management, like other forms of management, is mediated by focusing on what needs to be done to get results rather than the underlying rationale.

Unfortunately, there are a number of practical considerations that are not explicitly stated in this or other CoPs. One of these is related to the role of managers. As we have seen in Chapter 2, managers are responsible for balancing safety goals with other business goals, which can in some ways be incompatible. Thus, managers should also be held accountable, and an inspection authority should be given the power to not only request remedies for breaches but also to initiate legal proceedings against the company and its managers. Regrettably, this stipulation is not currently included in most CoPs. It is also disappointing that the legal requirements of the FIU (Safety Officers and Safety Supervisors) Regulations, which mandate the employment of registered safety officers in certain designated industries (described further below), are not reproduced in CoPs as they should be.

CoPs also often lack stipulations regarding accident investigation. Accident investigation involves multiple steps following the initial incident, including assessing fault, providing recommendations, and monitoring implementation of their remedial measures. Unfortunately, current CoPs do not emphasise that management should be proactive in their investigations and recommendations. Their recommendations should include preventive measures in addition to remedial actions following an accident. While there will always be some risks inherent in construction work, safety management can help to minimise the occurrence of accidents by trying to stay ahead. Although there are a number of points that should be included or better emphasised in each CoP, this section of the FIUO is an essential piece of legislation in the construction industry.

NON-LEGALLY ENFORCEABLE GUIDELINES

In contrast to ordinances, regulations, and CoPs, GNs do not have any legal power, but they should still be used to help direct relevant parties to comply with common safety practices. These GNs have an advisory role. Examples include "A Guide to the Factories and Industrial Undertakings (Lifting Appliances and Lifting Gear) Regulations", "Guidance Notes on Safety at Work for Maintenance of Low Voltage Electrical Switchgears", and "A Guide to Part VII of the Occupational Safety and Health Regulation (Manual Handling Operations)", among others.

DESIGNATING ENFORCEMENT AND RESPONSIBILITY

A discussion of the legal ramifications in the construction industry for non-compliance with applicable laws and regulations often leads to a question of who is ultimately responsible—and legally culpable—for their enforcement. In practice, while the enforcing officers from the Labour Department oversee their territory-wide application, regulations should also be enforced by occupational safety officers as well as the proprietor of the construction site. In this context, the "proprietor", as interpreted from the FIUO, is the person or persons on the construction site that, at that moment, has management or control of the business carried out on the said worksite. This can be a corporation, firm, or any occupier (or agent of such an occupier) of a construction site. This interpretation casts legal obligations across a range of persons on a construction site, including the resident safety consultants and site management staff charged with safety and health responsibilities. Management positions involved may include the project director, project manager, site agent, and worksite foreman. Therefore, legal enforcement and responsibility extend beyond the main contractor to other contractors or sub-contractors responsible for different kinds of work.

In accordance with this, a trend has emerged in the area of enforcement, whereby legal culpability has been extended to specific individuals in construction organisations. In fact, the Labour Department has implemented processes to charge all persons responsible, from the main contractor to all other safety personnel, when a duty or regulation is breached. For example, on 30 May 2014, a person responsible for a warehouse at Yau Tong was fined HK$20,000, sentenced to one month's imprisonment, and suspended for two years by the Kwun Tong Magistrates' Court after it was found that all three escape routes from the warehouse were obstructed, a violation of an OSHO regulation. On 15 May 2017, the owner of a suspended working platform (gondola) was sentenced to one month's imprisonment and suspended for two years by the West Kowloon Magistrates' Court for violating the FIU (Suspended Working Platforms) Regulation. The case involved two workers that were injured when the suspended working platform they were using for plastering work on the external wall of a building suddenly tilted. This trend in enforcement towards individual liability has pushed those charged with these roles and responsibilities to take safety legislation and compliance even more seriously.

Examples of the legal responsibilities being questioned for each party are outlined below.

Main contractor, co-contractors, sub-contractors, and sub-sub-contractors

The main contractor, co-contractors, or any sub-contractors working on the same site can be regarded as "proprietors" defined under the FIUO. This may also cover nominated sub-sub-contractors. Unfortunately, the complex contracting system, whereby various levels of contractors, sub-contractors, and sub-sub-contractors are responsible for various tasks, leads to the question: Can there be more than one "proprietor" on a construction site? This question was raised in *HKSAR v Chun Wo Building Construction Limited.*

HKSAR v Chun Wo Building Construction Limited (HCMA 749/1999)

This case, heard in the Court of First Instance, involved a breach of Regulation 19(1) of the FIU (Electricity) Regulations. The Court held that "the proprietor was the appellant and includes sub-contractors who had management or control of the business carried on in such an industrial undertaking". This decision indicates that there can indeed be more than one proprietor on the same construction site and, therefore, more than one responsible party. The laws apply to main contractors, sub-contractors, and sub-sub-contractors alike, and each person can be held accountable. This case is also discussed in Chapter 7.

The repercussions for the main contractor following a fatal or serious injury on their worksite can be significantly detrimental to the company, particularly if they are working for public contracts. When a serious injury case or site safety offence occurs, the Development Bureau (formerly the Works Bureau) will take administrative penal action. Notably, a "serious injury case" in this context refers to a case involving a fatality, a permanent bodily injury, or a dangerous occurrence that has attracted media attention or aroused general public concern. Furthermore, a "site safety offence" refers to any offence under the FIUO, Cap. 59; OSHO, Cap. 509; or the Shipping and Port Control Ordinance, Cap. 313. Site safety and environmental offences are separate. The penalties typically involve voluntary suspension of bidding for a set period, which will undoubtedly cause financial loss in opportunity costs for the contractor. Their name and brand may also be tarnished, leading to additional repercussions.

Owners of the plant or equipment

Effective 28 November 2003, an owner of any "suspended working platform", "loadshifting machinery", "lifting appliances", or "lifting gear" on a construction site has legal duties to ensure that these plant and equipment are safe. The term "owner" has been defined under the FIU (Suspended Working Platforms) Regulation, FIU (Lifting Appliances and Lifting Gear) Regulations, and FIU (Loadshifting Machinery) Regulation (see full definition in Chapter 3). According to these regulations, "owner" refers to all parties responsible for the control or management of the plant and equipment situated or used on a construction site. This can include the lessee or hirer, any overseer, foreman, agent, or person involved in these operations. It also includes the main contractor, co-contractors, sub-contractors, or sub-sub-contractors who have control over the way any construction work (including the use of said plant or equipment) is carried out on the construction site. These owners have a non-delegable duty with regard to enforcing legislation, regardless of there being other "proprietors" on the worksite. For example, when conducting the examinations and tests required under these regulations, the owner must take responsibility for any and all negligence and cannot pass the blame to the examiner if the assessment was not done properly. As any negligence may be accompanied by legal repercussions, the owner of the plant or equipment must be aware of the regulations stipulating criminal liability. This has been highlighted in *HKSAR v Shun Tak Properties Limited* in which an examiner knowingly delivered a false report to the owner, but the owner was still held responsible.

HKSAR v Shun Tak Properties Limited (HCMA 1014/2006)/ [2009] 3 HKLRD 299

The appellant was the owner of the Shun Tak Centre, a commercial and office building that also houses the Hong Kong-Macau Ferry Piers. On 7 October 2005, two workers were performing their cleaning duties on the 38th–39th floors, when the Eastern luffing jib of the suspended working platform they were on failed and dipped down. The Western jib remained normal and functional, thus tilting the suspended working platform and causing injuries to both workers. The accident led to a summons against the appellant under section 4(e) of the FIU (Suspended Working Platforms) Regulation. This section states that the owner of a suspended working platform shall ensure that it is not used for carrying persons unless "properly maintained". The Magistrate concluded that "passive reliance on a maintenance contractor to make reports on defects as and when they were found came nowhere near discharging the statutory responsibility to ensure the gondola was in a proper state of maintenance". The Court agreed with this during the appeal, stating that the word "ensure" denotes positive and vigorous measures to achieve a result or event, and the duty to ensure cannot be discharged by a passive reliance on others. The Court further indicated that this designation follows the common definition of the word "ensure" in the New Shorter Oxford English Dictionary. Thus, the owner was held accountable for all negligence. This case was also discussed earlier in this chapter as an example of a safety expert giving testimony and is quoted in *Hin Lin Yee and Another v HKSAR* (FACC No. 7 of 2009), which is discussed and described in Chapter 5.

An owner who contravenes the legal duties for these plant and equipment will face a maximum fine of HK$200,000 and imprisonment for 12 months.

Consultants, project managers, site agents, and foremen

Consultants, project managers, site agents, and foremen are also legally culpable in some circumstances and can be prosecuted. For example, criminal proceedings were laid against a site manager, site agent, and a foreman in an accident on 29 March 2017 during the construction of the Hong Kong-Zhuhai-Macao Bridge, which resulted in the death of two workers and injuries to three others. Further, on 11 April 2019, a project manager and a site agent were charged with failing to comply with the requirements made by an occupational safety officer. Both were fined HK$5,000 in the West Kowloon Magistrates' Court.

Safety officers and safety supervisors

Questions have been raised regarding whether registered safety officers who are employed by construction contractors would be more proactive in reporting their employers' non-compliance with safety and health requirements if they too were held accountable. This has been explored in multiple cases.

In one case, a registered safety officer was suspended for 12 months and another was de-registered as a result of using a false document to gain registration. The officer was charged under the Crime (Amendment) Ordinance. Another registered safety officer was charged for failing to take reasonable care of the safety and health of another person in the June 1993 passenger hoist disaster in which the hoist suddenly plunged 17 floors, killing 12 workers, of which one was a teenager. On 11 April 2019, one registered safety officer was prosecuted under OSHO, section 24(2)(a), for failing to comply with the requirements made by an occupational safety officer, and OSHO, section 26(a), for obstructing or delaying an occupational safety officer in the exercise of the power conferred upon him. The officer was fined HK$8,000 for both offences and might face disciplinary action (which will be determined by a disciplinary board, which may or may not be held, under the FIU (Safety Officers and Safety Supervisors) Regulations). In fact, under the FIU (Safety Officers and Safety Supervisors) Regulations, registered safety officers are required to fully and accurately complete the approved Form 2A on or before the last day of every month. Failing to do so may result in fines and disciplinary action.

Thus, the courts have made it clear that registered safety officers should take proactive steps to ensure that their employers are fully aware of the potential adverse implications and consequences of refusing to accept or neglecting their advice. The Labour Department stresses that should there be sufficient evidence that a registered safety officer has failed to perform his duties, at which point the department will take disciplinary or legal action against the safety officer concerned. Bogus safety practitioners should be de-registered.

Examiners

Examiners and inspectors, who are professional engineers, are commonly appointed by contractors to review construction plants and equipment, acting as the "competent examiners" specified by law. They too have been subject to prosecution for not reporting non-compliance on the worksite. For example, one survey company that had appointed an examiner to evaluate lifting appliances and passenger hoists was charged with corporate manslaughter following an accident in June 1993. During sentencing, the Judge stated that the company's conduct called for a sentence of "great severity". The company was fined HK$3 million. As the Judge indicated that the company director could not be sent to prison, an even more severe fine was required. In another case, an examiner engaged by a company was convicted of breaching statutory duty by failing to report defects detected during the course of his technical examination. The Court was told that the pinion of the passenger hoist had deteriorated to such an appalling condition that it would have been obvious to anyone inspecting it that the passenger hoist was unsafe. The examiner was charged with delivering a false certificate to the contractor of the construction site. Other High Court cases dealing with appeals from examiners for delivering incorrect certificates in examining and testing lifting appliances include *HKSAR v Michael M. NKasu* and *HKSAR v Sun Kam Sing Stephen*.

HKSAR v Michael M. NKasu (HCMA 479/2002)/[2002] HKCFI 715

The appellant was a registered professional engineer. He was charged under the FIU (Lifting Appliances and Lifting Gear) Regulations for delivering a false certificate to the owner of a crane he was inspecting. Interestingly, the reason for the charge was not brought up in the course of the trial. Normally, a defendant would be entitled to know the basis of the prosecution and the Court could order particulars to be provided. Even so, the appellant was convicted, on review, and later appealed against conviction and for costs incurred. Evidence was then provided showing that the certificate issued by the appellant contained incorrect data in column 6 of the scheduled form under the FIU (Lifting Appliances and Lifting Gear) Regulations and that the appellant only carried out part of the test. This case demonstrates that any crane test or examination should be carried out in full accordance with the law based on "Schedule 1 — Procedure for Testing and Examining Lifting Appliances and Lifting Gear" as specified under the FIU (Lifting Appliances and Lifting Gear) Regulations.

HKSAR v Sun Kam Sing Stephen (HCMA 27/2007)

Similar to the previous case, the appellant was a registered professional engineer. He was appointed to carry out an examination on a crane. In the certificate for his examination on 4 November 2005, he stated that the automatic safe load indicator (ASLI) — an essential device for safe operation of the crane — was in good working order. However, on 20 January 2006, about two and a half months later, it was discovered that the crane did not have an ASLI installed. The Court favoured the circumstantial evidence produced by the respondent and dismissed the appeal.

Employees

There is a strong belief amongst employers that enforcement officers should stress the responsibilities of each individual employee in the safety and health aspects of the workplace. It is also generally felt by employers that employees or workers should also be prosecuted for breaches of safety and health and non-compliance with legislation. Section 6B(1)(a) of the FIUO states: "It shall be the duty of any person employed at an industrial undertaking while at work... to take reasonable care for the health and safety of himself and of other persons who may be affected by his acts or omissions at work." However, even with this statement contained in the legislation, statistics show that few employees or workers are prosecuted for failing to comply with the law. In one of the few examples of this, one worker was fined HK$5,000 for failing to comply with the requirement made by an occupational safety officer on 11 April 2019.

The rationale for not prosecuting injured workers seems to include an element of sympathy. It is felt that the worker is adequately penalised when a bodily injury is sustained after failing to observe safety rules while at work. The injured worker will no doubt learn a hard lesson, which to most courts is a sufficient penalty.

REPERCUSSIONS

As indicated by the examples in the sections above, repercussions for non-compliance typically involve fines or imprisonment. For example, as of 1 January 2008, breaching a CS(S)Rs results in a fine of HK$10,000 to HK$50,000 depending on the severity of the breach. Although simultaneous imprisonment terms up to a maximum of 12 months have not been imposed by the court, suspended sentences have been enforced. Repercussions aim to improve worksite safety and to deter future breaches. The following quotations sum up the general legal stance on construction safety:

> If the prosecution in future leads evidence to show that current sentencing is failing to induce contractors to give more than lip-service to the safety regulations, the Magistrate should consider a gradual increase in the

starting point for sentence until a point is reached where it is cheaper for a contractor to enforce obedience to the regulations than to ignore them.

– Justice Leonard
AG v Hip Hing Construction Co. Ltd
(HCMA 440/1993)

[I]n light of the undisputed evidence that the hole (associated with the accident) in question had been covered for some two months prior to the accident and that it was regularly inspected, the last such inspection having taken place about two days previously, the Judge allowed the appeal, reducing the fine from $100,000.00 to $25,000.00.

– Justice Jackson
HKSAR v Paul Y-ITC General Contractors Ltd
(HCMA 347/2003)

[F]ines have not proved any deterrent at all.

– Justice Beeson
HKSAR v China State Construction Engineering Corporation
(HCMA 347/1997)

That the average fine was $21,000 reflects no more that the fact that fines, in the context of often heartless safety conditions on Hong Kong construction sites are (not infrequently) far too low.

– Justice Beeson
HKSAR v Teemway Engineering Ltd
(HCMA 1081/2003)

If my decision had been otherwise on ground one I would have raised a question of the adequacy of the fine of $15,000, not because the Magistrate did otherwise than apply the usual tariff but because that tariff, eaten away by inflation and the application of "average" fines (which includes those levied upon small contractors), has become outdated. I would be surprised if anyone thought that fining Hyundai Engineering and Construction Company Limited or the China Engineering Construction Corporation such a sum, whether together or singly, was adequate.

– Deputy Judge Line
HKSAR v Hyundai-CCECC Joint Venture and Another
(HCMA 530/2005)

> In no sense are they (fines) in any way excessive. Courts have repeatedly expressed concern over the state of safety on construction sites in Hong Kong and emphasized the duty that is imposed in law upon contractors and, now, persons who have direct control over facets of construction. If the figures claimed in this and other cases are in fact correct for the average fine being imposed in matters of this nature it may well be that the level of fines being imposed now is no longer commensurate, in many instances, with the breaches of that duty.
>
> – Justice Wright
> *HKSAR v Chuen Kee Construction Company Limited*
> (HCMA 986/2005)

Taken together, these High Court cases clearly indicate that they are prepared to impose fines to deter non-compliance unless and until there are sound and satisfactory mitigation factors. An appeal against excessive fines and the level of seriousness was made in *HKSAR v Dickson Construction Company Limited* (HCMA 92/2004), in which three workers were found wearing only parachute-style safety harnesses (no lanyards or fall arrestors were provided). These three workers were erecting bamboo scaffoldings and were working at height, over two metres from the ground. It was alleged that the appellant company failed to take adequate steps to prevent these on-site workers from falling from height. The Court held that the appeal against excessive fine was an unmeritorious appeal.

Finally, as companies, contractors, and workers begin to share the liability for non-compliance, it is important for the Labour Department to clearly communicate its prosecution policies. The relevant safety rules and regulations must explicitly state who is responsible for their enforcement and how they will be penalised if they are not complied with.

SUMMARY

To prevent accidents to the workforce and damage to plant and equipment, proprietors need to assess how they can be more involved in ensuring safety. The proprietor's main responsibility is to control the work—both its human and physical elements—and accidents are caused by failing to manage and control these aspects. They are not, as some believe, the result of straightforward failures of technology but typically involve interactions between social, organisational, and technical issues that lead to multifaceted accidents. Such issues often arise on construction sites where there may be more than one contractor, owner, or tradesman, all of whom will have different, and often incompatible, goals regarding progress, production, manpower, and project finance. Therefore, technical excellence, though important, is not enough and must be combined with preventive measures at the management and organisational levels.

Legal compliance with safety laws is one way to achieve minimum industry standards and prevent accidents on worksites. However, compliance with safety regulations alone is not enough if high safety standards on construction worksites are to be achieved. Further, legal repercussions are also responsive rather than proactive in nature. The courts are, therefore, not in a position to prevent accidents or to investigate the underlying causes of an accident. They can only interpret and clarify what each safety regulation means and punish those that do not comply.

Since their enactment, the subsidiary regulations in the FIUO, Cap. 59; OSHO, Cap. 509; and associated CoPs published therein have resulted in a number of court cases. Many proprietors and contractors have been fined or temporarily imprisoned. In some cases, these cases have resulted in changes to the laws themselves. Chapters 5, 6, and 7 describe court cases that specifically involve breaches of the FIUO, CS(S)Rs, and the FIURs, respectively, and highlight how the legal consequences of each case have impacted work in the construction industry. However, changes in construction safety standards and the processes required to legally enforce them take time. Although some in the field may feel that extending liability to individuals is a personal attack, the main purpose of enforcing safety laws and aggressively prosecuting companies and individuals for non-compliance is to enhance and improve safety standards. Ultimately, the top management of a construction company has to take the lead. Preventing worksite accidents calls for a commitment to safety at a senior level and the deliberate application of management skills. This is safety management.

FURTHER READING

Accident Prevention Advisory Unit of HM Factory Inspectorate (1976) "Managing safety: A review of the role of management in occupation health and safety", *HSE Occasional Paper Series: OP03*.

Construction Industry Training Authority in collaboration with the Labour Department, Hong Kong SAR Government (February 2000) *Case Studies of Construction Accidents in Hong Kong* (Third edition).

Environment, Transport, and Works Bureau, Hong Kong SAR Government (2003) *Technical Circular (Works) No. 2/2003: Regulation Action where a Serious Incident has or Site Safety or Environmental Offences have occurred on a Construction Site*, dated 2 April 2003.

Labour Department and Occupational Safety and Health Council (2003) *Analysis on Occupational Fatalities Casebook Volumes 1–3*.

Legislative Council, Hong Kong SAR Government (2019) *Occupational safety performance in Hong Kong, Panel on Manpower, LC Paper No. CB(2)563/18-19(4)*, 15 January 2019.

DISCUSSION QUESTIONS

1. What measures would you recommend to the management of a construction company to achieve high standards of compliance with safety law?
2. Discuss the following statement: "It is difficult for a construction company which has a series of safety convictions under the health and safety legislation to convince staff, clients, and other workforce that management is running a safe business."
3. Can fines by courts bring about a significant improvement in reducing accidents on construction sites? Discuss.

"The primary responsibility for doing something about the present levels of occupational accidents and diseases lies with those who create the risks and those who work with them"

– Robens' Report, United Kingdom (1972)

"Provision and maintenance of... systems of work...; Provision of such information, instruction, training and supervision"

– Section 6A of the Factories and Industrial Undertakings Ordinance, Chapter 59

5 Breaches of the Factories and Industrial Undertakings Ordinance, Chapter 59

INTRODUCTION

As discussed in Chapter 4, the legal repercussions for violating the Factories and Industrial Undertakings Ordinance, Cap. 59 (FIUO) can be severe. This chapter focuses on digesting breaches and legal proceedings based primarily on section 6A and section 13 of the FIUO.

SECTION 6A: DEFINING TERMS THROUGH LEGAL PROCEEDINGS

Section 6A, the general duties provision, was modelled on section 2 of the United Kingdom Health and Safety at Work etc. Act (HASAW Act) of 1974 and is the basis for numerous legal cases in the construction industry. Specific terms used in this section—namely, "system of work", "practicable", "reasonably practicable", and "supervision"—have been defined and scrutinised in legal proceedings in both the United Kingdom (UK) and the Hong Kong Special Administrative Region (SAR).

Legal precedence in the United Kingdom

Published in 1983, the United Kingdom Health and Safety Commission's (UKHSC's) guide defined a "system of work" as the way in which the work is organised and includes the layout of the workplace, the order in which tasks are carried out, and special precautions that have to be taken before carrying out certain hazardous tasks. This means that, for example, the plant or equipment itself and the way it is operated must both be safe. The operator must be competent, the workplace must be safe, and the operations must be conducted without unnecessary risks. Similarly, according to the UKHSC guide, if someone is prosecuted for failing to comply with a duty that is qualified by the term "so far as is practicable" or "so far as is reasonably practicable", then it is up to the accused to prove to the court that it was not practicable or reasonably practicable to do more to comply with the duty. There are authorities, all substantially to the same effect, which recognise that, in considering reasonable practicability, a court may have to consider the need to balance the likelihood of risk against the cost, time, and trouble necessary to avert the risk. In doing so, regard will be paid to what was known at the relevant time.

The following cases are presented chronologically to show how the definitions of these terms evolved in parallel over time, both before and after the UKHSC guide was published. Furthermore, as the focus of this book is on the Hong Kong experience, the cases in the UK are condensed to focus on their decisions and were selected based on their relevance to how the FIUO was to be understood in Hong Kong.

Speed v Thomas Swift and Company Limited [1943] 1 KB 557

In this case, the English Court attempted to explain the term "system of work" as follows:

> What is a safe system can only be determined in the light of the actual situation on the spot at the relevant time.... A system of working may consist of a number of elements. One element may be the sequence in which a particular job ought to be carried out. The decision as to which task is to be performed first appears to me [the Judge] to lie with the master's duty to decide, and in so doing, he must pay proper regard to the conditions

> affecting the safety of his men.... I [the Judge] do not venture to suggest a definition of what is meant by a system, but it includes in my opinion or may include according to circumstances such matters as the physical layout of the job—the setting of the stage, so to speak—the sequence in which the work is to be carried out, the proper cases of warnings and notices, and the issue of special instructions. A system may be adequate for the whole course of the job or it may have to be modified or improved to meet circumstances which arise. Such modifications or improvements appear to me [the Judge] equally to fall under the head of the system. The examples which I [the Judge] have given are not intended in any way to be an exhaustive list.

Schwalb v Fass and Son [1946] 90 Sol Jo 394, 175 LT 345

In this case, the Lord Chief Justice accepted the Oxford English Dictionary definition of "practicable" which is "capable of being carried out in action" or "feasible". Thus, a safety precaution must not be regarded as impracticable merely because it would slow down production or because it is difficult or inconvenient.

Edwards v National Coal Board [1949] KB 704

Lord Justice Asquith said that

> "reasonably practicable" is a narrower term than physically possible and seemed to me to imply that a computation must be made... in which the quantum of risk is placed on one scale and the sacrifice involved in the measures necessary for averting the risk (whether in money, time, and trouble) is placed in the other. If it is shown that there is gross disproportion between them—the risk being insignificant in relation to the sacrifice—the defendants discharge the onus upon them.

In other words, if there is foreseeable risk, then the precaution required must be "grossly and disproportionately" costly before the employer is justified in not acting.

Winter v Cardiff Rural District Council [1950] All ER 819

In this case, the English Court stated:

> It is always a question whether the negligence complained of is the failure of the employer to inaugurate and maintain a safe system or the casual departure from that system as the result of the negligence of an individual fellow workman. The difference is between a case where sufficient and adequate provisions have been made, which will, if carried out, protect the workman unless one of his fellows does not use proper care in carrying out the system, and a case where the system itself makes no such provision ... the employer ... should employ competent servants, should supply them with adequate directions as to the system of work or mode of operation, but this does not mean that the employer must decide on every detail of the system of work or mode of operation ... Where the system or mode of operation is complicated or highly dangerous or prolonged or involves a number of men performing different functions, it is naturally a matter for the employer to take the responsibility of deciding what system be adopted. The giving of proper instructions may well be part of a proper system of working, and the omission to give them may constitute a defect in the system of working. Or alternatively, a breach of the employer's obligation to take reasonable steps for the safety of those employed on the task ... On the other hand, where the operation is simple and the decision [about] how it shall be done has to be taken frequently it is natural and reasonable that it should be left to the (foreman) or workmen on the spot.

Pease v British India Steam Navigation Co. Ltd (1953) 1 Lloyd's Rep 207

Here, the Court held that:

> It does not mean that because something could have been done in some different way, the way in which it was done is an unsafe system. An unsafe system, I [the Judge] think, means ... that if the whole lay-out of the work, the whole plan of the work which it is for the employer to decide upon is such that it exposes the employees to an unnecessary risk, that may be said to be [an] unsafe system of work.

Marshall v Gotham Co. Ltd [1954] AC 360

Here, Lord Reid said that what is called for is an assessment of the situation at the material time and that if a precaution is practicable, it must be taken unless it would be unreasonable considering the whole situation. As men's lives may be at stake, a decision that a practicable precaution is unreasonable should not be made lightly.

R v Nelson Group Services (Maintenance) Limited [1999] 1 WLR 1526

In this case, the English Court of Appeal held that the question of what is reasonably practicable is a matter of fact and degree and it will be sufficient for an employer to show that everything reasonably practicable had been done, such as: (a) ensure that the person doing the work had the appropriate skills and instructions; (b) ensure that a safe system of work had been established; (c) ensure that the workers were provided with adequate supervision; and (d) ensure that the workers were provided with proper plant and equipment.

R v Chargot Limited and Others [2008] UKHL 73

In this case, the House of Lords held:

> These duties [to ensure the health and safety of employees at work] are expressed in general terms... They are designed to achieve the purposes described in section 1(1)(a) and (b) [of the HASAW Act]. The description in section 2(2) of the matters to which the duty in section 2(1) extends does not detract from the generality of that duty. They describe a result which the employer must achieve or prevent. These duties are not, of course, absolute. They are qualified by the words "so far as is reasonably practicable". If that result is not achieved the employer will be in breach of his statutory duty, unless he can show that it was not reasonably practicable for him to do more than was done to satisfy it.... It is the result that these duties prescribe not any particular means of achieving it.

Tangerine Confectionary Limited and Veolia ES (UK) Limited v The Queen [2011] EWCA 2015

When discussing the distinction between foreseeability of risk and reasonable practicability in this case, Lord Justice Hughes said:

> But in my view, the foreseeability of a risk is distinct from the question whether it was "reasonably practicable" to avoid it. Diplock LJ explained in *Taylor v Coalite*.... It is only *if* a risk is reasonably foreseeable and it was reasonably foreseeable that an injury would be caused that it becomes necessary to consider whether it was reasonably practical to avert the risk. Thus, for the purpose of deciding the issue of reasonable practicability, it is *assumed* that the risk is reasonably foreseeable.... Foreseeability of risk (strictly foreseeability of danger) is indeed relevant to the question [of] whether a risk to safety exists. That accords with the ordinary meaning of risk, as is demonstrated by the concept of a risk assessment, which is itself an exercise in foresight.... We note that this defence does not impose on an employer a duty to take every feasible precaution, or even every practicable one; it imposes a duty to take every *reasonably practicable* one. What is reasonably practicable no doubt depends on all the circumstances of the case, including principally the degree of foreseeable risk of injury, the gravity of injury if it occurs, and the implications of suggested methods of avoiding it.

Baker v Quantum Clothing Group Limited and Others [2011] 1 WLR 1003

In this civil action, the English High Court accepted that the words "reasonably practicable" imported a relative concept involving consideration of whether the risk of harm was considered acceptable by the prevailing standards at the time. The Court pointed out that it cannot be reasonable to put in place measures that are not known to be necessary. It may be practicable to do so, but it cannot be said to be reasonably practicable. The Court further held that reasonable foreseeability was relevant to the issue of safety as well as reasonably practicability. It is necessary to examine the context in which the question arose.

Legal precedence in Hong Kong

In Hong Kong, the Commissioner for Labour of the Labour Department, the regulatory authority on safety and health at work, in a letter addressed to the Hong Kong Construction Association dated 27 June 2012, said:

> A safe system of work must be in place, which includes the conduct of a comprehensive risk assessment by a competent person, preparation of a method statement to include necessary safety measures, and procedures for ensuring safety operations as well as provision of information, instruction, training, and supervision to ensure adherence to safety procedures and rules by workers.

While this statement reinforces the contents of section 6A of the general duties requirements on safe systems of work in the FIUO, the legal aspects of what constitutes a safe system of work, what is considered reasonably practicable, and what is a breach of the general duties have been long debated. Many of the legal proceedings in Hong Kong cited or referred to cases in the UK, while other decisions were unique to the region. While the cases in the previous section were condensed, as the main focus of this book is on experiences in Hong Kong, the selected cases described below include more discussion about the case itself and some of the insights gained.

R v Tai Fong Textile Finishing Work Limited (HCMA 264/1994)/[1994] 3 HKC 285/[1995] HKLY 317

This case concerned the fencing of a dangerous part of machinery in a factory. The judgment stated that "it is dangerous if it is a reasonably foreseeable cause of injury to anybody acting in a way in which a human being may be reasonably expected to act in circumstances which may be reasonably expected to occur". The Court further remarked that whether or not the accident was reasonably foreseeable by the appellant was a question of fact and degree with regard to the circumstances of the particular case. Thus, any plant or equipment must be safe (with no dangerous parts), and this is one of the basic requirements for a safe system of work.

The Queen v Ping On Foundation (Piling) Co. Ltd (HCMA 879/1995)

This was an appeal against a conviction for failing to provide and maintain plant and systems of work for the erection of sheet piles that was, so far as was reasonably practicable, safe and without risks to the health of all persons employed at the industrial undertakings, contrary to sections 6A(2)(a) and 6A(3) of the FIUO, which led to the death of a worker. The deceased was doing sheet piling work with two other riggers. It was not in dispute that the method used by the deceased on that occasion was not safe. Nor was it in dispute that the safe method of sheet piling was what was called the portal/frame method. It was accepted by all parties that the equipment necessary for the use of the portal/frame method was on-site and available but was not used on that occasion. The two riggers working with the deceased on that occasion both said that the method he used on that day was wholly exceptional and that they had never seen him use it before when they worked with him. No one could tell why the deceased departed from the use of the safe method on that occasion. The Court held that the deceased, for reasons known only to him, chose not to use the safe method. The Court went on to say that it was not reasonable to expect the appellant company to constantly be on hand to supervise each and every occasion when sheet piling was carried out. It was reasonable for the company to assume that the safe system of work that had always been used in the past would continue to be used. This case indicates that deviating or departing from a normal safe system of work by an experienced worker could be used as a defence for a company. Site supervisory personnel should advise or remind workers not to deviate or depart from an established safe method of work.

Cheung Ping v Pak Kee Transportation Company Limited and Another, B+B (HCPI 963/1997)

The appellant company was charged under section 6A(2)(a) of the FIUO after an incident involving the lifting of H-piles on a construction worksite. Two riggers (one being the plaintiff) and one crane operator were involved in the lifting operation. Each of the riggers was responsible for hooking up one end of the H-piles and they had to give hand signals to the crane operator who was performing the lifting motion. The hand signal was a V-sign made with the index and middle finger. This system was devised so as to ensure that when the crane operator started to lift the H-pile, the two riggers would be at a safe distance away from the H-pile being lifted. The H-piles were stacked to a height of about 10 feet from the ground. The crane operator had a clear view of both the riggers. When the H-pile was lifted by the crane, the H-pile swung towards the plaintiff, hitting him on the left leg and fracturing his left tibia and fibula. The Court held that the defendant had provided a safe system of work. The failure was not the system or any defect in the system but was the result of the other worker (the crane operator in this case) failing to adhere to the system. It was not normal practice for a foreman to be present throughout the operation since there was already a safe (and simple) system of work established. This case indicates that an operational error committed by an experienced worker in a safe system of work can be a defence for a company. Such a defence is admissible on the condition that the worker at fault admits an error in operation.

HKSAR v Lau Ping Sun (HCMA 725/1999)

A vehicle apprentice aged 16 or 17, while attempting to replace lorry batteries, was crushed to death by the falling lorry bucket. The apprentice was working alone and unsupervised. He was too young to have sufficient experience to know that additional support was needed to secure the lorry bucket before positioning himself directly underneath it to replace the batteries. The Court held that the whole system of work was not in compliance with the requirements of section 6A(2). An apprentice or new hire receiving on-the-job training should be more closely supervised, and solo work is punishable under the law.

HKSAR v Eastime Engineering Limited (HCMA 82/2000)/ [2000] HKCFI 798

The appellant company was prosecuted for failing to provide and maintain a system of work for telescoping up a tower crane on-site. It also failed to provide information, instruction, training, and supervision to those workmen involved in the accident. The Magistrate concluded that he was unable to determine how the accident occurred and who was responsible for it. The Court held that saying the *actus reus* (which gave rise to the prosecution) occurred is not enough for the appellant to be found responsible. The appellant company was acquitted of the charges under the FIUO, but no claims for costs incurred were allowed under the Costs in Criminal Cases Ordinance, Cap. 492. Thus, contractors should be aware that even if a prosecution case for a safe system of work has been acquitted or dismissed, it does not necessarily follow that the Court will award costs following the decision.

HKSAR v Ken On Concrete Company Limited (HCMA 1304/2000)

The Ken On Concrete Company appealed against convictions based on sections 6A(2)(a) and 6A(3) involving maintenance work being carried out inside one of their two concrete mixers. The accident happened while a worker was cleaning inside the mixer (which should have been rendered dead and unable to rotate). Unfortunately, the mixer began operating, causing fatal injuries to the worker. The investigation of the accident revealed that the malfunction of the micro-switch controlling the mixer was not due to improper installation but was instead a result of the system of maintenance being cursory and insufficient. The Court also found that safety training and supervision was lacking in the whole operation and there were no clear instructions for the controller concerning the required procedure before the worker entered the mixer. It held that experienced workers could become complacent and that it was the duty of the employer to ensure their safety. In this regard, supervision, even for cleaning work, would have ensured that workers did not take shortcuts.

This case specifically highlights how maintenance actions on critical items of a plant or machinery are considered to be part of a safe system of work. For example, for a truck-mounted crane or a loader mounted on a truck or lorry, the critical items may include the hydraulic systems, the slewing systems, the hooks and hook blocks, the boom, the outrigger, the limit switch, the automatic safety devices, and the age of service. For other plant or equipment, it is important to ensure that the critical items are adequately identified and their functions safely maintained. In tasks such as preventive maintenance on critical items, necessary steps are more likely to be omitted during reassembly than during the original disassembly (or the "garage floor" phenomenon). During the disassembly of a piece of plant or equipment, each step follows in a fairly obvious way from the previous one. The same is not true during reassembly when items like rings, washers, lubricant oils, and the like may be easily left out. It is essential for safety practitioners to advise on how to establish procedures to avoid these easy omissions.

HKSAR v Gold Ram Engineering and Development Limited (HCMA 912/2001)

This is a case about the people aspect of a safe system of work. Indeed, the qualifications and competency of personnel employed and appointed are considered to be an essential aspect of the safe system of work on worksites. Here, an 80-kilogram hammer (plant) was lifted up a rugged incline onto a wooden scaffolding platform, which affected the stability of the device being used to lift it. This case referenced *Marshall v Gotham Co. Ltd* [1954] AC 360 in the UK, discussed above. In the present case, the Court held that it is not its duty to determine the cause(s) of the accident. Instead, the Court has to consider whether there was

> any risk involved in the operation carried out, [and] if there was a risk, what precautions the company or its servants, had taken to ensure that it was a safe operation and whether these precautions, so far as reasonably practicable, if any had been taken, were sufficient.

Simply reminding workers to do their work slowly and safely is insufficient in a safe system of work. It is also unacceptable not to check the qualifications and competency of the workers engaged. The Court further stated that

> The information did not allege two distinct offences; rather its particulars instanced the two respects in which the appellant was alleged to have failed in its statutory duty towards his employees. The scheme of the section is that Section 6(1) imposes a duty on every employer to ensure, so far as is

> reasonably practicable, the safety and health at work of all his employees. Section 6(2) contains a non-exhaustive list of cases in which an employer fails to discharge that duty. Section 6(3) creates an offence of non-compliance with Section 6(1) and provides for the penalty.

Safety practitioners should advise site management that personnel employed on the worksite should be qualified and competent. Competency should be gauged on a worker's understanding of the relevant current best practices, awareness of one's own limitations in experience and knowledge, and willingness and ability to supplement existing experience and knowledge with ongoing professional development.

HKSAR v Leighton Contractors (Asia) Limited (HCMA 1029/2000)

In this case, the appellant was charged with failing to provide information and instruction under section 6A(2)(c) to a worker that was subsequently involved in a fatal accident in a hoist shaft. Judge Jackson stated:

> I find myself unable to agree with (the Magistrate) that, on the evidence, he could properly conclude that there was anything beyond a fanciful risk that a worker might place a part of his body above the closed gates and into the hoist shaft, or that it was necessary (and I stress that word) for safety instructions (in the circumstances of this particular case) to be given in written or diagram form. It seems to me that the evidence of the expert witness for the prosecution upon which the learned Magistrate appears to have placed great reliance was little more than an expression of ideals and a counsel of perfection arrived at in hindsight in an attempt to explain what, on the face of it, was inexplicable. ... To suggest as the prosecution expert appears to have been suggesting that this dreadful accident would not have happened if the deceased worker had received instructions in writing is speculative in the extreme.

This case is important in several respects, but one significant point is that safety practitioners must be aware that speculative opinions or views of a safety expert will not be accepted in legal proceedings.

Wong Tai Wai David v Hong Kong Cable Television Limited (HCPI 541/2001)

The plaintiff was employed by the defendant as a technician. When the plaintiff visited a subscribed household, there was a 14-inch TV set on the floor which had to be moved a short distance. He moved the TV set himself and sustained injuries to the wrist of his right arm. The claim for damages was dismissed. The Court found that moving or lifting a 14-inch TV set was a simple and uncomplicated operation. It was a one-person job and did not require the assistance of either a colleague or householder member. In the ruling, Deputy Judge Fung quoted the following from Lord Oaksey in *Winter v Cardiff Rural District Council*:

> In my opinion the common law duty of an employer of labour is to act reasonably in all the circumstances. One of those circumstances is that he is an employer of labour and it is, therefore, reasonable that he should employ competent servants, should supply them with adequate plant, and should give adequate directions as to the system of work or mode of operation, but this does not mean that an employer must decide on every detail of the system of work or mode of operation. There is a sphere in which the employer must exercise his discretion and there are other spheres in which foremen and workmen must exercise theirs.

HKSAR v Kum Shing (K.F.) Construction Company Limited (HCMA 645/2003)

This was a case charged under sections 6A(1), 6A(2)(a), and 6A(3) for failing to ensure the safety of a worker associated with an excavator for work near a hillside. When the excavator operator skewed the extended excavator arm and bucket in an anti-clockwise direction, the excavator arm struck a worker who happened to walk through the space between the hillside and the excavator, causing fatal injuries. The Court held that the appellant company should send a safety officer to carry out a risk assessment on every hillside during excavation work. This is necessary because each hillside might have its own inherent hazards; though, they might seem to be fairly common. The worker's disobedience to company safety rules was a non-point for appeal. A risk assessment is a precursor for a safe system of work for different work environments. The absence of a risk assessment for similar activities carried out in different environments is not acceptable as a defence. Safety practitioners should perform the role of coordinator in the risk assessment process.

HKSAR v Sunley Foundation Engineering Company Limited (HCMA 615/2004)

In this case, a worker was fatally hit by the bucket of an excavator being operated by another worker. Though the Court held that no system of work could be perfectly safe, it was legally accepted that, where an excavator is in operation and there is a risk of injury, there should be an assigned person responsible for blocking any person from entering into the excavation zone. The Court further held that the subsections of 6A(2)(a) of the FIUO are not mutually exclusive and can overlap. In operating an excavator on a site, another lookout worker should be assigned to form a safe system of work or the working area should be safely cordoned-off to prevent unauthorized entry.

HKSAR v Lee Fung Construction Company Limited (HCMA 1062/2005)

In this appeal, the Court held that section 6A was breached when the appellant company failed to carry out a proper risk assessment. Verbal instructions like "If you go to a site, be careful how you unload. Don't unload by the edge of the things that can be dangerous, where there is a drop or there is water or the like." are deemed too general to constitute a safe system of work. This case confirmed that verbal safety instructions such as telling workers to take care of themselves mean that management is off-loading the responsibility instead of accepting it. Such instruction delivered to workers cannot replace a proper risk assessment. Safety practitioners should remind frontline foremen of this and similar court rulings. In this case, like the *Gold Ram* case above, the court's view is clear that verbal instructions or telling workers to work safely are not monitoring or supervision on the safe system of work.

In general, supervision should be appropriate. It should be proportionate to the risks and consider the personnel involved. Levels of supervision are determined by the nature of the work and the competence of those on the worksite. While in some cases experienced operators will not require direct supervision every time they carry out a routine task and instruction may be minimal, for new hires or apprentices, "nanny-type" or "babysitting-type" of supervision may be necessary until they are fully trained. Regardless of the competency and experience of the workers, intermittent safety reminders are still required.

HKSAR v Juh Wang Engineering Co. Ltd (築泓工程有限公司) (HCMA 625/2008)

The appellant company was charged under sections 6A(1), 6A(2)(a), and 6A(3) of the FIUO. This case arose from an accident whereby a worker engaging in the installation of decorative lighting at the ceiling was injured. The ceiling was about three metres above the floor. The Court held that relying on an experienced worker and the availability of other wooden ladders for his own use are not a defence to these charges. Such excuses could not absolve the appellant company from their statutory obligation to provide and maintain a system of work that is, so far as reasonably practicable, safe, and without risks to health for the worker engaged in the work. Wooden ladders provided for three-metre-high ceiling work are not accepted as a safe system of work. A certificated mobile working platform might be an acceptable alternative. Ensuring that the company has a safe plant environment and equipment is one of the basic requirements of a safe system of work.

HKSAR v Otis (Hong Kong) Co. Ltd (HCMA 1018/2009)

This case involves an accident in which two workers using flammable cleaning agents at the bottom of a lift shaft were injured by another group of workers doing welding work above them. The appellant company was charged under sections 6A(2)(a) and 6A(2)(c) of the FIUO. This case references *Winter v Cardiff Rural District Council* tried in the UK and reinstates that a safe system of work should employ competent persons, supply workers with adequate plant and equipment, and should give adequate direction to workmen concerning the mode of operation. This case shows that having junior or peer workers deliver safety information, instruction, and supervision to the workers about how to safely handle and use flammables is not acceptable as a defence. Delivering safety information, instruction, and supervision should be charged to senior or experienced staff. Site management should avoid scheduling incompatible work that creates potential fire risks inside the lift shaft. This is a case that should be referenced by lift contractors who have to carry out work inside lift shafts.

HKSAR v Yau Hop Scaffolding Engineering Company Limited (有合棚廠工程有限公司) (HCMA 219/2012)

The appellant company was charged under sections 6A(1), 6A(2)(c), and 6A(3) of the FIUO after an employee, a scaffolder, was assigned to dismantle a scaffold for the Town Gas piping at height and fell. He sustained bodily injuries from the scaffold. It was found that he was appointed as a "senior worker" but had only received one day of safety training by another "senior worker". No assessment of the effectiveness of the training was available as evidence. The Court held that safety training delivered to the injured worker by a peer senior worker was insufficient and that a higher rank and authoritative person should deliver the safety training and information to the worker. The Court further held that distributing safety and health information material or pamphlets, though not mandatory, is a simple matter and can supplement safety information and instruction to workers. Such distribution of safety information is a reasonable, practicable, and preferred measure. Safety pamphlets issued to workers can, therefore, be accepted by the court as giving safety information and instructions. Safety practitioners should note that issuance of safety pamphlets with cartoons or pictures to workers who are illiterate can discharge the functions of delivering safety information and instruction.

HKSAR v Gammon Construction Limited (HCMA 426/2013)/(FACC No. 10 of 2014)

The following case involved an accident during a lifting operation using a mobile crane which resulted in a worksite death. The system of work comprised of two signalmen (or banksmen): one employed by the main contractor and one employed by the sub-contractor. There was a mobile crane operator and a rigger. Thus, a team of four persons was involved in the lifting operation. The crane and its operator were stationed on a metal platform constructed above the basement on the worksite. The rigger was down in the basement. There were two points of access to the basement, one on either side of the platform. Each point of access was surrounded by guard-rails. The mobile crane stood between the two sets of guard-rails. In order to lift up materials from the basement level through one point of access or to deposit material through the other point of access the counterweight of the crane had to turn, or slew, about a pivot point. The rear of the body of the crane would pass close to one set of the guard-rails. This would create what was described in the evidence as a "trapping zone" in which a person might be caught between the counterweight and the guard-rails. This is what happened to the signalman of the main contractor who was fatally injured. The issues in this case and the subsequent appeal concern the meaning and effect of sections 6A and 18 of the FIUO and, in particular, the nature of the duty imposed by section 6A on the proprietor of an undertaking in respect of the safety of employees and the requirements of section 18. The Court held that:

> It cannot be that the legislature intended that, if an accused failed to bring itself within the terms of defence, it would then still be possible for the accused to turn around and say that, even so, it honestly believed on reasonable grounds that it had done so. The effect would be to render the legislation meaningless. In my judgment, the common law defence is not available to the appellant in these proceedings as it is inconsistent with the statutory defence.

The intention of a piece of legislation is always within the considered views of courts. This case was later advanced to the Court of Final Appeal. During the appeal, evidence was shown that the sub-contractor's signalman used his walkie-talkie to instruct the crane operator to perform a lift. The lift was performed with a slewing action, not knowing that the main contractor's signalman was still in the trapping zone. It was indicated that the main contractor's signalman should have been the "boss" in charge of giving final signals for lifting. Nevertheless, evidence showed that the main contractor's signalman had seldom given signals to the crane operator.

This case and appeal provide significant food for thought to safety practitioners from a safety organisation point of view as it involves an issue of crew organisation akin to safety in the aircraft industry, whereby leadership and communication roles must be clearly defined. The judgment for this appeal generated the following guiding principles and observations:

1. An allegation of an offence against section 6A of the FIUO does not depend upon the occurrence of an accident, and, if an accident occurs and an employee is injured, the prosecution, in order to make out its case, does not need to establish a causal relationship between the alleged breach and the injury. Even so, a charge alleging a failure to comply with a proprietor's obligation as to workplace safety may be brought in circumstances where an accident has occurred, and the death or injury of an employee has resulted. In that event, as a matter of forensic reality, the accident is likely to become the focus of attention in the evidence and arguments given about the safety issues. Those issues will be resolved according to the terms of the FIUO, but *what* happened, *why* it happened, and *what could* and *should* have been done to prevent it are likely to be the primary matters that occupy the court. Section 6A(1) requires, subject to the qualification concerning reasonable practicability, the achievement of a result, that is, safety, as elaborated in subsection (2). The Ordinance was modelled on the UK legislation considered by the House of Lords in *R v Chargot Ltd and Others*, outlined above.
2. The duty imposed upon a proprietor is non-delegable. This follows from the creation of an obligation to "ensure" safety (so far as is reasonably practicable). This duty cannot be pushed to a sub-contractor.
3. In a case where a worker has been injured, and the circumstances of the accident are relied upon as evidence of a breach of section 6A,

negligence on the part of the worker is not itself an answer to the charge. The duty to ensure safety, qualified as it is by reference to reasonable practicability, extends to protect workers who fail to take reasonable care for their own safety. In the present case, a line of argument pursued at the trial and on appeal was that the case went far beyond mere negligence, and that the worker, regrettably, was entirely the author of his own misfortunate. That argument failed based on the facts of the case.

4. To describe a workplace or system of work as "safe" does not necessarily mean that no accident could possibly occur. It does not connote the elimination of every conceivable risk.
5. Risk assessment normally involves foresight, but standards of safety are often propounded with hindsight. It is one thing to say that safety does not require the elimination of every conceivable risk; it is another thing to say that it means an absence of reasonably foreseeable risks.
6. On the true construction of the FIUO, the obligations of a proprietor are to be considered in terms of the language of the Ordinance, and not as a reflex of the common law principles of negligence. The relevance of reasonable foreseeability, if it becomes an issue, will be to the question of the reasonable practicability of some measures to enhance safety. Indeed, according to existing Hong Kong authorities on the test of reasonable practicability, what safety measures are required depends on reasonable foreseeability of dangers, the consequences of such dangers, and the trouble and expense involved in minimising the danger.
7. There was a Code of Practice, which was tendered and discussed in the evidence of this case (i.e., the Labour Department has published a Code of Practice for Safe Use of Mobile Cranes in January 2004). The code calls attention to the risk associated with the absence of a clear line of authority and communication in giving signals to the operator of a mobile crane.
8. The Court of Final Appeal held that the system of signalling in this case was not safe.
9. As to section 18, the onus there referred to is a legal onus (to be discharged on the balance of probabilities) and not merely an evidentiary onus.

This case is the leading authority in Hong Kong on the construction of the general duties under sections 6 and 18 of the FIUO. Safety practitioners should be familiar with the lines of reasoning used by the Court in this case.

HKSAR v Ho Chun Wai (HCMA 634/2015)

This case is of particular interest as it involves charges against an employee as an individual rather than the company or contractor. The appellant was a forklift truck driver employed on the 14th floor of an industrial building to transport bags of rice from a container on the ground floor via a cargo lift. When driving the forklift backward away from the cargo lift, the forklift driver injured another worker who came out from the cargo lift into the warehouse while carrying out ventilation work. The Court found that the appellant was not cautious while driving the forklift truck. This case specifically references the decision in *Paul Y. General Contractors Limited v HKSAR* (detailed in the next section), whereby section 6B imposes a duty to take care of other persons, which has been interpreted as including persons other than the proprietor's employees. However, unlike the English law from which this section was adopted, the duty is on the proprietor's employee only, and not on the proprietor. The demarcation between occupational safety and public safety is not blurred here, whereby overall workplace safety is considered as a whole.

HKSAR v Penta-Ocean Construction Company Limited (ESS31076/2015)

This case was heard in a Magistrates' Court. The company was charged under sections 6A(1), 6A(2)(a)(c), 6A(3), and 13(1) of the FIUO. The real issue of this case was whether it was safe to use an electric breaker to chip plasters while standing on a kung-fu stool. The Court held that:

> After careful consideration, I [the Magistrate] am not totally convinced that the use of kung-fu stool in such circumstances can be described as "unsafe". Of course, there can be safer options as suggested by the prosecution's

> expert, such as mobile working platforms. However, I [the Magistrate] do not think the use of kung-fu stool is inherently unsafe.

The Magistrate went on to say that:

> PW1 was doing de-plastering when he got injured. I [the Magistrate] agree with the defence expert that it is not heavy-duty work. The height of the kung-fu stool is much lower than two metres. The ceiling height of the site was only 2.8 metre. So it is not unreasonable for a worker to use kung-fu stool for removing plastering. Considering the nature of the work, I [the Magistrate] tend to agree with the defence expert that a kung-fu stool is a convenient and safe tool. I [the Magistrate] am not saying a kung-fu stool is the perfect tool; nothing is but, considering all the circumstances, I [the Magistrate] am of the view that it is not unsafe to use it for de-plastering. More sophisticated mobile working platforms are, of course, good choices. While they might be safer than a simple kung-fu stool, at the same time, they may not have the same flexibility of the stool. In any event ... I [the Magistrate] cannot say the working system ... [was] unsafe.

The Magistrate finally held that: "I [the Magistrate] do not believe extra information or supervision is needed for an experienced worker ... when performing the work but, ... it is down to the worker himself to exercise reasonable care and diligence." Safety practitioners should note that kung-fu stools (less than two metres in height) of sound construction for plastering or concrete chipping are not prohibited on worksites. It is not an "unsafe" piece of equipment. However, it is also essential to be aware that it may cause danger when stationed close to large floor openings where a falling hazard is present.

HKSAR v Modern Terminals Limited (HCMA 680/2016)/ [2018] HKCFI 1003

The accident investigated in this case involved a forklift truck operating in a container terminal. The truck, together with the operator, fell into the sea while preparing for the mooring process. The mooring procedure was undertaken by two teams of workmen: one at the bow and one at the stern. Each team included a supervisor, three stevedoring workers, and a forklift truck operator. The truck was there to take a heaving line tossed ashore. The scene was casually captured by a CCTV camera. The truck was reversing at a speed of 1.57 km/hour towards the edge of the berth, crossed the rail of the quay crane, and fell into the sea. The operator, who was certified to be dead after being rescued, had over 12 years of driving experience. The forklift truck was examined and found to be in good working order after the accident. The company was prosecuted under sections 6A(2)(a), the "safe system of work summons", and 6A(2)(c), the "supervision summons", of the FIUO. The "safe system of work summons" demanded that kerbs or barriers, temporary or otherwise, be retrofitted at the berth edge in order to stop the forklift truck running into the sea as the crux of the safe system. The Magistrate held that there was no case to answer in respect of the "safe system of work summons" because of the reasonable practicality of retrofitting kerbs or barriers but convicted the appellant company of the "supervision summons" after the trial. The company then appealed against the ruling. The High Court held that the safety document of the appellant company stipulated that the supervision measure for preventing the risk of falling into the sea is to ensure that the forklift trucks do not operate on or beyond the rail of the quay cranes. The Court concluded that the necessary supervision in this regard must be the deployment of more manpower, such as signallers, behind the forklift truck to assist the operation supervisor to keep an eye on the driver. The defence did not provide evidence that the provision of necessary supervision (such as deploying a signaller to the forklift truck driver) was considered unreasonable or impracticable. The Court further held in favour of *HKSAR v Gammon Construction Limited* (detailed above) in that the prosecution does not need to establish a causal relationship between the breach and the injury. In this case, the operator was reversing the truck at a slow speed (1.57 km/hour). The truck crossed the rail of the quay crane, fell into the sea. The operator was not able to stop the truck even though the truck was in good working order. The Court did not consider the working experience of the forklift truck operator and instead focused on the direct and effective supervision that is required in the mooring process in a container terminal. Furthermore, safety practitioners should also take note of the Code of Practice, clause 5.3.9, on Mechanical Handling Safety in Container Yards issued by the Labour Department, which states: "If the visibility or range of sight of the operator is impaired by adverse weather conditions, strict supervision of the mechanical equipment operation should be exercised." This case highlights how cases involving "supervision" and "safe system of work" can be separate, allowing the appellate to be charged with both simultaneously or with either individually.

SECTION 13(1): PROSECUTING "LIKE OFFENCES"

Since its enactment in 2003, numerous breaches of section 13(1) of the FIUO by main or main contractors undertaking construction work have been prosecuted. The main contractor on a construction worksite is commonly the main proprietor under the law. The general duties of a proprietor are described in section 6A of the FIUO. Nevertheless, there will be other contractors of different trades and practices (multiple sub-contracting layering) and working on the same worksite. Under section 13, an unsafe work system adopted by a contractor or sub-contractor while working on a construction site would cause the main contractor or proprietor to be prosecuted for a "like offence". Section 13 is an unusual provision in that it may be used to impose safety liability on a proprietor (the main contractor and other contractors) in circumstances where: (a) the proprietor has neither performed nor failed to perform any act; (b) the proprietor is not at fault, and (c) the proprietor ensures, so far as reasonably practicable, the safety and health at work of all persons employed by him at the worksite as well as the safety and health of all persons employed by other proprietors (other contractors). Prosecutions of "like offences" under section 13 may come as a surprise to the proprietor, and some believe that they lead to further uncertainties or even unjust liability to the main contractor(s). Indeed, based on this section, any breach of the safety regulations under the FIUO on the worksite can bring a parallel prosecution to the main contractor or proprietor. Questions have been raised about whether or not these individuals can be fairly charged and what defence is available to them. This has led to a distinction being made between "section 6A proprietors" and "section 13 proprietors" in some legal proceedings. Even with these distinctions, there is still uncertainty concerning the reasonable practicability involved when multiple trades and practices are being conducted on a large and complex worksite, and the concept of proprietorship on a site where construction work is undertaken is amorphous. There is not a unique formula that is universally applicable in construction work. Two foremost cases highlight the application of this section and the fluid nature of proprietorship during legal proceedings: *HKSAR v Paul Y. General Contractors Limited* and *Lucky Engineering Company Limited v HKSAR*.

HKSAR v Paul Y. General Contractors Limited (FACC No. 4 of 2012)/ (2013 16 HKCFAR 487

This case concerns a contractual agreement between Paul Y. General Contractors Limited and CK Construction Management Limited, the owners or employer's representatives, for the former to undertake carcass work at a building in the Ho Man Tin area. The carcass work included aluminium cladding work, which was contracted to HH Robertson Limited by Paul Y. However, HH Robertson, in turn, sub-contracted the work to Ka Shing Engineering Company. On 20 September 2008, two employees of Ka Shing fell when an aluminium slab, which was six metres or more above the ground, on which they were standing, buckled. Tragically, one of the workmen died. The Court's decision rests heavily on how section 13 is read in combination with section 6A concerning the liability of proprietors.

Lucky Engineering Company Limited v HKSAR (FACC No. 5 of 2012)/ (2013) 16 HKCFAR 487

On 30 October 2002, a workman was electrocuted while installing floodlights on the wooden catwalk over the top of the indoor swimming pool at the Jockey Club's Happy Valley Clubhouse. The appellant, Lucky Engineering Company Limited, was the Jockey Club's contractor for upgrading its electrical power system at the swimming pool as well as the supply and installation of 32 250W floodlights (black lights). However, they were also responsible for the supply and installation of 18 400W floodlights (grey lights). The deceased was engaged in the installation of the grey lights when he was electrocuted. The deceased was not an employee of Lucky Engineering. Similar to the case above, the Court's decision involves both section 13 and section 6A of the FIUO.

The two cases above were then appealed together in the Court of Final Appeal.

Paul Y. General Contractors Limited and Lucky Engineering Company Limited v HKSAR (FACC No. 485 of 2012)/(2013) 16 HKCFAR 487

The following four questions put to the Court are summarised below.

1. Does section 13(1) of the FIUO, when read together with section 6A(1) of the same, permit a proprietor to be convicted of a "like offence" in relation to a person who was not employed by that proprietor?
2. If the answer above is in the affirmative, whether under the FIUO, any defence would be available to that proprietor, under those circumstances?
3. Under regulation 2(2)(a) of the Construction Sites (Safety) Regulations, can a contractor from whom other contractors do not derive their contracts, be deemed the main contractor?
4. Under regulation 2(2)(a) of the Construction Sites (Safety) Regulations, can a contracted "owner's representative" be precluded from liability of the main contractor?

The Court of Final Appeal gave the following answers to these questions:

1. Yes, but only insofar as the proprietor could be properly regarded as coming within section 13.
2. It would be a defence that the predicated offence has not been committed.
3. A contractor could be regarded as the contractor responsible even for contractors who had no direct contractual relationship with the sub-contractors employed by their own contractors and so on.

4. No. The question does not arise in this case.

The following guiding principles emerged from this case:

- The legislation is designed to ensure safety and health at work, and in pursuit of this aim, the net of criminal liability is cast widely.
- Section 6A imposes a general duty of care on a proprietor in relation to their own direct employees.
- An offence is committed under section 6A if the proprietor does not do all that is reasonably practicable to safeguard the safety and health of all their employees at the relevant industrial undertaking.
- Liability under section 13 is a derivative liability. It depends upon the commission of the predicate offence, such as the offence contrary to section 6A or other subsidiary offences made under the FIUO.
- Liability under section 13 does not impose a duty on a proprietor extending beyond their employees, but it does impose liability on a proprietor for a predicate offence committed by another proprietor.
- The scope of liability for the offence committed by a proprietor in relation to the failings of another proprietor is not entirely clear and may be uncertain. It seems to be limited to circumstances where the business of a "section 13 proprietor" encompasses or includes the work of a "section 6A proprietor". In the construction businesses, there are many trades and special occupations involved on a worksite as well as contractual layering, further complicating liability.
- When charged with a breach of section 13, a defence can be made for the main proprietor if they can show that the "section 6A proprietor" has done what is reasonably practicable to ensure the safety and health of his employees.

Safety practitioners should consider these principles when advising proprietors and contractors about worksite safety, regardless of the particular type of construction work is being performed.

The late Toby R.W. Jenkyn-Jones, a barrister-at-law, advanced the following criticism of section 13. First, when a section 6A proprietor of an industrial undertaking is guilty of an offence, any relevant section 13 proprietor is also considered guilty, regardless of their conduct or state of mind at the relevant time. This differs from the position taken under section 36 of the HASAW Act. Second, the concept of "proprietor", as Justice Litton acknowledged in the *Paul Y.* case described above, is "ill-defined and amorphous". He states:

> "Proprietor" in relation to any industrial undertakings or notifiable workplace includes the person for the time being having the management or control of the business carried on in such industrial undertaking or notifiable workplace and includes a body corporate and a firm and also the occupier of any industrial undertaking or notifiable workplace and the agent of such occupier.

Here, construction on a worksite is considered an industrial undertaking. Third, while it may be possible for a section 13 proprietor to avoid liability by proving that the section 6A proprietor ensured, so far as is reasonably practicable, the safety and health at work of all persons they employed at the relevant industrial undertaking, the section 13 proprietor cannot avoid liability by relying on the precautions carried out by another. In other words, liability is shared regardless of the safety precautions put in place by another proprietor. Even when the section 13 proprietor assiduously enforces and requires procedures and protocols to be followed by sub-contractors, if a section 6A sub-contractor deliberately and knowingly breaches these safe working protocols, then the section 13 proprietor will be found guilty of a "like offence". This is the case even in circumstances where the section 13 proprietor cannot possibly be expected to control or even know about the sub-contractor's actions in omniscient detail. Fourth, the defence identified by Justice Tang in *Paul Y. and Lucky* appeal above is unlikely to be workable because the section 13 proprietor is unlikely to be in a position to adduce evidence of the steps taken by the section 6A proprietor to comply with the general duties imposed by that section. At the very least, the section 13 proprietor is likely to be compromised or restricted in fully advancing his defence.

PRACTICAL GUIDES FOR IMPLEMENTING SAFE SYSTEMS OF WORK

Understanding section 6A and section 13, along with the terms "safe systems of work", "supervision", etc. as established in the legal cases discussed above, is essential to ensure safety on a construction site. However, a theoretical understanding is not enough, management and company leaders must also have a practical understanding of how to apply these case decisions and principles in their own work to avoid FIUO breaches and prosecution and to maintain a safe working environment. If site management can (a) provide safe plant and equipment, (b) engage competent workers, and (c) organise and manage construction work in a safe working environment and assess risks, then the odds of adhering to the stipulations of the FIUO and avoiding unnecessary risks are good.

Plant and equipment

Any plant or equipment used in construction work should be safe. There should be no inherent or manufacturing defects. As most of the plant and equipment used in construction work are not owned by the main contractor or sub-contractors, the manufacturer, its agent, or the hirer of the plant or equipment should give assurance that they are in good working order. However, the law is simple and straightforward regarding liability, whereby anytime plant or equipment, particularly lifting appliances, enters a worksite, the main contractor is considered the legal "owner". This is a legal responsibility that the main contractor must be aware of. The safety of plant and equipment is considered under section 13 of the FIUO as outlined above.

Thus, to select plant or equipment for a task, the following points should be considered: (a) the position of the plant or equipment within its life cycle and the risk of early failure, chance failure, or worn-out failure; (b) the maintenance records and examination certifications; (c) the safety standards; and (d) the design with or without ergonomic applications. Examples of undesirable plant or equipment are: an expired (or poor quality) abrasive disc cutter; an electric cable with a low index of protection; poor quality drill bits; second-hand excavators; tower cranes or mobile cranes with a known history of accidents; damaged electrical sockets; a makeshift electrical transformer; makeshift wooden ladders; aged or poorly maintained drilling rigs; unguarded dangerous parts of machinery inherent in an environment or piece of equipment; and a poorly maintained suspended working platform.

Unfortunately, providing safe plant or equipment alone cannot prevent construction accidents. In fact, even when the above safety measures are considered, one uncertainty proprietors and contractors face is if the plant or equipment is designed with inherent defects, which could ultimately contribute to an accident, can they be held responsible? The answer to this will be assessed on a case-by-case basis, and proprietors and contractors must do what they can to limit the risks. Furthermore, the points above only account for the physical elements of the plant and equipment, and there is a great deal more to safety at a construction site than just providing the right plant or equipment. Technical excellence in hardware is not enough, and there must be an effective and imaginative safe system of work employed as well as a commitment to eliminating or avoiding human error on the worksite.

To play it safe, the owner of the plant or equipment should obtain a maintenance manual (or a copy of this) from the manufacturer or an authorised agent as part of the safe system of work. For sophisticated plant or equipment (such as tower cranes or mobile cranes discussed in Chapters 8 and 9, respectively), a periodic technical audit from the manufacturer or its agent focusing on the maintenance actions carried out by the owner is highly recommended. This will add evidential points regarding the maintenance program undertaken by the owner in case of legal action.

Competent workers

Safety, being largely about people, is generally a far more complex issue than simply ensuring the physical plant and equipment are working properly and safely. Unlike engineering problems, there are no quick-fix safety solutions. Workers make errors. These can be unintentional slips or lapses of judgement or intentional mistakes or violations. They can be the result of a careless safety culture, a low morale workforce, inexperience, a poor safety attitude, inadequate physical capabilities, bad psychological conditions, lack of skill, a "macho-culture", a misguided "can-do" culture, misperception of risk, adrenaline addiction, drug abuse, inattention, rationalisation, normalisation, or unfamiliarity with the process. All errors can potentially result in severe consequences for the worker or their peers as well as the proprietor and anyone on the worksite. These human factors are a significant challenge in the construction safety field. Thus, it is essential to engage competent workers.

Worker competency should be a primary aspect of a safe system of work. In construction work, there is often a wide range of tasks occurring on a site at any given time, ranging from simple tasks to complex tasks that require a high level of professional skill. A competent worker will also need to be aware of how their work may affect others working on related or unrelated tasks. The need to engage competent workers, and replace incompetent workers as the case may be, was a relevant point in *HKSAR v Hin Lin Yee*. This case is unusual as it focuses on breaches in public health regulations, but it has significantly impacted the construction field.

HKSAR v Hin Lin Yee and Another (FACC No. 7 of 2009)/[2010] 2 HKLRD 826

This case involved two appellants (a medical practitioner and his assistant) operating in a clinic. The medical practitioner was charged under two separate ordinances: section 54(1) of the Public Health and Municipal Services Ordinance, Cap. 132, and regulation 36(1) of the Pharmacy and Poisons Regulation. The second appellant was only charged under the Public Health and Municipal Services Ordinance. The charge was for selling a drug (called "Pirtion", which contains an active ingredient called "chloropheniramine") which was unfit for human use because it was contaminated to varying degrees with isopropyl alcohol (the contaminant). The assistant was engaged in selling the contaminated medicine on four occasions. The drug was decanted from a large bottle into a 500 mL container. From this secondary container, the assistant dispensed four smaller bottles. There were also three additional 3.6 L bottles that were unopened and similarly labelled as "Chloropheniramine Melate 10 mg/5 mL" (or "CM 10 mg/5 mL"). It was discovered that the substance contained in these bottles was not the same as that registered with the Pharmacies and Poisons Board. This led to the medical practitioner being charged and convicted under regulation 36(1) for possession of the unregistered substances in those bottles. The medical practitioner maintained that he had been unaware of the fact that the CM 10 mg/5 mL in the bottles was unregistered but that it had been obtained from a reputable, long-standing, and trusted supplier. His rationale for appeal was that he did not know and could not with reasonable diligence have discovered that the substance in question was not registered with the Pharmacies and Poisons Board. Furthermore, both appellants maintained that they were unaware of the contamination with isopropyl alcohol and that the contamination must have been introduced before the drug was delivered. Thus, they were relying on a common law defence (section 18) on the basis that they had honestly and reasonably believed the medicine to be fit for its purpose when sold to the patients.

The Court stated that "if the contractor or employee is slack or careless or incompetent on the job, he has every incentive to make sure that the job is properly done and to replace contractors or employees who are not up to the task." However, the statement that "the so-called common law defence had no application to safety legislation" is far too broad. A "halfway house defence or intermediate defence" is available for defence in safety regulations, and the "honest but mistaken belief" can be a defence in cases. Treating all regulatory offences as offences of absolute liability is not fully acceptable, and cases need to be assessed on a case-by-case basis.

While this Court of Final Appeal case is seemingly unrelated to work safety in the construction industry, the judgment has been quoted in a number of construction safety cases, most notably in *HKSAR v Shun Tak Properties Limited* [2009] 3 HKLRD 299 (described in Chapter 4), which concerned the maintenance carried out on a gondola by the owner. In fact, in the first sentence in the judgment for the *Hin Lin Yee* case, Justice Bokhary states: "Neither the reasons of the Magistrate nor those of the appeal judge can be supported. The reasoning of the majority in *HKSAR v Shun Tak Properties Ltd* [2009] 3 HKLRD 299 is wrong and that of Stock JA in that case is right." To clarify, in the *Shun Tak* case, Justice Stock indicated that a common law defence (or halfway house) is, in certain statutory contexts, a defence for the accused to prove, on balance of probabilities, that they honestly, albeit mistakenly, held a belief which, if true, would have amounted to a defence. However, he went on to say that the word "ensure" implies a non-delegable duty, and the owner of the gondolas has restricted liability. Hence, the common law defence (or halfway house), which was advanced by the majority of the High Court and the Magistrate, was not applicable. This is what prompted Justice Bokhary's statement in the *Hin Lin Yee* case and the decision "that the so-called common law defence had no application to safety legislation". The appeal of this case is further discussed in Chapter 6.

The decision in the case above highlights a valid safety goal in theory, but in practice, this goal may not be compatible with those of other stakeholders, who may be focused on the timeline or financial input for the work. It is often difficult to get a timely replacement, and in some cases, the worker employed is one of only a few experts for that construction process. Thus, it is essential to focus on preventing errors through trade test certification and approved safety training courses conducted by institutions such as the Construction Industry Council. These can be used as baseline proof for competency. The safety requirements for that particular worksite should also be discussed early on.

One widespread safety issue is the relaxed use of personal protective equipment by some workers while in the work area. Examples include not wearing eye goggles, not attaching safety belts to independent lifelines or other anchorages, and not wearing earplugs. To instruct or enforce workers to wear personal protective equipment properly is not enough. It is necessary to understand why they choose not to wear personal protective equipment. By understanding their rationale, safety practitioners will be able to address the root cause of the issue. Ensuring worker competency through such on-site education is also the responsibility of management and safety practitioners.

Worksite management, organisation, and risk assessment

Section 6A(2)(c) requires supervision in a safe system of work. This was the basis for prosecution in the *Gammon* case tried in the Court of Final Appeal, discussed earlier in this chapter. This means that for any construction task, there should be a supervisor engaged or appointed. They must be a senior worker who is responsible for looking after groups of workers conducting particular trades. This supervisor will be entrusted with a list of safety responsibilities and assist a site agent in monitoring the progress of a particular project. An "effective" construction supervisor is someone who is aware of safety matters and has good supervision skills. This individual plays a key role in the execution of a safe system of work.

The organisation of the work environment is also part of a safe system of work. This will be a particular challenge for civil engineering. Most civil engineering sites operate in open space or in difficult site conditions, like underwater, tunnels (with or without compressed air), caverns, shafts, hills, confined spaces, underground or at extreme heights or altitudes (where weather conditions may change quickly), and during daylight or at night. Such difficult environments may involve an increased risk of error or other hazardous conditions and should be carefully managed. Emergency preparedness is essential, and recovery procedures that minimise damage to plant and equipment and mitigate bodily injuries to the workforce should be part of the organisation's safe system of work.

Lastly, safe worksite management and organisation require a comprehensive risk assessment. This assessment is a useful tool to minimise undesirable happenings using preventive measures in construction work. According to the IEC/ISO 31010 publications on risk management and risk assessment techniques, there are 30 tools available. These risk assessment tools involve visual risk assessment, brainstorming, and consequence/probability risk matrix development, or some combination of these. A consequence/probability matrix is used to rank risks, sources of risk, or risk treatments on the basis of the level of risk. This technique is commonly used in assessing risks in construction work. Additional instruments include Fault Tree Analysis (FTA) or Event Tree Analysis (ETA), which are probabilistic techniques applied to assess the risk of an undesirable event, and a Hazard and Operability (HAZOP) Study, which attempts to exhaust and predict the possibilities of foreseeable risks to personnel or equipment that could prevent efficient operation. These tools, depending on the availability of reliable data, can be semi-quantitative or quantitative.

Risk assessments are based on past experiences and harness the wisdom of asking the pertinent questions of what will go wrong before it goes wrong, applying a "what-if" model. Could undesirable events that have happened elsewhere happen to us? What would be the worst disaster that could happen on our worksite? While providing answers to these questions cannot necessarily guarantee that all the risks of a project are identified, they provide a starting point. Asking these questions can stimulate the implementation of necessary control or precautionary measures.

Risk assessments should be undertaken by a designated risk assessment team comprised of knowledgeable personnel who are selected for their skills, experience, and competency. The team should also include the safety personnel or practitioner, who will act as the coordinator. A comprehensive risk assessment should be demanded before any construction task occurs. It is a precursor for a safe method statement indicating that the safest method has been chosen, amongst other methods, and will be carried out in a manner with the lowest calculated risk, as is reasonably practicable. However, construction activities can never be risk-free. A risk assessment is meant to help translate hindsight (past known accidents) into foresight (planning for safe methods of work) and to assist management in deciding the best safe system of work.

After a risk assessment has been conducted for a task that involves people, time, plant, or equipment at the worksite, a written version should be made available to all workers. Any sub-contractor who conducts a task should carry out its own risk assessment. The sub-contractor's risk assessment should then be vetted by the proprietor, main contractor, or the contractor responsible. For complex or sophisticated engineering tasks or tasks that have not been undertaken at the site before, the assessment should be preferably vetted by an external and independent third party to ensure the correct input for hazard identification and adequacy of control measures.

Risk assessments should also be regularly reviewed in light of incidents or changes or modifications of plant or equipment. For exposure to hazardous substances or chemicals, for example, a Health Risk Assessment (HRA) based on the dosage and the exposure duration is recommended. An HRA requires input from occupational health professionals. A good reference regarding the toxicity of harmful or dangerous substances can be obtained from the American Conference of Governmental Industrial Hygienists (ACGIH) in the United States. Such references are updated and published regularly.

Ultimately, site management has to decide what level of risk is tolerable for each task, while at the same time ensuring that the business of the construction activities can stay competitive. The safety-at-work laws in Hong Kong and elsewhere around the world require that the risks on a worksite are kept as low as is reasonably practicable.

SUMMARY

The importation of the general duties in the UK's HASAW Act to section 6A of the FIUO in Hong Kong was both practical and philosophical. The imposition of general duties stimulates an analytical and assessment-oriented approach. It puts a comprehensive obligation on construction management to look at every aspect of its activities from the point of safety and health. It imposes a specific question for managers to ask themselves: what do I need to do to ensure the safety and health of operations within my area of responsibility?

The court cases outlined in this chapter indicate that delivering information, instruction, training, and supervision to the whole construction workforce are essential issues. Court decisions have played a significant role in defining terms and levels of liability, and this reliance on prosecution of breaches of the FIUO will likely persist in the future. There will almost certainly be more accidents and errors in every construction work activity because even the simplest of these requires people, plant, or equipment, all of which carry an inherent amount of risk. Incompatible goals between individuals, sub-contractors, contractors, and proprietors only exacerbate these risks. Moreover, production (time, money, progress, quality, manpower) goals and safety goals are also sometimes in conflict. In the long term, enhanced education and training seem to be the ultimate solution. One must learn to do the safe thing at the very start of a task, rather than correct an unsafe behaviour later. Management must lead and establish company or project-wide goals. These should be considered when employing contractors and workers and used to assess competency.

Thorough risk assessment is a pre-requisite for a safe system of work and the identification of potential hazards. However, even at its best, risk assessment is guesswork, particularly for activities that workers have little or no previous experience with, technically or procedurally. These tasks carry an inherent level of uncertainty. Humans can and will make errors and mistakes. Managing this human factor on the worksite is by far the most challenging aspect of safety in the construction industry.

This chapter is the first of several focused on regulatory breaches in the construction industry. Unfortunately, the flexible and fluid safety and health situation on construction sites is difficult to manage with an inflexible legislative instrument, even for a "catch-all" conceptual regulation like section 6A of the FIUO. Safety practitioners have repeatedly questioned if the section 6A general duties regulations work in the construction industry and if the enforcement of this section and the FIUO in general decreases the number of construction accidents, fatal or non-fatal. Is it time to review the effectiveness of section 6A or of the FIUO in general? This is a question safety practitioners and students will continue to grapple with. As the general duties section in the FIUO is not the only regulatory instrument used for prosecutions in the construction industry, the next two chapters will cover breaches of the Construction Sites (Safety) Regulations as well as of construction-specific FIU Regulations.

FURTHER READING

Cheung, S.O., Cheung, K.K.W., and Suen, H.C.H. (2004) "CCSHM: Web-based safety and health monitoring system for construction management", *Journal of Safety Research*, Vol. 35, pp. 159–170.

Labour Department, Hong Kong SAR Government (2004) *Safe Systems of Work*, Hong Kong Government Printer.

Shell Health, Safety and Environmental Panel (April 1999) *Risk Assessment Matrix*.

Tam, C.M., and Fung, I.W.H. (1996) "Effectiveness of safety management strategies on safety performance in Hong Kong", *Construction Management and Economics*, Vol. 17, pp. 49–55.

DISCUSSION QUESTIONS

1. Obtain a full copy of the judgment in *HKSAR v Hin Lin Yee and Another* (FACC No. 7 of 2009). What general observations can you

make concerning the common law defence that may be available in construction safety?

2. Obtain a full copy of the judgment in *HKSAR v Gammon Construction Limited* (FACC No. 10 of 2014). What general observations can you make concerning a safe system of work for lifting operations at construction sites?

"... take adequate steps to prevent any person on any place where the construction work is being carried out from falling from a height of 2 metres or more"

– Regulations 38B(1) and 38B(1A) of the Construction Sites (Safety) Regulations

"In 1988, during the construction of the Hong Kong Convention and Exhibition Centre, a landmark in Wan Chai, no fewer than 459 workers were injured. Of these, there were two fatalities, 36 workers were permanently disabled and 54 were seriously injured"

– The Hon. K.Y. Yeung
Government Secretary for Education and Manpower
20 November 1989

6 Breaches of the Construction Sites (Safety) Regulations

INTRODUCTION

Past safety studies at work shown that from 1981 to 1987, a total of 173 deaths were recorded as a result of falls on construction sites, including falls from working platforms or workplaces at height, falls from bamboo scaffolds or platforms on scaffolds, and falls from upper floors from over the edge or through floor openings. Another study showed that on average 1 fall in every 100 proved fatal from 1985 to 1995. A more recent study by the Labour Department showed that from 2012 to mid-2014 more than 75% (44 of the 58 fatal construction cases) were related to three types of work activities—namely, working at height (31 cases), electrical work (8 cases), and tunnelling or underground work (5 cases). These ad hoc studies lead to the question: what safety-at-work regulations have been enacted to address such events and to prevent future accidents, fatal or otherwise?

The Construction Sites (Safety) Regulations (abbreviated CS(S)Rs), a set of subsidiary regulations under the Factories and Industrial Undertakings Ordinance, Cap. 59 (FIUO), were introduced to specifically address such safety-at-work problems and various regulatory aspects of construction safety. Of these, regulation 38 in Part VA is clearly one of the most prosecutable regulations. Most, if not all, contractors are aware of or have previously been penalised for breaching this piece of safety legislation. Regulation 38 consists of sub-regulations concerning safe work using scaffolds (bamboo, metal, or a combination), working platforms, ladders, and other workplaces presenting falling hazards. This regulation (specifically regulation 38H) also prescribes an available legal defence for those being prosecuted.

The first part of this chapter focuses on important legal cases involving various CS(S)Rs and outlines the legal issues underlying these court decisions. These issues include how "construction work" and "construction site" are defined as well as the meaning of "monitoring" or "supervision" (particularly in relation to working at height under regulation 38B). The second part of this chapter explains strict liability under regulation 38 as well as the defence available to those prosecuted for breaches of this regulation.

DEFINING "CONSTRUCTION SITE" AND "CONSTRUCTION WORK"

Legally, the CS(S)Rs only apply to construction sites where construction work is being carried out. A "construction site", under the FIUO, refers to

> a place where construction work is undertaken and also any area in the immediate vicinity of any such place which is used for the storage of materials or plant used or intended to be used for the purpose of construction work.

Further, "construction work" is defined as

> the construction, erection, installation, reconstruction, repair, maintenance (including redecoration and external cleaning), renewal, removal, alteration, improvement, dismantling, or demolition of any structure or works specified in the Third Schedule.

To help clarify this, the list of "Specified Structures and Works" in the Third Schedule of the FIUO is reproduced below:

1. Any building, edifice, wall, fence, or chimney, whether constructed wholly or partly above or below ground level

2. Any road, motorway, railway, tramway, cableway, aerial ropeway, or canal (Amended 19 of 1976 section 32)
3. Any harbour works, dock, pier, sea defence work, or lighthouse
4. Any aqueduct, viaduct, bridge, or tunnel
5. Any sewer, sewage disposal works, or filter bed
6. Any airport or works connected with air navigation
7. Any dam, reservoir, well, pipeline, culvert, shaft, or reclamation
8. Any drainage, irrigation, or river control work
9. Any water, electrical, gas, telephonic, telegraphic, radio, or television installation or works, or any other works designed for the manufacturing or transmission of power or the transmission or reception of radio or sound waves
10. Any structure designed for the support of machinery, plant, or power transmission lines

Courts will also interpret this list when a case involves unspecified structures or works. For example, environmental enhancement work may include landscaping work, horticultural work, or weeding work associated with building or engineering construction, even though this is not explicitly defined in the Third Schedule. While the Commissioner for Labour has the power under the law to amend or add to the Third Schedule, it has not been revised since 1976.

For the CS(S)Rs to be applicable, the work must be "construction work" on a "construction site". While the definitions above are helpful to establish this, their practical application in Hong Kong is most evident in legal cases tried (or dismissed) based on their interpretation of "construction work" or "construction site".

AG v China Light and Power Co. Ltd (CA No. 1112/1981)

Following a worksite accident, this case involves a charge brought under regulation 47(1) of the CS(S)Rs for the safety of workmen liable to come into contact with live electrical apparatuses. On the night of the accident, the respondent company was engaged in the conversion of an electrical feeder line with a single transformer into a full electricity consumer with two transformers. To perform the conversion, the electrical current was disconnected between two substations situated at Kingsway Industrial

Building, Phase II, KCTL 311, and Milo, KCTL 161, located on either side of the intended new substation in Cheung Wing Road, KCTL 9B. The work that night involved the disconnection of circuits, testing those circuits to check they were live, wiring in new circuits, testing the new circuits, and finally reconnecting the altered system to the electricity supply. A qualified electrical engineer was in charge of the operation that night with an electrician and a linesman. The accident occurred at the switchgear feeding down from Kingsway to KCTL 98 where the new substation was being brought into operation when the linesman entered Kingsway to assist in completing the final testing and reconnection and was killed.

During the trial, it was questioned whether the qualified electrician, who was working with live electrical apparatuses in an electrical station, was doing "construction work" or not. If not, then the CS(S)Rs would not apply. The Court held that the work at Kingsway substation on the night of the accident was not construction work based on the fact that the contractor would be unable to do the work to comply with regulation 47(1) without contravening the same CS(S)R. Thus, the substation was not a "construction site" and the CS(S)Rs did not apply. This case shows that some works requiring specific expertise (e.g., certain electrical works, etc.) cannot be restricted or prosecuted for offences of the CS(S)Rs.

AG v Harbour Engineering Company Limited (HCMA 1098/1985)/ [1986] HKLR 613

The company involved in this case was responsible for excavation work to locate a blocked concrete telephone-wire conduit buried at the site and to remove the blockage. A trench was dug and while an employee of the respondent was using a pneumatic drill to break loose the concrete slab covering the conduit, the drill came into contract with a live underground electric cable. This resulted in an explosion, and three employees were injured. The Magistrate held that the work carried out by the workers was not "construction work" and the site was not a "construction site" under the CS(S)Rs. However, in the appeal, the High Court held the opposing view that "telephone installation" was indeed construction work, irrespective of size, and that the site was considered a "construction site". The High Court even stated that to accept the Magistrate's opinion would mean that in such cases the courts would be required to decide when a wall becomes a sizable wall, when a sewer becomes a sizable sewer, when a chimney becomes a sizable chimney, and so on. This could create significant confusion regarding precedence in addition to potentially consuming hours of valuable time in defining such parameters.

In the judgment of the case above, the High Court cited the *ejusdem generis* rule. According to *Halsbury's Laws of England* (Fourth edition):

> As a rule, when a statue uses general words following particular and specific words, the general words must be confined to things of the same kind as those specified ... It seems that the *ejusdem generis* rule can have no application where the general words precede the enumeration of particular instances, and may not be relevant for the construction of international conventions.

However, in the construction field, this rule must be applied with caution and is subject to the primary rule that statutes are to be construed in accordance with the intention of Parliament or the Legislature. For the *ejusdem generis* rule to apply, the specific words must constitute a category, class, or genus and the general words cannot by their nature exclude themselves from the category, class, or genus, so that, for example, a superior thing will not be held to be within a class of inferior things. If the particular words exhaust the whole genus, the general words must be construed as referring to some large genus. Thus, this legal term has specific repercussions in the construction field when it comes to defining "construction work" and "construction site".

AG v Marples International Limited (HCMA 803/1987)

This case stemmed from an accident in a borrow area in which a loader fell from the edge of a cut slope to a lower slope. The borrow area provided earth and rock to another site separated by a distance of one kilometre by road and half to one kilometre by sea and by an estate. The edge of the slope the loader fell from was not provided with a guard-rail. This case again raises the question of whether the work in the borrow area was "construction work" and whether the area was, therefore, a "construction site" to which the CS(S)Rs would apply.

The Court held that the words "including the laying of foundation and the excavation of earth and rock prior to the laying of foundation" in the definition of "construction work" under the FIUO were not words of limitation and were only examples of what went on during construction work. If that was the law, it could lead to absurd situations where the borrow area would have a dual purpose in the sense that when it supplied fill for reclamation, it would be deemed a construction site and would therefore need to be fenced according to the CS(S)Rs, while when it supplied rocks for crushing or some other purposes, it would be deemed a quarry and different regulations would need to be applied. The Court further held that the borrow area involved was not a "construction site" under regulation 2(1)(a) of the CS(S)Rs. It stated that this regulation did not entail work in a different location as being part of the same construction site and only preparatory work within the site where reclamation was to take place was "construction work".

AG v Cheung Kee Fung Cheung Construction Company Limited (HCMA 874/1989)

This case involved an accident which led to a fatal injury. On the day of the accident, a lorry loaded with cement bags arrived at the site and the driver was directed to unload the bags at a particular location on the site. On the lorry, apart from the driver, were three cement transportation workers employed by a sub-contractor. When they were preparing to unload the bags from the lorry, a lump of concrete fell while two scaffolders were dismantling nylon mesh on the scaffolding. The falling concrete struck one of the transportation workers, who was not wearing a protective helmet although there was one available for his use on the lorry.

The Court held that the bringing and unloading of the cement on the construction site for subsequent use in construction work on the site was considered "work involved in preparing for construction". The deceased was therefore considered a "workman" engaged in construction work because he was there for the express purpose of unloading the cement at the site. This ruling also extends to workers delivering steel bars, facades, windows, or other items for building or engineering construction and implies that they too are carrying out construction work, regardless of who employs the worker. The main contractor on the site is ultimately liable.

The Queen v Sime Darby Property Services Limited (HCMA 239/1993)

The case involved an accident which occurred during the maintenance of a cooling tower of an air-conditioning system installed on the roof of a two-storey building. Access and egress for the maintenance work required workers to walk over a 30-degree pitched asbestos roof. One worker was found lying unconscious below a hole in the asbestos roof, and the company was charged for a breach in the CS(S)Rs. The Magistrate initially held that this was indeed "construction work" on a "construction site", but the High Court later reversed this ruling, stating that the demolition of air-conditioning cooling towers installed and attached to the exterior of a building was not construction work as air-conditioning cooling towers were not an integral part of a building, and hence the CS(S)Rs did not apply. Furthermore, the cooling towers were also excluded from the category of "water installation" within item 9 of the Third Schedule.

The Queen v Tsui Wai Ping (HCMA 575/1993)/[1993] 2 HKC 675

This case involved a fatal accident of a scaffolding worker. Decoration work was being carried out on the 10th floor of a building. Following the work, while dismantling the metal scaffolding structures, the worker fell from the roof of an adjoining building where the he was transporting the bamboo posts from the 10th floor premises. The appellant was charged under the CS(S)Rs as if the accident occurred on the worksite proper. However, during the proceedings, the Court was asked: Should regulation 2(1) of CS(S)Rs be extended beyond the specific work premises, and if so, how far? In response, the Court stated that the statutory extension covers any area which is in the immediate vicinity of the place where construction work is undertaken and is used for the storage of materials for use in the work. However, the Court went on to explain that if the lift of the building was big enough to carry the scaffolding materials from the ground floor to the 10th floor and if the deceased had to carry the bamboo posts by stages into the lift, it would have been inevitable to leave some of the bamboo posts inside the lift while he went out to carry more. The Court then questioned: Would one sensibly regard the lift as an extension of the construction site on the 10th floor? Would one seriously regard the lift lobby as an extension of the construction site? Thus, it is reasonable to expect there to be limitations to what is considered the worksite. The Court finally agreed that the roof from which the deceased fell to his death could not be regarded as part of the construction site.

Leung Lai Yin v Yeung Kei Chi and Others (HCPI 317/1999)

This is a High Court Personal Injury Case (HCPI) where an employee was injured while using a circular saw in a residential flat of a building. Although the charges were not brought under the CS(S)Rs, it is another example of how the courts interpret the definitions of "construction work" and "construction site".

In this case, the Court held that "the definition of 'construction work' is 'the construction and maintenance (including redecoration) of any building'". However, the word "redecoration" has to be interpreted in context and not in isolation. Indeed, decoration or redecoration works are not considered construction work unless they form part of the maintenance work of the building. Obvious examples would be removing defective plaster, rendering the wall surfaces, covering up exposed concrete, and fixing decorative tiles or marble slabs. They have to be works that involve the "well-being" of the building as a whole. Redecoration work in common areas of the building, such as the external walls, lobbies, and corridors are common examples. It may also cover maintenance work of a structural nature inside individual flats of the building as a whole. However, this definition does not cover internal decoration or redecoration work inside individual units done for the personal enjoyment of individual owners, such as making cupboards, wardrobes, or beds.

HKSAR v Alliance Engineering Co. Ltd (HCMA 1154/2006)

This case stemmed from an inspection of a worksite at Hutchinson House in which a workman was found not wearing a suitable safety helmet while on the site. The appellant was charged under regulation 48(1) of the CS(S)Rs. The work at the site involved the installation of an air-conditioning system, drainage work, electrical work connected to the central system of the building, and water leakage preventive work, as well as painting and plastering work. It was contested that the work that was being undertaken at Hutchison House did not meet the statutory definition that would make the place a construction site.

The Court held that the description of the work being carried out falls under the category of "improvement, maintenance (including redecoration), reconstruction, repair". Thus, the Court found that the work at Hutchison House, regardless of size, clearly made it a construction site.

HKSAR v Otis Elevators Company (HK) Limited (HCMA 154/2008)/ [2008] 2 HKCLRT 73

The appellant was charged under regulation 44 of the CS(S)Rs for failing to effectively fence a dangerous part of machinery which resulted in an accident. A team of three lift technicians was sent to carry out maintenance and repair work for lift installation in a residential building. When the leader of the team was conducting "testing" and "fine-tuning", one of the technician's hands was trapped and injured by the steel gear of the driving unit while it was in motion. At the time of the accident, the protective guard of the driving unit had not been re-installed. During the case, an issue was raised as to whether the work was "construction work".

The Court held that the plant room, the driving unit, motor, and other gear traction systems as well as the lift passenger car, lift belts, and ingress/egress points are parts of the entire lift system. Because the lift under repair served various floors, all these parts formed an integral part of the building. This was the rationale underlying the Court's decision to consider this type of maintenance and repair of lifts in residential buildings to be construction work on a construction site.

HKSAR v China Geo-Engineering Corporation (TWS 847-9/2012)

This case was heard at a Magistrates' Court. A female worker fell fatally from a slope while she was doing weeding work. The Court held that weeding work was not construction work. This work involved the removal of unwanted plants during a period of establishment work, but it did not involve the installation of soil nails, nets, or drains. Thus, the Court viewed the work at the time of the accident as being related to planting and not related to the maintenance of the drainage of the slope.

HKSAR v Tsang Lik Services Limited (HCMA 199/2015)

During a visit to the site, two occupational safety officers from the Labour Department found two workers were doing cleaning work on the podium of a building at a height more than two metres above ground level. The cleaning work involved using water jets to remove rubbish which had accumulated and clean the area. The appellant company was charged under regulation 38B(1) of the CS(S)Rs because of the risk of falling at a height greater than two metres.

The Court held that such cleaning work can be classified as "maintenance (including redecoration and external cleaning)" and is, therefore, deemed to be "construction work" and the workplace a "construction site". It is important for contractors and sub-contractors undertaking cleaning work in buildings to be aware that such labour falls under the purview of the CS(S)Rs.

PROSECUTIONS INVOLVING REGULATIONS 38B(1) AND 38B(1A) OF THE CS(S)Rs

Of the sub-regulations under regulation 38, construction contractors are frequently charged under regulation 38B(1) and 38B(1A). Regulation 38B(1) stipulates that the contractor responsible for any construction site shall take adequate steps to prevent any person on the site from falling from a height of two metres or more. This is also called the six-feet rule. Regulation 38B(1A), introduced in 2003, is similar to this but stipulates that *any contractor who has direct control over any construction work* shall take adequate steps to prevent any person on any place where construction work is being carried out from falling from a height of two metres or more. A key difference is the use of the term "direct control", which is legally defined as

> in relation to any construction work, process, excavation, operation, or erection, substantial addition, alteration or dismantling of scaffold means control over the way the construction work, process, excavation, operation, or erection, substantial addition, alteration, or dismantling of scaffold, as the case may be, is carried out.

The "adequate steps" stipulated in these regulations include the provision, use, and maintenance of one or more of the following: (a) working platforms; (b) guard-rails, barriers, toe-boards, and fences; (c) coverings for openings; and (d) gangs and runs. Further, every working platform must comply with the provisions set down in the Third Schedule of the CS(S)Rs.

Both regulations can be used to prosecute one or more contractors on a single site if found to be responsible. The following selected appeal cases summarise the courts' rulings on the standard of safety measures stipulated and the definition of terms in these regulations. The cases are separated into those before 2003 and those thereafter to highlight how the enactment of the "direct control" term has affected legal proceedings. These cases are also dependent on the "2-metre rule" and have shed light onto the meaning of "monitoring" and "supervision" when working at height.

Before 2003

The cases before 2003 specifically involve regulation 38B(1).

HKSAR v Hip Hing Construction Company Limited (HCMA 1253/2000)

The Court held that a workman standing astride an A-frame ladder while carrying out repairs to a fluorescent light fixture in the ceiling breached regulation 38B. In this case, the top of the ladder was 2.72 metres above the ground, the legs of the ladder were 1.13 metres apart, and the feet of the workers were 2.39 metres above the ground. He was therefore 0.39 metres (or 16 inches) above the height limit specified in regulation 38B. The light fixture was about 4.17 metres from the ground. The Court held that "[b]ecause of the height of the ladder and the height of the light fitting there existed a real danger that the worker might fall unless other adequate steps were taken such as the use of a more stable platform". Safety practitioners responsible for site safety should note that using short A-frame ladders for high-ceiling work is punishable by law.

HKSAR v Hip Hing Construction Company Limited (HCMA 509/2001)

This was an appeal case against a material irregularity during the course of the trial that regulation 38H(1) was not given due consideration to an offence under regulation 38B(1) of the CS(S)Rs. The appeal was allowed, thus quashing the conviction, setting aside the fine, and directing that the case should be remitted for retrial. The facts of the case were that on 8 August 2000 an occupational safety officer visited a construction site and he noticed workers at that site working on the construction of a metal canopy which was about five metres above the ground and which was attached to the wall of a building. He also noticed that there were some voids or openings in two sections of the canopy and *inter alia* he formed the view that there was a risk of the workers falling through those voids and that the workers were not wearing safety belts and there was no ladder, scaffolding, or platform allowing access to or egress from the canopy. However, the workers were in fact filling the voids with metal sheets as the canopy was being constructed, and indeed, this was what the workers were employed to do. The defence indicated that it was impracticable for the workers to somehow cover the voids or openings temporarily with some material because that would prevent the work from being performed. It was also impracticable to construct a platform from which to do the work.

HKSAR v Hyundai Engineering Construction Company Limited (HCMA 815/2002)

This case was heard before Deputy High Court Judge Line. It arose from a site inspection. The officer saw a man standing with one foot on the top bar of a tower scaffold and the other foot on the very top step of an

A-frame ladder which was leaning unsecured and unrooted against a wall. The man was standing fully erected and working with his hands above his head on the ceiling above him. His feet were 2.78 metres above the ground. He was making measurements and marking the ceiling in order for suspended piping to be fixed to it. The ceiling was 4.5 metres above the floor. He wore no safety belt, and there was no suitable anchorage for one. No safety nets were in place. If he had lost his balance or footing or if the ladder had slipped or the tower moved there was nothing to prevent his falling to the ground. A photograph was taken by the officer as prosecution evidence. The Court held that "falling risks are acceptable when the height from which a man may fall is below 2 metres. They are not acceptable over that limit." The Court rejected the availability of a defence and held that "adequate steps" had not been taken to prevent a person on the site from falling.

HKSAR v Paul Y-ITC General Contractors Limited (HCMA 347/2003)

The company was charged for failing to comply with the requirements of the Third Schedule of the CS(S)Rs. In this case, there was a rectangular hole on the top of a platform, which was part of a junk collection structure. The hole was unguarded but would be protected by guard-rails and toe-boards when the building was completed. On the day of the incident, a three-man painting team began hauling up planks to lay them on the top of the scaffolding to act as a working platform. They did this by passing up the planks in a chain or relay up the scaffolding. A member of the team was standing on the platform of the junk collection point to receive the planks and then pass them upwards. In dealing with a plank and manipulating it, this member of the team stepped backward with the plank and fell through the hole. He fell to the ground and sustained a head injury. The case for the appellant was that, at some stage, a heavy metal plate had covered the hole. After the incident, a metal plate was found on the floor of the refuse collection point. There were lurking doubts as to when and who removed the heavy metal plate that covered the hole.

However, the Court held that the hole was uncovered prior to the commencement of the work and that if the appellant's safety officers had inspected the site prior to the commencement of the work, then this issue would have been detected. Because they failed to do so, the appellant was found guilty, and the appeal was dismissed. Thus, safety practitioners should look for any floor openings that may present falling hazards during their safety inspections. Such hazards require immediate rectification. Unfortunately, there is still some question as to what size an opening must be for a worker to fall through. Accident records showed that floor openings resulting in accidents ranged from 640 mm × 640 mm, 1200 mm × 540 mm, 1700 mm × 1700 mm, 950 mm × 2200 mm, 2400 mm × 660 mm, 1830 mm × 900 mm, and 2380 mm × 480 mm.

HKSAR v Teemay Engineering Limited (HCMA 1081/2003)

The case, heard by Justice Beeson, involved a worker using an electrical arc-welding set to weld metal plates forming the cover of a walkway. The worker was on the top of an A-frame ladder which was positioned on the "first floor" of the walkway which was 2.8 metres high above the ground and 1.5 metres wide. The overall height of the temporary boarded fence around the worksite (also known as the hoarding) was 5.8 metres. The unfinished length of the hoarding at the working location was more than 24 metres. No safety netting was erected at the walkway, and no guard-rails or toe-boards were in place. No independent lifelines had been slung, and no fall arrestors were in place. The Court held that these offences should be dealt with by deterrent sentences, and any appeal against excessive fines should be dismissed.

After 2003

The cases tried after 2003 involve regulation 38B(1) as well as regulation 38B(1A), which expands liability to those with "direct control".

HKSAR v China Overseas Engineering Company Limited (HCMA 781/2004)/[2005] 4 HKLRD 771

The appellant company was prosecuted under regulation 38B as a result of an inspection by an occupational safety officer. The case involved a worker who was seen working above six metres from floor level on a bamboo scaffolding. No Form 5, a prescribed statutory form certifying the safety condition of the scaffolding, was displayed. He was standing and working on a wooden plank measuring 2.5 metres long and 1.2 metres wide. The plank rested on the bamboo scaffolding and created a void space which was 0.53 metres long and 0.39 metres wide between the bamboo poles of the scaffoldings. Thus, a fall through the void space was foreseeable. The worker admitted that he was aware of this unauthorised practice, but he continued his work anyway, making the breach a deliberate act. Nevertheless, while it may have been the worker's own decision, the company was held accountable by the Court.

Safety practitioners should be aware that if there are no safety precautions or warnings, a company cannot form a defence based on the act being a "frolic of the worker". Companies are expected to assess risks and post warnings. Site management should note that if bamboo scaffolding is not ready or safe for use or is still under the erection process, a warning notice "not allowed to use" must be prominently posted.

HKSAR v Fai Lung Exploitation Limited (HCMA 1189/2005)

Here, the appellant was charged under regulation 38B(1A) of the CS(S)Rs following an inspection by an occupational safety officer from the Labour Department in which two workers were found working at the unfenced edge of the third floor of a new school annex. A scaffold has been erected next to that area, but it was half a metre from the floor edge, leaving a void of that size from the third floor to the ground floor, a distance of 12 metres. Workmen were expected to move across the void while carrying articles such as planks. There were no safety nets or harness anchorage points. There was also no warning notice.

A second violation was also observed. An open lift shaft was found by the inspecting officer with workmen working in the immediate vicinity. The lift shaft opening was neither fenced off nor covered in any way. No lifelines or safety nets were installed at or near the shaft. No warning notices were posted. A worker falling down the shaft would fall for 3.6 metres from the third floor to the floor slab on the second floor of the annex.

The Court held that an unfenced floor edge a half metre from a scaffold created a void space and that an unfenced lift shaft opening is dangerous to workmen in their immediate vicinity. Falls of over two metres were foreseeable in these situations. Hence, regulation 38B of the CS(S)Rs applied. This case highlights how strict the courts are with regard to the 2-metre rule and that an accident need not occur to trigger a prosecution.

HKSAR v Chun Fai Construction Company Limited (HCMA 161/2005)

The appellant company was convicted under regulation 38B(1) for failing to take reasonable steps to prevent a person from falling from a height of two metres or more. In this case, a proper working platform was alleged to be provided for concrete pouring. However, it was held by the Court that despite the presence of a working platform, the worker who had to stand and carry out the work on the platform could not control the concrete pouring that had to be carried out. He had to step up and walk over the platform, which resulted in injury.

Safety practitioners should note that even when properly constructed working platforms are provided, they must be suitable to the ergonomics of the workers carrying out the work in order to be considered a safe working platform.

HKSAR v Chuen Kee Construction Company Limited (HCMA 986/2005)

The case involved workers who were found by an occupational safety officer to be working at a height more than two metres at unfenced building floor edges and near concrete columns which were still under construction. These workers were not wearing any type of safety belts, and there were no independent lifelines or safety nets installed. The company's defence was that the workers involved were acting on their own initiative and added that sub-contractors and workers on construction sites will, from time to time, disobey direct instructions and cut corners if it will mean that the work will be completed more quickly. The Court ruled against this and referred to *Carr v Mercantile Produce Company Limited* (2 All ER531; 1949, 2 KB601), in which Justice Stable stated: "[T]he Factories Act is there not merely to protect the careful, the vigilant and the conscientious workmen, but human nature being what it is, also the careless, the indolent, the inadvertent, the weary, and even, perhaps, in some cases, the disobedient."

HKSAR v Adrian Engineering Limited and Another (HCMA 561/2007)/ [2007] HKCLRT 597

This prosecution was brought following an inspection by an occupational safety officer from the Labour Department. He found that three workmen were working on a slope on the site without proper fall prevention measures in place as specified in regulation 38 of the CS(S)Rs. The appellant argued that these workmen were merely labourers and were not required to work on the slope, so it was not their responsibility to provide fall protection measures.

The Court held that the term "any person" as stated in regulations 38B(1) and 38B(1A) of the CS(S)Rs was broadly defined as meaning any person working on the worksite. Further, the statue does not stipulate that different types of workers would be afforded different levels of protection, meaning that any person on the site should be protected against any foreseeable risk of falling. In fact, the Magistrate in this case noted that the scope of "any person" even covers criminals who have entered a site to commit a crime. Thus, site management must be aware that even though criminals may not be the best example for illustrating the scope of the term "any person", the Court's ruling in this case indicates that identifying the injured as "unknown persons" is not a valid defence.

HKSAR v Chun Wo Construction & Engineering Co. Ltd and Another (HCMA 1190/2006)/[2007] HKCLRT 711

The appellant was charged under regulation 38B(1A) of the CS(S)Rs. The case involved an inspection by an occupational safety officer of the Labour Department on the site. He saw a worker squatting on the working platform of the formwork near a duct at L8/1 on level 3. He observed the worker for about 3 minutes while he was hammering a plank on the platform. The platform was about 3.30 metres from the ground of level 3. The platform was 0.7 metres long on one side and about 0.5 metres long on the other. No guard-rail was installed on either side of the platform to prevent people from falling, nor was there any fall arrestor, safety strips, or safety net. The appellant based their defence on the fact that the worker was not directly employed by the company. However, the Court ruled against this based on the view that the term used in the regulation is "any person", not "any worker" or "any worker employed by the contractor".

HKSAR v Kaden Construction Limited (HCMA 757/2010)

During an inspection by an occupational safety officer of the Labour Department, a workman was observed at the swimming pool area on the second and third floors of the worksite standing on three partially overlapping horizontal battens which were themselves placed on two perpendicular wooden battens, forming an H-shaped platform. The worker was not wearing a harness or safety belt. There was no fence or guard-rail. The officer was of the opinion that the worker could easily have fallen from the primitive structure.

The appellant was the "carcass contractor" of a construction site, and it had further contracted the formwork to a sub-contractor. Both contractors were charged under regulation 38B(1A). The sub-contractor pled guilty, but the appellant company did not. They instead indicated that they should not be charged under regulation 38B(1A) and should be rightly charged under regulation 38B(1), so the case against them should be dismissed. The Court held that in accordance with the contract document signed between the appellant company and the sub-contractor company, both of them have direct control of the works undertaken. Therefore, both companies should rightly be charged under regulation 38B(1A). The Court further held that "the intention of the legislation here clearly is to increase the safety on building sites and the amendment in year 2003 was to catch all parties with respect to being in direct control over the work on the construction site". Claiming that they are a "carcass contractor" who had contracted out the control of safety and health matters was not a valid defence.

This case highlights an essential consideration for companies when drafting contracts. Such contracts should have safety duties and responsibilities well written and defined regarding the parties concerned. However, the company contracting out the work will still be responsible to ensure that the proper safety measures are being used.

HKSAR v Cheung Kee Fung Cheung Construction Company Limited and Another (HCMA 813/2012)

Here, the appellant was charged under regulation 38B of the CS(S)Rs after an occupational safety officer from the Labour Department observed suspicious behaviour on a construction site. When he arrived at the 15th floor of the building, he heard the sounds of welding, saw welding flames, and smelled welding fumes. He also saw two workers on the floor. These workers immediately stopped their welding work in the lift shaft when they saw the occupational safety officer. The workers were wearing safety harnesses but were not anchored to any independent lifelines. The risk of falling down the lift shaft was evident.

In this case, the Court asked: if workers were provided with adequate and sufficient personal protective equipment to prevent falling from heights of more than two metres during welding work, then why did they need to stop work while the occupational safety officer was present? The Court went on to ask: if the welders were provided and actually wearing safety harnesses and provided with independent lifelines and fall arrestors, then why did they need to put on all these protection devises when the occupational safety officer came to inspect the premises? The Court finally asked: why did the workers involved not continue to weld safely? The appeal against conviction was dismissed.

This case indicates that it may be considered a "red flag" when workers stop doing dangerous or unsafe work or quickly put on the required safety gear only to avoid detection by an occupational safety officer. Doing so does not make the company immune from being prosecuted for unsafe practices.

HKSAR v Optimum Engineering Limited (卓領工程有限公司) (HCMA 423/2012)

During an inspection, an occupational safety officer found that workers employed by the appellant company were carrying out waterproofing work at a height without any safety protection. The appellant was charged under regulations 38B(1) and 48(1)(b) of the CS(S)Rs. The appellant company appealed against the ruling, arguing that it was not the main contractor and that the estate management company should be responsible. The Court held that employers are responsible for their employees. The estate management company's staff carried out a risk assessment, conducted safety inspections, and reported progress status, thus fulfilling the safety aspects of its management role on behalf of the estate, but they were not performing the role of a main contractor. This case simply confirmed that any contractor undertaking construction work shall be held responsible for their workers. They should carry out their own safety inspections, provide suitable personal protective equipment, and ensure workers are wearing such equipment properly while at work.

HKSAR v Goldenwall Engineering Limited (HCMA 731/2013)

Here, an accident occurred involving a female labourer who fell more than two metres through a floor opening. The contractor was charged under regulation 38 of the CS(S)Rs. At the time of the accident, the labourer believed that the wooden board covering the floor opening should be removed and disposed of as trade waste. In doing so, she fell through the opening. The appellant company argued that the labourer was assigned to remove and dispose of trade rubbish only and was not actually doing any construction work on the site.

The Court held that a contractor is still considered to have direct control of the construction work undertaken at a site which had a lot of holes previously made by another contractor. Thus, the new contractor on the site must make such hazards safe before any work is allowed to commence. Safety inspections for unfenced holes on the site were also suggested by the Court. This case shows that although the hazards on the construction site were there from the previous contractor, and not the doing of the current contractor, it is still the latter's responsibility to ensure worksite safety and adherence to the CS(S)Rs.

HKSAR v Leighton Contractors (Asia) Ltd (KTS 17711/2017)

This case concerning ergonomics has been detailed in Chapter 4 with regard to the use of testimony from safety experts, but it also has implications regarding liability under the CS(S)Rs. It was tried in a Magistrates' Court, and the Magistrate held that it would be negligibly possible or almost impossible for workmen to completely fall through a floor opening 0.41 metres × 0.42 metres in size while they were working nearby. The floor opening that existed was temporarily used for lifting pipes with the use of a chain block anchored in the wall. The case was ultimately dismissed.

Does regulation 38B apply? Understanding the "two-metre rule"

In its enforcement, any fall from a distance of two metres or more is prosecutable under regulation 38B. The example cases above show that this is a rigid line, and companies have been prosecuted regardless of whether the fall resulted from an accident, with or without bodily injury, or is objectively foreseeable.

To prevent falls from a distance of two metres, companies must provide: (a) anchorage points, such as independent lifelines and anchor bolts or eye bolts; (b) safety belts or full-body harnesses; and (c) connections, such as lanyards and fall arrestors. These are considered the "abc" standard for safety. Failing to provide or to ensure any of these items is prosecutable, although this may or may not occur under regulation 38B of the CS(S)Rs. It could, however, fall under other parts of regulation 38 and would certainly qualify as prosecutable under the safe systems of work. The two cases below highlight how the courts have viewed the application of the "2-metre rule" in relation to other parts of regulation 38.

HKSAR v Skyfield Construction Limited (天域建築有限公司) (HCMA 747/2013)

This case resulted from an accident investigation into a fall from a working platform approximately 1.8 metres high. There were no guard-rails or toe-board installed on the working platform, which was provided for carrying out maintenance working on the ceiling, 3.93 metres from the floor. The injured person admitted that he fell from the working platform because he took the wrong step. While the 2-metre rule did not apply, the appellant company was charged under regulation 38C, which states that

> [w]here work cannot be safely done on or from the ground or from part of a permanent structure, the contractor responsible for the construction site concerned and any contractor who has direct control over the work shall provide, and ensure the use of, a scaffold, ladder, or other means of support, all of which shall be safe for the purpose, having regard to the work to be done.

The Court held that since no evidence was produced to show that the working platform was unsafe and since the working platform, which was less than two metres high, did not require guard-rails or toe-boards, the appeal was allowed. In its ruling, the Court indicated that it is also possible to fall from a ladder, but this does not render the use of a ladder for simple tasks (such as replacing a light bulb) unsafe.

HKSAR v Tsang Lik Services Limited (HCMA 199/2015)

In this case, the Court held that the falling hazard from two metres is unlikely when working at a distance of 1.5 metres from the floor edge, with or without anchoring one's lanyard to an eyebolt. However, prior to this case, there was no regulatory rule indicating how far from the floor edge a worker must be to be considered safe. This case is the current judicial reference, whereby a distance of 1.5 metres or more from an unfenced floor edge is an acceptable safe distance.

The meaning of "monitoring" and "supervision"

While the cases above provide precedence regarding instances when the two-metre rule does not apply, the courts have been less clear on how the use of personal protective equipment should be supervised. Some court rulings are for such supervision and some rulings are against. This is understandable as there are many trades of workers with different skills in the construction industry, all requiring different protective equipment. Problems also arise when determining how much supervision is necessary: would a professional scaffolder with many years of working experience and no previous breaches in safety need the same level of supervision as a novice? Is "nanny-type" supervision necessary at all if workers are provided with adequate personal protective equipment against falling and given initial training to use it? What happens if a worker stops wearing the personal protective equipment he has been provided? In theory, an occupational safety officer will prosecute a worker who is not following the proprietor's system of work without bringing a parallel prosecution against the proprietor for failure to do all that is reasonably practicable to ensure that the system is actually implemented and maintained. In practice, there is more grey area. The selected cases below highlight situations where the courts were required to make rulings concerning the meaning of "monitoring" and "supervision" as well as what are considered "adequate steps" to ensure safety.

HKSAR v Dragages Hong Kong Limited (HCMA 510/2013)

This case arose from an accident investigation into a fall involving a worker undertaking flooring installation work. The worker fell from an edge 9.1 metres high from the ground level. At the time of the accident, he had forgotten to tie up his lanyard. The loose lanyard became tangled with the chain slings attached to the lifting object, a prefabricated flooring board. As the chain sling was lifted by the tower crane, the worker was pulled off the edge and fell onto the ground. The appellant company was charged under regulation 38B(1).

The system to protect a person from falling in such a case was the use of the Sala block, a device that can push and pull a worker using a collapsible wire attached to a fixed anchorage. In this case, the lanyard should be attached securely to the Sala block at all times, until or unless the worker was well away from any danger, in which case the lanyard could be disconnected from the Sala block. However, the injured worker did not use a Sala block, which was available on-site, so no fall protection was applied. At the time of the accident, he forgot to tie the one-metre lanyard to his body when the lanyard should have been secured to his full-body harness when not in use and not be left in a tangled state. The injured worker was trained how to use a lanyard. He was also trained on how to use the Sala block with the lanyard during the flooring installation process. Thus, the appellant had provided all reasonable steps to ensure the proper use of the safety belts by the worker. The Court held that, though strict supervision or monitoring might not be required in this case, it is still necessary for companies to check that workers engage the Sala block and attach their lanyards before commencing work.

HKSAR v Projexasia Limited (博建(香港)有限公司) (HCMA 345/2014)/ [2015] 5 HKLRD 501

This case arose following a safety inspection by an occupational safety officer. During his inspection of a construction site, he found four scaffolders working on an external wall between the third and fourth floors, at a height of 8.4 metres above the ground. The four workers, employed by a sub-contractor, were seen wearing a parachute-type safety harness with a karabiner on the lanyard attached to a fall arrestor, which should be attached to an independent lifeline to ensure the worker would not fall. However, none of the scaffolders had attached his safety harness to the independent lifeline along the external wall. The occupational safety officer observed the situation for about 10 minutes. He saw the workers were moving from side to side on the bamboo scaffolds at the same height. No planks were laid on the scaffolds. No safety net or working platform was seen near the scaffolds to prevent the workers from falling. The appellant was thus prosecuted under regulation 38B(1) of the CS(S)Rs.

In this case, a risk assessment had been carried out, and falls were identified as a potential risk. The workers were provided with safety belts. The workers attended "toolbox talks" in the morning before commencing work. The workers obtained "safety cards" after attending two safety training sessions. A full-time safety supervisor was employed by the appellant to monitor site safety on a daily basis. At 10:00 a.m. on the day of the incident, a responsible person from the sub-contractor had carried out another round of inspection and had noticed a worker was in violation of the rules by failing to attach his safety belt properly in the course of moving between bamboo poles. At 11:10 a.m., the occupational safety officer from the Labour Department observed the four workers described above. The Court held that the measures taken by the appellant could have given rise to an honest, reasonable belief on the part of the appellant that the regulation had been complied with. The Court also agreed that the appellant could not be the "nanny" of the workers on the site. Thus, the appeal against the conviction was allowed.

HKSAR v Cheung Kee Fung Cheung Construction Company Ltd and Another (HCMA 328/2016)

These two appellant companies (one main contractor and one sub-contractor) were respectively charged under regulations 38B(1) and 38B(1A) of the CS(S)Rs. These cases were brought as a result of an occupational safety officer observing a worker doing welding work without attaching his lanyard to the independent lifeline. The worker was standing and working on metal planking placed amongst some bamboo scaffolding with space existing between them. The companies had installed 60 eyebolts and independent lifelines, and the worker was provided with a safety belt. If the worker had attached his lanyard to the independent lifeline, then he would have been protected from the risk of falling. The main issue in these cases was whether "adequate steps" had been taken by the two companies for workers while doing welding work at height on bamboo scaffolding. The height from which the worker could have fallen was about 4.5 metres from the ground. The Court held that the phrase "one or more of the following" safety provisions in regulation 38B does not mean just "one of the following". The appeal was dismissed as the working platform (in this case, metal planking placed amongst bamboo scaffolding) was considered unsafe.

HKSAR v Aggressive Construction Co. Ltd and Another (HCMA 204/2016)

These two appellant companies (one main contractor and one sub-contractor) were charged under regulation 38B(1A) of the CS(S)Rs for failing to provide "adequate steps" to prevent five workmen from doing levelling marking work at a height of more than two metres from falling. These workmen were not protected by any guard-rails, toe-boards, safety nets, or any other fall protection device. The appeal argued that these workmen were doing preparatory marking work for the erection of guard-rails and barriers and that the work would be of short duration (only 10 to 15 minutes). Moreover, temporary removal of guard-rails or barriers is acceptable under the Third Schedule of the CS(S)Rs, even if guard-rails or barriers are installed. However, the removal of one safety provision is best countered by the use of another, such as safety belts. In this situation, there were no anchorage points for safety belts (had they been provided and worn by the workmen). The Court held that since the appellants were well aware that there would be no suitable places to install such anchorage points, the workmen were in danger of falling while working near the edge of the formwork. Preventive steps should have been taken in advance. The appeal was dismissed.

STRICT LIABILITY UNDER THE "SAFETY LEGISLATION"

Legislation dealing with occupational safety and health in general, and regulation 38 of the CS(S)Rs in particular, deviates from common law rules (discussed in relation to construction safety in Chapter 5) by imposing strict liability, sometimes called absolute liability. In theory, an offence has strict liability if it is one in which the defence has no case or rebuttal once the prosecution has made out a *prima facie* case or, more specifically, has definitively proved that the accused is responsible for the criminal act or breach. This begs the question: is an offence under the CS(S)Rs one of strict liability?

To answer this question, reference must be made to three exemplary cases, one from the United Kingdom (UK) and two from Hong Kong. Interestingly, none of these three cases deal directly with construction safety or even with events on a construction site. However, these cases share the views of statutory offences in general, and courts frequently use them for reference in cases concerning construction safety.

Tesco Limited v Natrass [1972] AC 153

The English Court held that:

> If Parliament has put an absolute duty on some individual, he cannot evade that duty by delegating it to somebody else. So far the principle is unexceptionable. Any legal duty whether arising at common law or imposed by statute, may generally be performed by the person upon whom it is imposed through the agency of some other person. But if it is not performed, the person upon whom the duty is imposed is liable for its non-performance. It is irrelevant that he instructed a servant or agent to perform it on his behalf, if that servant or agent failed to do so. All that is relevant is that the duty was not performed. When the duty is imposed upon a person by statute and non-performance is made a criminal offence without any requirement of *mens rea* and that is what is meant by an offence of "strict liability".

This case demonstrates that the courts in the UK do not favour such a "halfway house approach" or the common law defence.

Gammon (Hong Kong) Limited v AG [1985] 1 AC 1

This is a Hong Kong case that advanced to the UK Privy Council. It concerns a statutory offence under the Buildings Ordinance, Chapter 123, after the company deviated from approved plans and carried out works in a manner involving increased risk and a higher likelihood of injury or damage. Before 1997, this case was the leading authority on the issue of strict liability. In the ruling, Lord Scarman of the UK Privy Council stated:

(1) there is a presumption of law that *mens rea* is required before a person can be held guilty of a criminal offence;
(2) the presumption is particularly strong where the offence is "truly criminal" in character;

(3) the presumption applies to statutory offences, and can be displaced only if there is a clear or necessary implication on the effect of the statute;
(4) the only situation in which the presumption can be displaced is where the statute is concerned with an issue of social concern, and public safety is such an issue;
(5) even where a statute is concerned with such an issue, the presumption of *mens rea* stands unless it can also be shown the creation of strict liability will be effective to promote the objects of the statute by encouraging greater vigilance to prevent the commission of the prohibited act.

AG v Fong Chin-yue and Others [1995] HKC21

This Hong Kong-based case is the genesis of the "common law due diligence defence". It concerns a statutory offence under the Dutiable Commodities Ordinance, Chapter 109. It was a case involving the dealing with, possession of, and buying dutiable cigarettes on which duty had not been paid. The Court identified four theoretical alternative regimes in relation to the mental requirements of those provisions which can be summarised as follows: (1) that the prosecution must prove *mens rea* beyond reasonable doubt, that is, prove knowledge, intention, or recklessness, the presumption not having been displaced; (2) that the prosecution need not set out to prove *mens rea*, but if there is evidence capable of raising a reasonable doubt that the accused may have performed the prohibited act in the honest and reasonable belief that the circumstances were such that, if true, liability would not attach, that the accused must be acquitted unless the prosecution proves beyond reasonable doubt the absence of such exculpatory belief or that there were no reasonable grounds for such belief; (3) that the presumption has been displaced so that the prosecution need not prove *mens rea* but that the accused has a good defence if he can prove on the balance of probabilities that the prohibited act was done in the honest and reasonable belief that the circumstances were such that, if true, he would not be guilty of the offence; and (4) that the presumption is displaced and the offence is one of strict liability so that the prosecution succeeds if the accused is proved to have performed the *actus reus*, regardless of his state of mind.

The Court held that:

1. It would be a defence to the four offences in question if the accused could prove on a balance of probabilities that he believed for good and sufficient reason, though erroneously that the provisions of the Ordinance had been complied with. This included a reasonable belief that the duty had been paid.
2. A Magistrate should approach such a defence with fairness and common sense. Relevant consideration should be the quantity and the values of the goods involved; whether the accused gained or stood to gain by offending; the extent of such gain and how it compared with what he could earn by honest means.

This case ultimately opened the door for allowing a common law defence in such cases, instead of treating them as offences of strict liability. It implies that an intermediate basis of liability exists.

There are also several cases related to strict liability that deal directly with construction work.

AG v Liu Ching-sun trading as Sun Lee Air Condition Company (HCMA 438/1986)

In this case, the respondent was charged under regulation 38C of the CS(S)Rs for failing to ensure that a scaffold was only altered under the immediate supervisor of a competent person and by competent workmen possessing adequate experience of such work. The Court held that regulation 38C of the CS(S)Rs made the contractor responsible for the construction site and also made the contractor responsible for the scaffolding being performed on that site. The defence argued that "plant" as defined in regulation 2 of the CS(S)Rs does not encompass scaffolding. Thus, the respondent was not liable under regulation 2(2)(b) of the CS(S)Rs. However, he was found liable under regulation 2(2)(a) of the CS(S)Rs, which was a strict liability offence. The respondent was, therefore, strictly liable for *inter alia* the erection, installation, maintenance, alteration, removal, or dismantling of the scaffolding concerned.

HKSAR v Hip Hing Construction Co. Ltd (HCMA 376/2002)

This case arose from the fall of a formwork worker. Around the time he was to go off duty, he fell down the side of a parapet from A5-A6 of the building into the basement 2.71 metres below. There was nothing to prevent his fall. The worker indicated that he had fainted and did not know the full circumstances of his fall. The appellant company was charged under regulation 38B(1) of the CS(S)Rs based on their failure to take adequate steps to prevent a person on the site from falling from a height of two or more metres. The Court held that this was a strict liability offence, and the appellant company was convicted.

HKSAR v Hyundai Engineering Construction Co. Ltd (HCMA 815/2002)

The details of this case are described in an earlier section of this chapter. It involves prosecution under regulation 38B(1) of the CS(S)Rs for failing to take "adequate steps" to prevent a person on the site from falling from a height of two metres or more. The case also has implications regarding strict liability. Judge Line held that "as a matter of law, the common law defence of honest and reasonable belief is necessarily excluded". He also said that "safety regulations of the type in question in this case have a long history both here and in England and Wales. They have long been dealt with on the basis of strict liability." This decision thus rejected the common law defence. The Judge went on to say:

> In my judgment, the same considerations and reasons that justify offences of strict liability for safety regulations make it right to construe them as excluding the claimed common law defence. This is not heavy handed. The statutory defences, which the legislature has provided to meet the rigour of the regulation, are available in deserving cases and honest effort is good

> mitigation, especially in respect of regulatory offences. ... I can thus see no need to upset the established law that has seen Magistrates try such safety cases on the basis of strict liability without the claimed common law defence for decades. I can see good reason to exclude the defence as its availability opens up a host of issues and complexities that should have no place in summary trials of regulatory offences.

This case has been referred to in numerous subsequent decisions, including that in *HKSAR v Shun Tak Properties Limited* [2009] 3 HKLRD 299 (described in Chapters 4 and 5).

DEFENCES AVAILABLE UNDER HONG KONG LAW

Considering the above cases and discussion of strict liability, what defence is actually available to those who are prosecuted for breaches in the CS(S)Rs? Before 1997, the presumption of *mens rea* as laid down by the Privy Council's decision in the *Gammon* case was applied to statutory offences in Hong Kong. It was decided that statutory offences are construed either (a) as requiring the prosecution to prove *mens rea* (the presumption of *mens rea* not having been displaced); or (b) where that presumption is supplanted, as an offence of strict liability, with nothing in between. Where the offence is absolute, proof by the prosecution of the external *actus reus* elements of the offence will sufficiently establish liability, regardless of the defendant's state of mind.

However, after 1997, in order to alleviate the harshness on the accused charged with a strict liability offence (and the possibility of being wrongly convicted), the courts have been more inclined to allow an intermediate defence (or a halfway house defence), in which the accused can rely on the common law defence that they had an honest and reasonable belief in a state of facts which, if shown to exist, would make them innocent. In general, section 18 of the Factories and Industrial Undertakings Ordinance (FIUO), Cap. 59, provides such a defence in relation to "a duty or requirement to do something so far as is necessary, where practicable, so far as is reasonably practicable, or so far as practicable or to take all reasonable steps, all practicable steps, adequate steps or all reasonably practicable steps to do something". As explained in Chapters 3 and 5, this defence applies to all cases, including those involving breaches of the CS(S)Rs. For offences of strict liability, it is also not unusual to find special statutory defences expressly provided in the same statute creating the offence. For example, regulation 38H of the CS(S)Rs provides defences to regulations 38B(1), 38B(1A), and 38C. Regulation 38H applies only to breaches of the CS(S)Rs. Hence, leaving aside special statutory defences, the choice of defence depends on the *mens rea* and application of strict liability to the case. Further, for regulatory offences that have their own statutory defences (like regulation 38H), whether the existence of such a defence would automatically exclude the concurrent availability of a common law defence has been a controversial question raised in several appeal cases.

The following cases summarize the approaches and decisions of the courts in Hong Kong at different stages regarding the above general principles in determining whether a statutory provision creates an offence of strict liability or an offence which allows the common law defence of honest and reasonable belief.

R v Nishimatsu Construction Company Limited (HCMA 1441/1996)

This case involves an accident which occurred when a retaining wall formwork collapsed during the pouring of concrete for that retaining wall. The appellant was charged under the former regulation 38A(b) of the CS(S)Rs. At the time of the accident, a worker employed by the appellant was working inside the formwork and died as a result of the accident. The formwork was found to have collapsed because round bars were used instead of threaded bars for stability. Threaded bars were the original design, and the Court was told that the threaded bar system was safer than the round bar system. However, an expert in the trial stated that round bars could be safely used and were considered reasonably practicable and safe. The Magistrate held that the appellant failed "to ensure that a place on the site which a person at any time worked so far as reasonably practicable, was made and kept safe for the person working there".

In the appeal, the Court observed that the Magistrate had based his decision on whether there was a safer system than that in use at the time of the accident rather than whether the system in use at the time of the accident was "reasonably practicable" and "made and kept safe for the person working there". Since the wrong test had been applied, the appeal against conviction was allowed. This case demonstrates that practising a safe system of work is sufficient for a defence, even though a safer system is demanded by the enforcement body.

HKSAR v China Road and Bridge Corporation and Two Others (HCMA 192/2010)

This case concerned a breach of regulation 38A(2) under the CS(S)Rs regarding safe access to and egress from upper-floor balconies to a workplace. Here, the common defence of honest and reasonable belief advanced was not accepted. The appellant honestly believed that the workman, who was injured as a result of the breach, was verbally informed that he should seek permission from authorised personnel to gain access and egress to the workplace through another location on the site (in this case, a nurse changing room). The workman did not follow these instructions and attempted to gain access and egress through the outside balconies and sustained his injuries.

HKSAR v Paul Y. General Contractor Ltd (HCMA 828/2012)

Like the case above, this case also concerned regulation 38A(2) and the safe access and egress via a fixed metal ladder connecting the basement floor and the pump room floor through a three-metre-high opening of one metre by one metre square. Here, the defence of honest and reasonable belief was advanced. The appellant believed that the workman could access and egress by the fixed ladder which was built for the purpose. There had been no mishaps reported by other users.

In the appeal, this defence was found to have been inappropriately allowed and that the Magistrate had used the wrong test as she accepted the suggestions by the prosecution to make the access/egress ladder "safer" but that did not necessarily mean that the original access/egress ladder was "unsafe". There were insufficient findings to support the Magistrate's conclusion that the access/egress was not a suitable and adequate one.

Like the China Road and Bridge case above, this appeal case indicated the application of section 18 as a defence is wider and requires more than the common law defence of "honest and reasonable belief". It requires proof of actual precautionary steps taken or appropriate things done.

The leading authority about the use of a common law defence by contractors is now the Court of Final Appeal case in *Hin Lin Yee and Another v HKSAR* (2010) 13 HKCFAR 142.

Hin Lin Yee and Another v HKSAR (FACC No. 7 of 2009)/(2010) 13 HKCFAR 142

The original case (FACC No. 7 of 2009) is described in Chapter 5 with regard to competent workers. It also has implications about strict liability and the application of the common law defence, whereby the Judge of the appeal held that the basis for the Magistrate's finding could not stand as the Magistrate wrongly concluded that the contamination was intentional by the appellants. He nevertheless held that the convictions should be sustained. He decided that section 54(1) of the Public Health and Municipal Services Ordinance, Chapter 132, created an offence of strict liability and that the common law defence had no application to safety legislation. The Judge also confirmed the conviction under regulation 36(1) of the Pharmacy and Poisons Regulations, Chapter 138A.

The Court of Final Appeal provided the following legal principles which were applied to this case. They can also be extrapolated for use in determining whether a statutory provision creates an offence of strict liability or an offence that will admit the common law defence of honest and reasonable belief. The following points were stated in the case:

1. The proper starting point for ascertaining the mental requirements of any statutory offence or any external element of such an offence was to presume that the prosecution must prove

mens rea in respect thereof. That presumption may be displaced expressly or by necessary implication. If it was not displaced, the *mens rea* requirement persisted.

2. If the presumption was displaced, three possible alternatives arose under Hong Kong law, namely whether the legislative intent was (i) to allow a defence if the defendant could prove on the balance of probabilities that the prohibited act was done in the honest and reasonable belief that the circumstances were such that, if true, he would not be guilty of the offence; or (ii) to confine the defences open to the accused in relation to his mental state to the statutory defences expressly provided for in relation to the offence charged; or (iii) to make the offence one of absolute liability so that the prosecution succeeded if the accused was proved to have performed or brought about the *actus reus*, regardless of his state of mind.
3. On its true construction, a statute may expressly or by necessary implication provide for special defences which represented its own halfway house, to the exclusion of any other possible middle course. The key question was whether the statutory defence, properly construed, was inconsistent with the availability of the common law defence. If so, only the statutory defence could be relied on.
4. The suggestion that the common law defence be excluded broadly in cases of safety legislation could not be supported. A desire to avoid complexity in summary trials was not an acceptable basis for treating all regulatory offences as offences of absolute liability. It did not justify convicting defendants who had demonstrably acted reasonably, diligently, and without actual fault. Further, in the context of industrial safety, there may be sound reasons for concluding that some offences were absolute, but the compelling rationale of a halfway house was that the statutory objectives may well be attainable by adopting an intermediate basis of liability in many, if not most, cases.
5. In the present case, the presumption of *mens rea* was displaced in relation to section 54(1)(a)'s requirement that the medicine sold be unfit for human use. The legislative intent was to confine the defences available to those contained in subsections 70

and 71 of the Public Health and Municipal Services Ordinance, Cap. 132 such defences being inconsistent with the concurrent availability of the defence of honest and reasonable belief (paras 170–184, 198(d)).

6. The appellants had not brought themselves factually within either subsection 70 or 71 and the 1st appellant had no reasonable prospects of being able to do so if given an opportunity to attempt this on a trial. Likewise, for the offence under regulation 36(1), the 1st appellant could not establish a defence under regulation 36(1C) as he was unable to show that he could not have discovered with reasonable diligence that the substance in his possession had not duly been registered (paras 185–197, 198(e), 198(f)).

PRACTICAL DEFENCES FOR REGULATIONS 38B(1) AND 38B(1A) OF THE CS(S)Rs

While section 18 of the FIUO and regulation 38H of the CS(S)Rs provide defences for individuals that are being prosecuted for CS(S)Rs breaches, the following are practical guides for the defendant to help establish conditional evidence.

1. Provide workers with suitable fall prevention and protection equipment while working at height. The personal protective equipment may include full-body harnesses (parachute-type), lanyards, safety helmets, etc. Specify the standards for the personal protective equipment provided. Such standards should preferably be higher than the legal requirement. Keep records of issuance.
2. Provide adequate anchorage points, independent lifelines or Sala blocks, or other suitable designated anchor points. Such points should be tested for structural adequacy. Anchor points should be able to withstand a minimum pull-out force of 5 kilonewtons (kN).
3. Conduct practical training for workers on how to use fall prevention and protection devices. Take photos of such practical

training as evidence. Keep records for the workers who receive this training. Refresher courses or periodic training should also be arranged. In addition, workers should be trained in the use of two lanyards for alternative movements when they are positioning themselves at great heights.

4. Carry out periodic safety observations to see whether the workers are wearing (or not wearing) such personal protective equipment and fall protection devices. Record these safety observations and immediately remedy non-conformance. Advisory or warning letters should be sent to the workers' direct employers if the worker concerned is employed by a sub-contractor. Discuss such observations in site safety committee meetings.
5. Take a picture and keep the photo as evidence of monitoring and supervision before the commencement of any work at height. It is a good practice to see that all workers are wearing their personal protective equipment properly.
6. Conduct periodic inspections of such openings to ensure that they are securely fenced in accordance with the Third schedule of the CS(S)Rs. If there are temporary floor openings in the building or structure under construction, it is important that such openings be identified and marked to connote danger.

If the above measures are properly taken by both the main contractor and other sub-contractors who have direct control, then a case can be made on firm evidence in their defence. These measures will also go a long way to help them conform to the regulations and enhance safety on the construction site in general.

SUMMARY

The CS(S)Rs involve safety at work, and breaches can result in injury and death. One of the most prosecutable CS(S)Rs is regulation 38, which requires any contractor who has "direct control" to be held responsible for the construction site and indicates that they need to take "adequate steps" to prevent any undue risk to workers. These steps should comply with the Third Schedule of the CS(S)Rs which lists the specific requirements for certain safety equipment. Nevertheless, practical compliance with the Third Schedule is a challenge in construction work, where some situations simply cannot allow compliance. Thus, what is considered an "adequate step" remains one of the most arguable aspects of the CS(S)Rs, and it has been necessary to settle non-compliance in the courtroom.

The courts have also been called upon to help delineate what is considered a "construction site" and "construction work" as well as how the specific regulations apply. For example, court rulings regarding the 2-metre rule in regulation 38 have been incredibly strict. But what happened if the fall is less than two metres? Is it still considered to be working at height? Practically, it should be, and there have been guidelines promulgated by interested bodies that do not have the legal power to mandate their compliance. Perhaps one legal solution would be the introduction of a set of special regulations for the safe use of working platforms or publication of an enforceable code of practice for the prevention of falls less than two metres. A similar situation is present for the size of temporary floor openings which require added protection. These distinctions are highlighted in the cases outlined in this chapter. Similarly, various legal decisions have been used to clarify the meaning of "monitoring" and "supervision".

Legal precedence is heavily relied upon to help the courts assess the facts of a prosecution based on a breach of one of the CS(S)Rs as well as other regulations in the FIUO. Regarding strict liability under the CS(S)Rs, the appellant's defence can be derived from section 18 of the FIUO or regulation 38H of the CS(S)Rs. The application of section 18 depends on the specific wordings of the regulation and the particulars of the case. However, one ruling is very clear. It is the meaning of the word "ensure". Once this word is encountered in the safety regulation, the court will treat the case as strict liability. The leading authority for the application of a common law defence based on section 18 is the *Hin Lin Yee* case.

Construction activities are necessarily complex and involve a range of parties doing physical tasks with different backgrounds, skills, and experiences. These individuals are pooled together in a single work environment. Even for one single trade, there could be several contractors on a worksite. Compliance with safe work practices, both from a legal standpoint and a practical standpoint, is essential. Thus, contractors, workers, and occupational safety officers need to be familiar with the CS(S)Rs as well as with the legal precedence established by cases tried in court. Beyond breaches of the general duties of the FIUO and the CS(S)Rs, there are also construction-specific FIU Regulations that will apply to different trades and across worksites.

FURTHER READING

Construction Industry Council (November 2016) *Guidelines on Work-Above-Ground Safety, Version 1, Hong Kong.*

HKSAR v Hin Lin Yee and Another (FACC No. 7 of 2009).

HKSAR v Gammon Construction Limited (FACC No. 10 of 2014).

Hong Kong Housing Authority (2018) *Site Safety Handbook, Volume 2, Chapter 7*, Hong Kong Government Printer.

Labour Department, Hong Kong SAR Government (March 2018) *Overview of Work-at-Height Safety*, Hong Kong Government Printer.

Selwyn, N.M. (1982) *Law of Health and Safety at Work*, Butterworths.

DISCUSSION QUESTIONS

1. What innovative technology do you think should be introduced to prevent falls on construction worksites?
2. What advice would you give a contractor to help them comply with regulation 38B of the CS(S)Rs?
3. What is meant by "strict liability" or "absolute liability" in breaches of construction safety regulations?
4. Comment on the "Guidelines on work-above-ground safety" (Version dated 1 November 2016) published by the Construction Industry Council.

"Those who cannot remember the past are condemned to repeat it"

– George Santayana (1905)

"'I believe it is rather because of the advancement of modern technology which outdated the Regulations and made part of its provision incompatible or inapplicable.'... If that is the position it is not for the Magistrate to try and force the square peg of the fact situation into the round hole of the legislation just because a summons has been drawn up"

– C.-M. Beeson
Judge of the Court of First Instance
(In response to the quote from the Magistrate)
HKSAR v China Merchants Container Services Ltd
(HCMA 597/2001)

7 Breaches of Construction-specific Factories and Industrial Undertakings Regulations

INTRODUCTION

Within the Factories and Industrial Undertakings Ordinance, Cap. 59 (FIUO), there are 30 sets of subsidiary regulations (FIURs). Of these, 22 are fully applicable to construction work (described in Chapter 3). One of these is the Construction Site (Safety) Regulations (covered in Chapter 6) and another is the main FIURs (covered in Chapter 5). The other 20 sets of subsidiary regulations are detailed below. Many of these applicable regulations have been amended since their enactment in response to legal proceedings and experience gained in light of their enforcement. Some sections in the regulations have themselves become new sets of subsidiary regulations that carry specific repercussions for non-compliance. This chapter outlines some of the important legal cases involving breaches in some of the FIURs.

A NOTE ABOUT OTHER SAFETY LEGISLATION RELATED TO THE CONSTRUCTION INDUSTRY

Before detailing the cases involving specific FIURs, it is important to mention some of the other safety legislation that has been enacted in relation to these regulations. The list below highlights some of the additional ordinances and regulations that have been established, either to avoid future accidents or in response to a particular legal case. All of those listed can in one way or another be applied to construction work, worksites, or workers. Thus, in addition to understanding the FIURs, it would be wise for registered safety officers and safety practitioners to be familiar with these documents, some of which are referred to in the cases detailed later in this chapter.

- Boilers and Pressure Vessels Ordinance, Cap. 56
- Buildings Ordinance and Regulations, Cap. 123
- Employees' Compensation Ordinance, Cap. 282
- Mining Ordinance, Cap, 285
- Dangerous Goods Ordinance & Regulations, Cap. 295
- Radiation Ordinance & Regulations Cap. 303
- Air Pollution Control Ordinance Cap. 311
- Shipping and Port Control Ordinance, Cap. 313
- Limitation Ordinance, Cap. 347
- Pneumoconiosis and Mesothelioma (Compensation) Ordinance, Cap. 360
- Noise Control Ordinance, Cap. 400
- Electricity Ordinance & Regulations, Cap. 406
- Builder's Lifts and Tower Working Platforms (Safety) Ordinance, Cap. 470
- Construction Workers Registration Ordinance, Cap. 583
- Lifts and Escalators Ordinance, Cap. 618

FACTORIES AND INDUSTRIAL UNDERTAKINGS (SAFETY OFFICERS AND SAFETY SUPERVISORS) REGULATIONS

The introduction of this set of regulations (abbreviated FIU(SO&SS)Rs) in the 1980s was used as a way to engage professional safety officers and to assist proprietors and contractors to prevent accidents on construction sites. Over time, various court cases have been tried, which have further shaped how these regulations are applied. The following summary of a case described in a press release from the Labour Department gives a glimpse of the present scene.

Registered safety officers may be prosecuted by the Labour Department under the FIU(SO&SS)Rs if they fail to discharge their legal duties outlined in the OSHO. On 11 April 2019, one site safety officer was fined HK$8,000.00 in court for failing to comply with the requirements made by an occupational safety officer under the OSHO section 24(2)(a) and obstructing or delaying an occupational safety officer in the exercise of the power conferred upon him under OHSO section 26(a).

Once a registered safety officer is found breaching any of the FIU(SO&SS)Rs, they may be subject to a suspension of their registration if the Labour Department, through legal procedure, finds that they are unable to discharge the legal duties entrusted to them. In the past, the Labour Department issued advice to registered safety officers when they did not perform their statutory duties under this set of regulations. This would be the case, for instance, if a registered safety officer failed to satisfactorily complete a scheduled Form 2A under the FIU(SO&SS)Rs.

Concern has been raised about whether registered safety officers who are employed by construction contractors are able to be proactive in reporting their employer's non-compliance with occupational safety and health requirements. One reason registered safety officers may be unable to discharge their legal functions in this situation is that once they are employed by a contractor working on a construction project there may be some confusion and difficulty balancing the competing desires from the company's management. When hired, a registered safety officer is supposed to advise the project manager and the site management team to safely perform the work. However, this duty may conflict with the expectations of the site management team, who may believe the role of the safety officer is to help them find ways to avoid compliance or delay the repercussions of non-compliance. This role may be further complicated by the expectations of the proprietor, who may expect the safety officer to help them avoid prosecution and evade penalties for unsafe practices. There may also be confusion about whom the safety officer should be reporting any issues to. Indeed, in many cases involving breaches of the FIU(SO&SS)Rs, the independent role of the safety officer has been compromised or even usurped. This employment arrangement is not desirable and greatly hinders the ability of the safety officer and the company to achieve and maintain high standards of safety. Safety standards cannot be viewed as simply needing to comply with the law and prevent accidents—this is just the starting point. As safety practitioners play a pivotal role in ensuring the safety and health of workers on the worksite, the Labour Department has specified that only those persons who remain competent, fit, and professional should retain their status as registered safety officers. Thus, a certain level of independence from the company, site management, proprietor, etc. must be maintained and a hard line must be held in terms of legal compliance with the FIU(SO&SS)Rs and other regulations.

There is currently no CoP published by the Hong Kong Labour Department related to this issue, but there is a professional code of ethics issued by the Society of Registered Safety Officers in Hong Kong. The code outlines the principles that safety practitioners should practise and follow. These practices will not only help registered safety officers adhere to the FIU(SO&SS)Rs, but they will also help them avoid other compliance issues and maintain a professional relationship with their employers.

FACTORIES AND INDUSTRIAL UNDERTAKINGS (LIFTING APPLIANCES AND LIFTING GEAR) REGULATIONS

Breaches of the FIU (Lifting Appliances and Lifting Gear) Regulations (abbreviated FIU(LA&LG)Rs) often result in legal proceedings because the nature of the accidents with lifting appliances commonly result in serious injury. To understand the legal ramifications and cases, it is important to define various terms and concepts.

Automatic safe load indicator, safe working load, and rated capacity indicator

The mandatory installation of an automatic safe load indicator (ASLI) on a crane was introduced in the Hong Kong Legislative Council session on 21 July 1993. In the FIU(LA&LG)Rs, an ASLI is defined as "a device intended to be fitted to a crane that automatically gives an audible and visible warning to the operator thereof that the crane is approaching its safe working load and that automatically gives a further audible and visible warning when the crane has exceeded its safe working load". In practice, an ASLI is simply an indicator of safe working load (SWL), which is the value or set of values representing the strength and stability of a lifting appliance based on the hoisting radius (or the hoisting angle). The SWL value or set of values is fixed.

In the UK, the UK Construction (Lifting Operations) Regulations, 1961 required cranes to be fitted with an approved type of ASLI. Approval by the UK Minister of Labour was necessary for any ASLI fitted on a crane. In 1998, under the UK Lifting Operations and Lifting Equipment Regulations, the term ASLI was replaced with a new term: rated capacity indicator (RCI). This change was necessary to reflect the safe operation of modern lifting appliances which depend on a catalogue of interactive safety factors rather than just a single, fixed SWL. While an ASLI system measures only safe working load, the RCI system monitors a range of other factors that are displayed on a screen installed in the operator's cabin. These other monitoring factors include operating speeds, levelling conditions, wind speed, hydraulic conditions, traveling speed, slewing speed, hoisting speed, lowering speed, upper and lower moment limiter, etc. As each of these factors can contribute to mis-operation, they too must be monitored in addition to the SWL. In modern mobile cranes, these factors are available on a monitoring screen inside the driver's cabin. The SWL is displayed as a load capacity chart of the load moment, or the product of the load multiplied by the distance from the centre of the crane (kNm). Exceeding the safe load moment may result in an accident.

Definition of lifting gear

The FIU(LA&LG)Rs defines lifting gear as "a chain sling, rope sling, ring, or similar gear, and a link, hook, plate clamp, shackle, swivel, or eyebolt". The term webbing sling is not explicitly expressed. However, in Singapore, the term webbing sling is included in the definition of a lifting gear, which includes "any chain, rope, chain sling, webbing sling, rope sling, ring, hook, shackle, swivel, or eyebolt, and any cage or work platform used for carrying persons while suspended from the load line of a crane". The webbing sling was included as lifting gear in the Hong Kong definition following the *Kwan On Construction Company* case in 2017, the details of which are explained in the list of cases below.

The definitions of "lifting appliance" and "lifting gear" are overdue for an update and clarification in the law. For the regulations to be effective, it must be clear what machinery, equipment, plants, and worksites they apply to. One example which requires clarification is the use of drilling rigs on land and at sea for land reclamation. These drilling rigs have a lifting action in their design but their main function on these sites is to move and connect drilling rods as well as to drill, bore, and collect earth and rock samples. Are such drilling rigs still considered "lifting appliances" under the existing regulations? Similarly, spreader beams, gas cylinder storage cages, man cages, material buckets, and concrete skips are all commonly used on construction sites to lift and move items. Are they defined as "lifting gear"? The law needs to be updated to avoid confusion for workers, companies, and registered safety officers and to promote safety across the construction site.

Safe working load versus work load limit

Part of the issue with items such as the webbing sling being included in the definition of lifting gear relates to the application of SWL to such appliances, which may not be practical or even appropriate. Webbing slings are made from synthetic fibres. The history of Nylon fibre begins just before the beginning of the Second World War when the chemical giant DuPont had been experimenting with synthetic plastic fibres, with an initial version of Nylon being developed as early as 1935. Nylon webbing slings, which utilise tightly interwoven Nylon strands to provide a wide surface area for smooth lift, are flexible enough that they avoid tarnishing surfaces and decrease damage to softer materials.

Manufacturers of webbing slings do not specify any SWL but have introduced the working load limit (WLL) in the BS EN 1492-1:2000+A1:2008 Standard instead. This standard, published in Europe, was established to ensure the safe use of textile slings that are made from flat woven webbing slings of man-made fibres. It defines the WLL as "the maximum mass which sewn webbing component of a flat woven webbing sling is designed to sustain in straight pull and which a sling or sling assembly is authorized to sustain in general lifting service". It also includes a reference table which provides the WLL based on mode factors for a range of lifting configurations, such as straight lift, choked lift, basket hitch, and two-leg, three-leg, and four-leg slings. The geometry and sewn webbing components of a webbing sling also affect the WLL. In fact, the width, as the primary aspect of this metric, is colour-coded on the sling—violet (one-tonne), green (two-tonne), yellow (three-tonne), grey (four-tonne), red (five-tonne), brown (six-tonne), blue (eight-tonne), and orange (ten-tonne and above)—and corresponds to a range of allowable safe lifts. Moreover, the material from which the webbing sling is made is also identified by colour on the sling itself, on a durable label fixed directly on the webbing. The colours green, blue, and brown correspond to polyamide, polyester, and polypropylene, respectively.

While the use of WLL is standard in the field, it has not been introduced into the existing lifting legislation. Similarly, how webbing slings should be tested or examined for safety has not been produced in any CoP or Guidance Notes by regulatory bodies. Taken together, this means that registered safety officers must be aware of the difference in SWL and WLL when webbing slings are used on a worksite in order to ensure that the proper safety measures are adhered to.

Cases involving breaches in these regulations

As mentioned earlier, many cases of non-compliance with the FIU(LA&LG)Rs result in serious injury and a subsequent investigation or trial. The cases listed below are those that carry the most weight with regard to how this set of regulations is understood and applied.

The Queen v SOGEA/CAMPENON BERNARD SGE/FRANKI JOINT VENTURE (HCMA 890/1995)

This case involved the use of an earth excavator to carry out lifting operations on a construction site, a process such devices are not approved for. Such misuse was treated as unsafe by the prosecution. The excavator was treated as a "crane" by the regulatory body. The Court held that since any excavator and any "crane" is distinguishable under law, the misuse or wrongful use of an excavator cannot be settled under law but by introducing specific law to deal with such misuse or wrongful application.

Modern machines are now designed with excavating-cum-lifting functions. This means an excavator can be used as a lifting appliance and vice versa. This is a good example of how the law lags behind innovation in technology.

R v Kone Elevator (HK) Limited (HCMA 452/1995)

This case involved an accident which occurred during the use of a pulley block and a wire rope for the installation of passenger lifts inside a building. The appellant company was charged under regulations 7J(1)(b) and 19(b) of the FIU(LA&LG)Rs as a result of the slipping or displacement of a part of the load while lifting as well as regulations 18(1)(d) and 19(a) for not ensuring that the wire rope used was tested and thoroughly examined by a competent examiner under the same regulation.

There was a main building contractor on-site who had sub-contracted the installation of lifts to the appellant. The appellant was a company which constructed lifts but did not assemble them. The assembly work was sub-contracted by the appellant to another company which had the responsibility of assembling the lifts and putting them in place. It was while employees of this sub-sub-contractor company were working that the accident occurred. The Court allowed the appeal and held that the main building contractor is still the "owner" of the lifting appliance and should be prosecuted instead. The respondent (in colonial Hong Kong this was the Queen) agreed that the wire rope was not a lifting appliance, so therefore the second limb of the definition of the "owner" does not apply. The appellant company did not own the wire rope as it was not the contractor responsible for the construction site. This appeal was also allowed. Taken together, this case demonstrates that the main building contractor technically owns the pulley block, the lifting appliance used by a sub-contractor (or sub-sub-contractor) doing the physical work, and will be held accountable for any accidents or breaches in safety regulations.

HKSAR v Hip Hing Construction Company Limited (HCMA 858/1998)

This case arose from an accident which occurred when two bundles of town gas pipes (the load) were hoisted up the side of a building by a crane to an elevated position. The bundles were secured together by strips and then secured to the crane by chain slings which were rigged around the load. For the fifth load of the day, after the load had been secured, the crane lifted the load a short distance (about five feet) and the load was checked again to see that it was securely rigged. When the load was then raised higher, the pipes broke free from the chain sling and scattered to the ground, causing bodily injury to one of the workers stationed beneath. The appellant was charged with failing to prevent slipping or displacement of a load under regulations 7J(1)(b) and 19 of the FIU(LA&LG)Rs.

The Magistrate inferred four possible causes to the accident:

> "1. the load was not adequately secured;
> 2. the metal strip of the packing of the two gas pipes was broken;
> 3. the load bumped against something on its way up; and
> 4. the chain sling broke."

She concluded that there must have been a fault in the securing of the load or that the strips securing each or one of the bundles of pipes had failed, discounting the rest possible causes. The Court found that her findings were unassailable, and the appeal was dismissed.

Rigging metal town gas pipes with metal chain slings is not the preferred safety option. This is because both are metallic surfaces and rigging friction between them is not enough to prevent slipping. In addition, there may be void space between them, leading to displacement. A safer choice is the use of synthetic or Nylon webbing slings for the rigging to increase friction and contact with the surface of the load. Such webbing slings can also avoid unnecessary damage to the surface of the load.

HKSAR v China Merchants Container Services Limited (HCMA 597/2001)

Following a fatal accident in which the driver of a loader was killed when he was not in his driving cabin in a container yard that operated in a grid pattern, the appellant company was prosecuted under the FIU(LA&LG)Rs for failing to provide a signaller. The prosecution treated the loader as a "lifting appliance" since the loader can lift containers.

The Court held that the loader was in fact a forklift truck and the charge should instead be brought under the FIU (Loadshifting Machinery) Regulation. The Court agreed that "it is rather because of the advancement of modern technology which outdated the Regulations and made of its provisions incompatible or inapplicable". The Court also dismissed the appeal for the requirement that a signaller be appointed.

This judgment is akin to that in the *SOGEA/CAMPENON BERNARD SGE/FRANKI JOINT VENTURE* case described earlier in this section in that an excavator used in lifting operation cannot be treated as a crane as excavators are excluded from the definition of a "crane". The word "vicinity" written in the regulation refers to the load being lifted and not to the area surrounding the loader. This is in line with the UK Factories Act.

HKSAR v China State Construction Engineering Corporation (HCMA 1188/2001)

The charges for this case arose from an accident. Workers were concerned with moving "bundles" of water pipes from the ground into the second level of a structure through an opening in the roof of that structure. In the course of that transportation, a worker was injured by the water pipes which fell when they were dislodged while being lowered by the crane driver into the structure. The water pipes which were to be lifted through the roof of, and into, the structure were tied up in bundles of five. The length of each bundle was six metres and the width was 1.08 metres. The roof opening of the structure into which the pipes were to be lowered measured 7.2 metres in length and 2.54 metres in width. This being so, there was not much room for manoeuvring or error on the part of the crane driver who, from his position in the crane cabin, could not see into the structure itself or where the pipes were to be placed. The appellant was charged for two counts: the load being lifted was not adequately secured as a result of slipping or displacement and no signalman was employed in ensuring safe lifting, under regulations 7J and 15B of the FIU(LA&LG)Rs, respectively.

This case demonstrates that lifting a load through an opening is a high-risk operation as the load may strike against the sides of the opening, causing the load or part of the load to collapse and fall. For example, the tower crane operator at his driving cabin at the top may not have a clear and unobstructed view of the load to be lifted through the opening. The lift will be a "blind lift". When the lifted load is of a lengthy or an oddly shaped object through an opening, the size in terms of the length and width or adequacy of the opening space should be considered. A rule of thumb should state the size of the opening in terms of length and width; the size should be 50% more than the size of the object, in terms of its length and breadth, to be lifted. In addition, signalman posted en route is required.

HKSAR v Michael M. NKasu (HCMA 479/2002)/[2002] HKCFI 715

This case is also detailed in Chapter 4. The appellant was a registered professional engineer. He was charged under the FIU(LA&LG)Rs to deliver to the owner of a crane a certificate which was, to his knowledge, not complete as to a material particular. He was convicted, on review, at the Magistrates' Court and appealed against the conviction and for costs incurred. The certificate issued by the appellant was that the data put into column 6 of the Certificate was incorrect. This reason for the charge was not brought up in the course of the trial. Normally, a defendant would be entitled to know the basis of the prosecution and the Court could order particulars to be provided. While doing the test, the appellant did not carry out a full assessment in accordance with the law. The appeal was allowed.

This case demonstrates that any crane test or examination carried out by competent persons should be carried out in accordance with the Schedule 1—Procedure for Testing and Examining Lifting Appliances and Lifting Gear under the FIU (Lifting Appliances and Lifting Gear) Regulations. If the test or examination procedure on a piece of equipment or plant (e.g., lifting buckets, cages for oxy-acetylene cylinders, spreader bars, etc.) is not prescribed under this Schedule, owners of the piece of equipment or plant should be aware of the existence of section 6(2)(a) of the FIUO, whereby they are expected to provide or maintain safe plant and systems of work. The owner, in these circumstances, may refer to other international standards or best trade practices.

HKSAR v Paul Y. Construction & Engineering Company and Another (HCMA 161/2007)

This case, which involves a tower crane accident and a breach of regulations 4(a), 4(b), and 19 of the FIU(LA&LG) Rs, is also mentioned in Chapter 4. While the crane was being used to perform a lifting operation, it collapsed, and the crane operator was killed. It appears that the pins securing the bottom legs of the tower crane failed, causing instability and collapse. The locked pins that caused the collapse were found. They had not been supplied or approved by the crane manufacturer or its appointed agent. The Court dismissed the appeal.

This appeal demonstrates the maintenance requirement for connecting pins used in tower cranes. Unapproved connecting locked pins or pins not recommended by tower crane manufacturers or its approved agent must not be used.

HKSAR v Sun Kam Sing Stephen (HCMA 27/2007)

This case, described in Chapter 4, is a prime example of how the courts will penalise competent examining engineers responsible for checking the presence and the effectiveness of an ASLI. The appellant was charged under regulation 21(2) of the FIU(LA&LG)Rs and the appeal was dismissed after it was discovered that there was no ASLI installed.

HKSAR v VW-VES (HK) Ltd and Others (HCMA 742/2013) (FAMC 69/2014)/(2015) 18 HKCFAR 84

This case, held in the Court of Final Appeal, involved charges under the FIU(LA&LG)Rs and deals with absolute liability. It is also a binding case which set precedence. The four appellants were all charged with breaches of regulations 7J(1) and 19, regulations 18A(a) and 19, and regulations 18(1)(e) and 19. The offences related to a lifting operation carried out at a construction site in Tuen Mun where a sludge treatment facility was being constructed. The first appellant was the main contractor for the site. They sub-contracted the construction work to the three appellants, who formed an unincorporated joint venture for the project. The lifting operation involved the use of a truck-mounted crane which was being used to lift a stack of wooden boards and battens. The Magistrate held that the regulations created offences of absolute or strict liability that the appellants were each an owner of the lifting appliance and gear and even if the offences were not strict liability, the defence of honest and reasonable belief was not established. On appeal to the Court of First Instance, the Judge upheld the Magistrate's conclusion but certified two questions involving important points of law:

> Whether a joint venture could properly be the subject of prosecution for offences under the Regulations? [designated Question 2]
>
> Whether evidence that a joint venture was an "owner" within the meaning of the Regulations was, without more, evidence that each individual party to the joint venture was to the same extent an "owner" within the meaning of the Regulations? [designated Question 3]

However, she declined to certify a third question:

> Whether the offences created by regulations 7J(1), 18A(a), 18(1)(e), and 19 of the Regulations were offences of absolute liability or whether the offences admitted of a defence of honest and reasonable belief which, if true, would have rendered the acts of the defendants innocent? [designated Question 1]

At the hearing, the appellants applied for leave to appeal on the ground that all three questions were raised and on the basis that substantial and grave injustice had been done to the appellants. In dismissing their application, the Court held that:

> "1. Whilst the question of whether a statutory provision created an offence of strict liability or admitted of the common law defence might, depending on the circumstances, give rise to a point of law of great and general importance, it did not in respect of the particular offences in the present case. The Magistrate's conclusion that the offences in question were ones of absolute or strict liability, based on her careful analysis of the regulations and applying of the relevant principles, was plainly correct and leave to appeal should be declined in respect of Question 1.

2. The Appeal Committee retained a discretion to refuse leave to appeal, notwithstanding the Judge's certification of questions as ones of great and general importance. Leave to appeal should also be refused in respect of the other two questions. The applicants were prosecuted as individual members of the joint venture; it was therefore academic whether the joint venture could properly have been prosecuted (Question 2).
3. It was not clear that Question 3 arose in the present case. The Magistrate did not find that each of the individual applicants was an 'owner' within the meaning of the Regulations simply because the joint venture was such an 'owner' (i.e., 'without more'). Rather, the Magistrate scrutinised the evidence to determine whether each of them was a 'contractor who had control over the way any construction work which involved the use of the lifting appliance or lifting gear was carried out' and concluded that it did (para 15).
4. In any event, as framed, Questions 2 and 3 were fact and case-specific and therefore neither posed a point of law of great and general importance (para 16).
5. To succeed on the substantial and grave injustice ground it must be shown that there had been to the applicant's disadvantage a departure from accepted norms so serious as to constitute a substantial and grave injustice. None of the arguments advanced involved any departure from accepted norms to the applicants' disadvantage such as to constitute substantial and grave injustice."

This *VW-VES (HK)* case has been frequently referred to and quoted in cases involving regulation 7J of the FIU(LA&LG)Rs for absolute liability offences. This is because the phrases "reasonable steps" or "practical steps" are not in the regulation.

HKSAR v Kwan On Construction Company Limited (HCMA 11/2017)/ [2018] HKCFI 1640/[2019] HKCFI 474

The appellant of this case was summonsed for an offence contrary to regulation 18A(a) and 19 of the FIU(LA&LG)Rs. The offence aroused from an inspection by an occupational safety officer of the Labour Department. The officer witnessed two workers lifting a stack of triangular metal frames from a lorry compartment and lowering them to the ground with a mobile crane. The stack of triangular metal frames was tied with two fibre slings, and the upper ends of the sling legs were directly connected to the hook of the mobile crane and not connected by a shackle, ring, or link, as specified in the regulations. Two arguments were put forward: one regarding the definition of what should be considered "single", "double", or "multiple" slings, and the second regarding the definition of what should be considered a "fibre sling". The Court held that two fibre slings are a "double sling" within the ambit of the regulation and that the regulation clearly covers fibre slings as "lifting gear". Furthermore, the Court in *obiter* said that "when multiple slings are hinged altogether on the hook of a crane directly without a shackle, the ends of the slings might overlap and rest unevenly at an angle of the U-shape of the hook. It might be easier for a sling to come off the hook. Therefore, a ring or shackle linking the ends of the slings together before they are hinged to the hook of the crane would provide better safety measure". This ruling implies that when multiple slings are used in lifting, a ring-type or shackle should be used.

FACTORIES AND INDUSTRIAL UNDERTAKINGS (NOTIFICATION OF OCCUPATIONAL DISEASES) REGULATIONS

At present, there have been no High Court cases reported or recorded involving breaches of this regulation.

QUARRIES (SAFETY) REGULATIONS

The quarry industry is one of the oldest industries in Hong Kong. At present, there is only one active quarry situated at Lam Tei in the New Territories. It will continue production subject to regular renewal from the Hong Kong Government, specifically the Civil Engineering and Development Department.

Historically, the Commissioner of Labour was also the Commissioner of Mines. However, in 1991, this title was passed to the Director of Civil Engineering, and the Mining Ordinance, Cap. 285, is now administered by the Civil Engineering and Development Department (CEDD). This means that the Hong Kong SAR Government is directly involved in the storage and transport of explosives, whereas in other places they will allow the users to store and transport these items themselves. In October 2011, the CEDD engaged a consultant to carry out a review to assess the long-term demand and strategy for the supply of crushed rocks products, to identify potential new quarry sites, and to carry out a Quarry Development Master Plan for the future.

Notably, this set of regulations applies only to quarries. While no High Court cases have been tried under this regulation, there have been laws enacted related to this work. For example, on 28 October 1987, the Legislative Council passed a new law to increase the protection of workers against pneumoconiosis (also known as silicosis), the lung diseases caused by the inhalation of silica dust, such as silica and asbestos. Silicosis is one of the major health hazards of quarry work. Thus, this law has specific applications related to these regulations.

FACTORIES AND INDUSTRIAL UNDERTAKINGS (BLASTING BY ABRASIVES) SPECIAL REGULATIONS

Sand, which consists of free silica, was originally used as an abrasive to blast off impurities during the casting of iron pipes. This kind of process has since been abandoned and is no longer in use. This set of regulations can, therefore, be considered as obsolete. There have been no reported or recorded cases tried under this set of regulations.

FACTORIES AND INDUSTRIAL UNDERTAKINGS (WOODWORKING MACHINERY) REGULATIONS

This set of regulations only applies when a circular saw is operated on wood. If a circular saw is operating on other materials, such as plastic, this set of regulations does not apply (they would instead be charged under the FIU (Guarding of Machinery) Regulations under group 10 or under regulation 44 of the CS(S)Rs). Modern bench circular saws have been developed so that the saw blade retracts down into the bench table when an operator's hand is too close to the revolving saw blade, thus avoiding hand injuries. Such innovation and modern design make this set of regulations largely obsolete. However, there has been one significant case tried under these regulations which has shaped their application.

Leung Lai Yin v Yeung Kei Chi trading as Shun Hing Furniture Decorating Construction and Another, a decorator company (HCPI 317/1999)

The plaintiff, aged 32, was a master carpenter employed by the first defendant who sub-contracted the carpentry work to the second defendant, a decorator company. While cutting one of the wooden boards, which happened to be a little longer than the others, the board hit the wall and bounced upward. As a result, the plaintiff lost his balance and staggered forward. His left hand was injured as it hit the unguarded saw blade. The plaintiff's case against the second defendant is based on the first and second defendants' breach of statutory duty to cover the saw by a strong and easily adjustable guard and to keep a suitable push-stick available for use at the saw bench. The statutory duties relied upon are those under regulation 10(4) and regulation 11 of the FIU (Woodworking Machinery) Regulations.

The Court ruled in favour of the plaintiff against the first defendant in the amount of HK$1,991,140.70 with costs. The plaintiff's claim against the second defendant was dismissed with costs against the plaintiff. Factors like "momentary inadvertence", "disobedience to order", or "reckless disregard by a workman of his own safety" must be proved before the worker can be held contributory negligent.

FACTORIES AND INDUSTRIAL UNDERTAKINGS (CONFINED SPACES) REGULATION

When this regulation was introduced to the Hong Kong Legislative Council on 18 April 1973, the Commissioner of Labour said: "Between 1st January 1968 and the end of February 1973 my staff has investigated 16 such accidents in which, out of 34 persons involved, 14 were killed ... one was in [a] well, three in manholes, seven in caissons and three on board ships." During the motion to pass this set of regulations, a question was raised concerning whether the open pits (about 4 to 5 five feet deep) used for public utilities, such as telephone and power, should require a safety certificate before workers can work therein. The primary issue is that such pits can contain dangerous fumes, thus putting workers at risk. Similarly, specific areas of the sewage system in Hung Hom, Yau Ma Tei, Kwai Chung, Sha Tin, and Tung Chung have recorded "confined spaces" incidents, which have resulted from dangerous fumes. In fact, fatalities in confined spaces have been caused by carbon monoxide, carbon dioxide, methane, hydrogen sulphide, and oxides of nitrogen. The *Lee Yu Kee* case is one such incident involving dangerous fumes in a confined space. Amended in 1999, this set of regulations lists five foreseeable "specified risks" in a "confined space". It requires the production of a "risk assessment report" by a "competent person" and demands the engagement of "certified workers" in carrying out confined space work. These competent persons and certified workers are also required to attend and complete an approved course recognised by the Commissioner for Labour.

AG v Lee Yu Kee Ltd (Criminal Appeal No. 325 of 1981)

This case involved three workmen employed by the defendant company who were overcome by gas in the course of their work in an underground sewer in Kwai Chung. These workmen subsequently died. The defendant company was convicted by the Magistrate on two summonses laid under regulations 6 and 9(1) of the FIU (Confined Spaces) Regulations. The defendant appealed against these convictions. The issue on appeal concerned the interpretation of regulation 4 to which regulations 6 and 9(1) were subject. The Court allowed the appeal and quashed the conviction based on evidence from an occupational hygienist. This expert explained that hydrogen sulphide is produced by the decomposition of organic matter and that it is always present to some extent in human sewage. However, neither the Magistrate nor Counsels, so far as we can judge by the record of the trial, directed their attention to whether the level of the hydrogen sulphide was liable to be sufficiently adverse on the particular afternoon of the incident. Furthermore, the prosecution could not provide toxicity evidence to show that the level of gas present was sufficient to cause the accident.

To eliminate incidents inside confined spaces, including underground tunnels, robotic drilling tunnel machines have been developed and employed for water pipes, sewer pipes, gas pipes, and electric cable pipes. Modern plant and equipment can help eliminate the dangers of employing workers to work inside underground tunnels. This regulation was amended in 1999.

FACTORIES AND INDUSTRIAL UNDERTAKINGS (ABRASIVE WHEELS) REGULATIONS

An abrasive wheel is usually defined as a wheel consisting of abrasive particles bonded together with various substances. There are two main types of bonding agents: inorganic and organic. Inorganic bonded types are used for grinding, while organic bonded types are used for fettling and cutting off. This set of regulations does not make a distinction between an abrasive wheel for abrasion and grinding purposes and an abrasive disc for cutting only. Under the First Schedule of the FIU Regulations, the "bursting of a grinding wheel moved by mechanical power" is considered a Dangerous Occurrence event scheduled under the law. There is one case of particular note involving this set of regulations.

Tom K Engineering & Construction Company Limited v R (Criminal Appeal No. 2 of 1978)

This case resulted from a fatal accident in which a sub-contracted workman was killed when using an abrasive wheel which was mounted and guarded by a piece of fibreboard. This "guard" was found by the Court to be totally inadequate for the protection of the worker. The appellant, the main contractor, was prosecuted for two counts under regulation 8(1) of the FIU (Abrasive Wheels) Regulations for failing to provide a guard for abrasive wheel and regulation 7(1) of the same regulations for failing to properly mount an abrasive wheel. The appeal against regulation 8(1) was dismissed as the appellant company was a registered contractor under the Buildings Ordinance, Cap. 123, and its subsidiary regulations. As the wheel lacked a guard, the case should have been prosecuted under regulation 9 of the same regulations. It should not have been brought under regulation 7. The Court went on to say that the sub-contractor who owned the abrasive wheel should have also been prosecuted.

It is important for safety practitioners to be aware of the abrasive wheel marking system that refers to BS EN12413:1999 and its periodic updates. This marking system includes the restrictions for use. Examples include:

- RE1: Not permitted for hand-held and manually guided grinding
- RE2: Not permitted for hand-held cutting-off machines
- RE3: Not suitable for wet grinding
- RE4: Only permitted for totally enclosed working areas
- RE6: Not permitted for face grinding

A use-by date from the date of manufacture should also be shown. A bar code or traceable number to indicate the source and manufacturing details of the wheel will also be present.

FACTORIES AND INDUSTRIAL UNDERTAKINGS (WORK IN COMPRESSED AIR) REGULATIONS

This long and complex regulation has a simple objective — to ensure that adequate precautions are taken to protect workers from sickness and ill-health arising from working in an environment of compressed air. It was introduced in 1975 when Hong Kong was about to construct its first Mass Transit Railway (MTR) line. This set of regulations was derived from similar regulations in the UK, as updated by the Construction Industries Research and Information Association (CIRIA), but they were tailored to Hong Kong's special circumstances. Although there have been breaches in these regulations noted by safety officers, no High Court cases have been reported or recorded.

FACTORIES AND INDUSTRIAL UNDERTAKINGS (SPRAYING OF FLAMMABLE LIQUIDS) REGULATIONS

Introduced in 1976, this set of regulations was established to control the use of thinners, varnishes, lacquers, sealing compounds, and petroleum-based adhesives. When using these substances, the flammable liquid vaporises rapidly and so creates a high concentration of gases in the local environment which is potentially explosive and can easily catch fire. A disastrous event like the fur treatment factory explosion in October 1986 was associated with the use of these flammable liquids. However, while breaches of these regulations are apparent, no cases have been tried in relation to their enforcement.

FACTORIES AND INDUSTRIAL UNDERTAKINGS (CARTRIDGE-OPERATED FIXING TOOLS) REGULATIONS

In introducing this set of regulations in the Legislative Council on 8 March 1977, the Commissioner for Labour said:

> Cartridge-operated fixing tools are widely used as an easy method of fastening attachments to walls and ceilings, and provide a simple and inexpensive alternative to drilling. They are mainly used in building construction industry and in the installation of air-conditioners and electrical fixtures.

Since 1973, there have been 41 reported accidents, including 4 fatalities, arising from the use of cartridge-operated fixing tools. These accidents occurred mainly because the operators had not been properly trained and therefore did not appreciate the possible hazards arising from the incorrect use of this type of tool. This was the rationale for drafting this set of regulations. There is only one related case.

The Queen v LO Hing Tang trading as LO'S Engineering Company (Criminal Appeal No. 1395 of 1983)

The prosecution of this case arose from an accident in which the operator attempted to pull the trigger of a Komet gun. A Komet gun is used to shoot fixing spikes. The operator did not break the gun open to see if it had a cartridge in it but put it against the wall of a metal container that was lined with wood. He obviously did not expect an explosion, and it seems likely that he believed that even if the gun went off, the fixing spike would not pass through the wall. However, the fixing spike did in fact go through the wall. It proceeded to hit a metal door jamb and ricochet at an angle, eventually going through the head of another worker on the site, with fatal results.

The appellant appealed based on the fact that the operator was employed by a sub-sub-contractor for the purpose of carrying out air-conditioning work and that the main contractor should be held responsible and prosecuted instead of the appellant company. The Court dismissed the appeal and held that the appellant was a "contractor" doing "construction work" on a "construction site". (Notably, if this case had happened after the enactment of section 13(1) of the FIUO, then the main contractor could also be prosecuted as a "like offence".)

FACTORIES AND INDUSTRIAL UNDERTAKINGS (PROTECTION OF EYES) REGULATIONS

Eye protection is essential for all persons on a worksite. During the introduction of the FIU(Protection of Eyes)Rs on 4 May 1977, the Commissioner for Labour stated:

> Unfortunately, accidents to eyes are all too frequent, and in recent years the number of workers who have received eye injuries in the course of their employment has risen annually by about 12% from 600 in 1973 to 836 in 1976. Fortunately none of these were fatal. However, any eye injury, even a trivial one, is highly unpleasant, and severe injury to both eyes can result in a 100% loss of earning capacity.

While accidents involving the eyes are frequent, there has only been one predominant case brought under these regulations.

HKSAR v Leighton Contractors (Asia) Limited (HCMA 604/2014)

An occupational safety officer inspected a worksite and found a worker using a portable electric concrete breaker to break concrete on the ground in a tunnel. The worker was not wearing any eye protection but produced a pair of goggles, which for reasons unknown were not seized and produced in court. They were merely photographed. No effort was made to test or show that these goggles were "approved" eye protection as defined in regulation 4 of the FIU(Protection of Eyes)Rs. The Court allowed the appeal based on the fact that the prosecution failed to prove the eye goggles produced on-site were not in the "approved" list of eye protectors as defined in regulation 4 of the same regulation.

These regulations can be enforced in tandem with regulation 43 of the CS(S)Rs for failing to provide suitable goggles and ensuring their use for the protection of workers. In fact, it seems that prosecutions for failing to provide eye protection and ensuring use are brought up much more under the CS(S)Rs than this set of regulations. Such cases brought under the CS(S)Rs include, for instance, *HKSAR v Chun Wo Construction and Engineering Co. Ltd* (HCMA 251/2003) and *HKSAR v Nishimatsu Construction Co. Ltd* (HCMA 503/2015). The following Magistracy case shows how regulation 43(a) for the provision of eye goggles and regulation 43(b) for the use of the goggles are applied in court.

In a prosecution proceeding in a Magistrates' Court, the defendant company was prosecuted under regulation 43(a) of the CS(S)Rs for not providing proper eye protection to workers, which resulted in an injury on the worksite. However, when the injured worker was called to give evidence for the prosecution, he changed his statement to indicate that eye goggles were in fact provided on the site and that sufficient numbers were kept in the site office. He also stated that the site foreman had advised him to wear the goggles when carrying out his stone breaking and hammering work. Upon hearing such evidence, the defence counsel submitted that the defendant should have no case to answer. At this stage, the Magistrate interrupted and looked through the regulations. He held that the offence was still covered by regulation 43(b) of CS(S)Rs, specifying that the workman must use the goggles, and amended the summons by virtue of section 27 of the Magistrate's Ordinance. The defendant was subsequently convicted and did not appeal.

In general, prosecution for failing to provide and ensure wearing of safety goggles on construction sites would most often be brought under the CS(S)Rs and not the FIU(Protection of Eyes)Rs, unless the work process was one of that specified under the FIU(Protection of Eyes)Rs.

FACTORIES AND INDUSTRIAL UNDERTAKINGS (ELECTRICITY) REGULATIONS

This set of regulations, introduced in 1982, was based broadly on the Electricity Regulations in the UK Factories Act. Before the enactment of these regulations, there were already other items of safety legislation applicable during the use of electrical apparatuses. For example, regulation 47 of the CS(S)Rs deals with live overhead cables, and regulation 6 of the FIU (Cargo Handling) Regulations deals with the protection of electrical equipment used in docks, quays, or wharfs. Thus, this set of regulations was established to further monitor breaches in the safety procedures necessary during work involving electricity.

The Director of Electrical and Mechanical Services is responsible for matters related to the control of registered electrical contractors, electrical products, quality of installation and workmanship, etc. under the Electricity Ordinance, Cap. 406 and its regulations. This set of legislation is also applicable to electrical works carried out on construction sites. There are several High Court cases related to the application of these regulations.

HKSAR v Southa Technical Limited (HCMA 566/2007)

This case arose from an electric flash which occurred inside a transformer switch room with three-phase 280 volt AC. At the time of the accident, the transformer room could not be rendered electrically dead because it required humidity control. The injured worker, the prosecution's witness, received flash-induced burn injuries to his chest and arms when he attempted to peel off the plastic adhesive tape surrounding the electrical wire. The appellant was an electrical sub-contractor charged under regulations 6, 31(1), and (2). The Court held that an electrical conductor should be effectively insulated to prevent such electrical hazards. The appeal was dismissed. This case demonstrates that in order to carry out electrical work, a permit-to-enter a transformer room and a permit-to-work inside is a required safety procedure.

HKSAR v Sun Fook Kong Construction Limited and Another (HCMA 298/2009)

During a worksite inspection on 14 April 2008, three occupational safety officers noted that the power supply cable of an electric arc-welding machine was not insulated or effectively protected so as to prevent electrical hazards. The two appellants, the main contractor and a sub-contractor, were both charged under regulation 6 of the FIU (Electricity) Regulations.

The Court held that the conviction was unsatisfactory and unsafe. The reasons for this decision were that there was conflicting evidence tendered by the prosecution's three witnesses (an occupational safety officer, a foreman employed by the sub-contractor, and the site safety officer employed by the main contractor). The occupational safety officer claimed he saw a worker doing welding when he arrived on the site and then discovered the broken cable, but the site safety officer and the site foreman gave a direct contradictory account of what happened.

HKSAR v Chun Wo Building Construction Limited (HCMA 749/1999)

This case, also briefly mentioned in Chapter 4, involved a worker who was electrocuted while working on a construction site. The appellant company, a main contractor, was charged under regulation 19(1) of the FIU (Electricity) Regulations when no adequate precautions were taken during work that had to be carried out on a conductor, so as to ensure that the work might be carried out without undue risk from electrical hazards, contrary to regulations 31(1) and (2) of the said regulations. This lack of safety measures resulted in a fatal accident in which a worker without any certification was employed by a sub-sub-contractor to carry out the electrical work.

The appellant company argued that under section 34 of the Electricity Ordinance, Cap. 406, the appellant not only could not do the electrical work itself but could not even attempt to supervise or coordinate or monitor the efforts of the sub-contractors to ensure that the Electricity Regulations and other regulations were complied with. However, the Court did not agree and held that the main contractor should be held responsible and that the safety duties in respect of electrical work were not delegable. The appellant company further argued that it was not the proprietor as such, but the Court held that there could be more than one "proprietor" on the site and that the appellant was one of them.

The Court held that it was an absolute duty. Justice Nguyuen specifically stated that the FIUO was enacted "to ensure that places of work, including factories and industrial undertakings, should be safe for the people working therein.... Clearly the statute is concerned with an issue of public safety, and it can readily be said that the creation of strict liability for all offences created under this Ordinance will be effective to promote the objects of the statute by encouraging greater vigilance to prevent the commission of prohibited acts.... In my judgement, therefore, the offence in question is clearly one of strict liability." This appeal was dismissed.

FACTORIES AND INDUSTRIAL UNDERTAKINGS (ASBESTOS) SPECIAL REGULATIONS

There are no High Court cases reported or recorded in respect of this set of regulations. Furthermore, this set of regulations may become obsolete as building materials containing no asbestos are becoming more prevalent. However, until all older buildings and worksites using asbestos are refurbished using other materials, it is important to understand how this set of regulations could apply.

FACTORIES AND INDUSTRIAL UNDERTAKINGS (DANGEROUS SUBSTANCES) REGULATIONS

On 8 October 1986, an explosion took place in a fur dressing and treatment factory in Kwai Chung, New Territories, and as a result over a dozen workmen were killed and a few dozen were injured by the fire. The cause of the explosion was the use of a chemical sold and labelled as X-55B, which was a petroleum spirit with a flashpoint of less than 23°C. The X-55B was mixed with sawdust for use in the fur dressing process, which also contributed to its instability and volatility. This accident triggered the enactment of this set of regulations related to the use of dangerous substances. A list of 231 commonly used substances was identified. There have been no dangerous substances added since its inception.

When dealing with a chemical or substance hazardous to health, safety practitioners should refer to the Material Safety Data Sheet (MSDS) provided by the manufacturer or approved supplier of the substance. A well-prepared MSDS should contain the following information:

1. Identification of the substance or preparation and company
2. Composition and information on ingredients
3. Hazard identification
4. First-aid measures
5. Fire-fighting measures
6. Accidental release measures
7. Handling and storage
8. Exposure control and personal protection
9. Physical and chemical properties
10. Stability and reactivity
11. Toxicological information
12. Ecological information
13. Disposal considerations
14. Transport information
15. Regulatory information
16. Other information

Any MSDS that does not contain the above 16 items is not a well-informed document. An MSDS should be sourced from the substance manufacturer and the information supplied should be regularly updated. A useful reference document of dangerous substances is the annual publication by the American Conference of Governmental Industrial Hygienists (ACGIH). The document includes general toxicity data, threshold limit values (TLVs), and safety and environmental information for chemical substances or substances hazardous to health.

There are currently no reported court cases related to these regulations.

FACTORIES AND INDUSTRIAL UNDERTAKINGS (NOISE AT WORK) REGULATIONS

This set of regulation works in tandem with the Noise Control Ordinance, Cap. 400, in respect of operations on construction sites. To avoid hazards to operators and nuisance to nearby residents, site managers may wish to use plant and equipment that only generate low levels of noise in order to avoid regulatory action from this set of regulations. Thus, while noise violations have been noted, there are no recorded or reported High Court cases in relation to this set of regulations.

Notably, piling machines equipped with hammer-heads, which produce loud, high-impact noise, have been involved in numerous fatal accidents, but these are not related to noise but to mis-operation during installation, operation, or dismantling.

FACTORIES AND INDUSTRIAL UNDERTAKINGS (SUSPENDED WORKING PLATFORMS) REGULATION

In general, there are two categories of suspended working platforms: permanent and temporary. The former is designed and permanently attached to high-rise buildings or structures for their external cleaning and maintenance. The latter is installed temporarily for providing a workspace for construction workers at the external faces of a building. These temporary platforms will be dismantled and removed when the building or structure is at an advanced stage of completion. This regulation specifically controls the safe use of suspended working platforms, commonly called gondolas. The "owner" of any suspended working platform is responsible for its safe installation, operation, and dismantling. The repercussions to such owners following accidents or breaches flagged by safety officers are discussed below.

HKSAR v Poon Wing Lam and Another (HCMA 520/2006)

This case stemmed from photographs of a temporary suspended working platform installed on a building roof taken by an occupational safety officer after a site inspection. The set-up was identified as unsafe by the prosecution. Both appellants were charged with three summonses related to a temporary suspended working platform installed on a construction site. Two charges were concerned with the failure to ensure the proper installation of outriggers of the suspended working platforms, and one summons was concerned with the failure to provide workers with safety belts and independent lifelines under the FIU (Suspended Working Platforms) Regulation. The prosecution's case was that the L-shape supports for the two suspended working platforms were merely resting on the top side of the parapet wall without any anchor or fixing. The defence's case was that it was a "lashing-type outrigger" which is not the style of "outriggers" defined in the CoP, meaning it was a safe system. Both of them appealed against the first two charges (installation) for costs incurred, which were acquitted on a technicality, but they pleaded guilty to the latter charge (safety belts and lifelines).

HKSAR v Cheung Kee Fung Cheung Construction Co. Ltd (HCMA 600/2011)

The appellant company was a main contractor. It contracted out work that required the use of suspended working platforms to another contractor. This contractor hired three suspended working platforms from another company that physically owned the three suspended working platforms. During an inspection by an occupational safety officer, it was found that the two statutory forms on the three suspended working platforms hired (scheduled Form 2 and Form 3) were not displayed. The appellant company appealed the case based on the question of whether the company, which was the technical owner (not the physical owner) of these three suspended working platforms, would incur "absolute liability" or "strict liability". The Court held that it was a strict liability case because the statutory requirement of the forms in regulation 25(2) of the FIU (Suspended Working Platforms)Rs uses the word "shall" and not "ensure". The appeal was allowed.

In its judgment, the Court referred to five precedent cases, including *HIN Lin Yee and Another v HKSAR* [2010] 3 HKC 403 (described in Chapters 5 and 6) and *HKSAR v Shun Tak Properties Limited* [2009] 3 HKLRD 299 (described in Chapters 4 and 5).

This Magistrate's case, which involved an unnamed company, was detailed in a press release by the Labour Department. On 15 May 2017, an owner of a suspended working platform was sentenced to one month's imprisonment and suspended for two years at a Magistrates' Court for violation of regulations 4(a), 4(e), and 14(1) of the FIU (Suspended Working Platforms) Regulation. The case involved two workers performing plastering work on a suspended working platform against the external wall of a building in Kwai Shing West Estate. The suspended working platform suddenly tilted, causing leg injury to one worker and finger injury to the other.

Based on the cases above, it is obvious that one of the primary hazards of any temporary suspended working platform is the strength and stability of the outriggers installed. Any outriggers should be: (a) of adequate length and strength; (b) properly installed and supported; (c) firmly anchored at the inner ends; and (d) securely fastened to any ballast or counterweights. An inverted L-shaped support for a suspended working platform which rests on the top edge of a parapet wall without any anchor or fixing is an unsafe design. When the support is designed only with makeshift back-tie and side fixing ropes, it is liable to displacement when loaded with workers and equipment. This may lead to tilting or even collapse of the support and cause unstable movement of the suspended working platform. If back-tie and side fixing ropes are used, they should be designed by a professional engineer for safety and be securely fixed. Similarly, inverted

U-shaped anchors mounted on the top edge of parapet walls fixed by screw force are not desirable and can be displaced or dislodged from the parapet wall because of eccentric movement of the suspended working platforms in the process of performing the work. A put-through parapet wall bolt anchor, for example, is a preferred choice, being both safe and reliable, particularly if space on the roof is not available for any ballast or counterweights.

Notably, a CoP on "Access for External Maintenance" was published by the Buildings Department in February 2021. The CoP provides maintenance and repair access to these permanent platforms and safety requirements for their use while at height, supplementing the legal requirements under the FIUO and OSHO.

FACTORIES AND INDUSTRIAL UNDERTAKINGS (SAFETY MANAGEMENT) REGULATION

Introduced in 2002, this regulation requires contractors to appoint registered safety auditors or safety review officers to carry out safety audits or safety reviews of any construction work they conduct. It also requires the engagement of safety practitioners to assist in the promotion of safety on worksites by carrying out scheduled safety management system audits or reviews, detecting any weaknesses, and recommending improvements in the safety management systems. However, based on the number of accidents, injuries, and fatalities on worksites, it seems that the effectiveness of these audits or reviews by registered safety auditors or safety review officers is limited, and these individuals are far from able to detect or prevent certain issues on construction sites. While all construction activities are subject to safety audits or safety reviews, the auditors or reviewers should pay attention to the following six systems principles: (a) comprehensive risk assessment and method statement; (b) hierarchy of hazard control; (c) a fail-proof checking system; (d) a thorough safety inspection system with follow-ups; (e) coordination and communication system; and (f) effective safety training and information. Construction managers are ultimately accountable for implementing such principles. The following two cases were charged under this regulation.

HKSAR v FEWA Chinat Construction Limited (HCMA 439/2018)/[2019] HKCFI 1736

In this case, the appellant company, FEWA, a sub-contractor, was charged, amongst others, after failing to develop, implement, and maintain a safety management system under section 8(1) of the FIU (Safety Management) Regulation. The appellant company undertook a contract value of HK$100 million or more with the main contractor, Leighton Contractors (Asia) Limited. Workers of the appellant company were in the process of extending a working platform when the platform collapsed underneath them and they fell more than seven metres to the ground.

The Court held that the appellant company was responsible for the working platform and, therefore, should have had a safety management system for its construction. This case demonstrates that sub-contractors should have their own safety management system under the FIU (Safety Management) Regulation when the work value exceeds HK$100 million or more. Reliance on the main contractor's safety management system to encompass its administration to sub-contractors is not a valid defence.

HKSAR v Hong Dau Construction Company Ltd and Two Others (HCMA 186/2017)/[2018] HKCFI 1462

The appellant company, the main contractor, was charged under section 8(1) of FIU (Safety Management) Regulation, amongst other safety regulations, after they failed to develop a set of in-house safety rules to provide instruction for achieving safety management objectives at a worksite following an accident. At the time of the accident, one wing of a tower working platform snapped when the sub-contractor's workers were doing refurbishment work. The snapped tower working platform belonged to a sub-contractor and the two deceased workers were employed by another sub-contractor.

The Court held that in-house safety rules must be developed, implemented, and maintained. The failure to do so by the appellant company was unacceptable. However, the seriousness of the offence would have likely been reduced if the rules were present but not effectively enforced. While this could be used as a mitigating factor to reduce the fines imposed, it does not substitute the need for safety rules to be established and enforced.

FACTORIES AND INDUSTRIAL UNDERTAKINGS (LOADSHIFTING MACHINERY) REGULATION

No High Court cases have been reported or recorded regarding this regulation. However, as mentioned in the details of *HKSAR v China Merchants Container Services Limited* (HCMA 597/2001) above, this case should have been brought under this regulation as the loader involved is considered a "forklift truck" rather than a "lifting appliance".

FACTORIES AND INDUSTRIAL UNDERTAKINGS (GAS WELDING AND FLAME CUTTING) REGULATION

No High Court cases have been reported or recorded for this regulation.

OTHER LEGAL PROCEEDINGS RELATED TO REGULATIONS

Registered safety officers must be conscious of the other sets of subsidiary regulations above as well as the CS(S)Rs and main FIURs, which are listed in Chapter 3. However, they should also make themselves aware of all the work being conducted on the construction site in order to ensure that they understand the regulations that apply and must be adhered to. Indeed, while some regulations are not considered to be directly related to construction work, it is important for safety officers to be aware of their contents and any related legal cases.

SUMMARY

This chapter highlights the construction-specific regulations that have been introduced to prevent accidents on worksites and the legal cases that have shaped their enforcement. Most of the regulations in this chapter have rarely or never been tried in court. In contrast, other sets of regulations, including FIU(LA&LG)Rs, FIU (Electricity) Regulations, and FIU (Suspended Working Platforms) Regulation, have been repeatedly tried in higher courts. This distinction is, in part, dependent on the nature of the work being done and how much risk is inherent in the process. However, in other cases, the regulations need amendments or revisions, while others are completely outdated or obsolete. The wrongful application of some of these regulations has also been pointed out in the cases above.

The Hong Kong SAR Government has indicated that practitioners registered under the FIU (Safety Officers and Safety Supervisors) Regulations should be more proactive in advising their site management in accident prevention. This is also applicable to registered safety auditors or appointed safety review officers under the FIU (Safety Management) Regulation. There will even be repercussions targeted at safety practitioners who are not performing up to a professional standard. Thus, it is essential for safety officers and students to be well aware of the legal cases involving all of the FIURs.

This chapter concludes the section on the legal stance on construction safety. The cases outlined in these chapters are meant to be a brief overview of the legal repercussions of some of the ordinances and regulations related to construction work. It is highly recommended that practitioners and students research the cases which may be applicable to their specific work. The next section will consider specific examples of plant and equipment common in Hong Kong, which local safety officers will need to be familiar with.

FURTHER READING

Buildings Department, Hong Kong SAR Government (September 2019) *Code of Practice on Design for Safety—External Maintenance* (First issue).

Shell Hong Kong Limited (January 2001) *Safety Data Sheet for Formula Shell Super Unleaded.*

Singapore WSH Council (2014) *Code of Practice on Safe Lift Operations in the Workplaces.*

Singapore Standards Council (2014) *Specification for Lifting Gear; Part 1: Wire Rope Slings*.

United Kingdom Health and Safety Executive (1992) *Personal Protective Equipment at Work* (Second edition).

United Kingdom Health and Safety Executive (Reprinted 2003) *Safety in Working with Lift Trucks*.

United Kingdom Health and Safety Executive (Reprinted 2005) *Safety in the Use of Abrasive Wheels*.

United Kingdom Health and Safety Executive (2014) *Safe Use of Lifting Equipment—Lifting Operations and Lifting Equipment Regulations (Approved Code of Practice and Guidance)* (Second edition), L113 HSE Books.

DISCUSSION QUESTIONS

1. Is there a way to enhance the role of registered safety officers in accident prevention? What steps should be taken? How can independence be maintained?
2. What construction-specific regulations or codes of practice do you think need urgent amendment or revision?
3. Compare and contrast the FIU(Asbestos)Rs with the Air Pollution Control Ordinance, Cap. 311, in the control of asbestos at work.
4. Wearing personal protective equipment is a last resort if engineering solutions are not feasible. How would you try to change the attitude and behaviours of an individual who persistently refuses to wear the personal protective equipment provided? What are some of the things to consider that could affect your success in bringing about any behavioural changes?
5. What detailed information can be obtained from a Material Safety Data Sheet (MSDS)?

PART III

EXAMPLES AND APPLICATION IN HONG KONG

LEARNING OBJECTIVES

Part III is dedicated to three types of equipment commonly used on construction sites in the Hong Kong SAR: tower cranes, mobile cranes, and bamboo scaffolding. Example court cases involving regulatory breaches or accidents are also cited and summarised for reference. Upon completion of Part III, one should be able to:

1. Understand the basic mechanics and stability of tower cranes, mobile cranes, and bamboo scaffolding;
2. Describe how tower cranes, mobile cranes, and bamboo scaffolding are erected, operated or climbed, and dismantled as well as the foreseeable hazards associated with these processes;
3. Detail the safety precautions for preventing accidents from an organisational and managerial perspective and devise how these process can be implemented on-site; and
4. Carry out basic investigations into accidents and recommend preventive measures.

Work accidents associated with tower cranes, mobile cranes, and bamboo scaffolding are often serious and fatal. Thus, understanding their basic mechanics and safe operation is essential.

"The sky is the limit"

– Tower cranes

"No matter how well defended the system, nor how remote the hazards, someone will find a way of defeating the protective measures. If something can go wrong, it will go wrong"

– Murphy's Law

8 Tower Cranes

INTRODUCTION

Tower cranes were introduced in Hong Kong for building construction in the late 1960s. They are now widely used, not only for high-rise construction, but also for material handling in steel bending yards and container handling work. Depending on the construction activities being performed on a worksite, hundreds or thousands of tower cranes may be in operation.

Notably, Hong Kong does not manufacture tower cranes, and all of those in use across the city are therefore imported. Some of the imported cranes are brand new and some have untraceable or unknown maintenance histories and accident records. Different brands of tower cranes found in Hong Kong include Potain, Liebherr, BKT, Kroll, Wolff, SCM, SYM, Yongmao, Simma, Terex (Comedil), Commensa, Jarlway, Favco, Zoomlion, CSC, Lianyun, SAEZ, and others. As there may be slight differences in how each brand and model of tower crane operates, it is advisable to secure a copy of the handbook for the particular crane being used on the worksite. Unfortunately, accidents involving tower cranes are prevalent and occur on virtually every high-rise building worksite. Skyscrapers and high-rise buildings are under near-constant construction or refurbishment in Hong Kong, which means tower crane-related accidents make up a large portion of the total accident rate on construction sites.

To better understand how to prevent tower crane accidents, this chapter explains the basic mechanics, construction, phases of erection, climbing, operation, and dismantling of tower cranes in general. Each phase of operation has its own foreseeable hazards and operational risks, making it essential to understand the basics in addition to becoming familiar with the operation and safety handbook for the particular brand and model on the worksite. The chapter concludes with a discussion of how human error contributes to accidents—errors of contractors, owners, crane operators, crane safety inspectors, examiners, and maintenance personnel.

TYPES OF TOWER CRANES

There are two principal types of tower cranes: the static-mounted crane and the climbing tower crane. They can be either hammer-headed (with or without A-frame) or luffing-shaped (shown in Figure 8.1). The without A-frame type is becoming more common because of its ease of dismantling after use. The static-mounted and standing cranes are available for up to a 100-metre clear distance between the hook and ground level. To increase the height further the crane must be tied to the structure under construction. It is usually preferable to position the crane outside the building as this makes easier erection and dismantling and also avoids the costs associated with leaving holes for the crane in the floor slabs within the building's structure during construction (as highlighted in Figure 8.2). Because external site space is at a premium and is determined by both the shape of the building and the surrounding area (particularly in densely populated areas), climbing tower cranes tend to be more popular than static-mounted cranes in building construction.

Table 8.1 explains the features of static base and climbing tower cranes. For small to medium building work, a tower crane with a 30-metre jib and minimum 4-tonne tip load capacity may be sufficient. For large housing work, which often utilises mechanised construction methods, a large crane with a 50-metre jib and 10-tonne capacity is required.

FIGURE 8.1: Types of tower cranes: (a) luffing tower cranes on the ICC; (b) zoomed view of the luffing tower cranes; (c) hammer-head tower crane; and (d) A-frame tower crane

FIGURE 8.2: Telescoping tower crane operating through a floor opening

TABLE 8.1: Comparative features for static base and climbing tower cranes

Feature	Static Tower Cranes	Climbing (or Self-rising) Tower Cranes
Base support	Concrete expendable base section to the maker's requirements	Erect at the existing foundation of the building or some designed opening within a building to maker's requirements
Erection	Require a mobile crane to unload from transport and to position the base carriage on rails. Self-erecting but mobile crane needed to assist with jib assemblies and positioning of ballast	Stay at a "static" base but the base will climb from floor to floor
Coverage	Full circle swept out by jib for a single crane; otherwise, an anti-collision device should be installed to avoid overlapping hitting hazard	Full circle swept out by jib for a single crane; otherwise, an anti-collision device should be installed to avoid overlapping hitting hazard
Operating height	Adequately tied into the building or structure by maker's specifications	Limited only by winch drum capacity and power to deal with rope weights and loads lifted
Climbing frames	Not required unless changes in mast heights are made after installation	Require climbing frames of suitable design to transmit vertical and horizontal loads to the structure
Operation	See load at all times unless picking up loads over the building, which may briefly obstruct vision	Operate under blind-lift conditions, particularly lifting load at ground level
Dismantling	Require a self-dismantling mobile crane for removal of ballast and loading of traveling base and crane sections to transport vehicles	Dismantle on roof of completed building or structure. Require a tripod or derrick crane to dismantle. Extra care is necessary to prevent damage to the finished building

THE BASIC MECHANICS OF TOWER CRANES

The following sections break down the general structure of various tower crane types in relation to the conditions of tipping as well as protocols for erection and climbing. As accidents often occur during the dismantling of tower cranes, there is a detailed section explaining the protocols and specific safety measures that should be implemented.

Basic crane structure and condition of tipping

The "condition of tipping" is defined as the threshold for a crane that cannot be increased by even a small amount without causing the crane to fall over. The overturning forces on a tower crane may be greater when it is out of service than when it is working. The tipping load of a tower crane with a luffing jib is calculated using the principles explained in Figures 8.3 and 8.4, excluding side loads. In contrast, the tipping load for a hammer-head jib crane can be calculated using the notations in Figures 8.5 and 8.6.

Figure 8.7 details the hoisting rope revving arrangement in a tower crane, while Figure 8.8 shows a diagram of how a trolley travels outbound and inbound along the crane. Figures 8.9 and 8.10 highlight the process of hoisting up and down. These mechanisms will function in a manner similar to what is shown in these figures. However, the operating details for each brand and model of tower crane may differ slightly.

Tower crane erection

Before assembly, the base, which provides the support for a static or climbing crane, must be properly designed by an engineer. Full information about the horizontal and vertical loads, together with the condition of tipping, must be obtained from the manufacturer. The supplier's catalogue usually provides information regarding the mast composition, the hook height and weight, and the moments and forces involved during both in-service and out-of-service conditions. When in doubt, one should seek clarification from the manufacturer.

A crane is initially assembled at ground level. Thus, there must be ample space for laying out the crane components as well as for mobile

FIGURE 8.3: Forces acting on a luffing-jib tower crane

(adopted from Harris, 1989, p. 146)

$$Wr + J\frac{r}{2} = Cx$$

$$W = \frac{Cx}{r} - \frac{J}{2}$$ where W is the tipping load

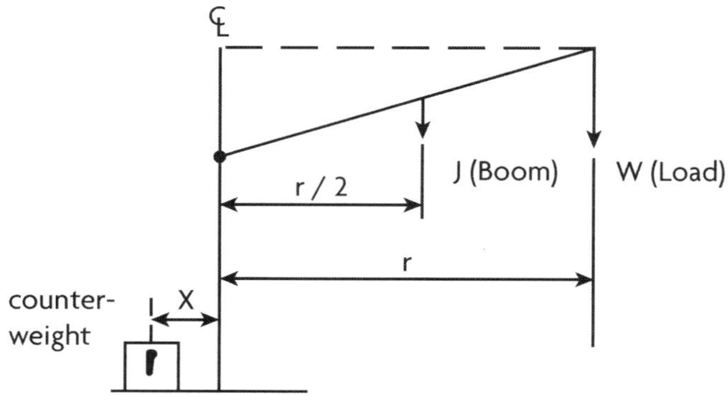

FIGURE 8.4: Load-radius diagram for a luffing-jib tower crane

(adopted from Harris, 1989, p. 146)

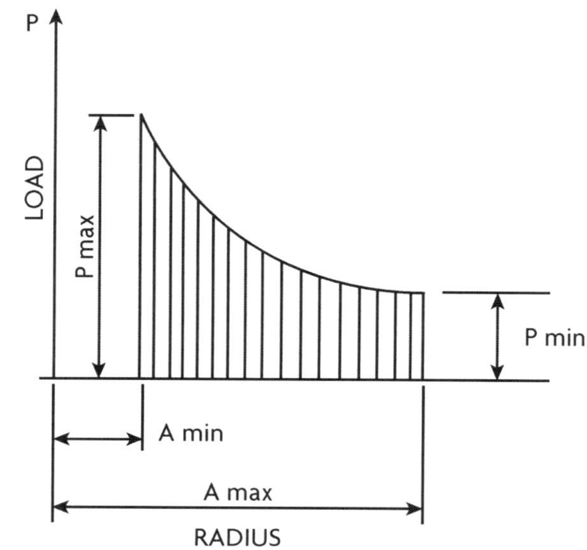

FIGURE 8.5: Forces acting on a hammer-head tower crane

(adopted from Harris, 1989, p. 147)

$$Wr + Jl = C_1x + C_2y$$

$$W = \frac{C_1x + C_2y + Jl}{r}$$

where W is the tipping load

$$P = W - \textit{margin for safety}$$

where P is the safe working load

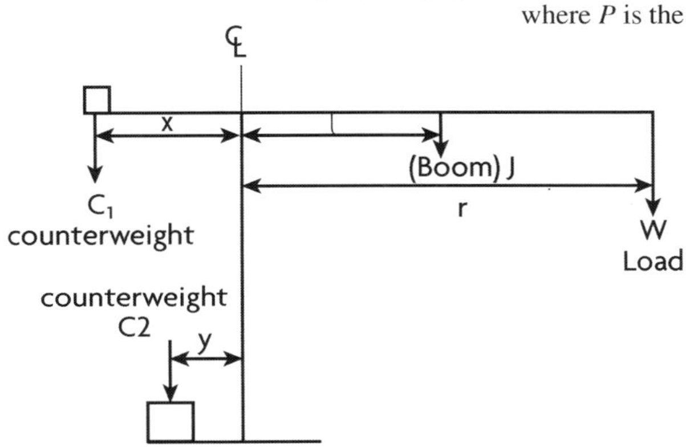

FIGURE 8.6: Load-radius diagram for a hammer-head crane

(adopted from Harris, 1989, p. 147)

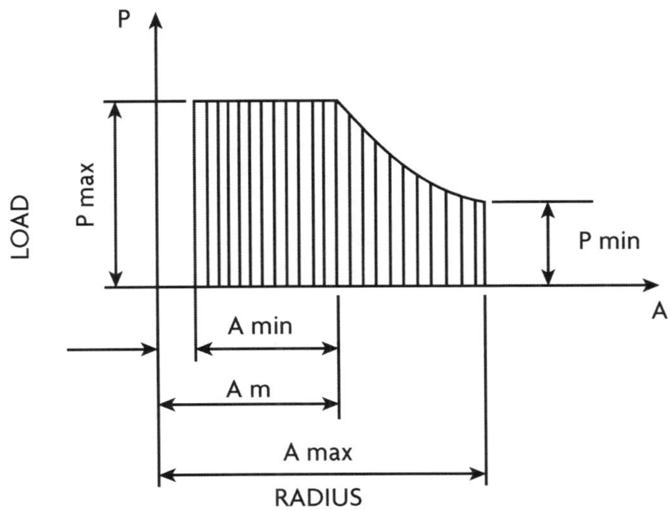

FIGURE 8.7: The hoisting rope revving arrangement in a tower crane

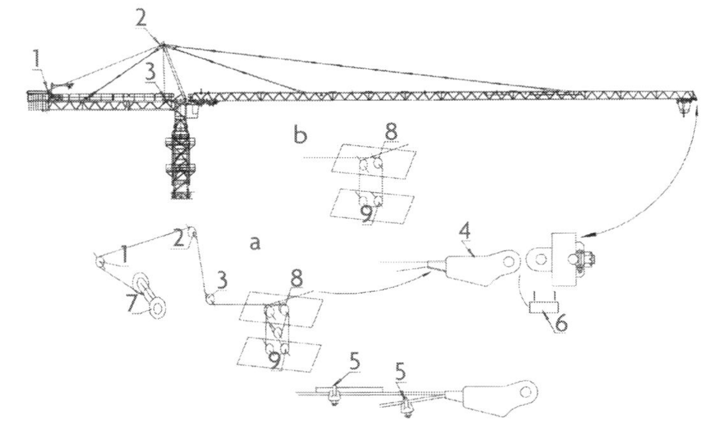

1: Hoist drum; 2: Dynamometric ring; 3: Jib foot pulley;
4: Jib end stretch device; 5: Wire clip; 6: End wire clip; 7: Hoist rope drum;
8: Trolley pulley block; 9: Hook pulley

FIGURE 8.8: Schematic explanation of a trolley travelling outbound and inbound

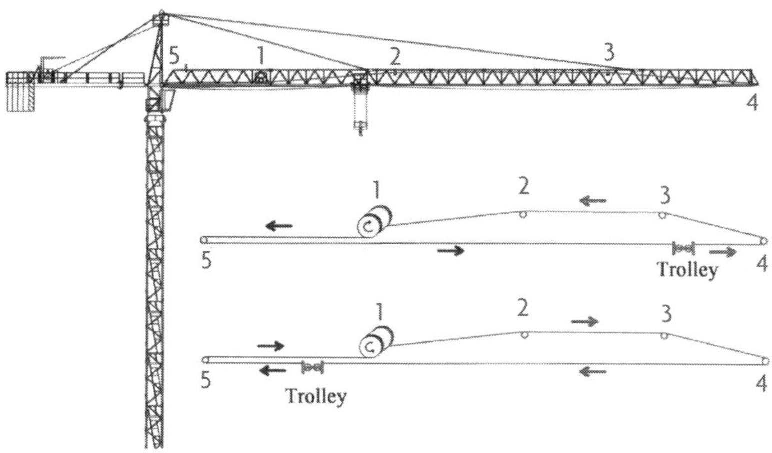

FIGURE 8.9: Schematic explanation of hoisting down

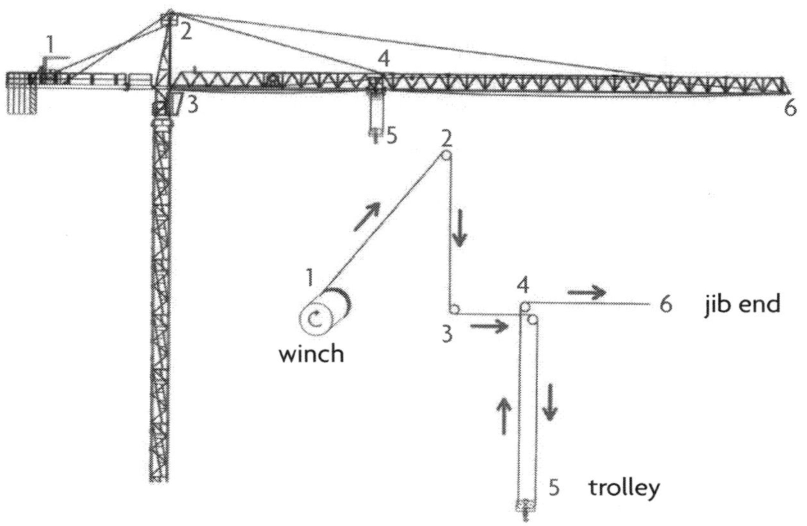

FIGURE 8.10: Schematic explanation of hoisting up

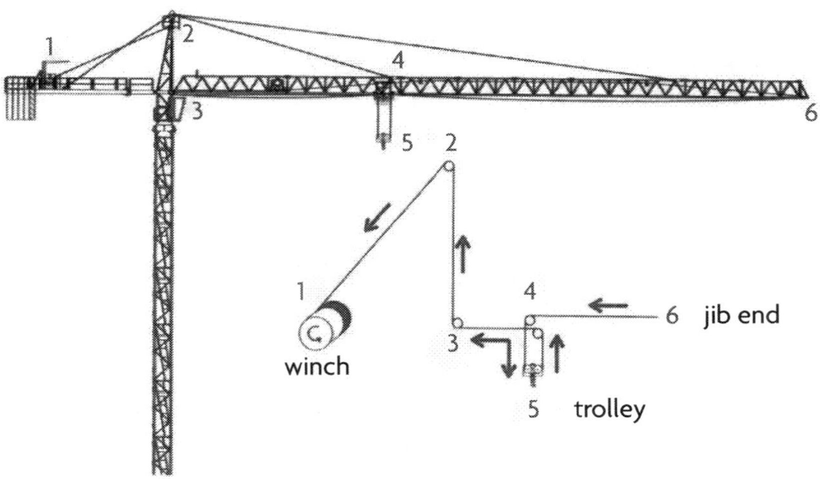

crane use for assembly. The area must also be able to be accessed for off-loading of materials and pre-assembling activities. To begin assembly, the mast section should be erected with the legs anchored to the concrete base by bolts or the expendable base cast in situ. The counterweight jib can then be lifted by the mobile crane and pin-jointed to the tower head at the top of the mast. The jib can then be tilted slightly to connect the pendant. The loading jib is similarly installed by repeating this procedure. Some manufacturers require part of the counterweight to be installed before joining the loading jib. Erection of a tower crane normally requires a team of five to six workers and takes approximately two days.

Climbing

Once the crane is assembled and in service, its weight is transferred, by means of the resting bars, to the supporting frame, which in turn passes the load to the building structure (Figure 8.11 shows a schematic diagram of climbing crane equipment). As a single floor slab is unlikely to support the crane's weight and the load it carries, shores are installed on the three floors below the supporting frame to distribute the weight to multiple levels of the building's structure (Figure 8.12).

The overturning and torsional moments that occur during crane operation as well as the wind shear are transferred to the building structure as horizontal forces. This is achieved by installing wedges between the crane mast and the floor slabs at two levels (Figure 8.13).

Climbing collars are fixed on the supporting frames, which should be installed at three levels (except for the first telescoping level, where only two collars are required). The necessary distance between two collars will be specified in the manufacturer's instructions. Any deviation from these instructions is dangerous and may result in accidents. Each collar consists of two lateral hollow beams. One beam carries a support for the hydraulic jack, two supporting points for the anchorage struts, and two other supporting points for wedges. The other beam has only four supports for wedges to block the tower crane horizontally and to maintain its correct vertical alignment. The wedges will be replaced by guide rollers during telescoping to ensure a smooth upward movement.

A team of six workers, including a chargehand, a crane operator, a jack operator, and three riggers, is required for the telescoping operation,

FIGURE 8.11: Schematic explanation of external climbing crane equipment

(adopted from UKHSE Investigation Report, 2000, p. 72)

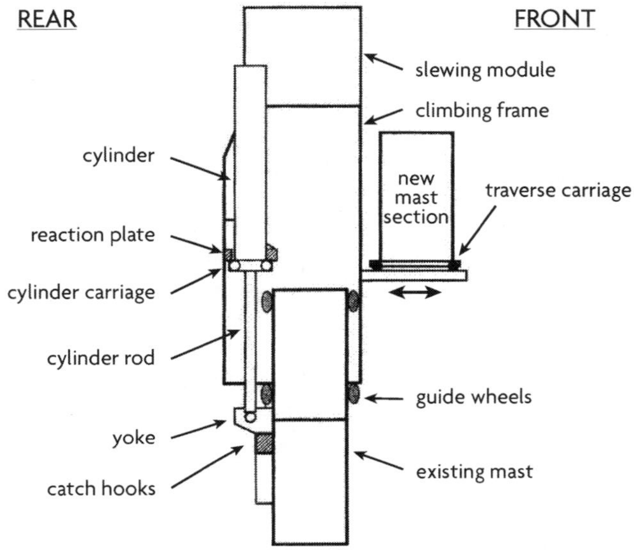

FIGURE 8.12: Elevation of climbing crane installation and support base

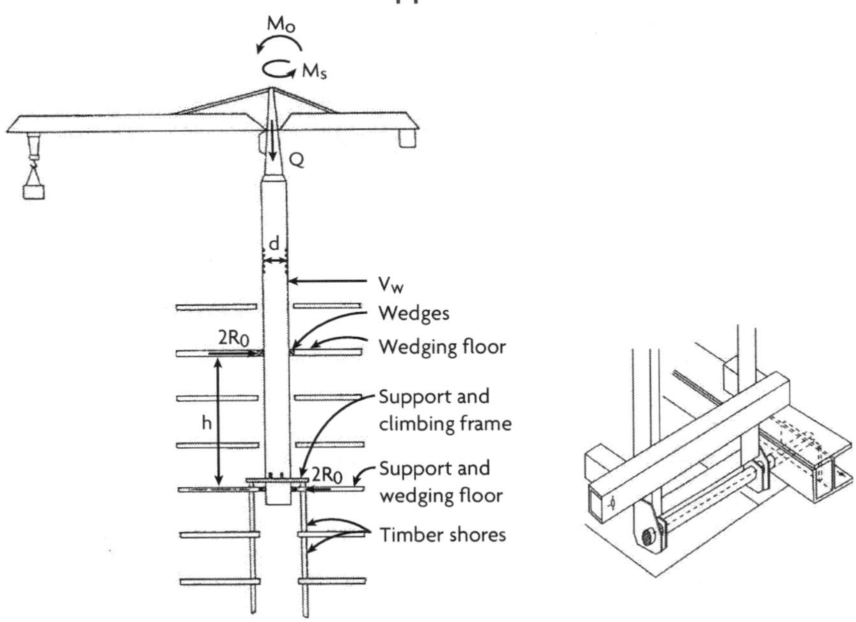

FIGURE 8.13: Wedge and distribution of upper wedge-level reactions, showing the (a) torsional; (b) overturning; and (c) wind shear forces

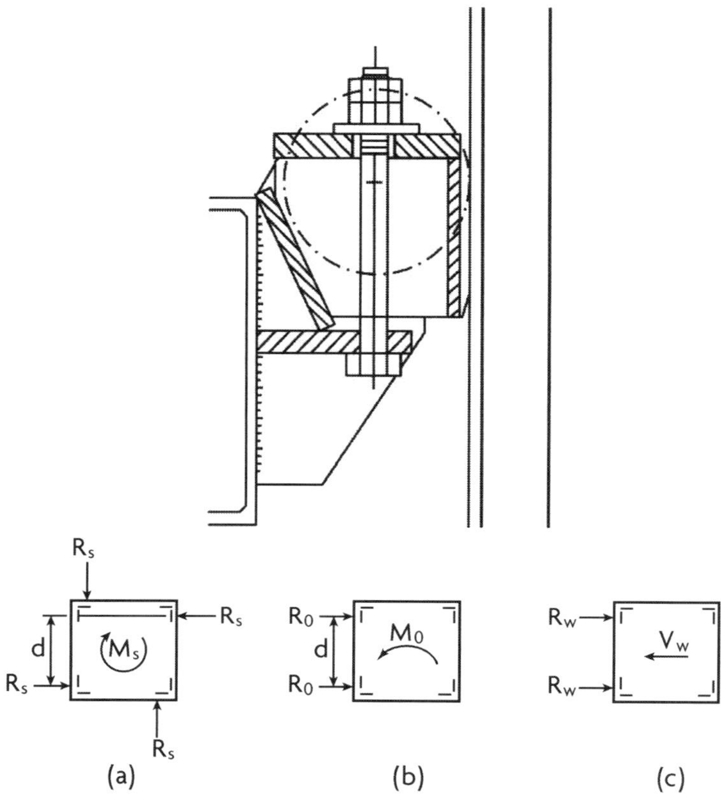

The reaction at the wedge is made up of three parts:

1. Torsional moment M_s: $R_s = M_s/2_d$, where d is the distance between the wedges
2. Overturning moment M_o: $R_o = M_o/2_h$, where h is the distance between the upper and the lower wedging levels
3. Wind shear R_w: $R_w = V_w/2$, where V_w is the total lateral wind force

The maximum reaction ($R = R_s + R_o + R_w$) occurs at the upper-level wedge which involves jacking the crane upwards. Before telescoping, the crane should rest on the Nth floor and will be jacked to the N+3th floor (Figure 8.14). The riggers are responsible for cutting the protruded reinforcement bars using an oxy-acetylene torch at the floor opening where the crane is installed. The telescoping yoke and the hydraulic jack are raised by a chain block from Nth floor to N+3th floor. The jack can then be installed on the climbing collar and all wedges can be replaced by guide collars. During the upward movement of the telescoping device, a counterweight is suspended from the hook to balance the crane.

After connecting the oil pump to the piston, telescoping can be started. Pumping will continue until the telescoping yoke is securely hooked under the saddles of the mast. The resting bars should then be removed, and the jack can be activated until the two anchorage struts hook at the saddles (Figure 8.15). In this way, the crane remains anchored during the retraction of the piston. The jacking operation is repeated until the base of the crane reaches the climbing collar on the N+3th floor. The crane will then be supported on the collar again through the resting bars with all guide wheels replaced by wedges. The whole operation will normally take a full day.

Dismantling

After completing its lifting operations, the tower crane should be dismantled as soon as possible. It is a time-consuming process. Dismantling of the four Favco tower cranes used in the construction of the 118-floor International Commerce Centre (the highest building in the Hong Kong SAR), for example, was done in stages and took a full year. Detailed planning for dismantling is necessary to avoid any dangerous consequences. It is a high-risk process. Foreseeable hazards include:

- wrongly choosing, installing, and operating a smaller crane or another lifting appliance for dismantling can lead to accidents;
- mis-operation of the smaller crane may cause damage to the newly constructed building or structure;
- possible fall of a person and falling objects;
- any lapses of the work may extend damages to third parties outside the worksite;

FIGURE 8.14: Sketch of a tower crane under telescoping

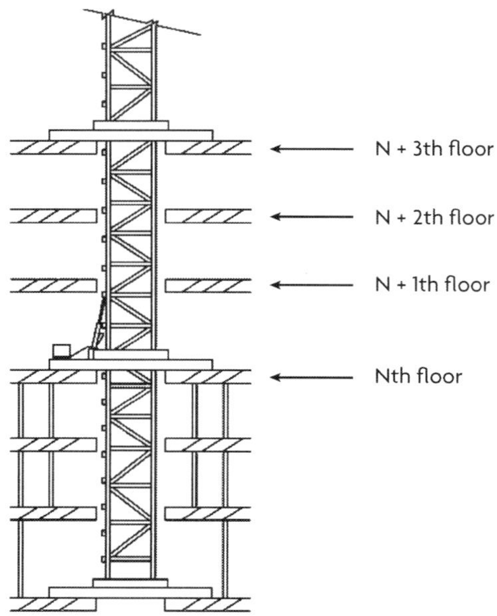

FIGURE 8.15: Sketch showing a telescoping device

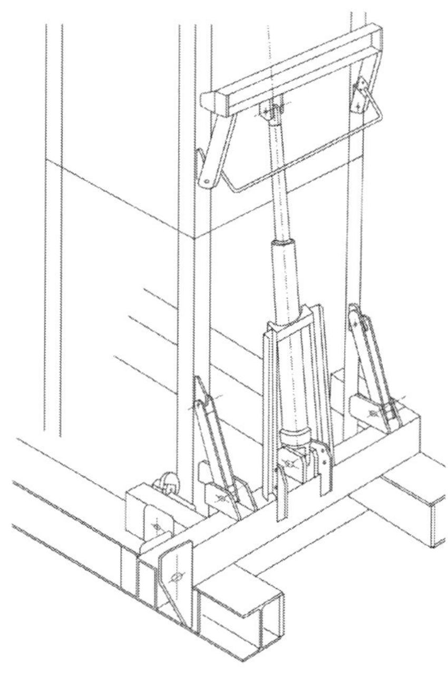

- neighbouring activities, on-site or off-site, may introduce unintended dangers; and
- recovery and rescue measures as a result of any accident will also have inherent risks when such measures are being carried out.

Notably, these are the foreseeable risks, and the list does not include the added risks when safety measures are neglected or the inherent risks caused by human error (discussed in later sections).

For most tower cranes, particularly when used to construct high-rise residential or commercial buildings, the dismantling appliance requires a luffing-jib crane (derrick crane) to be supported and installed on the roof of the building. The general steps for derrick crane installation and the subsequent tower crane dismantling as well as a suggested audit are outlined in the sections below.

Derrick crane installation

1. Select a proper and suitable derrick crane for dismantling the tower crane that was used for the construction work. Check the structural adequacy of the roof for supporting the equipment and its accessories as well as the space surrounding the building. This primary check should be carried out at the initial stages of building construction.
2. Conduct a risk assessment and provide a safe system of work (safe method statement) for the derrick crane's erection and its subsequent dismantling and removal after dismantling the tower crane.
3. Ensure the derrick crane selected and installed on the roof complies with the local regulations as specified in the FIU (Lifting Appliances and Lifting Gear) Regulations, namely regulations 5, 6A, 7A, 7B, 14(1), and 15A(1). Compliance with such regulations shall be certified by competent registered professional engineers.

Tower crane dismantling

1. Obtain a copy of the tower crane manual from the crane's manufacturer. Make reference to the terminology, quantities,

sections, identification numbers, sizes (L × H × W), and weights of all the items. Mismatching or cross-matching the sections can lead to hidden dangers. When in doubt, consult the manufacturer or an approved agent.

2. Dismantling can generally be considered the reverse of assembly. Thus, it can be helpful to reference the assembly procedure and erection sequence for the tower crane. Secure a copy of the safe method statement for erection. Notably, many of the erection hazards also apply to dismantling.
3. Inform on-site and off-site staff who may be affected by the dismantling process.
4. Train and instruct the dismantling crew in precautionary measures and safety procedures.
5. Ensure the dismantling crew understands the step-by-step and item-by-item procedures.
6. Hold pre-dismantling meetings with the crew. The crew members should be conversant with the brand and type of tower crane they are going to dismantle. All crew members should hold valid certifications. Crew members that are new to the dismantling process require strict supervision.
7. Appoint a qualified, experienced, and skilful supervisor to monitor the dismantling process. The supervisor's safety duties and responsibilities should be clearly defined and executed.
8. Ensure adequate space for the dismantled crane on-site and arrange transport off-site.
9. Prepare an emergency preparedness plan for possible failures during the dismantling process. The plan should cover recovery measures such as medical emergency response, calls for third-party assistance, etc.
10. Provide written procedures for the whole dismantling process in the form of a safe method statement based on the relevant risk assessment. The risk assessment should address foreseeable hazards such as wind speed, inclement weather, falling objects, fall of persons, pinch points, diagonal pulling, bump hazard, etc., and assume the worst-case scenario.
11. Cordon off the dismantling site as far as is practical. Unauthorised entry to the cordoned-off site should be strictly prohibited.

12. Monitor the local wind speed online.
13. Comply with any other additional safety requirements imposed by third parties.

An audit checklist for tower crane dismantling

Table 8.2 shows a proposed checklist for dismantling a tower crane when it has completed its lifting function. This checklist can be used to help ensure safe dismantling. It can also be similarly applied during tower crane erection. However, when used for this reverse application, some items will not be applicable but should still be noted as they will apply in the later dismantling of the crane. Site safety officers can carry out the audit, but all workers involved in tower crane erection and dismantling should be aware of these steps. Deficiencies noted during the audit should be rectified before the dismantling/erection process begins.

The geometry of dismantling

Conducting the audit above will go a long way to help the dismantling process proceed smoothly. In addition to the steps of the dismantling process, workers and safety officers involved in tower crane dismantling must also be aware of the geometry of the process.

During dismantling, part or all of the counterweight of the crane will be disconnected from the counterweight jib and then lowered by the derrick. The slinging of the derrick is then fixed to the jib of the crane. This is followed by the activation of the derrick to support the jib's weight. The pendant bar should then be disconnected from the cab tower, and the jib set free by removing the locking pins which connect the jib to the crane. These actions will trigger a sudden release of load, both static and dynamic, the geometry of which requires careful examination. The following is an example of the calculations for the slinging geometry when the jib is tilted to slacken the load on the pendants for a tower crane with A-frame, as shown in Figure 8.16. It is necessary to calculate what the optimum angle of tilt is before slackening the load. The calculations assume a tilting angle of 20 degrees.

Based on the calculations in Figure 8.16, if F_1 is excessively larger than F_2, the slings will not share the load equally. This situation can be

TABLE 8.2: A proposed audit checklist for tower crane erection and dismantling

Hardware

- What type of crane or lifting appliance will be used for the tower crane lifting?
- Does the crane have enough capacity? Does the jib?
- Is there enough headroom?
- What type of derrick will be used for the lifting?
- Is the proposed derrick a safe choice?

Design

- Is there a lifting plan for the erection and dismantling?
- Does the choice of crane or derrick comply with the manufacturer's manual for erection and dismantling? Is the climbing frame or equivalent device supplied with an operating manual?
- Is the environment conducive for the positioning of the crane or the derrick?

Procedure

- Is the manufacturer's manual for erection and dismantling available? Is it in English? In Chinese?
- Has the supervisor(s) of the erection or dismantling team(s) had the opportunity to read the manual? Do they understand the manual? Are there any questions or concerns?
- Has a risk assessment been carried out? Is there a written safety method statement?
- Who is responsible for the implementation of the safety method statement? Record their names and working experience.

Training and instruction

- Are members of the erection and dismantling team(s) trained in the erection and dismantling of tower cranes of the specific type and brand being used?
- Are the workers experienced and trained with regard to construction site safety?
- Are the riggers trained?
- Are the signalmen trained?
- Are the workers who will be required to work at height trained in how to wear and use a full-body harness?

Personal protective equipment

- Are workmen each provided with a full-body harness if required to work at height?
- Are workers provided with a safety bump cap with a chinstrap?
- Are workers provided with a pair of suitable safety shoes? With anti-slipping treads?
- Are workers trained in how to use such personal protective equipment?

TABLE 8.2: Continued

Safety organisation

- Who is the supervisor(s) of the erection and dismantling team(s)? Do they have appropriate experience? Are they competent?
- Who is the tower crane operator or the derrick crane operator? Record their names and qualifications.
- Are drivers appointed in writing, and are they certificated?
- Are all workers engaged, competent, and experienced?
- Are there any new crew members? Who will be supervising these new crew members?

Maintenance

- Are the maintenance manuals for the tower crane, climbing frame (or equivalent device), mobile crane, and derrick crane available?
- Are the manuals in a suitable language so that personnel can refer to them?
- Is the crane or derrick well maintained? Is the climbing frame well maintained?
- Is the tower crane well maintained?

Error-forcing conditions

- Are the workers working for the first time on this type of tower crane?
- Are there unreasonable deadlines for the erection or dismantling?
- Are the workers working under undue stress or in an unsafe environment?
- Is the team coordinated? Have they worked together before?
- Is the working area cordoned-off appropriately?
- Is the weather conducive for the erection or dismantling?

Housekeeping

- Is the work area clean and tidy? Are there obstructions or waste? Are there other contractors or workers working nearby?
- Has the team been provided with the appropriate tools and equipment?
- Are there containers or receptacles provided for the components of the crane?

Communication

- Has the erection or dismantling process been properly communicated to the client? To other sub-contractors working on the construction site? Are walkie-talkies available to workers?
- Has the erection or dismantling process been adequately communicated to all members of the erection and dismantling team(s)? Has there been a pre-work briefing?

FIGURE 8.16: Lifting off the jib section from the main mast

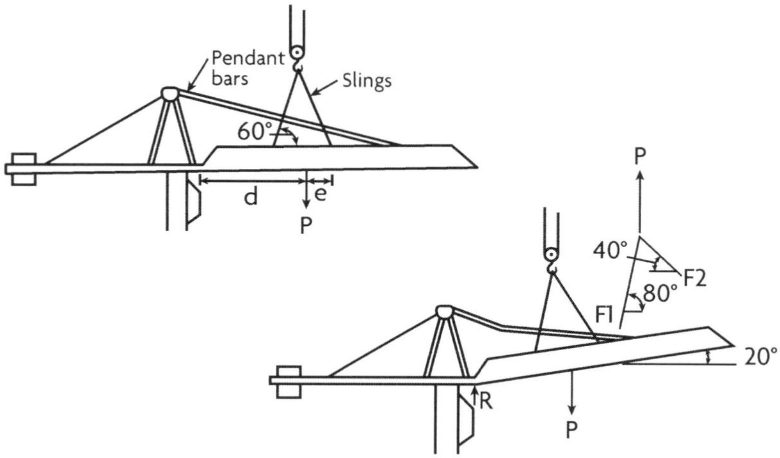

Resolving the forces horizontally, we have:

$$F_1 \cos 80^\circ - F_2 \cos 40^\circ = 0 \quad \text{(equation 1)}$$

Resolving the forces vertically, we have:

$$F_1 \sin 80^\circ + F_2 \sin 40^\circ - P + R = 0 \quad \text{(equation 2)}$$

Taking moments at reaction R:

$$F_1 (d - e) \sin 80^\circ + F_2 (d + e) \sin 40^\circ - Pd = 0 \quad \text{(equation 3)}$$

Solving equations (1) and (3)

$$F_1 = \frac{P}{1.1305 - 0.8391\ e/d}$$

Let D = 1.1305 – 0.8391 e/d

$$F_1 = \frac{P}{D}$$

$$F_2 = \frac{P}{4.41D}$$

Therefore, $F_1 > F_2$

dangerous if the weight of the jib is not equally shared or if the whole weight of the jib is taken solely by one of the slings. Once the jib weight is taken on equally by the slings, the jib can be lowered onto the roof or to the ground level. The jib sections on the roof should be further dismantled to smaller parts suitable for lowering onto the ground by the derrick crane.

TOWER CRANE ACCIDENTS

Accidents involving tower cranes can be very costly, involving substantial financial losses, severe injury or loss of life, and possible prosecution of stakeholders for negligence. This section includes some general examples of tower crane accidents in Hong Kong and details a specific case study which can be used to understand the safety measures necessary to erect, operate, and dismantle tower cranes.

General examples of accidents

The following are records of tower crane accidents and exemplify various situations that could result in accidents.

- A tower crane was lifting up a skip of concrete from the ground level to the 17th floor of a building under construction. The hoisting rope of the crane suddenly failed. The skip of concrete fell through the top of a workman's shed at ground level. A workman who was working inside the shed was killed as a result.
- A tower crane collapsed after a fire. A team of three workers was assigned to cut and dismantle the collapsed crane part by part using oxy-acetylene gases. Another crane was used to hold up the A-frame of the collapsed crane. While cutting, the crane mast sprang up suddenly. The three workers were thrown into the air and fell either onto the crane mast or down to the ground. They all sustained injuries.
- While a workman was working on the deck of a flyover under construction, some of the mould boards being lifted by a tower crane became displaced from the hook and fell. The falling boards hit the workman and fatally injured him.

- During the dismantling of a static-mounted tower crane, the counterweight trolley, with ballast blocks, moved towards the mast and struck directly against it. The mast section broke instantly, causing the lifting jib to fall and hit the ground. As a result, two workers helping to dismantle the crane were killed and five were injured.
- A self-climbing tower crane was used to detach a metal formwork from a building under construction. During lifting, a triangular section of the counter-jib collapsed, fell, and killed a workman below.
- During the erection of a tower crane, three workmen were required to position the counterweight ballast blocks to the head of the counterweight jib. In doing so, the whole jib, together with the three workmen, fell to the ground some 35 metres below, killing the three workmen.
- While raising a self-climbing tower crane using a hydraulic jack, the entire crane came down and damaged the concrete works on the upper-most floor under construction.
- While a workman was working near a formwork panel, above which a metal panel was being lifted by a tower crane, the metal panel swung and knocked off the formwork panel. The formwork panel fell and fatally injured the workman.
- A large panel formwork, when being lifted by a tower crane, dropped suddenly. No workmen nearby were injured. The sudden drop was caused by the failure of the braking system of the crane. There was no secondary braking system installed.
- A tower crane erected at a construction site collapsed while being operated. The operator's cabin, situated high up on the crane mast, plunged to the ground. The operator was killed. The collapse was caused by a strength defect of the four mast "legs" embedded into the concrete. Each leg is composed of hollow square tubes joined by locking pins.
- A tower crane technician was doing inspection work on the trolley on the jib section. Both of his legs were riding on the trolley rails (an unsafe act). While performing running out-and-in tests on the trolley in the jib section, his left leg was badly bruised by the running trolley.

Accident case study

The following is an analysis of a tower crane accident using the TRIPOD theory of accident causation described in Chapter 2. In addition to the background of the case and what the investigation uncovered, this section also describes how it could have been avoided.

Background

A luffing-jib static tower crane was installed for the demolition of a high-rise commercial building, being used to move demolished materials from the upper floors down to the ground level. The crane had a lifting capacity of 25 tonnes. The jib radius was about 40 metres. The luffing jib could be raised or lowered by varying its angle. It was a self-erecting and self-dismantling crane. The main crane mast was tapered and anchored to the main building under demolition.

At the time of the accident, a seven-member crew (one supervisor, one crane driver, and five riggers) was trying to remove a mast section of the crane as the demolition progressed down the building. To accomplish this, they had engaged an external climbing frame and hydraulic lifting gear. The crew was employed by a contractor solely for this job. They had varying experience and skills in handling the type of climbing frame being used here for disconnecting and removal of the mast sections.

The climbing frame had a large opening in its front face, allowing space for the mast section to move out (lowering down) or insert in (raising up). It was measured to have an overall height of about 9.3 metres. The front half and the rear half were not symmetrical. When in use, the two halves were bolted together, but they were detachable. On the opposite side, there was a hydraulic cylinder with an extendable cylinder ram. The cylinder was resting on two reacting lugs fitted on the main mast. The ram would move up and down so as to enable a mast section to leave a space to move out (or insert in) a mast section.

There were guide wheels designed to guide the movement of the climbing frame and the mast section of the crane. They ran on the corners of the mast sections when in use. Such guide wheels were intended to keep the frame in line with the mast of the crane. The lower part of the climbing frame was fitted with four guide wheels, each positioned at the corners of the uprights of the frame. The upper part of the climbing frame was also fitted with four guide wheels. Thus, there were a total of eight guide wheels, about 3.15 metres apart. Each guide wheel, measuring about 228 mm in diameter, was housed and provided with a V-groove (about 45 degrees) to fit the uprights of the climbing frame with the four corners of the main crane mast. In this arrangement, when the crane is balanced, the force acting on the guide wheels, in theory, should be zero. In practice, they transmit any forces acting on the frame onto the mast.

At the time of the accident, a section had been removed from the main mast, and the hydraulic jack was in the process of retracting down. The top part of the crane, weighing 100 tonnes, was being supported by the climbing frame. While lowering, the tower crane suddenly bent and collapsed, falling to land on the eighth floor, where demolition work by pneumatic breakers was in progress. Tragically, two crew members died, and three were injured. No one working on the eighth floor was hurt.

Investigation of the accident

An investigation indicated multiple safety management failures across the worksite. At the time of the accident, only two of the crane anchors remained tied to the building, and the top anchor was found to be distorted after the crane collapsed. Furthermore, two out of the eight guide wheels fixed to the climbing frame were found to be dislodged, one in the lower part of the climbing frame and one in the upper part, while the other guide wheels were still attached to the climbing frame. Further investigation of the dislodged guide wheels revealed that they had been sheared off from the uprights of the climbing frame. This appears to have occurred because of the high pressing force acting against the crane mast and the guide wheels.

The climbing frame was found distorted in an S-shaped, indicating severe buckling had occurred during the accident. The climbing gear was also disrupted, with the yoke being found bent and completely detached from the two lugs on the main mast. The hydraulic lift cylinder body was distorted, and the piston rod was extended. This implies that the piston rod was indeed in the process of retracting down the top part of the crane, which means that it was holding the top part of the crane (about 100 tonnes) at the time of the accident. Thus, the forces being exerted on the crane and climbing frame likely played a significant role in the collapse.

In addition to investigating the effects of the collapse on the crane and climbing frame, an assessment of the entire worksite was conducted in relation to the accident. As mentioned above, pneumatic breakers were in use for breaking up reinforced concrete structures on the eighth floor. It is possible for these breakers to generate impact forces that can vibrate through the building. This could have had an effect on the anchoring frames holding the crane mast.

When checking the safety apparatuses of the equipment, it appears that the crane slewing module was locked to prevent unintentional slewing, but it failed. However, other safety measures were lacking. For instance, while the weather was good on the day of the accident, there was no anemometer fitted to monitor the local wind speed. The vertical limitation of the crane was also not being monitored during use. It was also discovered that this particular climbing frame had been involved in a previous incident during the assembly of a crane (i.e., an issue while raising a mast section). Thus, although the collapse occurred while lowering a mast section, this climbing frame should not have been used before being serviced and checked.

The investigation also highlighted significant communication issues and relaxed safety training. For instance, the operation manual (written in English) for the dismantling procedure was not available to the dismantling crew. Even had it been available, none of the crew members understood English. Thus, no procedural guidelines on how to perform the removal of mast sections were provided. In fact, it was discovered that the crane crew did not actually participate in the risk assessment process concerning the use of the climbing frame, but the main contractor on the worksite prepared a written risk assessment on their behalf. This led the crew to use the wrong balancing weight at the wrong radius compared to the manufacturer's recommendations, which may have contributed to the accident. Moreover, the tower crane being used was unnecessary as there was already another tower crane being used for the demolition site, and it was shown to be working safely. The crane that collapsed had been added to hasten the demolition process.

Taken together, the accident is believed to have been caused because of an accumulation of site management failures. These include design failures in the tower crane itself; inadequate training and experience of the crane crew; lack of communication among contractors and workers;

skipped safety checks of the climbing frame hardware; and incompatible goals regarding safety at work and the work demolition schedule.

How it could have been avoided

The foreseeable risks while lowering a tower crane using a climbing frame include:

- the inherent risks during assembling and dismantling of the climbing frame;
- loss of support from the climbing frame;
- risk from the wind;
- altered alignment and slewing of the luffing jib of the crane;
- disrupted balance of the crane by the crane operator;
- extending beyond the vertical limits of the mast section during dismantling;
- poor fit of the climbing frame to the mast by the guide wheels;
- risk of falls of people or material while operators stand and work on the climbing frame; and
- various combinations of the above.

Thus, it is essential to make safe and appropriate choices. This particular accident could have potentially been avoided if the contractor had chosen a crane with a special climbing frame for the removal of the mast sections (or at least a climbing frame that had a clean incident history), if an appropriately experienced and trained dismantling crew had been engaged for the job, if the necessary safety checks had been conducted, and if the removal of the crane had been scheduled at a time when other work (i.e., the use of pneumatic breakers) was paused. A deeper discussion of various ways to avoid tower crane accidents can be found in the next section. This accident is a useful example of how multiple site management failures contribute to the safety of the worksite as a whole.

This incident is similar to the collapse of a tower crane in the Canary Wharf in East London in May 2000. The collapse happened as the erection team was increasing the height of the tower crane by adding another section using a "climbing frame". As a result of this accident, the United Kingdom Health and Safety Executive (UKHSE) published technical information to prevent similar tower crane accidents in future.

MITIGATING THE RISKS OF TOWER CRANE ACCIDENTS

This section explains various ways to decrease the probability of tower crane accidents on a construction site. Such steps include enhancing the processes of design, manufacturing, and supply of tower cranes; increasing the training and education of crane operators and engineers; requiring regular health checks and safety training refresher courses; decreasing error-forcing conditions; increasing awareness of incompatible goals on the worksite; ensuring crane maintenance and service; and strictly adhering to safety laws, codes of practice, and guidance notes.

Enhance the design, manufacturing, and supply of tower cranes

The role of crane designers, manufacturers, and suppliers (or their agents) in crane accidents and their prevention is rarely discussed in the context of Hong Kong because tower cranes are all imported. However, while we are at the far end of the designer-user chain, understanding these earlier processes can shed light on tower crane function and the mitigation of risks.

Tower crane design is not an exact science, and for any given problem related to tower crane operation, there may be no ideal or entirely reliable solution. An examination of tower crane accidents indicates that not only are design parameters often inexact (because designers may lack information or foresight), but the ways in which the design is realised tend to be subject to human error. Human error can be unintentional or intentional. Most tower crane accidents are believed to be unintentional errors contributed by workmen, such as slips, lapses, or mistakes. There will always be some possibility for these failures to occur. This is not to deny the contributions made to safety by the design engineers, but their contribution is finite. Factors of safety built into the design of tower cranes are a tacit admission of the limits of design knowledge and manufacturing capabilities. There are few feedback mechanisms that travel from users back to the designers. Establishing such channels would be a significant step towards preventing future crane accidents.

One example of a design flaw that could be addressed is the lack of an effective measure to avoid deliberate or inadvertent slewing of the jib during climbing or dismantling. This slewing can significantly jeopardise the cranes and cause unnecessary safety issues. A suitable design change could include the provision of a positive locking device to prevent unintentional slewing as well as a means of interlocking the slewing motor and power supply to the hydraulic motor of the cylinder. The UKHSE suggests that any interlock device needs to be of robust construction and difficult to bypass, thus decreasing both unintentional and intentional human errors. Another hardware improvement is to design and install a secondary braking system to prepare for and remedy a sudden failure of the primary braking system. Failure of the primary braking system may be caused by (a) the sudden stoppage of the power supply; (b) the excessive rotation of the hoisting (winch) drum; (c) the motor speed does not synchronise with the allowable speed limit; or (d) other unforeseen abnormalities.

In addition to the role of designers, manufacturers also have a responsibility in ensuring the safety of tower cranes. Training using the manufacturer's technical guide should be a must for worksite crews as well as the manufacturer's own staff. Direct training for crane maintenance, testing, examination, and other related operations by the manufacturer should also be conducted. Location-specific "worst-case scenario" questions should also be asked. In Hong Kong, such questions could include: what precautionary measures are necessary for tower cranes before a typhoon?

Suppliers of tower cranes are also in a position to help increase safety. The tower cranes designed and manufactured in Europe satisfy the European machinery directives in safety requirements and design criteria. These requirements may not exactly fit those in Hong Kong or elsewhere in the world. It is important for suppliers to be well versed in the differences in tower crane designs and safety measures, and these should be explicitly explained to the user.

At present, there are currently no relevant statutory liabilities for designers, manufacturers, or suppliers under the existing safety and health regulations in Hong Kong. However, those involved in these processes should do what is in their power to prevent tower crane accidents and enhance safety on worksites.

Increase training and education

Crane operators

The term crane operator in this chapter is not restricted to tower crane drivers, it also applies to those who install, alter the height of, dismantle, and maintain tower cranes. This being so, training and education of crane operators should apply to anyone involved in these tower crane processes. Records indicate that these workers account for the highest fatality cases in tower crane accidents.

The foremost consideration is to attract and recruit suitable persons to be crane operators. In Hong Kong, a person can get a job as a crane operator by obtaining a license from an approved training institute or taking a training course at an approved training institute. These are basic competency requirements. However, the law for these requirements is simple: only "competent persons" shall be allowed, thus leaving it to the courts to decide what the term "competent" means. However, courts are not in a place to prevent accidents or to identify their specific cause(s). Thus, to prevent or minimising tower crane accidents, employment ability tests, occupational tests, and personality questionnaires should be established for crane operators. There needs to be synchronicity between the educational achievements of the individual and the particular demands of the job.

Another form of training that is used in the field is simulation. Programmed simulators are now available for the training of crane operators. Such simulation training can put the operator into life-like situations involving dysfunctional tower cranes and accidents. Crane operators should be trained in such a way to prepare them for the worst-case scenarios and to avoid human error in crane operations.

Engineers

Testing and examining tower cranes must be performed by a competent, registered professional engineer. To examine a particular tower crane, the tower crane designer and the manufacturer have to provide information about the "ideal working conditions" for the specific brand and model. Unfortunately, there is much to be desired in the way of educating engineers about such conditions. It is recommended for crane designers and manufacturers to organise training programmes for engineers. Such training programmes should be mandatory and include competency assessments at the end of the programmes. While many engineers have become experts in assessing certain brands and models of tower cranes, it would be difficult for them to be fully versed in the ideal working conditions for all tower cranes in operation without assistance from those who design and manufacture the cranes.

Require regular health checks and safety training refresher courses

Another issue is the pre-employment medical examination of tower crane operators. Areas of medical concern for operators include sudden loss of consciousness through illness, visual defects, disorders causing sensory or muscular abnormalities, psychiatric diseases, and severely reduced exercise tolerance as a result of cardiac or respiratory disease. Operators should have their health checked regularly. While many consider the costs for regular checks too high, the consequences are far greater if a health issue or episode leads to a worksite accident.

In addition to health checks, the safety behaviours of tower crane operators should also be monitored. While the initial training is essential to correctly explain safe behaviours, refresher courses can also be used to remind crane operators what behaviours are considered safe and unsafe. Many workers involved in the erection, operation, and dismantling of tower cranes have been working in the industry for many years and may have picked up bad habits or are not acquainted with the most up-to-date safety protocols. Refresher courses, therefore, serve the dual purpose of helping workers correct their behaviours and to disseminate new information in order to keep the worksite safe.

Avoid error-forcing conditions

Most (if not all) accidents can be attributed to "error-forcing conditions"—a term used by industrial psychologists to describe the collective factors leading to accidents. It is also defined by the International Labour Organization as "failures due to poor quality of the working environment, with respect to circumstances that increase the probability of mistakes".

Mistakes are an unavoidable part of being human but certain situations tend to increase the chances of errors, which fall into three categories: skill-based slips and lapses, rule-based mistakes, and knowledge-based mistakes. Skill-based slips and lapses occur when an action deviates from what is planned in some unintended way. Rule-based mistakes occur when a rule is applied incorrectly or skipped, such as failing to notice a warning and failing to follow the manual.

Knowledge-based mistakes are usually disastrous. It occurs when one's knowledge is limited or inadequate to cope with an unforeseen situation. One has no rules on which to base their decision. Worse still, one does not know what one does not know.

Table 8.3 shows a short list of "dos" and "don'ts" when it comes to error-forcing conditions. These are all based on experience as well as investigations into accidents involving tower cranes. Notably, the list of error-forcing conditions on a worksite can be additive. Site management should avoid error-forcing conditions and apply their organisation's safety protocols. This may include improved training of tower crane operators, re-training and requiring safety refresher courses, and providing better or more information and instruction to enhance knowledge.

Increase awareness of incompatible goals

Incompatible goals on construction worksites are common and must be continuously monitored. Contractors, sub-contractors, sub-sub-contractors, nominated contractors, and their workers on the worksite are all pursuing multiple goals, some of which will overlap while others are at odds with each other. These goals might be related to safety, production, time, costs, or other factors. Conflicts between these goals should be recognised early on to avoid lapses in safety. The following are examples of incompatible goals when tower cranes are being used:

- To shorten the time needed for demolition work, a higher capacity tower crane might be assembled without acknowledging that the crane crew will not have enough operating experience or training with the higher capacity crane. In this case, either a new crew (with experience on the higher capacity crane) should be hired or expectations about the timeline of the work should be managed in advance.
- Site management may view post-erection tower crane maintenance as "downtime" or "non-production time" and try to avoid it even if they perceive an issue (because this may cause delays or extra financial costs). Tower crane maintenance should be carefully planned ahead, and buffer periods should be worked into the schedule in advance to manage expectations.

TABLE 8.3: Some dos and don'ts of error-forcing conditions

Do...	Don't...
✓ Observe local wind speed while in operation ✓ Ensure clear communication with the banksman ✓ Watch out for induced vibration from neighbouring sites ✓ Operate a brand of the crane that one is conversant with ✓ Ensure crane crew members do not face family problems ✓ Be aware of the verticality tolerance of the crane ✓ Acquire basic mechanics knowledge and an understanding of the structural limitations of the crane ✓ Read and understand the crane operation manual ✓ Undergo training for the brand of crane and understand its safe indicators, such as sampling period of anemometer, additional weights imposed by hook blocks, parking radius when the crane is not in use, etc.	× Don't perform "blind-lift" operations × Don't operate the crane in lightning weather × Don't impose time limits for or skip maintenance actions × Don't forget to lock the slewing module while doing height alteration work × Don't carry out "free-fall" operations × Don't use the crane to perform oblique pulling or dragging loads × Don't operate the crane when wind speed is above the allowable limit × Don't operate the crane when you are not feeling well

Ensure crane maintenance and service

Generally, tower cranes are used constantly during a working day, meaning finding time for maintenance and testing can be difficult. While the phrase "ensuring crane maintenance" describes a result to be achieved rather than the means of achieving it, there are pre-requisite conditions for cranes to be properly maintained. These are available in the manufacturer's operational and maintenance manuals. These manuals should be in a language that maintenance personnel and crane operators can read and understand. In Hong Kong, a Chinese language version is usually preferred. All maintenance personnel should be regularly assessed to ensure that they can discharge their duties safely and effectively. Such an assessment for competency should be carried out on appointment and at regular intervals thereafter.

When carrying out routine maintenance checks on a tower crane, the following items (at the very least) should be assessed: tower section and upper parts, hoisting unit, slewing unit, trolley and luffing unit, and any safety devices. It is imperative that records of these checks are kept by the contractor and owner of the tower crane, along with copies of the certifications of the maintenance personnel, a list of any previous incidents involving the crane, and other general information about the crane. The "birth date" of the crane (i.e., the year it was manufactured) as well as the brand, model, and other identifications should be included in this information. This will also help determine how long the crane has been in or out of service and help to adhere to a strict maintenance schedule while also highlighting any hidden dangers. It is recommended that a tower crane can be continuously operated in Hong Kong for not more than 10 years, provided it undergoes planned preventive maintenance. This recommendation is based on the reliability engineering theory underpinning the "bathtub" curve of a piece of equipment or plant, whereby the rate of failure increases with age. Any tower crane being operated for 8–10 hours a day, 25 days a month, for 12 months would clock up to approximately 2,500 hours annually. Thus, cranes operating at this yearly level are classified as performing medium to heavy duty, which requires certain considerations with regard to engineering design and maintenance.

A periodic technical audit, in addition to statutory testing, should be carried out on every tower crane. It is recommended that tower crane owners should invite the crane manufacturer or its appointed representative to carry out safety checks and inspections of cranes at appropriate intervals. During these inspections, the crane should be out of service, rather than kept on-site, and dismantled if necessary. One lesson learned from a previous tower crane accident is that strength-carrying bolts or pins should not be replaced in situ. Instead, the whole crane should be dismantled before any such bolts or pins are replaced. If the crane requires repairs or updates, then subsequent tests should be conducted after any changes.

The storage of a crane when it is temporarily out of service is also important. The storage space and facilities should offer good and safe shelter to protect the crane from inclement weather and damage. Keeping the crane in good working order even when out of service will help stay on the set maintenance schedule and avoid any unnecessary delays in use.

Strictly adhere to safety laws, codes of practice, and guidance notes

Tower cranes are generally regarded as a type of lifting appliance. The safety law governing the safe use of tower cranes on construction sites is the FIU (Lifting Appliances and Lifting Gear) Regulations. Its usage and safe systems of work are governed under the FIUO, Cap. 59.

A Code of Practice (Second edition) for the safe use of tower cranes was revised and published in October 2011 by the Labour Department. These revisions were necessary after a serious tower crane accident in July 2007 (the accident described and analysed as a case study above). Because technological advances often out-pace changes in the law, it is important to regularly revisit the legal requirements for operation. It is also dangerous for compliance to take precedence over wider safety considerations, and stakeholders should not simply adhere to the legal requirements but should maintain safety standards above this threshold to avoid accidents.

In Europe, tower cranes must comply with the specifications of Machinery Directive 2006/42/EC, and cranes manufactured and sold in Europe must have configurations certified by the European Declaration of Conformity (EC mark). Cranes that are EC marked have been subjected to conformity assessment with the Essential Health and Safety Requirements (EHSRs) and other relevant standards. This standard can be used as a reference for those who are concerned with the safer use of tower cranes.

SUMMARY

Tower cranes are essential lifting appliances for building and engineering construction. This chapter summarises the lessons learned from accidents involving tower cranes in Hong Kong. Understanding these lessons can positively prevent or significantly minimise accidents arising from the use of tower cranes across the construction industry. Establishing checklists for dismantling tower cranes, a high-risk operation, which occurs at great heights is one of the methods proposed for accident prevention. A detailed analysis of a real-life tower crane accident using the TRIPOD theory of accident causation has also been described. The analysis diagnoses the management failure types which require intervention. This is an example of top-end accident prevention.

To conclude, modern education and training techniques, such as running accident scenarios on simulators, are recommended to reduce skill-based, rule-based, and knowledge-based mistakes committed by crane operators. Stakeholders on all fronts should contribute to prevent future tower crane accidents occurred on worksites. While this chapter focuses on tower cranes, the next chapter moves on to mobile cranes.

FURTHER READING

Harris, F. (1989) *Modern Construction Equipment and Methods*. Longman Scientific & Technical.

Labour Department, Hong Kong SAR Government (October 2011) *Code of Practice for Safe Use of Tower Cranes*.

United Kingdom Health and Safety Executive (2000) *A Report about the HSE Investigation into the Collapse of a Tower Crane in Canada Square London E14, on 21 May 2000*.

United Kingdom Construction Plant-Hire Association's Tower Crane Interest Group (TCIG) (2008) *Technical Information Notes: Maintenance, Inspection and Thorough Examination of Tower Cranes*, CPA Best Practice Guide.

Workplace Health and Safety Queensland (2017) "Tower crane safety on construction sites—A complex sociotechnical system perspective", *Safety Science*, Vol. 109, pp. 95–108.

DISCUSSION QUESTIONS

1. List ten critical items of a modern tower crane.
2. What safety features would you advise a contractor to hire or purchase with a modern tower crane?
3. What safety precautions would you recommend to a tower crane contractor when a typhoon signal no. 10 is hoisted?
4. Should there be a working platform established in the construction industry in the Hong Kong SAR to give feedback concerning tower crane accidents to overseas crane designers or manufacturers? If so, who should take up this task?

"The power of lifting"

– Mobile cranes

"Force, Mass, and Gravity"

– Sir Isaac Newton (1687)

9 Mobile Cranes

INTRODUCTION

In addition to tower cranes, mobile cranes are also widely used on construction sites in Hong Kong. At its most basic, a mobile crane is a lifting appliance. It can be truck-based (crawler-based) or tyre-based and can have a fixed lifting lattice jib or telescopic jib (the boom) mounted with the driving cabin, turntable, winches, and counterweight (the superstructure). The whole unit is powered by a diesel engine. Unlike static tower cranes, mobile cranes are necessarily mobile and are able to move around the worksite to perform lifting functions on a piece-meal basis of short duration.

Mobile cranes are multipurpose machines that can be fitted with different attachments. These can be used for lifting operations as well as for other duties, such as piling operations, drilling operations, demolition and balling operations, grabbing, and magnet services. In addition to lifting work, mobile cranes can also drive other hydraulic machinery such as vibrators and drilling machines.

The following mobile crane brands are commonly found on worksites in Hong Kong: Liebherr, Kobelco, Tandano, Kato, Hitachi, IHI, Sany, and others. These brands of mobile cranes may have different designs and operational configurations. Thus, a copy of the brand manufacturer's handbook must be kept on-site.

Like tower cranes, mobile crane use is also associated with a certain level of accident risk. This chapter explains some of the basic mechanics, capacities, and capabilities of mobile cranes, as well as some safety considerations. It then goes on to explore the role of various stakeholders in crane operation and safety. Notably, lorry-mounted cranes or excavation-cum-lifting equipment equipped with a hook (for lifting) in their buckets are not included in this chapter, even though these appliances are equally defined as lifting appliances under the law.

CONFIGURATIONS OF MOBILE CRANES

When used for lifting operations, mobile cranes must follow certain design criteria to be suitable for certain actions. For instance, they have to consider if a high or low number of load cycles or low or extreme dynamic loading are required as well as if it needs a weight-optimised design or if there are rough environmental conditions. The operating sectors for the crane will depend on the crane type and configuration (for examples, see Figures 9.1 and 9.2).

THE BASIC MECHANICS, CAPACITIES, AND CAPABILITIES OF MOBILE CRANES

There are three main factors that determine the capacity and capability of a mobile crane:

1. Stability of the base machine (e.g., chance of overturning or upset)
2. Structural strength of the crane equipment and structural parts such as the jib (e.g., possibility of breakage of the jib)
3. Mechanical hoist component and wire rope strength (e.g., risk of wire rope breakage or winch drum failure)

Of these three factors, the one with the smallest numerical value determines crane performance, as shown in Figure 9.3. Each of these three factors, as well as a discussion about the transport, assembly, and disassembly of mobile cranes, is further detailed in the following sections.

FIGURE 9.1: Mobile crane operating sectors for various crane configurations

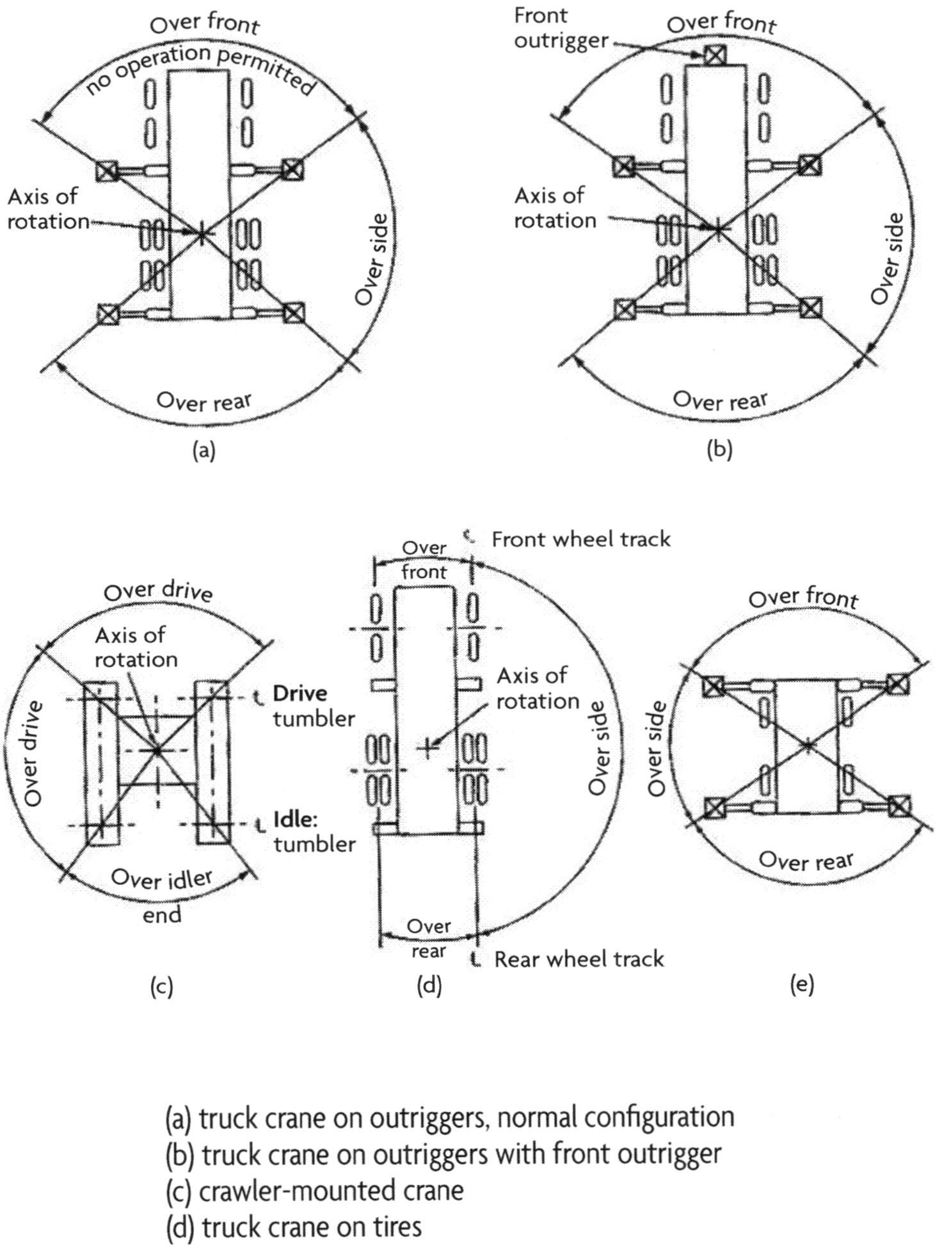

(a) truck crane on outriggers, normal configuration
(b) truck crane on outriggers with front outrigger
(c) crawler-mounted crane
(d) truck crane on tires
(e) rough terrain crane on outriggers

FIGURE 9.2: Plan view of a truck crane

(Note how the outrigger beams are offset from one side to the other to permit telescoping. Never lift at the front.)

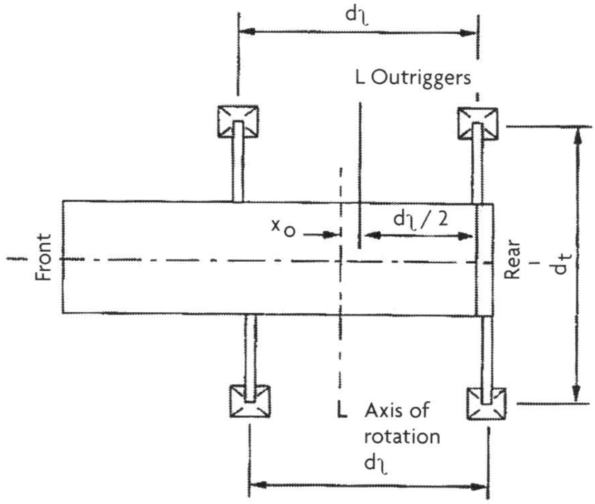

FIGURE 9.3: The relationship between the three factors for crane stability

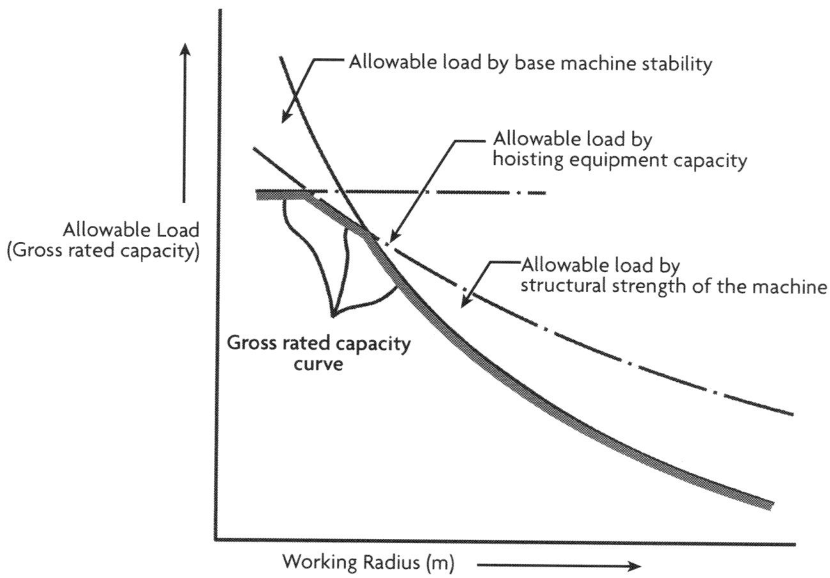

Stability

Mobile cranes are constructed to the stability requirements of the former British Standard 1757 Specification for power-driven mobile cranes. There are other standards, such as the EN directives (Europe) or Gaobiau (China). The EN 13000:2010 has been updated to EN 13000:2010+A1:2014. The margins specified are commensurate with the crane size. A higher safety margin for a heavier load is the basic rule. Some standards specify a tipping load equal to a safe working load plus 50% for crane free on pneumatic or other flexible tires.

Stability also involves the tipping load and working load. The "condition of tipping" is defined by the *British Standard 1757: Specification for Power Driven Mobile Cranes* as follows: "A crane is deemed to be in the condition of tipping when it is impossible to increase the load by even a small amount without causing the crane to fall over." It is, therefore, preferable to operate a mobile crane on a flat and well-prepared surface. The relationship between tipping load and working load is highlighted in Figure 9.4 and can be determined by using the specified formula.

Structural strength

This is normally the limiting factor at short radii. The permissible stresses of cranes are covered by standards such as the British Standards or the EN machinery and plant directives or others. A load factor is usually specified. The "load factor" is taken as the difference between the stress produced by the maximum permitted load and the stress producing the yield. It should be noted that the yield value (not the ultimate value) is the upper limit of a crane's structural strength.

Rope and mechanical component strength

Mechanical components are: winches, drives, gearboxes, brakes, clutches, etc. As an example of the safety margins of such components, the brakes should have a torque of at least 25% in excess of the maximum braking torque required.

Rope factors of safety are also specified by location-specific manufacturer standards. In specifying the load factors, the number of hours in service and the duty performed by the crane will be assigned. Some manufacturers show which factor (or factors) limits the safe

FIGURE 9.4: Tipping load and working load diagram and calculation formula

(adopted from Harris, 1989, p. 102)

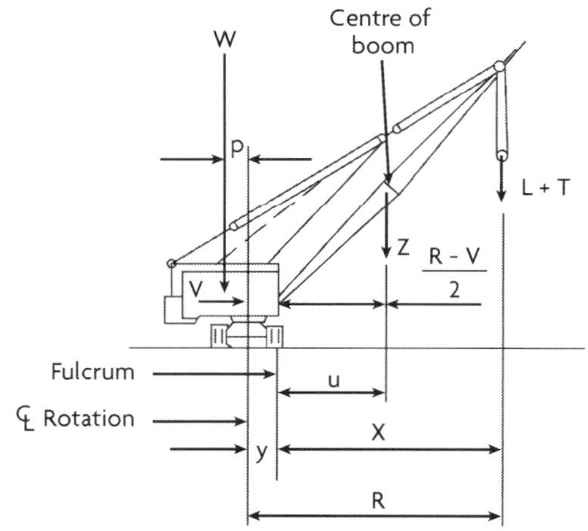

$$L = \frac{W\,(p + y) - Zu}{x} - T$$

where

L = tipping load of the crane;
W = weight of the machine without the boom (but including counterweights);
Z = weight of boom;
T = weight of head sheave;
R = radius to load from centre of slewing ring;
y = fulcrum distance;
p = centre of gravity of machine without boom to centre line of slewing ring;
v = connection point of boom to centre line of slewing ring;
x = R – y;

$$u = \frac{(R - v)}{2} + v - y$$

= distance between the centre of boom to fulcrum

Therefore, safe working load (P) = L – margin for safety

working loads at various radii on their duty charts, and this information is useful when investigating crane accidents.

Transport, assembly, and disassembly of mobile cranes

The mobile crawler crane is not intended to be self-transporting and will travel at only a little more than walking speed. It must be moved from the storage yard to the worksite on a lorry-loader truck. The choice to use a mobile crane is therefore not practical when the lifting operations are only required for a short period of time (hours or even a few days) as the time necessary to load, transport, unload, and prepare for work may require a full day or more. More importantly, hazards and risks exist in all these activities. If mobile cranes are used on a worksite, then it is necessary to train workers in the safe operation of all these activities.

LOAD CHARTS AND SAFETY CONSIDERATIONS

The load chart is a diagram showing the safe working load plotted against the crane's working radius. It is presented in a tabulated format. Graphically, the chart is always boot-shaped. For relative lateral strength, it denotes constant safe working load over the radii range. Within the normal range, the primary limiting criterion is structural strength. Outside of this range, stability (overturning or upset) becomes the significant factor.

Load charts are useful in the selection of a suitable crane to perform a safe lift. During selection, the reach (hoisting angle and any en-route obstructions), the vertical movement (boom or lattice length or height), and horizontal movement (working radius) should be critically considered. It requires a three-dimensional approach. The crane's stability also involves the weight of the hook block, together with any slings, etc., so these factors must also be considered when selecting a crane of suitable lifting capacity.

Digital load charts for mobile cranes are displayed in the driver's cabin. It is advisable for crane users or crane operators to seek information and instructions from the manufacturers on how to read and understand the background mechanics and the design geometry from the load charts. This is the first step in a lifting operation. In case of doubt, it is advisable to clarify from the crane manufacturer or its approved agent. The ability to read and understand the load charts is essential for safe lifting.

As a mobile crane ages over time, its load level will typically be scaled down to ensure safety. If this scaling down is necessary, approval has to be obtained from the manufacturer to determine the appropriate amount to scale down as the load ratings may drop in a non-linear way. This is particularly important when using second-hand mobile cranes.

The crane operator should perform the following checks with regard to the load charts. The permissible load capacity should only be determined when all the conditions are considered together.

- Check load chart presentation. The presentation will be different for a fixed lattice jib compared to that for a telescopic boom with retractable sections, particularly when a flying jib is fitted. When a fly-jib is attached but not in use, the safe working load should be reduced in accordance with the manufacturer's recommendations.
- Check the permissible wind speed. If it exceeds the indicated value in the load chart, crane operations must be terminated.
- Check the strength capacity of all boom sections. For a telescopic boom with retractable sections (some cranes are provided with six retractable sections) used in lifting, the strength capacity will vary. In general, the structural strength of the most distant section (smallest in size) is lesser than that of the closer sections.
- Check the outrigger support base. For mobile cranes fitted with outriggers, the support base (length × width) must be identified to determine the necessary extension of the crane's hydraulic supports for a corresponding safe load. Failure to observe this limitation may trigger an overturn failure during the lifting process.
- Check left- and right-side stability. Outriggers in mobile cranes are not bilaterally or symmetrically designed. When performing any lift, the right and the left side of the crane must both be checked for side stability.
- Check the size of the counterweight. The counterweight provides balance necessary to perform a stable and safe lift of a particular load. If this is not checked, the load could possibly lift the crane during the operation instead of the crane lifting the load.
- Check whether the crane can perform 360 degrees slewing or if there are any slewing limitations.

- Check the charts when operating close to the upper or lower limitation angles for any boom length. For the same crane, the upper or lower limitation angles will be different for different boom lengths. Failing to observe this could cause overturning or upset of the crane. Examples of the upper and lower limits are shown in Figure 9.5.

Taken together, the crane operator should refer to the load charts to select the correct crane with the right lifting configuration based on the environment to carry out a safe lift. Samples of load charts in modern mobile cranes are also shown in Figure 9.5.

Notably, like tower cranes, the term automatic safe load indicator (ASLI), used in Hong Kong, has been dropped in the UK and in Europe. Terms like rated capacity limiter (RCL) and load moment limiter (LML) are being used instead. RCL and LML are rated capacity indicators (see Figure 9.6). These terms more accurately describe their functions. While an ASLI only indicates the safe load, an LML indicates the combined safe load and its safe working radius, providing a more reliable bi-functional indication.

MOBILE CRANE ACCIDENTS

Like tower cranes, accidents involving mobile cranes can be costly for all stakeholders. This section includes some general examples of mobile crane accidents in Hong Kong and overseas.

Examples of accidents in Hong Kong

The following are records of mobile crane accidents.

- A worker was fatally struck by a load of concrete suspended by a mobile crane when the hoisting rope broke. The rope had been overloaded and poorly maintained.
- While lifting bundles of reinforcement bars, the telescopic boom of a mobile crane yielded and collapsed, causing injuries to a nearby worker.

FIGURE 9.5: Boom length and limit angles (a) and the upper and lower limit load chart (b)

(adopted from Liebherr (HKG) Limited)

- The upper limit angle turns off luffing up the boom and accessories at the upper end of the load chart.
- The lower limit angle turns off luffing down the boom and accessories at the lower end of the load chart.

Example 1:
ULA and **LLA** at a **boom** length of 60 m

Example 2:
ULA and **LLA** at a **boom** length of 30.1 m

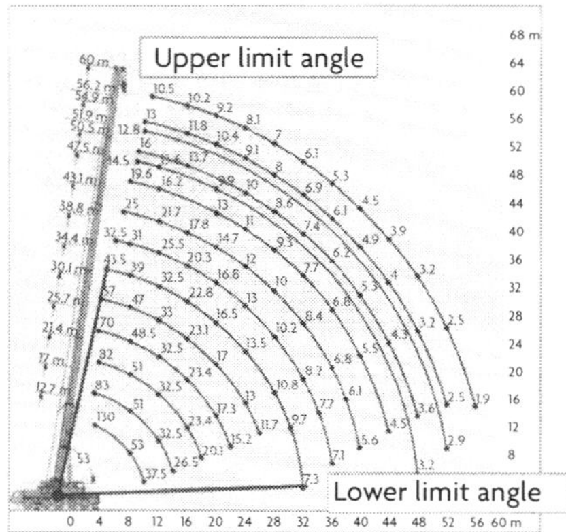

Upper and lower limit angle

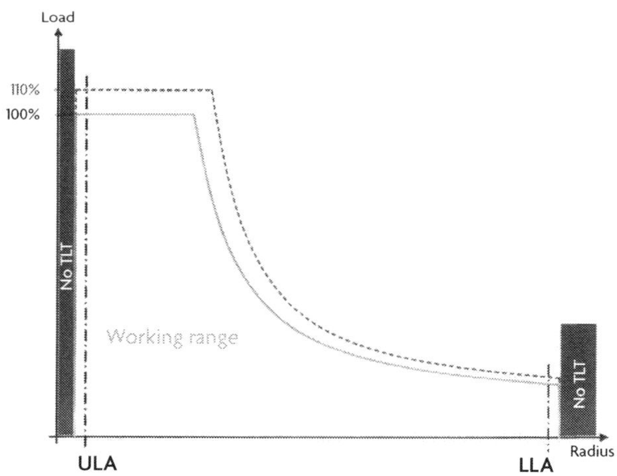

- Existing load chart (working range)
- Upper limit angle (ULA) and lower limit angle (LLA)
- Exceedance of shut off limits up to max. 110%
- No load chart is available

FIGURE 9.6: Examples of rated capacity limiter (RCL) screens

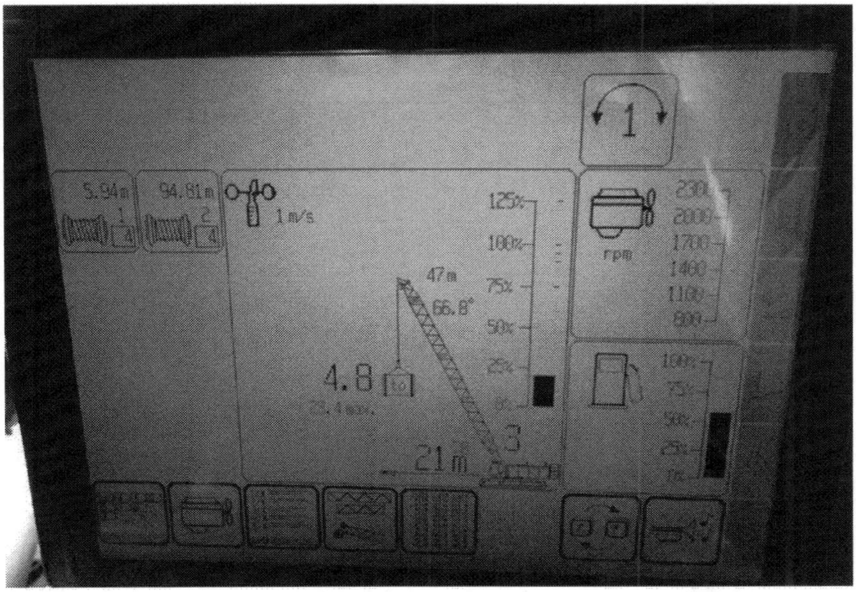

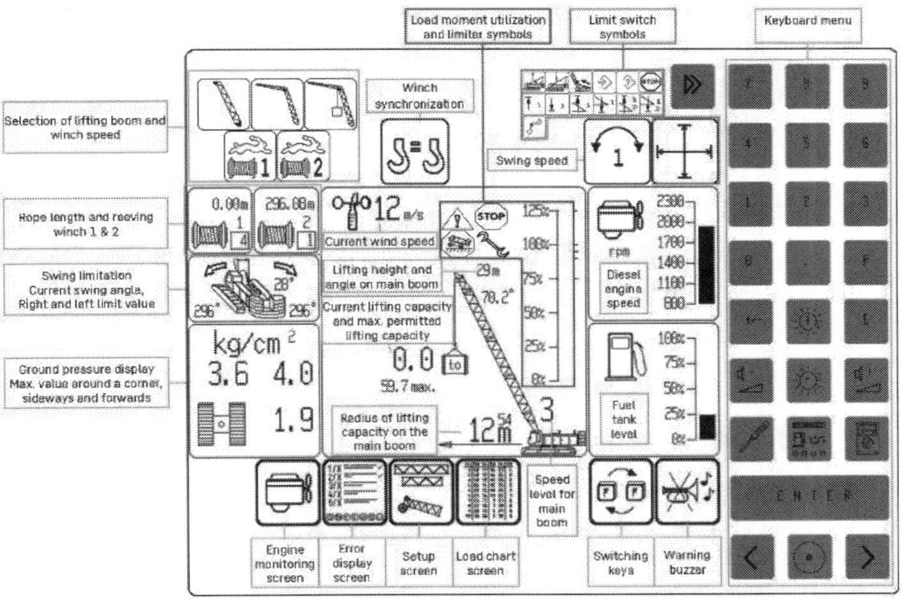

- A mobile crane was used to lift an air-conditioning unit onto a lorry at a worksite. The outriggers had to be levelled as the crane was parked on a slope. After levelling, the crane suddenly slipped backwards and trapped a worker between the crane and the lorry. The trapped worker died as a result.
- A worker was riding on a 20-foot container being lifted by a mobile crane. During the lifting operation, he fell from the top of the container and died.
- An H-pile was being lifted by a mobile crane. During lifting, the pile swung and hit another pile trapping a worker between them. The worker died.
- A worker was working on the carriage of a truck about 1.6 metres away from a mobile crane. The jib of the mobile crane suddenly collapsed while lifting a bundle of scrap metal and hit the worker. The injuries were fatal.
- During a hoisting operation, the upper H-pile of a mobile crane suddenly swung, causing it to dislodge from another H-pile down below to which it was temporarily welded. The sudden swing caused hand injuries to a welder close by.
- A telescoping mobile crane overturned as it lifted a pre-cast sea-wall concrete block from a lorry. The crane overturned, and the driver's cabin was seriously damaged. The driver sustained bodily injuries.
- A mobile crane overturned into the seafront while performing a lift. The driver could not escape from the driving cabin and drowned. An investigation revealed that the escape door on the roof of the driving cabin was obstructed and could not be easily opened by the driver from within.
- A crane operator performed an inadvertent free-fall operation while lifting a bore-pile casing with workers in the vicinity. The casing dropped and a worker stationed nearby was killed as a result.
- While preparing to transport a mobile crawler crane from worksite, a worker's foot was injured as he was helping to put the transport steel wire rope into its mounting via a rope ring. The injury was caused by the tilting back of the A-frame (more than 75 degrees). The worker's foot was crushed between the A-frame and the crane body.

- Workers were not aware of the "pinch point" or "nip point" hazards of a mobile crane, which refer to when a crane is used in a limited space with narrow clearance and the accessible area between the cab/counterweight and any stationary object (such as a building, wall, a parked vehicle, or a barrier) is minimal. Invariably, bodily injury occurs when a crane is located in an access way that invites workers to stand or walk nearby, whereby they can be injured. In this case, a worker was crushed.
- In dismantling and preparing a 300-tonne mobile crane to be transported out onto a public road, the crane driver, while walking and working on the deck of the crane, fell onto the ground and sustained fatal injuries.

Examples of accidents overseas

Various mobile crane accidents have also occurred in other locations around the world.

- In Canada in April 2011, a large capacity mobile crane rolled over while being moved on an unpaved dirt road. It was in a fully rigged condition with the long boom plus lifting luffer elevated to about 30 degrees, complete with full ballast mounted on the rear of the crane. The crane was about 224 tonnes in gross weight with an axle weight of 32 tonnes per axle. The weight of the crane along with the configuration it was in while being moved resulted in the rollover.
- In Brazil on 27 November 2013, there was a crawler crane disaster caused by the lack of timber mats under the tracks of a high-capacity machine crane rigger with above 102 metres of jib. During the accident, the crane travelled forward on the damp ground with 420 tonnes on the hook and killed three men.
- At Alphen on 3 August 2015, an accident resulted from poor planning of a complex tandem lift involving two large capacity mobile cranes lifting a bridge section weighing 187 tonnes while mounted unchained on two separate pontoons on water. Although (surprisingly) no one was fatally injured during this accident, there was significant damage to equipment.

SAFETY IN A MODERN MOBILE CRANE

To avoid accidents, modern mobile cranes incorporate man-plus-machine applications. To satisfy the ergonomic factors, the control elements and display are arranged in a particular way to make them easy to operate and read. Furthermore, the crane driver's seat is adjustable to suit the anthropometric data of most individuals.

As crane stability (or instability) and operational errors are the two main factors behind accidents, these two factors are controlled through the crane control system, which includes input elements, a central processing unit, and output elements. Safety devices such as limit switches, an electronic load moment limiter, sensors, a rated load indicator, an override key, etc. are used as input elements to prevent incorrect operation or misjudgements by ensuring all the crane's functions satisfy the appropriate input elements first.

Real-time monitoring and fault message storage are also carried out by the database system, allowing maintenance staff and management to monitor the machine and its operator from time to time. This data-logger system functions like a "black box" and is useful for incident investigation. A data-logger can be installed in all mobile cranes. Data are recorded at an interval of about 5 seconds. Special software is required to read out and analyse all the data.

Unfortunately, even with so much automation, there is still an element of human error that can lead to mobile crane accidents. Crane operators, being human, can err when operating a mobile crane. Thus, to minimise crane accidents, contractors should demand the use of a modern ergonomic mobile crane for their operators. Mobile cranes without ergonomic designs and built-in safety control system should be the least preferred option. Safety should be the top priority for all stakeholders on the worksite. The following sections focus on certain safety measures that should be considered for the crane operator, crane examiner, signalman, and lifting supervisor.

The crane operator

Most (if not all) crane accidents involve the crane operator, in one way or another. There are three main aspects to consider: licensing, training, and mental competency.

Licensing

To proactively prevent crane accidents, worksite contractors should not assume that a crane operator is competent simply because they possess a valid certificate issued by a licensing authority. In fact, the possession of a valid trade test certificate issued by an approved authority should only be a starting reference for operational competence and safety. It is by no means a license to operate any brand of crane or at any load capacity at any time. The unquestioning acceptance of such a certificate by site management to ensure compliance with the law opens the possibility of crane accidents. There is also no de-licensing penalty for mobile crane operators if they are found to operate a crane unsafely.

Moreover, experienced workers are sometimes adversely affected by technological changes in modern cranes. The changing technology means they cannot solely depend on their accumulated experience. The use of a crane with a changed design, however small, should be accompanied by some form of re-training prior to its operation. This is particularly important when reading and understanding the load charts in the digital form displayed in modern mobile cranes. Licensing alone does not address this requirement and further training should be required.

Training

In addition to the certificate issued by a licensing authority, crane operators should continue to attend training courses and refresher courses organised by crane manufacturers or through their approved agents. Safety training, in principle, is part of other types of training such as school training, on-the-job training, special education, etc. However, general safety training is only a small part of the training that is needed to act safely when operating a mobile crane. As discussed in earlier chapters, an increased amount of training is not always the solution, but increased safety may require smarter training and more specific training for the operations a worker will be responsible for on a worksite. In short, safe operators should be carefully recruited and selected by site management.

On-the-job training is useful but has definite disadvantages. These include: (a) the didactic qualities of experienced or older workmates are not warranted; (b) the educational process is difficult to control; and (c) there is an initial period in which the workers are not fully trained. Thus, it is best for on-the-job training to be used in conjunction with other forms of training, such as theory courses offered by the manufacturer or their authorised representative or agent. Another form of training is the use of a simulator. Simulators are now available for the training of crane operators. Such simulation can put the operator into real-life situations and theoretical accidents so they can be prepared and avoid such scenarios.

As mentioned above, cranes are often modified or updated in terms of its software or hardware. This requires re-training to emphasise the changes and the appropriate safe practices. There is also an urgent need for training courses focused on mobile crane assembly and dismantling. Such courses should explain the hazards encountered during these situations and the necessary safety precautions.

Medical examination

The competence of a crane operator depends on licensing and training as well as the operator's mental and physical limitations. Thus, operators should undergo regular medical examinations to ensure they possess good vision and are in good general health. Persons with colour blindness, cardiac problems, epilepsy, extremities problems, or who have consumed drugs or alcohol within 24 hours of work should not be allowed to operate any crane. It is the responsibility of the operator as well as the contractor(s) to ensure safety on the worksite.

The crane examiner

Mobile cranes are periodically tested and examined by competent registered professional engineers under the Factories and Industrial Undertakings (Lifting Appliances and Lifting Gear) Regulations. A competent examiner should be a person who is knowledgeable about the current periodic technical examination requirements, recommendations, and instructions issued by the crane designers and manufacturers. When appointing the crane examiner, site management should be aware of these requirements. In carrying out crane inspections, the following points may prove useful as a general checklist.

- Obtain the crane manufacturer's manual and operating instructions—check jib length, jib combinations, fly-jib, and any extensions, safe working loads, maximum and minimum operating radii, and any other restrictions.

- Understand the erection and dismantling procedures for the specific brand and model of crane being examined.
- Inspect all test and examination certificates and other statutory reports.
- Inspect general condition of the crane — check for damage, rust, serious wear on ropes, condition of all mechanical parts, etc.
- Inspect safety devices such as the rated capacity indicator — never ask for the crane to be overloaded to demonstrate any safety device, stability margin, or factor of safety.
- Inspect all safety devices and check that they are correctly connected and that the rated capacity indicator is in good order.
- Verify with the crane manufacturer for the inputs in the automatic safe load indicator.
- Inspect ground conditions — check that these conditions are satisfactory for the crane to operate. Use a carpenter's level or programmed indicator.

Signalman

A signalman is a key person in the lifting operation associated with a mobile crane, assisting the crane operator in blind lifts, high-rise lifts, or other difficult lifts. They are responsible for overseeing the entire crane operation and, therefore, have authority over the whole lifting team. Thus, as the "commander" of the crane, the signalman should:

- understand the basic operation of the type and brand of mobile crane used;
- undertake an approved signalman training course for lifting operations;
- obtain a driver's license for the type and brand of mobile crane used;
- be able to communicate clearly with the crane operator;
- be aware of the dos and don'ts of the operations of a mobile crane; and
- be certified physically and mentally fit.

Lifting supervisor

When a lifting operation is assessed to be difficult and challenging, a lifting supervisor should be appointed. In appointing such a supervisor, a contractor should consider the individual's previous lifting operation experience. A minimum of several years of relevant lifting experience should be considered a pre-requisite. The practical working experience considered should include both signalling and rigging.

DESIGN FAILURES LEADING TO ACCIDENTS

Design failures in mobile cranes can be broken down into three parts: the knowledge gulf, the execution gulf, and the evaluation gulf. Knowledge gulf failures involve discrepancies between what is known by the designers compared to users. Designers have what can be called "knowledge-in-the-head", while crane users, including the operator, supervisor, signalman, etc., have "knowledge-in-the-world", which may be incomplete or inaccurate. Designers may not know what the users do not know, and this gulf may lead to design-induced errors and accidents. To bridge this gap, it is not necessary for designers to learn the same "knowledge-in-the-world" as users, but they must be able to interpret this knowledge for error-free crane operation. What they may understand about crane use in theory needs to accommodate crane use in the real world. Thus, it is necessary for crane designers to interact with crane users and observe how the crane is used on a worksite in order to narrow the knowledge gulf.

In execution gulf failures, the inner workings of a crane or the range of safe actions are opaque. The available information may not reveal what the operator must do in order to achieve a particular lifting goal. This can result in a failure to execute the action necessary for a correct or safe operation.

In evaluation gulf failures, it is not obvious to operators (a) what the results of their actions were or (b) what the current state of the crane is. Dangerous errors occur because crane operators are unable to accurately gauge the consequences of their actions. An obvious example in crane operation involves the decision to override the rated capacity limiter. This action may be viewed as a way to enable incorrect crane usage, which can lead to an accident. Of course, the override key that limits the rated capacity of a crane is designed as a safety device for crane operations, but when used inappropriately, it could create an unsafe situation.

To avoid the types of errors above, it is essential to bridge the gap between the crane designers/manufacturers and the crane operators. This can be accomplished to an extent by all stakeholders being aware of the local and international standards for crane use. The BS EN 13000:2010+A1:2004 is perhaps the most updated engineering standard for mobile cranes in Europe but this standard was not referred to in the Code of Practice published by the Hong Kong Labour Department in September 2017. In the current standard, for example, the removal of the override key in mobile cranes by designers and manufacturers also removes the temptation to use it and as such is regarded as a significant development in driving up crane safety standards worldwide. Ultimately, crane designers and manufacturers should receive feedback from crane operators, and crane operators should be receiving operating tips and training from crane designers and manufacturers. This will go a long way to reduce mobile crane accidents.

ERROR-FORCING CONDITIONS

In addition to the design failures explained in the previous section, there are other error-forcing situations. The following conditions, if not well managed and organised on the worksite, tend to increase the chance of a crane accident.

- Use of an imported "second-hand" or "many-hand" mobile crane with doubtful or untraceable or incomplete maintenance and service records.
- Site management puts "production first" rather than "safety first" as these two goals are not easily compatible. Individual crane contractors have their own long-term, medium-term, or even short-term goals. When priority is given to work progress rather than safety, the crane operator may operate at a fast

slewing speed, drag a load (performing diagonal lifting), or "cut corners" (by shutting off the override key).

- Site management engages a large capacity crane for a small site area that cannot comfortably accommodate the assembling or dismantling of the crane, shortcutting necessary safety precautions.
- No timely planned preventive maintenance is carried out on the crane during its period of operation. This may lead to missing wing mirrors, broken rear-view mirrors, deformed safety catches, deformed wire ropes not being immediately replaced.
- The crane operator is under the influence of alcohol or drugs.
- The operator is working excessive hours, continuously for more than 3 or 4 hours without taking any break or rest period.
- The driver's cabin is full of items or personnel belongings that should not be kept inside the driver's cabin, or the cabin is not temperature-controlled.
- The crane operator is performing at a dry-bulb temperature of 34 degrees centigrade and is under heat stress.
- The crane's disassembling team is not given enough time for disassembling sections of the lattice jib, which might allow a section of the jib to fall.
- The crane operator has been instructed to hastily lift a load or object that, in terms of safety, should never be lifted from the rear quadrant to the side quadrant, or they have been instructed to lift sheet piles embedded in a rock layer, etc.
- The ground conditions on the worksite are not strong enough to support the crane and its load, which may cause the crane or part of the crane to collapse.
- The crane operator is performing a "blind lift" or a "high lift" or a combination of the two. A blind lift is a lift in which the view of the crane operator, rigger, or signaller is blocked so that they cannot see one another or in which the site where the load to be placed cannot be seen.
- The crane operator is performing "blind slewing". A blind slewing is a rotation of the crane base without seeing clearly what is surrounding the crane.
- The crane is equipped with "killer" hooks. A killer hook is equipped with a "safety" catch that makes it easy to displace or

dislodge from a load, which can cause the load to fall during the lifting process.

- A new crane is purchased which neglects the optional in-situ safeguards because of additional or extra costs.
- The crane is operated near the seafront, and the operator is not aware of how to escape from the driver's cabin should the cabin overturn and become submerged in water.
- The crane operator unsafely performs a free-fall operation. A free-fall operation is an unsuspected or unintentional release of the wire rope that supports the load.
- The crane operator does not have the proper education to operate a technical or sophisticated crane or any tandem lift.
- There is no supervision by site management, or the site management displays a careless attitude. No lifting supervisor has been appointed for lifting operations.
- The crane has been wrongly selected to lift a load of an awkward shape, and its centre of load was not understood (an eccentric loading lift).
- The crane operator does not extend the outriggers as it is not perceived to be a potential hazard, particularly on soft ground causing subsidence or because of insufficient space.
- The crane operator is not aware of the upper limit angle or the lower limit angle of the mobile crane. These angles are designed to vary with the length of the lattice jib (or telescopic boom).
- The crane operator is not aware of the maximum wind speed the crane can operate or does not reduce the load when the allowable maximum wind speed is reached.
- The crane operator chooses to perform a telescopic lift at the front of the crane rather than reverse the crane to the rear.
- The crane operator lifts a load with a crane that is not fitted with an anemometer that detects the wind speed.

MOBILE CRANE ACCIDENT INVESTIGATION

A registered safety officer may be called in to assist with an investigation after a mobile crane accident. The following points may prove to be useful in the investigation. They can be used in conjunction with the information provided by the crane manufacturer with regard to the safety measures particular for that crane.

- Check that all the crane operations have been performed in accordance with the duties, instructions, and limitations specified in the manufacturer's duty chart and operating manual.
- Check all statutory certificates and reports.
- Weigh the load at the time of the accident, if possible.
- Note the conditions of the ground.
- Accurately establish the radii of the operation being performed at the time of the accident. Note the operating quadrants, such as rear to front or front to rear, as well as the position of the load. Measure all rope lengths, bridle attachments, and pendants. This information can be plotted on a sketch to determine the radius.
- Check the mechanics of the crane and any rope damage.
- Determine any structural failure, instability, ground sinkage, etc.
- Prepare a sketch of the position of the crane in relation to its surrounding at the time of the accident.
- Interview the crane operator, signalman, previous examiners, or any eye-witnesses to the accident. Assess the competency of the operator and members of the lifting team.
- Perform an aftermath check on the rated capacity indicator or load moment limiter.
- Invite outside experts to assist (e.g., the manufacturer or their agents), if in-house expertise is not available.

SUMMARY

This chapter has outlined the general configurations of mobile cranes, explained the roles of various stakeholders in crane operation, and detailed situations in which failures and accidents occur. To improve the safety of mobile crane operations, crane operators have to contribute by undergoing continual training, instructing, and supervising.

Hong Kong is an exceptional place for crane operation because of the limited space on many worksites. This means that certain practices are required here that may not be applicable elsewhere. For example, modern mobile crane manufacturers have designed a unique system which enables each individual crane support to be extended to an arbitrary length for the outriggers. The load moment limiter within the control system ensures that the crane can operate safely. This is in contrast to what is recommended in the Hong Kong Code of Practice, which indicates that all outriggers in mobile cranes should be fully extended during use. In practice, this may not be possible because of space limitations. Similarly, to address safety in facing wind conditions, anemometers can be mounted on the jib head section and on the bottom of the head section. The control system compares the two measurements and always displays the higher wind speed and provides a warning to the operator. Such a requirement is currently absent in the Hong Kong Code of Practice. Thus, in future revisions of the Hong Kong Code of Practice, it is suggested that modern mobile cranes should be mandated to have monitors designed inside the crane to calculate the maximum load capacity precisely for situations with limited space and conditions on the actual site. Another consideration for future revisions involves mobile crane disassembly. During this process, it is necessary to walk and work at a height on the mobile crane at the deck, which involves a foreseeable risk of falling. This highlights the need for a collective fall prevention arrangement on the crane using railings that can be easily erected as well as adequate handles for body contacts, retaining points for the secure positioning of ladders or stools for access and egress to the crane, and non-slipping walking paths on the crane. While the current Code of Practice does not include these measures, safety officers and construction worksite management and workers should keep them in mind as a way to pre-emptively avoid accidents.

The next chapter shifts to a type of equipment unique to Hong Kong: bamboo scaffolding.

FURTHER READING

British Standard Institution (2010) *Cranes—Mobile cranes BS EN 13000:2010.*

ISO 4306-1, Cranes—Vocabulary—Part 1: General.

ISO 7363, Cranes and lifting appliances—Technical characteristics and acceptance documents.

ISO 11629, Cranes—Measurement of the mass of a crane and its components.

ISO 13202, Cranes—Measurement of velocity and time parameters.

ISO 14518, Cranes—Requirements for test loads.

Labour Department, Hong Kong SAR Government (2017) *Code of practice for Safe Use of Mobile Cranes* (Second edition), Hong Kong Government Printer.

Occupational Safety and Health Council (2017) *Survey on Occupational Health of Mobile Crane Operators, Hong Kong.*

DISCUSSION QUESTIONS

1. List ten items you believe are critical for operating a modern mobile crane.
2. What competency would you recommend for a professional engineer assigned to carry out the examination and testing of a mobile crane?
3. Lifting operations such as a blind lift or high-rise lift involve a rigger, signalman, and crane operator. What communication failures must be avoided by this crane crew?
4. Similar to mobile cranes, lorry-mounted cranes also lack an appropriate Hong Kong Code of Practice for safe use. Lorry-mounted cranes are a hybrid between different brands of lifting items mounted onto different brands of lorry. These lifting items are mounted between the driving cabin and the lorry-tray or at the very end of the lorry, resulting in altered or undefined lifting geometry for the crane's operation. Monitors for this variation of outrigging cannot be retrofitted. What kind of safety features should be implemented? How will these features need to differ from those of standard mobile cranes?
5. Crew Resource Management (CRM) is a safety management technique used in the aviation industry that makes optimum use of all available resources (i.e., equipment, procedures, and people) to promote safety and enhance the efficiency and safety of flight operations, where human errors can have devastating effects. It focuses on interpersonal communication, leadership, and decision-making in the cockpit. Can this safety management approach be introduced to the training and education of crane drivers, riggers, signallers, lifting supervisors, and other co-workers so they could work together safely in mobile crane operations on worksites? What aspects would need to be specific for the construction industry?

"Bamboo Scaffolding—the most flexible, economical, and indispensable for builders"

– Dr Francis Y.S. So
Chairman of Wui Loong Scaffolding Works Limited (2009)

"Man can live without meat, but man cannot live without bamboo"

– A translated Chinese saying

10 Bamboo Scaffolding

INTRODUCTION

There is currently no judicial authority for the meaning of a "scaffold". However, the Construction Sites (Safety) Regulations (abbreviated CS(S)Rs) state:

> "Scaffold" means any temporarily provided structure on or from which persons perform work in connection with operations or works to which the CS(S)Rs apply, and any temporarily provided structure which enables persons to obtain access to or which enables materials to be taken to any place at which such work is performed, and includes any working platform, gangway, run, ladder, or step-ladder (other than an independent ladder or step-ladder which does not form part of such a structure) together with any guard-rail, toe-board, or other safeguards and all fixings, but does not include a lifting appliance or a structure used merely to support such an appliance or to support other plant or equipment.

This definition casts a wide meaning to include any temporary structure from which persons may perform work. In fact, such a generality seems to cover every possible temporary structure that may relate to structural steel works, such as I-beams, H-columns, U-shaped sheet piles used in constructing beams, columns, or struts. Such structural steel works are widely found in civil engineering and construction work. Such structures, though temporary, are designed by professional engineers and approved by independent checking engineers. Unfortunately, the Code of Practice (CoP) and guidelines issued under the law do not adequately reflect how they should be applied to structures that may (or may not) be classified as "scaffold" as defined above. The simple question is: are temporary structural steel works classified as "scaffolds" under the CS(S)Rs? Furthermore, how does this definition and the CoPs and guidelines apply to "scaffolds" of varying materials, such as bamboo or mixed metal-bamboo systems?

Bamboo scaffolding has been used in construction work by builders in Southern China for hundreds of years. Its use is considered both an art and a science. This chapter explains some general information about bamboo scaffolding as well as some structural considerations and safety requirements. Metal scaffolding and metal-bamboo matrix system scaffolding are also briefly outlined. The text goes on to explain the role of various operators in scaffolding procedures and describes various legal cases involving scaffolding and how the courts have defined and applied the law.

THE BASICS OF BAMBOO SCAFFOLDING

There are 70 genera and 1,200 species of bamboo in the world. Mao Jue (毛/茅竹, *Phyllostachys Pubescens*) and Kao Jue (篙竹, *Bambusa Pervariablilis*) are the most commonly used varieties for scaffolds on worksites.

In general, the percentage of lime and water determines the strength and rigidity of the bamboo. When the water content drops below 10%, the bamboo piece becomes dry and brittle, and cracks may appear. When this occurs, the bamboo is no longer safe for scaffolding purposes. In contrast, if the percentage of lime content in the bamboo is too high, the bamboo will become rigid and may be more prone to breaking. Fibre content also affects the bending and tensile strength of a piece of bamboo. Generally, a bamboo piece that is three to four years old has ~50–58% fibre content and ~1.5% lime content, which together present the optimal strength conditions. This period is, therefore, the best time to harvest for use. After cutting, the bamboo can be used safely for one year, or at most one and a half years. There is a Chinese saying about using bamboo pieces for construction purposes: "retain at 3, cut at 4 and never at 7". A guideline for the design and construction of bamboo scaffolding recommends that the effective diameter of Mao Jue should be no less than 75 mm with a wall thickness of 10 mm, while the effective diameter of Kao Jue should be no less than 40 mm. In Hong Kong, Mao Jue is the variety used for all standards and ledgers for the first lift of scaffolds.

The wide use of bamboo scaffolding on Hong Kong construction sites is based on its various advantages. For one, bamboo is incredibly strong and flexible. In fact, it was once used to create shelters during wartimes. Even if bombs exploded nearby, they often only damaged the scaffolding and not the structures or buildings they were protecting. Bamboo pieces can also be cut and modified based on the environment. Even on ground that is uneven, the level of the horizontal ledgers and working platform can be adjusted to suit the situation. It is also a material that is easy to repair and maintain. To take out and replace a broken piece of bamboo within a scaffold lattice is straightforward and requires little effort. Bamboo scaffolding has also been shown to maintain its structure even if the pull-push ties have been removed because the weight of the united scaffolding is diverted and shared by other ties. Metal scaffolding will collapse in similar situations, meaning bamboo is a safer alternative. Furthermore, bamboo is very light. The weight of a seven-metre piece is less than 9 kg, compared to 17 kg for a hollow metal tubing of the same length with a diameter of 48.6 mm and a wall thickness of 2.3 mm. The cost of a piece of bamboo is also about 15–20 times cheaper than the corresponding metal tubing, making it incredibly economical. The installation process for bamboo scaffolding is also five to six times faster than the corresponding installation of other scaffolding types, while dismantling bamboo can be completed about 12 times faster than other types of scaffolding. Since time is money, the sooner a building project can be completed, the lower the development costs (including any loan interest). When not in use, bamboo is easy to store and dispose of. This is a particularly important advantage in Hong Kong, where land space for equipment storage is scarce. Because they are organic, bamboo pieces can be either set on fire in a designated compound or left in a certain area to rot after they fulfil their lifetime of use.

While the advantages above explain why bamboo is often the scaffolding material of choice in Hong Kong, the material also comes with some disadvantages. For instance, bamboo will crack in low humidity, and strength will be reduced in high humidity. In Hong Kong, the humidity varies greatly depending on the season. Other weather hazards, including high winds or monsoons, also affect the structural strength of the bamboo, particularly when being used for scaffolds around high-rise buildings over 240 metres from the ground, which are common in Hong Kong's skyscraper-heavy environment. To overcome these issues, there are stringent safety measures that have been put in place to ensure bamboo scaffolds can be used safely.

STRUCTURAL SAFETY OF BAMBOO SCAFFOLDING

The following sections describe the general bamboo scaffold formation, tie-systems, and strip locking of the bamboo poles, as well as details concerning the erection and dismantling procedures. In addition to the integrity of the bamboo itself, these processes are particularly important in maintaining safety when using bamboo scaffolding. To further support the safe use of such scaffolding, there are various CoPs and guidance notes to consider.

Pole formation

Bamboo scaffolding generally utilises a double-row (layer) configuration erected around a building's façade. The outer vertical posts and inner vertical posts should be footed at ground level with vertical standards spaced evenly between. The inner layer, at about 150–300 mm from the building face, is known as the finishing layer. The outer layer will be constructed at about 700 mm from the inner layer, or approximately 1,000 mm from the building face. Working platforms should be erected between the inner and outer layers. Horizontally, it is the ledgers that join the posts. Transoms should be placed on top of parallel ledgers to form the support for working platforms. The vertical distance between two ledgers is typically about 750 mm. Diagonal bracings should be fixed at the external side of the scaffolding in an "X" conformation and are usually positioned at an angle between 60 degrees to 70 degrees. The outer posts should be tied back to the structure of the building by metallic put-logs, using 6 mm diameter mild steel wire. To prevent objects from falling while working on the scaffolding, contractors will typically put up nylon mesh nets to cover the whole bamboo scaffolding structure and projected fans consist of galvanized zinc sheets laid on them at the outer layer.

The connection ties should be placed about every three metres vertically and horizontally along the structures. There is flexibility in positioning in that there may be places where the ties cannot be inserted. At every tie position, a short length of bamboo with an effective diameter not less than 40 mm should be connected between the inner scaffold and the building facade to restrict any inward movement of the scaffolding. For existing reinforced concrete buildings, the tie-system should use Hilti (or equivalent) bolts fixed into the existing building structures with mild steel bolts 6 mm in diameter.

The tie-system

In reinforced concrete building construction, the bamboo scaffolding will be raised in advance of the building structure itself. The bamboo scaffolding structure is usually tied to the main building frame to secure structural stability (for an example of this, see Figure 10.1). There are two commonly used tie-systems. The first system uses anchor bolts to secure the scaffold to the building structure. The bolts used should be 10 mm in diameter with a safe working load of 2 kN. The second tie-system uses mild steel rods 6 mm in diameter embedded into the steel-reinforced structure of the permanent building façade and loop-tied to the bamboo poles. Both options can help to prevent the bamboo scaffolding from collapsing.

Strip locking

Polypropylene (PP) or polyethylene (PE) (co-polymer) strips (for tying purposes) replaced bamboo strips in the late 1970s. Such strips are made of plastic materials and are commonly referred to as "nylon"

FIGURE 10.1: Example tie-system

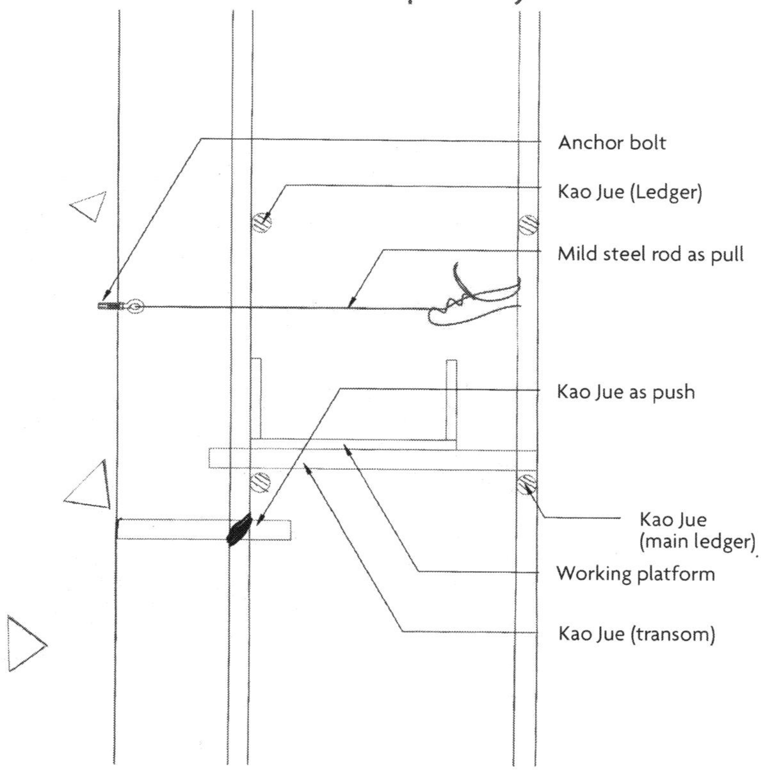

strips. Anti-UV and anti-aging materials are also added to the PP and PE strips during the extrusion process. A PP strip normally measures about 0.80 mm (thickness) by 6.0 mm (width) and is about two metres in length on average. Its tensile stress is about 210 Newtons per mm^2. Laboratory tests have confirmed that such plastic strips have a bearing capacity of multiple tonnes for six loops. Thus, these strips have the advantage of higher endurance to weather damage and less deterioration over time, making them more reliable. Indeed, the use of bamboo strips for fastening and connecting standards, ledgers, transoms, bracing, and ties is almost non-existent today. These "nylon" strips perform the function of a coupler (used to lock metal tubular scaffolding). The general tying rule for strip locking uses the cardinal principle of "three-pin five-strip" (三針五篾) (Figure 10.2).

FIGURE 10.2: The "three-pin five-strip" principle

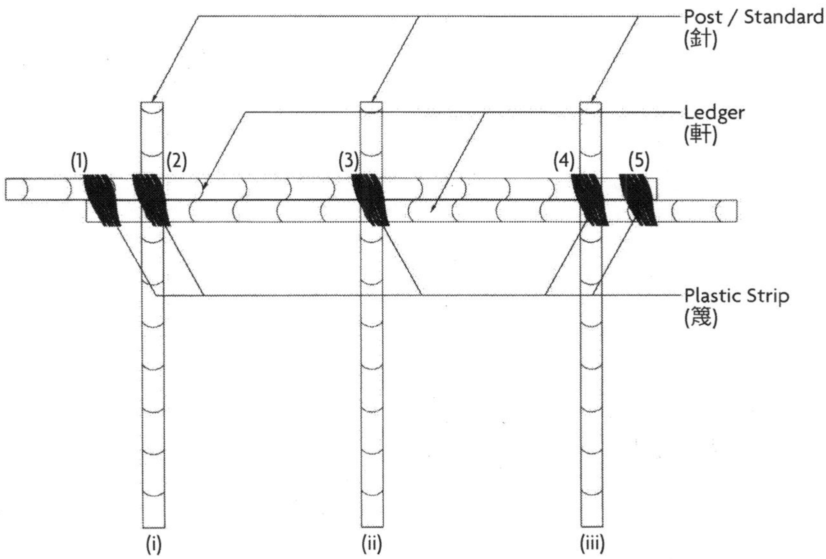

Scaffold erection

The most controversial safety issue concerns the erection of the first tier of bamboo scaffolding. The general process is shown in Figure 10.3. The bamboo scaffolders have to start the erection when there is practically no space for the provision and installation of independent lifelines or the use of fall arrestors. The only option is for the scaffolder to choke-hitch his lanyard to the bamboo cross-joints directly next to or lower than his body. This is a risk that bamboo scaffolders must be trained to handle. While being erected, the bamboo scaffolding itself provides access and egress points as it is tailored to the anthropometry of the scaffolders themselves. In fact, the spacing of the ledgers is typically equal to the inseam length of a scaffolder's leg. Although the erection process can be very dangerous, there are surprisingly very few cases of falls or accidents

FIGURE 10.3: The erection process for bamboo scaffolding

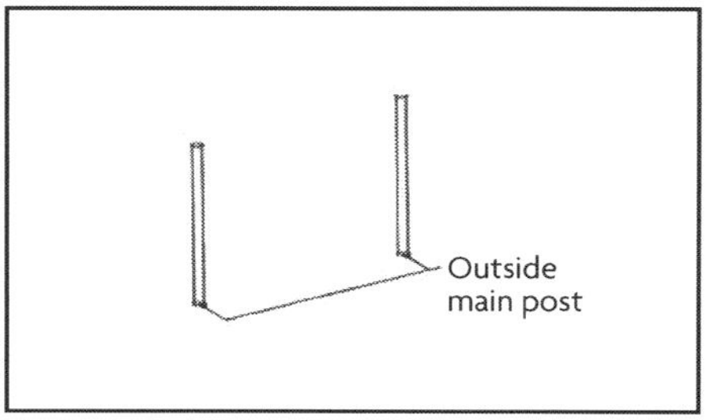

Step 1: Add external scaffold (SK–01)

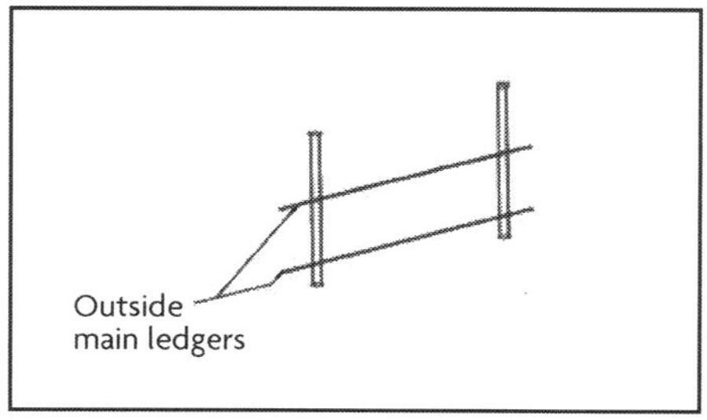

Step 2: Add main ledger (SK–02)

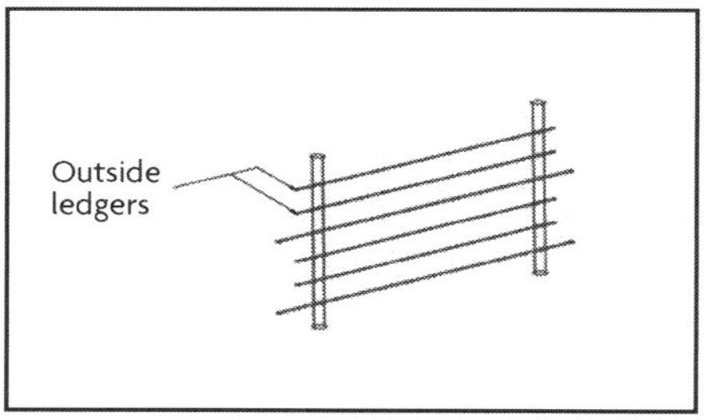

Step 3: Add outside ledger (SK–03)

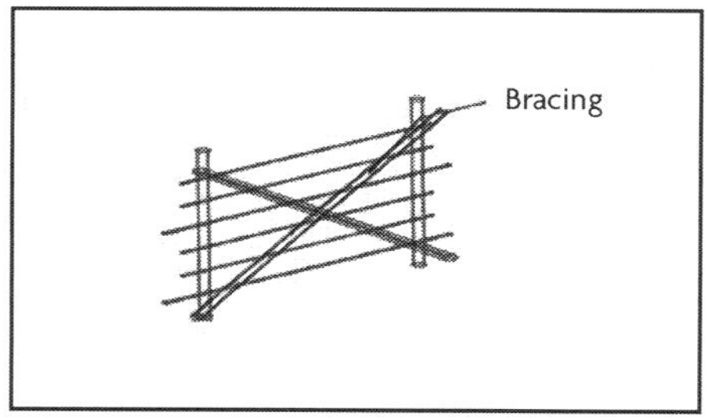

Step 4: Add bracing (SK–04)

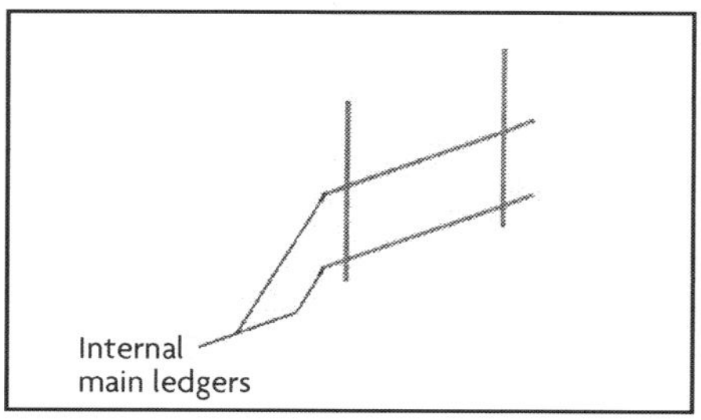

Step 5: Add internal scaffolding (SK–05)

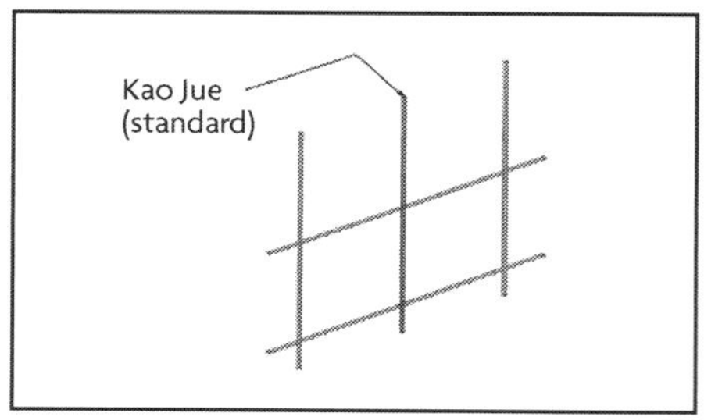

Step 6: Add standard internal (SK–06)

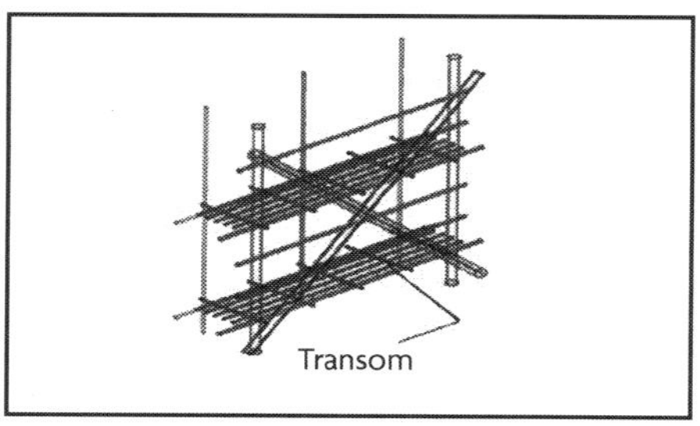

Step 7: Add transom (SK–07)

reported or recorded for first-tier bamboo scaffolders. Accident statistics show that their chance of falling is extremely low compared with workers of other trades.

Scaffold dismantling

When dismantling bamboo scaffolding, the sequence of removing or disassembling the tie-system built into the building or structure has to be carefully planned and executed, otherwise, the whole structure may collapse while the bamboo scaffolders are still secured to the scaffolding. They may endanger themselves if the sequence is not closely followed or if there is a misjudgement.

In general, bamboo scaffolding surrounding a structure or building will be dismantled by a team of several scaffolders. Depending on the size and height of the bamboo scaffolding, either two or three workers will be positioned at the upper-most level. Their tasks are to cut off the PP strips and remove the ties. If a two-member team is positioned in the upper-most level, the rest of the dismantling team will take a Y-formation (2.1.1... whereby the two members are located at the top, followed by a single member on each lower level). If a three-member team is positioned in the upper-most level, they will take a T-formation (3.2.1.1... whereby the three members are located at the top, followed by another two members on the level below, and then a single member on each lower level). The workers that are positioned in staggered formation in the rows below these upper-most workers are engaged to hand down or transfer downward the bamboo poles to the ground level or to a level where the poles can be stored and stacked temporarily. The number of workers positioned down below depends on the height of the bamboo scaffolding above the ground or above the storage floor. The dismantling team will follow the general procedure shown in Figure 10.4.

For a 24-storey building or more, a lifting system, such as a tripod installed at the roof level, may be used. Notably, the tripod is a lifting appliance and will need to be examined and tested under the Factories and Industrial Undertakings (Lifting Appliances and Lifting Gear) Regulations.

A checklist has been provided in Figure 10.5 to help perform a risk assessment and should form part of the safe system of work for dismantling bamboo scaffoldings.

FIGURE 10.4: The dismantling process for bamboo scaffolding

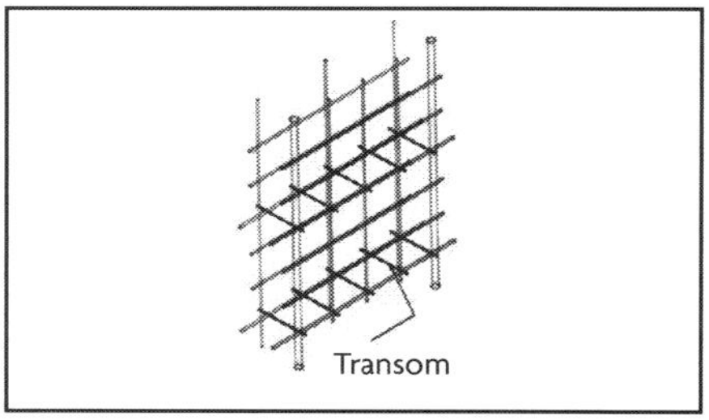

Step 1: Remove bracing (SK–01)

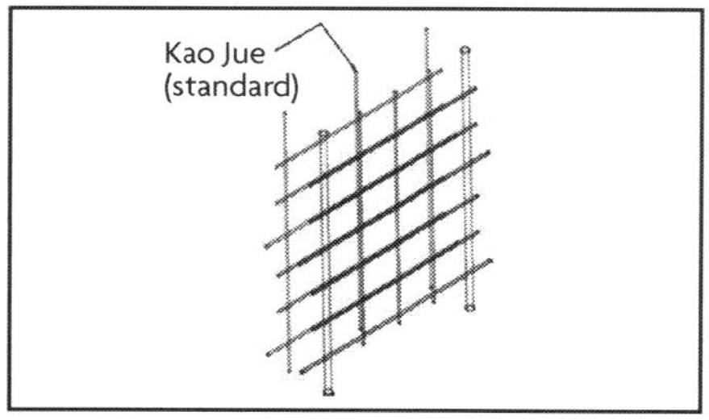

Step 2: Remove transom (SK–02)

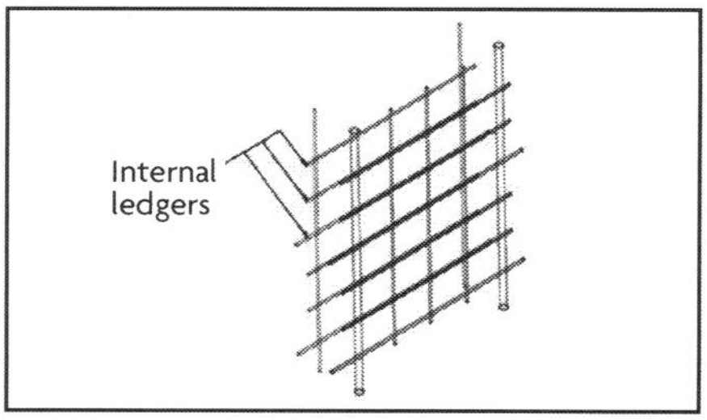

Step 3: Remove Kau Jue
(standard) (internal) (SK–03)

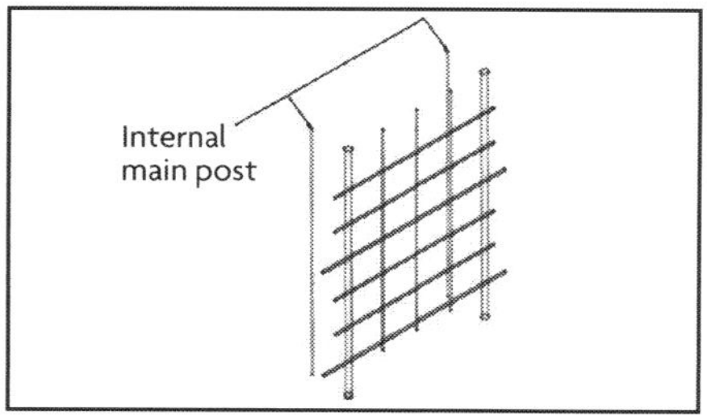

Step 4: Remove internal ledgers (SK–04)

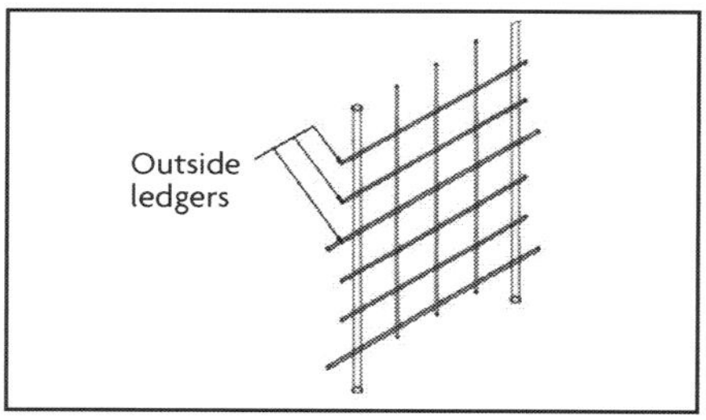

Step 5: Remove internal main post (SK–05)

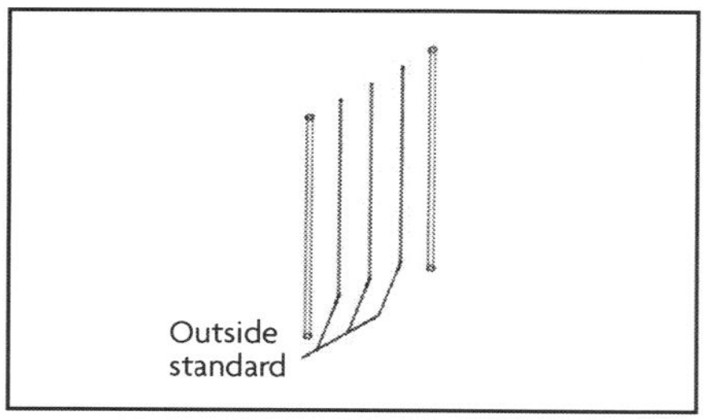

Step 6: Remove outside ledgers (SK–06)

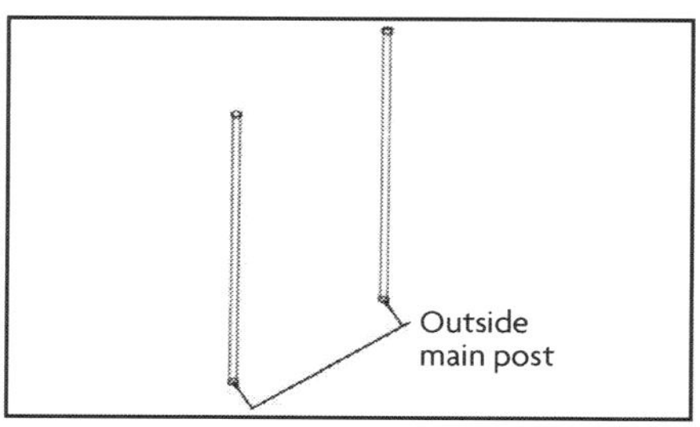

Step 7: Remove Kau Jue
(standard) (outside) (SK–07)

FIGURE 10.5: A safety checklist for dismantling bamboo scaffolds

Location of dismantling work: ____________________

Date & time of dismantling work: ____________________

Date & time of inspection: ____________________ Checked by: ____________________

Contact Tel. No.: ____________________ Signature: ____________________

Item No.	Description	Yes	No	N/A
1	Certified bamboo scaffolder(s) are appointed to supervise dismantling work			
2	Certified and fit bamboo scaffolders are engaged for dismantling work			
3	Bamboo scaffolds have been inspected and tied back in a secure and stable condition before the commencement of dismantling work and the sequence of tie removal has been thoroughly discussed			
4	Suitable personal protective equipment (including a safety helmet, safety belt/harness, fall arrestor, etc.) is provided and worn by every scaffolder			
5	Scaffolders are trained in the use of lanyards/harnesses/fall arrestors • Note any doubtful anchorage points • Only choke-hitching the lanyard to bamboo-pole joints with adequate strength is used, preferably 2×2 or 2×1 or 1×2 joints (if independent lifelines cannot be comfortably reached)			
6	Anchorages and independent lifelines are provided, including the following points: • Installation at intervals not exceeding five metres • Independent lifelines are suspended by the anchorages from the roof down to the ground level • Competent workers are employed for securing the independent lifelines onto the anchorages • The anchorages and independent lifelines are confirmed to be in good working order and have been certified by a Registered Professional Engineer			
7	The certification of the "lifting appliances and lifting gear" has been concluded, including completing the "weekly inspection form"			
8	The working area below is fenced off with warning signs displayed for the prohibition of unauthorized entry			
9	Throwing bamboo poles/materials from height is strictly prohibited. The bamboo poles/materials must be properly and safely lowered by lifting appliances or conveyed manually down to the ground level			
10	Others			

Codes of Practice and related Guidance Notes

The Buildings Department in Hong Kong has issued various safety codes and guidelines intended to keep the use of bamboo scaffolding safe. These include:

- a Code of Practice for Bamboo Scaffolding Safety;
- a Guideline on the Design and Construction of Bamboo Scaffolds; and
- a Code of Practice for Site Supervision.

A CoP for bamboo scaffolding safety was published by the Commissioner for Labour under section 7A of the Factories and Industrial Undertakings Ordinance (FIUO), Chapter 59. The CoP was published in 1995, 2001, 2009, and 2014, and the existing fourth edition was published in September 2017. The Guidelines on Planking Arrangement for Providing Platforms on Bamboo Scaffolds, published by the Hong Kong Construction Industry Council in September 2017, are in parallel with the CoP published by the Labour Department. First and foremost, in section 4.4.1(c) of the CoP, it is stated that the latest Guidelines on Planking Arrangement for Providing Working Platforms on Bamboo Scaffolds issued by the Construction Industry Council should be observed in fulfilling the safety responsibilities of laying planks as working platforms on bamboo scaffolds so as to ensure safety on the worksite. The CoP also recommends that bamboo poles used for scaffolding should be harvested at three years old. However, the bamboo poles used in Hong Kong are sometimes less than three years, highlighting a discrepancy between safety measures and common practices. The CoP also does not address the reliability and effectiveness of PE or PP strips in terms of their potential creep and fatigue behaviour.

Notably, the CoP indicates that bamboo scaffolding should not be used for anchoring safety belts, even temporarily. The Guidance Notes on Classification and Use of Safety Belts and their Anchorage Systems also suggest avoiding anchoring the lanyard of a safety belt to bamboo scaffolding. This recommendation is arguable amongst safety practitioners, with some being for and some against. Such differences between the opinions of safety experts regarding the safe anchorage of safety belts to bamboo scaffolding were clearly demonstrated in a related court case (see *The Queen v Otis Elevator Co. (H.K.) Ltd* (MA 931/1985) outlined in a later section). The appeal case was allowed as the Court could not rule for or against. As this is a significant issue and one that is frequently encountered by first-tier bamboo scaffolders as well as by other workers using the scaffolding, the following section is devoted to further exploration and discussion.

A question of temporary safe anchorage

When bamboo scaffolding is being erected or used, circumstances may be that (at least at that moment) there are no places for workers on the scaffolding to anchor to an independent lifeline. Under such special circumstances, should the bamboo scaffolding itself be used as a temporary safety anchorage? To answer this question, there are other sub-questions that must be considered.

- Can the lanyard of the safety belt or harness be correctly anchored to the bamboo scaffolding?
- Should the lanyard be "choke-hitched" around the bamboo scaffolding?
- Are there configurations of the scaffolding joints (intersections) present that are appropriate for lanyard attachment or "choke-hitching"?

From the above, the main considerations are the joints in the scaffolding and the means of connection using the lanyard of the safety belt or harness. The joints can have a configuration of 1+1, 1+2 (2+1) (as shown in Figure 10.6), or 2+2. These joints can have a combination of bamboo standard, ledger, or transom.

The author is of the view that choke-hitching on bamboo scaffolds may not be the ideal safe practice, but it is, sometimes, under special circumstances, possible to choke-hitch bamboo joints safely. Thus, it is not possible to disregard this option, which may be the only practical choice in a given situation.

To check the safety of lanyards choke-hitched to bamboo scaffolding, a basic experiment can be conducted. In the following example, two configurations of joints were tested. One was a 1+1 bamboo-pole joint,

FIGURE 10.6: The 1+1 and 1+2 joint configurations

and the other was a 1+2 bamboo-pole joint. The bamboo poles used in the experiment were about 40–45 mm in diameter and had been in use on various construction sites for about six to nine months. The ties were standards ties used for bamboo poles, using five loops of PP strips, with a total of ten loops being formed. The PP strips were tested with a tensile stress of about 210 Newton per mm^2. The safety lanyards were then choke-hitched to the bamboo poles. A dummy weight of 76 kg was chosen to fall vertically for a distance of two metres—a falling distance reflecting that allowed by the lanyard of a full-body harness normally used by scaffolders. The set-up for this experiment is shown in Figure 10.7. Notably, this experiment did not test other types of anchorage lifelines or repeat the testing to check for statistical reliability. It does, however, highlight a system that should be employed to test such anchorages on bamboo scaffolding.

The results of the experiment show that (a) the "drop test" did not cause any visual damage to the joint of the bamboo poles for either configuration; (b) the joints could indeed serve as a secure anchorage point for such a lanyard under conditions similar to those in the experiment;

FIGURE 10.7: Images showing a "drop test" on a 1+1 joint

and (c) the statement that bamboo scaffolding "should not be used for anchorages purposes" (as stated in Code 6.2.15 of the Code of Practice for Bamboo Scaffolding Safety) is far too broad a statement and lacks experimental verification. Thus, while such an anchorage may not be the first choice, this test indicates that there is no experimental evidence that the joints of a bamboo scaffold should not be used as a temporary safe anchorage point for choke-hitching lanyards. Whether all the joints are suitable for such anchoring of independent lifelines is subject to other experiments, and "drop tests" should be conducted. In fact, the effectiveness of an anchorage depends on the conditions of the bamboo scaffoldings in terms of its age and size, as well as the wholesomeness of the PP or PE strips. In addition, the body weights of the scaffolder(s) or worker(s) need to be considered. Taken together, the CoP should be reviewed after more research is conducted into the structural stability and reliability of bamboo scaffolding as a temporary anchorage point. Such studies should be conducted by various stakeholders, including academics, safety practitioners, engineers, and bamboo scaffolding companies.

There are also various other corrections and additions that should be made to the CoP to ensure accuracy and stress the safety requirements for using bamboo scaffolding on a worksite. For instance, Figure 4 of the CoP should be redrawn as it currently (and incorrectly) shows steel wires connected to the inner row (layer) of bamboo scaffolding, which is not a current practice in the construction industry. Structurally, they should connect to the outer row (layer). Moreover, the CoP should explicitly prohibit alterations to the bamboo scaffolding by workers of other trades for their own convenience, such as cutting the 6 mm diameter tying steel rods during plastering work or for the convenient transport of sanitary pipes under installation. Such actions disregard safety and should be penalised.

METAL SCAFFOLDING

In addition to bamboo, metal is also a medium used for scaffolding, and there are a number of proprietary systems using metal scaffolding to construct working platforms for building and construction activities. In the Hong Kong SAR, a CoP for the Safe Use of Metal Scaffolding has been published by the Labour Department. However, metal scaffolding has its limitations, particularly with regard to the space available for its installation, which must be considered before use. Furthermore, the cost of using metal scaffolding (even that without working platforms) in terms of materials, labour, and transportation is twice that for bamboo scaffolding. When working platforms are required, the installation cost can be three times that for bamboo scaffolds.

METAL-BAMBOO MATRIX SYSTEM SCAFFOLDING

In order to synergise the advantages of bamboo scaffolding and metal scaffolding, a new method was pioneered in Hong Kong around 1998/2000. This method, first explained by So (2009), is geared specifically towards scaffolding with working platforms during the construction of high-rise residential buildings. Metal-bamboo matrix system scaffolding (MBMSS) combines the advantages of both bamboo scaffolding and metal scaffolding while minimising their disadvantages. MBMSS can rise to a height of 240 to 300 metres above ground level and provide safe and proper working platforms at various heights. As mentioned previously, bamboo scaffolding generates inadequate structural strength at such great heights, particularly during high wind conditions. Metal scaffolding, on the other hand, can resist high winds at this height, but its heavy weight and inflexibility present a challenge for its handling by scaffolders. Thus, the combination of the two types of scaffolding allows for a stable and easy-to-handle structure to be built. In essence, the substitution of steel tubes for bamboo pieces as the load-bearing members in the scaffold system ensures that the stability of the scaffold is not affected as much by the surrounding environment. Table 10.1 highlights how MBMSS can accommodate certain challenges.

In addition to the advantages over metal and bamboo materials when used alone, MBMSS needs to be constructed in a way that addresses the functional requirements on the worksite, load requirements, safety requirements, structural elements, anchorage mechanisms, support mechanisms, and accessories. A general double-row layering of MBMSS is shown in Figure 10.8. The inner row (layer) is similar in design and arrangement to the outer layer.

TABLE 10.1: Comparison of different scaffolding systems

	Metal scaffolding	MBMSS	Bamboo scaffolding
Load capacity	0.75 kPa	0.75 kPa	0.75 kPa
Handling weight	1.4	1	0.5
Wind resistance	all heights	all heights	below about 240 metres

FIGURE 10.8: A double layer arrangement of metal-bamboo matrix system scaffolding (MBMSS)

(adopted from Wui Loong Scaffolding Works Limited)

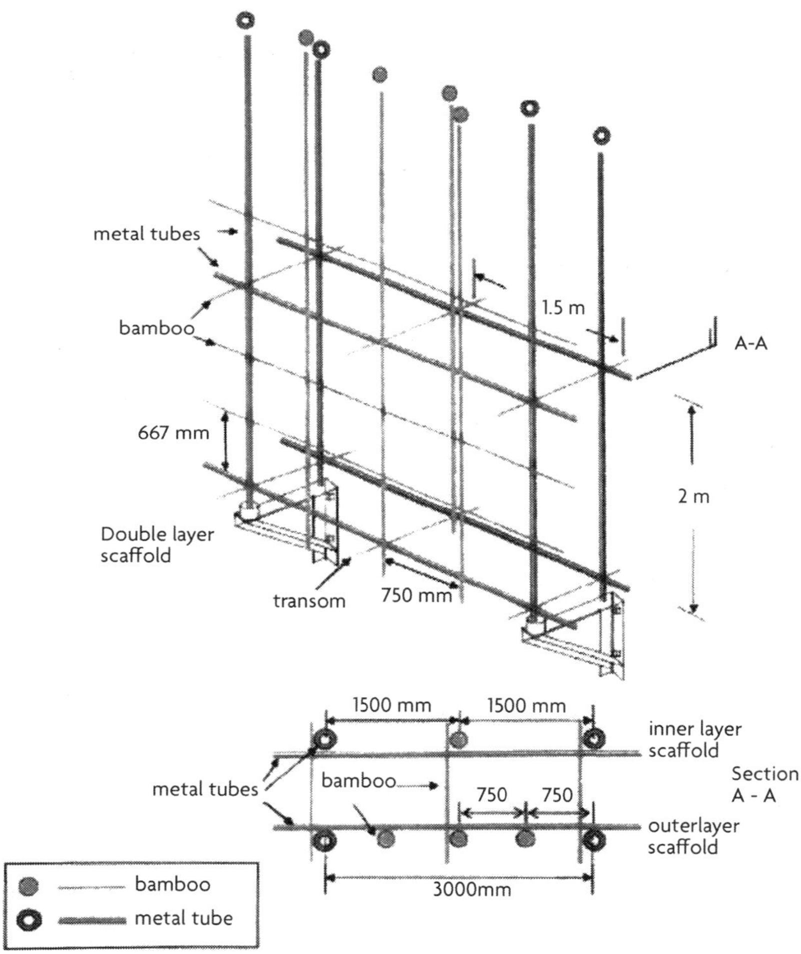

The vertical metal poles used in MBMSS have to be about 50 mm in diameter and 2.5 mm in tube thickness. The two inner tubes will be connected to each other by a metal tube ledger. The connection between the metal poles and tubes is achieved by using metal couplers, each of which can bear a loading force of 2 kN. The inner layer of MBMSS will be connected to the external layer by two pieces of bamboo transom of similar diameter and thickness at the two ends of the scaffold. The length of the transom will depend on the required width of the internal passageway for workers to walk and work on.

To maintain stability as a temporary working platform at great heights, a standardised anchorage system must be developed and used. An L-shape put-log anchorage should be affixed from the vertical metal poles at both ends to the concrete wall at minimum intervals of seven metres (apart) by four metres (high). Such an anchorage arrangement is shown in Figure 10.9.

As mentioned previously, MBMSS can be erected up to a height of 240–300 metres from ground level, which is suitable for high-rise buildings commonly demanded in Hong Kong. The scaffolding can either be erected from the ground level or may be positioned on a triangular steel bracket at an elevated level (normally about two metres above ground, thus avoiding excessive settlement of unconsolidated ground soil). Presently, there is no practical code or documented notes related to the design of MBMSS for its construction and safe use which has been found to be acceptable by all stakeholders.

BAMBOO SCAFFOLDERS VERSUS WORKERS ON SCAFFOLDING

When it comes to scaffolding work, any discussion of "stakeholders" must include the two categories of workers associated with bamboo scaffoldings: those who erect, alter, or dismantle bamboo scaffoldings; and those who have to work on or use bamboo scaffolding as their working platform.

Scaffolders

Bamboo scaffolders can be further distinguished into two groups: those who erect and alter the scaffolding, and those who dismantle the

FIGURE 10.9: The MBMSS anchorage arrangement

scaffolding. Interestingly, bamboo scaffolding dismantlers receive higher daily pay than those who erect and install them.

The tools used by bamboo scaffolders are simple and include hand-saws for cutting bamboo poles, hand-sickle knives for cutting PP strips, and snipers for cutting metal wires. Scaffolders often make use of their leg inseam lengths and their hands' "zone of convenient reach" to make measurements during scaffold erection. Measurement rulers or tapes are, therefore, not needed.

Within the groups of scaffolders erecting the bamboo structures and those who dismantle them, there are two classes of scaffolders categorised in the safety laws. These are "trained workers" and "competent persons". Only trained workers are allowed to carry out the erection, alteration, and dismantling of bamboo scaffolds under the immediate supervision of competent persons. The following sections list the requirements and responsibilities for each of these groups.

Trained workers

Under the Hong Kong safety law, a bamboo scaffolder should:

- be a "trained worker" defined under the CoP issued by the Labour Department.
- hold a valid Mandatory Basic Safety Training Certificate.

- have attended and successfully completed training courses organised by the Construction Industry Council. The courses include a basic craft course, short course, refresher course, and tailor-made course. The learning process can be a mixture of art and sensation. The skills necessary for tying the "nylon" strips (bamboo "skin" or "sheath" in the past) with the bamboo pieces are essential. The rigidity and strength of the scaffold rely heavily on whether or not the ties are tight enough. Such skills must therefore be mastered in the training course. Practical trade tests will be conducted for erecting and dismantling a set of double-row scaffolding.
- not be working under the influence of drugs or alcohol.
- be able to engage a fall protection system during their work.
- be able to wear personal protective equipment, such as a safety helmet, safety belt, safety harness, and fall arrestor.
- check the wholesomeness of the independent lifeline prior to work.
- evaluate the effectiveness of the free-fall arrestor prior to work.
- check the lifeline securely anchored with at least four knots.
- ensure the lifeline is not in contact with any sharp objects before commencing work.
- report defects if found and stop work in case of doubt.
- stop unsafe acts and report these to his senior competent person.

Competent persons

A "competent person" is interpreted as a person:

- who has satisfactorily completed their formal training in bamboo scaffolding work, such as an apprenticeship in the trade under section 28 of the Apprenticeship Ordinance, Cap. 47, or one-year full-time basic craft course on construction scaffolding work offered by the Construction Industry Council Training Academy (CICTA), or other similar bamboo scaffolding training courses or programmes; or has satisfactorily passed the trade test for bamboo scaffolder of the CICTA.
- who possesses 10 years of experience or more in bamboo scaffolding work (inclusive of experience under the formal training period).

- who has the ability to read and understand the scaffolding plans, design drawings, specifications, and method statement of the scaffolding work in order to competently supervise the installation and dismantling of the scaffolding and certify that the scaffolding is in safe working order. They should also be capable of identifying existing and predictable hazards in their surroundings or working conditions that are unsanitary or hazardous to employees.
- who has been appointed in writing and has authorisation to take prompt corrective measures to eliminate the existing and predictable hazards mentioned above.
- who is authorised to sign the Form 5 prescribed under the CS(S)Rs. A Form 5 is a statutory form indicating the bamboo scaffolding is in safe order for workers to perform their required work.

Those working on a scaffold

The latter category of workers that may operate on bamboo scaffolding include workers of other trades, such as plasterers, painters, mosaic tile workers, or those with a need to use bamboo scaffoldings as their working platforms but are not scaffolders. The majority of bamboo scaffolding accidents involve these workers.

ACCIDENTS AND THE COURTS

Past studies of accidents, including fatalities, associated with bamboo scaffolds found that most of the accidents occurred in single-row (layer) bamboo scaffolds. The major failure of single-row (layer) bamboo scaffolds was caused by either sub-standard working platforms or the lack of space for working platforms. The lack of working platforms on single-row scaffolds is not altogether surprising as it is difficult to provide such spaces when there is no second scaffold to attach to, meaning workers have to ride or stand on the scaffold ledgers to carry out their work. Because of the high risk of accidents on such scaffolds, the courts ruled against the use of single-row bamboo scaffolding (see *The Queen v Associated Coating*

Limited (MA 864/1990) described below). The majority of accidents and failures of double-row (layer) bamboo scaffolds are also related to sub-standard working platforms. As working platforms create such high-risk conditions, bamboo scaffolding companies and workers should refer to and follow the Guidelines on Planking Arrangement for Providing Working Platforms on Bamboo Scaffolds, version 2, published by the Construction Industry Council in September 2017.

One of the key contributing factors in all these accidents—for single- and double-row bamboo scaffolds—was the sudden breakage of the vertical bamboo poles and misjudgements concerning the strength limitations of the bamboo scaffolds. One notable example is the total collapse of a 17-storey double-row bamboo scaffold that was installed for hotel maintenance and repair work carried out inside a light well. The area of the light well was measured to be about 50 metres by 25 metres. The accident occurred on 9 December 2002 and resulted in one fatality and 16 injuries. At the time of the collapse, there were 36 workers (non-scaffolders) carrying out different activities on the bamboo scaffolds. Contributing factors for the collapse might include that the hotel was still in business and that the working platforms were paved with carpets to reduce noise nuisance caused to hotel residents. The time for the work was also limited.

Other accidents involving bamboo scaffolding occur during typhoon season. Typhoons hitting Hong Kong tend to have extreme wind conditions, heavy rains, and severe flooding in low-lying areas. Thus, it is essential that precautionary measures be taken to avoid accidents. For example, the plastic sheeting used to cover bamboo scaffolding can be removed when a tropical cyclone warning signal or a strong monsoon signal is announced. Moreover, the height above the top-most floor or any structure should not be over-extended, and sufficient ties of adequate strength should be provided to secure the cantilever portion at the top-most floors.

While measures can be taken to prevent issues, accidents will naturally happen, sometimes at no fault to anyone involved. However, in some situations, the courts have been relied upon to determine who is at fault and how to avoid such accidents in future. The following cases represent the current understanding of such situations. Safety officers should be familiar with these to ensure safety on worksites.

The Queen v Otis Elevator Co. (H.K.) Ltd (MA 931/1985)

As mentioned above, this case deals with the use of temporary anchorage points on bamboo scaffolding. Following an accident, charges were filed based on regulation 38Q(3) of the CS(S)Rs, whereby the appellant failed to provide suitable and sufficient anchorages and suitable fittings for safety belts. The prosecution's case was simply that the bamboo scaffolding cage, erected inside the lift shaft, was not a safe anchorage for the safety belts worn by those working therein. During the proceedings, safety experts were called for both the prosecution and defence and provided conflicting views about the safety of temporary anchorages on bamboo scaffolding. The Court allowed the appeal as no effort was made to resolve the conflict between these two experts. The Court finally held that when using safety belts in connection with bamboo scaffolding, a satisfactory anchorage and satisfactory fittings must be provided. (Note: Regulation 38Q(3) was later replaced by the current existing regulation 38H(3) of the CS(S)Rs.)

The Queen v Associated Coatings Limited (MA 864/1990)

Following an accident on a single-row bamboo scaffold involving workers painting the external wall of a building, the use of such single-row bamboo scaffolding was ruled out by the Court. The Court accepted the opinion of a safety expert that bamboo scaffolding could not be used as a working place for such work. Single-row bamboo scaffolding is now considered insufficient and unsuitable for standing or riding by workers (non-scaffolders).

The Queen v Hsin Chong Construction (Asia) Limited (MA 708/1993)

Similar to the case above, in this case, the Court (having considered the opinion of the prosecution's safety expert), held that caulking cannot be safely done from a single row of bamboo scaffolding. In this case, there was a safety harness provided to the worker doing the caulking work, and there was an independent lifeline installed. However, this was not deemed as safe working conditions. In contrast, other courts have accepted the excuse of not anchoring a safety belt while riding on the top-most level of the bamboo scaffold as there is no practical place or space for anchoring or looping one's lanyards.

Ta Xuong v The Incorporated Owners of Sun Hing Building (HCPI 496/1995)

This case involved a 37-year-old worker who used bamboo scaffolding erected outside of a building to climb out of a window to investigate a leak. The scaffolding collapsed, and the worker fell and suffered bodily injuries, leaving him a quadriplegic. The High Court delivered a judgment for the worker for HK$25 million in compensation. This case demonstrates the financial consequence caused by unsafe bamboo scaffolding. Furthermore, this and other cases have had a significant impact on the insurance premiums of workers working on bamboo scaffolding.

Secretary for Justice v Hong Dau Construction Company Limited (FAMC No. 7 of 2019) and *Secretary for Justice v Expand Scaffolding Limited* (FAMC No. 8 of 2019)

As these cases refer to the same accident, they will be discussed together. Hong Dau, the first appellant, was the contractor responsible for the scaffold, while Expand, the second appellant, was the contractor who had direct control over the erection of the scaffold. At the time of the accident, two bamboo scaffolders were working together to erect bamboo scaffolding alongside an external wall of a carpark building for maintenance work. One scaffolder, while attempting to return from the external wall to the interior of the building, fell approximately 10.9 metres from the third-floor level to the ground level. He died as a result. Charges were brought against the appellants based on regulation 38E of the CS(S)Rs, whereby no scaffolds can be "erected on the site or substantially added to, altered, or dismantled except by workmen who are: (a) adequately trained and possess adequate experience of such work; and (b) under the immediate supervision of a competent person."

The issue in these two cases was the term "supervision". When there are two certified scaffolders working together in parallel and as a team—a common trade practice—is it acceptable by law that one of them is considered to be supervising the other? During the case, the Magistrate posed two questions:

> "(a) Did I err in the holding that under regulation 38E, workmen can be under the immediate supervision of a competent person who is engaged in the erection of scaffold?
> (b) If the answer to (a) is 'No', were my findings that there were reasonable doubts that each of them [Mr Kong and the deceased] was under the immediate supervision of the other perverse?"

In the High Court, the Judge answered the first question "Yes". Although the second question only arose if he had answered the first question "No", the Judge nevertheless dealt with the second question, also answering it "Yes".

These judgments by the Magistrate and the High Court thus allowed these two cases to advance to the Court of Final Appeal for a ruling. The ruling by the Court of Final Appeal was that the supervision referred to in regulation 38E of CS(S)Rs involves both the safe condition of the scaffold and the safety of the scaffolders. These interests are inextricably linked, and such supervision is not confined to the time when scaffolders are actually moving or perched on a scaffold but extends to when they are climbing on or off a scaffold—situations that may also be hazardous, as this accident clearly and tragically demonstrates. The Court of Final Appeal held that supervision in scaffolding work has to be "one-on-one". The ruling casts additional interpretation of "supervision" as stated in section 6A of the FIUO. (Such an interpretation of the regulation was also made in the judgment of *HKSAR v Modern Terminal Limited* (HCMA 680/2016), described in Chapter 5, which involved the operation of a forklift truck in a container terminal.) The ruling of this case should also be considered to apply to scaffolders working on metal scaffolding as well as to scaffolders not actually doing scaffolding-specific work at the time.

One impracticality and caveat to this ruling may occur when multiple scaffolders are working at heights varying from 15- to 20-stories from the ground level. During this situation, how would one scaffolder stationed on the ground level (or at any level) be able to supervise the work? Thus, the "one-on-one" rule on a team of bamboo scaffolders may not be applicable in large-scale bamboo scaffolding work. However, in practice, bamboo scaffolders should be trained to coordinate amongst themselves and work in parallel. Trained bamboo scaffolders have skills in working on the bamboo poles, including where to stand safely and how to secure themselves using their feet and ankles. Each scaffolding team member is trained to work in tandem with the others and at the same speed. Thus, while the "one-on-one" ruling in these cases must be considered, the practical working relationships within a team of scaffolders are at the heart of maintaining safe working conditions.

SUMMARY

Bamboo scaffolding can be used to provide temporary working platforms for short duration building maintenance work, renovating building facade work, sign-board installation work, external sewage pipe repair work, etc. The efficient and practical use of bamboo scaffolding will likely continue in the Hong Kong SAR for the foreseeable future. Indeed, the total replacement of bamboo scaffolding with metal scaffolding is unlikely, until perhaps there is another material discovered that has all the advantages of bamboo and eliminates all its disadvantages. In the meantime, MBMSS seems to be the most reasonable emerging alternative for high-rise building construction, particularly that exceeding 200 metres in height. However, while the future of bamboo scaffolding usage in Hong Kong and elsewhere appears to be secure, there is a significant need to carry out studies and research to establish applicable safety laws that are supported by scientific and technical data. These studies should include assessing the:

- bamboo species with ideal structural integrity and longevity;
- application of biotechnology to identify such species;
- use and limitations of bamboo frames or joints as safe anchorages for lanyards;

- reliability of PP or PE as joints couplers;
- structural strength of bamboo poles, including their depreciation caused by inclement weather such as rain or sunshine;
- legal requirements and processes for the safe replacement and inspection of bamboo scaffolding materials;
- effects of wind on the stability of bamboo scaffoldings and the precautions that can be taken to avoid collapse before and after a typhoon;
- size and stability of bamboo scaffolding platforms for working or storage purposes; and
- loading, static or dynamic, limitations of bamboo scaffolds.

Over the years, critics of bamboo scaffolds have advocated for discontinuing and banning their use, insisting that they are comparatively not safe. However, there are safety considerations for all types of scaffolding. Indeed, if the bamboo scaffolding materials have suitable botanical characteristics (e.g., proper age, flexibility, etc.), are properly installed, are suitably maintained, and comply with the approved CoP issued by the Labour Department or equivalent good practices, then such bamboo scaffolding can be considered to be a safe place to conduct construction work.

This concludes the section on examples of common construction safety situations in Hong Kong. The next section shifts to a more detailed view of safety practitioner assessment tools, starting with accident economics.

FURTHER READING

Chang, C.C., and Yu, T.X. (2002) *An Engineering Study for Improving Safety and Reliability of Bamboo Scaffoldings (Final Report) Submitted to the Occupational Safety and Health Council 14 June 2002.*

Hong Kong Occupational Safety and Health Council (2017) *Study on the Redesign of the I-shape Metal Bracket for Truss-out Bamboo Scaffoldings.*

Labour Department, Hong Kong SAR Government (2017) *Code of Practice for Bamboo Scaffolding Safety* (Fourth edition), Hong Kong Government printer.

Lee, H.K. (2002) *Bamboo Scaffolds—Past, Present and Future from a Safety Practitioner's View Proceedings of International Seminar on Bamboo Scaffolds in Building Construction*, INBAR, 101-104.

Wong, F.K.W. (April 1998) *Bamboo Scaffolding: Safety Management for the Building Industry in Hong Kong.*

DISCUSSION QUESTIONS

1. Compare and contrast the safe use of metal and bamboo scaffoldings.
2. What improvements would you recommend in the use of bamboo scaffolding to provide safe working platforms?
3. Read and discuss the Guidelines on Planking Arrangement for Providing Working Platforms on Bamboo Scaffolds, version 2, 2017, published by the Construction Industry Council.

PART IV

PRACTITIONER ASSESSMENT TOOLS

LEARNING OBJECTIVES

Part IV provides guidance for carrying out accident costing and safety audits. To evaluate the economic costs of accidents and incidents, two models are described, one simple and one advanced. Further, two safety auditing schemes are furnished to assess a company's safety management system. Upon completion of Part IV, one should be able to:

1. Cost a workplace accident or incident in financial terms;
2. Determine the optimal investment in safety, health, and environmental matters for a specific construction project;
3. Understand the Factories and Industrial Undertakings (Safety Management) Regulation and the applicable elements;
4. Choose an effective safety audit scheme for a construction company or project;
5. Assess and engage value-added safety auditors.

To ensure safe practices are being applied on a construction worksite, it is necessary to perform such assessments regularly. Understanding the financial burden of accidents can also help to encourage management to take a proactive view of safety. Ultimately, safety should be a top priority for all stakeholders.

"The first duty of business is to survive and the guidance principle of business economics is not the maximization of profit — it is the avoidance of loss"

– Peter Drucker (1910–2005)

"The Law of Diminishing Return operates in the health and safety field as it does elsewhere"

– James D.G. Hammer, CB
Deputy Director-General,
United Kingdom Health and Safety Executive (1989)

11 Accident Economics

INTRODUCTION

In a 1993 study, the United Kingdom Health and Safety Executive (UKHSE) indicated that accidents cost up to 8.5% of the contract price for construction projects. Thus, when accidents occur, it is essential to understand their full effects and if or how such costs can be justified.

This chapter shares two practical accident costing schemes developed in Hong Kong. Both schemes are tailor-made and are practical for construction companies that are conscious of accident economics and costs. The first scheme, published by H.K. Lee (1991) (the same author as the present book), was developed from overseas studies of historical cost models and focuses on the relevant costing items applicable to the Hong Kong construction industry. A real-life accident costing example is provided using this scheme. The second scheme was extensively researched and developed by Tang et al. (1997) and is also specific to the Hong Kong construction industry. This scheme is refined and sophisticated, and uses cost optimisation techniques. It is an advanced model for companies that primarily consider accident economics in a financial sense. The final section explains why accident economics matter and how the costs of an accident are related to safety performance.

ACCIDENT ECONOMICS: A COST-BENEFIT APPROACH

Historically, there have been a number of studies on accident costing in other countries. Some of these are highlighted in Table 11.1. The following subsections focus on some general considerations for safety practitioners to understand with regard to accident cost analysis in the construction industry and then explain the details of the two studies conducted in Hong Kong.

General accident considerations

These two costing schemes described in the next sections are incredibly useful when assessing the financial burden of an accident. There are also some general points that must be considered. These considerations will affect the costs in each category of both schemes.

1. The definition of "accident" is important. Use one that is suitable for and acceptable to the company or organisation. This will help identify what situations should be costed and how they should be described. A suggested definition is that defined under the Employees' Compensation Ordinance, Chapter 282, whereby an accident occurs when an employee is off duty for more than three days when injured or fatally wounded at work. If this definition is used, situations involving property and material damage would not require a costing exercise.
2. Depending on the insurance policy of the main contractor, any accident incurred by a sub-contractor should be costed and assessed. It is therefore important to fully understand the company's policies as well as the contractual agreements with any sub-contractors.
3. For both schemes, a "financial loss" refers to a loss in monetary terms by a company or an organisation, whereas an "economic loss" refers to a loss incurred at the societal level.
4. Major contracts will typically include a penalty clause to be invoked in the event of late completion of the accident costing evaluation. Should this occur, then the penalty fee must also be apportioned towards the cost of the accident. This can be entered in the "Other costs" category of both schemes.

TABLE 11.1: Accident cost studies listed by author and country

Author (Year)	Country
Heinrich (1927)	United States
Heinrich (1930)	United States
Simonds (1950)	United States
United States Department of Labour (1956)	United States
Simonds and Grimaldi (1956)	United States
Wallach (1962)	United States
Beckingsale (1963)	United Kingdom
United States Department of Labour (1965)	United States
Beckingsale (1976)	United Kingdom
Fletcher and Douglas (1971)	Canada
Engineering Employers Federation (1971)	United Kingdom
Sinclair et al. (1972)	United Kingdom
National Federation of Building Trade Employers (1971)	United Kingdom
Health and Safety Executive (1993)	United Kingdom
H.K. Lee (1991)	Hong Kong
S.L. Tang et al. (1997)	Hong Kong

5. The costs of accidents are restricted to a contractor, including the site where the accident occurred, through the district or site office, and onto the head office, including the resultant effects on output, turnover, insurance, and profits.
6. These schemes involve construction work on construction sites (both defined in the Construction Sites (Safety) Regulations, see Chapter 6). Depending on the type of work the contractor or sub-contractor are undertaking, certain activities may require other items to be included or excluded from the accident costing evaluation.

The 1991 study by H.K. Lee

The previous studies in Table 11.1 leading up to the 1991 study recognised a total of 26 costing items. However, not all of these are considered practical or applicable to the Hong Kong construction industry. H.K. Lee trimmed this list down to only 12 items. These items, listed in the accounting sheet in Table 11.2, are considered to be simple to understand, easy to compute, and realistic to apply. The following subsections explain each item in greater detail.

Safety administration

The first item considered in this scheme is the cost of safety administration, which includes the charges for the time of the safety officer and other safety personnel while investigating the accident, expenditures for completing the necessary forms and reports, and fees related to liaising with outside bodies, such as the occupational safety officer, police officers, solicitors, insurance company investigation personnel, and engineering consultants. It also includes the cost of secretarial time required to mediate these activities. Costs related to personal protective equipment, such as safety helmets, safety shoes, and eye goggles, are also listed in this category when costing an accident.

Medical services and expenses

This category considers the financial losses related to the first-aid equipment used during the accident and the cost of taking the injured worker to a hospital by company car or a taxi when emergency treatment is required. The aftercare medical expenses are also included in this cost. In accidents involving a fatality, the costs associated with funeral arrangements for the family of the deceased should also be included in this category.

Lost time of the injured person

This cost covers the loss of time for which the injured person has been or will be paid under the Employees' Compensation Ordinance, Cap. 282. In some cases, this loss of time may extend to the period after they resume work.

Lost time of other employees

This cost factors in the time taken by the foremen in assisting the injured person, in investigating the accident, and in compiling accident reports afterwards. It also includes the costs for the time taken by other employees

TABLE 11.2: Accounting cost items for construction accidents based on Lee, 1991

Cost item	Separate total	Item total
1. Safety administration		
1.1. Safety officers	$	
1.2. Safety supervisors	$	
1.3. Secretarial support	$	
1.4. Cost of protective equipment	$	$
2. Medical services and expenses		
2.1. First-aid equipment	$	
2.2. Cost of transport	$	
2.3. Aftercare medical expenses	$	$
3. Lost time of the injured person		
3.1. Loss of time by the injured person	$	
3.2. Loss of time (aftercare)	$	$
4. Lost time of other employees		
4.1. Site foreman	$	
4.2. Ganger, etc.	$	
4.3. Other employees involved in the investigation	$	$
5. Replacement labour		
5.1. Replacement labour	$	
5.2. Advertisement costs	$	$
6. Welfare and other payments		
6.1. Fatal welfare payment	$	
6.2. Non-fatal welfare payments	$	$
7. Lost production		
7.1. Production measurement	$	
7.2. Suspension of work by regulatory bodies	$	$
8. Replacement or repair of damaged plant or equipment		
8.1. Damage costs for replacement	$	
8.2. Repair costs	$	$
9. Damaged materials or products		
9.1. Damaged material cost	$	
9.2. Cost of labour from damaged materials or products	$	
9.3 Damaged product cost (ready for certification and measurement)	$	$
10. Fines and legal expenses		
10.1. Court fines	$	
10.2. Solicitor fees	$	
10.3. Time spent by company personnel in attending court proceedings	$	$
11. Insurance costs		
11.1. Increase in premium (estimated)	$	
11.2. Extra accident coverage (estimated)	$	$
12. Other costs (investigation by third parties, revoking suspension notices, etc.)		$
	Accident Cost Total	**$**

in assisting the injured person and investigating the accident (if involved in such inquiries), as well as any subsequent loss of time as a direct result of the accident.

Replacement labour

This cost focuses on the financial losses incurred to hire a replacement worker or workers brought onto the job following the accident. In the construction industry, professional and skilled personnel are difficult to replace under certain circumstances. In fact, advertisements for these positions often highlight higher pay or other bonuses in order to attract applicants.

Welfare and other payments to the injured person

As the name of this category suggests, accident costing must consider any payments made to the injured worker. In non-fatal cases, this normally includes a lump sum payment as well as any additional medical expenses. In fatal accidents, a payment package is typically granted to the dependents of the deceased (not including the funeral costs, which are included in the medical services and expenses category).

Lost production

These costs arise because of the non-availability of manpower as a result of injury or the non-availability of materials or machinery as a result of damage during an accident. To account for such production losses, the output of the injured person or damaged materials will need to be measured. These costs may overlap with the lost time of the injured person. Unfortunately, such costs can be difficult to measure, particularly for general workers, for whom there is no direct reference (as opposed to skilled tradesmen with significant experience and identifiable financial measures of production).

Replacement or repair of damaged plant or equipment

This cost includes the labour charges incurred to carry out repairs on damaged plant or equipment as well as the cost of replacing parts to restore the equipment to working order. This cost only applies to the plant and equipment owned by the company.

Damaged materials or products

This cost includes the replacement costs of any materials damaged in the accident and any labour costs associated with the work already done on the damaged products. There may also be re-work costs associated with certain items. While these re-work costs may not be a loss per se, there are still financial considerations regarding these processes.

Fines and legal expenses

If the accident resulted in prosecutions by the authorities, then the fines imposed by the courts must be included in the costing evaluation. Legal expenses, such as lawyers' fees, should also be included in this category. The time spent by company personnel to attend court proceedings as witnesses will also involve a financial loss.

Insurance costs

This category covers any changes in the insurance premium or other charges for added coverage following an accident.

Other costs

This final category of the costing scheme covers any other miscellaneous cost items which are incurred as a result of an accident but are not included in any of the above items. Such financial losses may include the fees for engaging an external and independent investigation consultant or revoking a suspension notice issued as a result of the accident.

Example cost assessment using Lee, 1991

The following example shows how the costs of an accident can be accounted for using the criteria established by H.K. Lee (1991). The accident being assessed occurred in 1988 and involved a tower crane that was being used to hoist a bundle of wooden planks at a construction site. The wooden planks slipped and dropped while being hoisted up. The planks struck the concrete drum of a mixer truck parked at ground level. The driver of the concrete mixer truck was injured. Table 11.3 lists the various costing items used in the evaluation, their individual costs, the total cost for that category, and finally, the total cost for the accident. As this example highlights, there are numerous "hidden" costs that are associated with an accident. Each of these must be evaluated, calculated, and included in the costing evaluation.

The 1997 study by Tang et al.

In the other study conducted specifically for construction projects in Hong Kong, Tang et al. (1997) refer to nine costing items. These are outlined in Table 11.4 and described in the following subsections.

Loss due to the injured person

The first category of the costing scheme focuses on the compensation paid to the injured person by the contractor. In Hong Kong, the compensation to be paid is four-fifths of the injured person's wages for every day they are absent from work. On top of this, the contractor will also have to pay disability compensation, the amount of which depends on the percentage of disability that the injured person suffers because of the accident. A medical doctor must be consulted to determine this percentage under the Hong Kong Employees' Compensation Ordinance. The amount for fatal cases is also determined based on this ordinance. The age of the deceased employee is classified in three brackets—under 40, 40 to 56, and 56 or above—which are associated with varying compensation amounts—84 months' earnings, 60 months' earnings, and 36 months' earnings, respectively. To help simplify this while auditing an accident internally, a company can estimate using the industry average for fatal accidents at that point in time. At the time of writing this book, the average maximum compensation for a fatal case is HK$2.4 million, and very few contractors pay over this amount for a single case.

Loss due to the injured person after resuming work

When the injured worker recovers and returns to work, they are not expected to initially work at 100% efficiency. Thus, it is important for

TABLE 11.3: Example costing evaluation following an accident (HK$)

Cost item	Separate total	Item total
1. **Safety administration**		
• Investigation (assistant plant manager and safety officer)	$ 420.00	
• Report writing — 1 day	$ 240.00	
• Secretarial support — 0.5 day	$ 60.00	
• Cost of photograph	$ 50.00	$ 770.00
2. **Medical services and expenses**		$ 0
3. **Lost time of the injured person** (See Item 11 — injured person was not an employee but a concrete worker)		$ 0
4. **Lost time of other employees**		
• Project supervisor — 0.5 day	$ 300.00	
• Foreman — 0.5 day	$ 150.00	
• Mechanic — 0.5 day	$ 115.00	$ 565.00
5. **Replacement labour**		$ 0
6. **Welfare and other payments**		$ 0
7. **Lost production (and claims incurred)**		
• Overtime paid to 16 concreter's labourers	$ 11,900.00	
• Working hours compensated to 3 plasterers	$ 300.00	
• Overtime paid to 5 labourers	$ 1,700.00	
• Overtime paid to 5 P&M workers	$ 1,012.50	
• Extra payment for pump truck and the workers involved	$ 4,620.00	
• Penalty for delaying work progress (3 × 25,000.00 per day)	$ 75,000.00	
• Claims raised by the following sub-contractors for lost work		
– Steel benders, 12 workers — 3 days each	$ 13,320.00	
– Carpenter's labourers, 21 workers — 3 days each	$ 12,500.00	
– Concreter's labourers, 15 workers — 1 day each	$ 5,550.00	$ 125,902.50
8. **Replacement or repair of damaged plant or equipment**		
• Tower crane		
– Repair of winch drum and gearbox	$ 2,500.00	
– Labour for installing new winch drum	$ 2,600.00	
– Replacement of hoisting cable (made in Japan)	$ 7,000.00	
• Mixer truck (replacement of concrete drum)	$ 17,000.00	$ 29,100.00
9. **Damaged materials or products**		$ 0
10. **Fines and legal expenses***		$ 0
11. **Insurance costs (Third-party claim)****		$ 16,840.00
12. **Other costs**		
• Fee for checking the cause of failure of the hoisting winch conducted by surveyors	$ 1,000.00	
• Fee for the tower crane after the installation of new winch drum, gearbox, and hoisting cable	$ 320.00	$ 1,320.00
	Accident Cost Total	**$ 174,497.50**

* The incident was a Dangerous Occurrence and while there was no prosecution at the time, it could be filed by the Labour Department in subsequent accidents. The amount for the fine and legal expenses was not available at the time of assessment.

** The injured concrete worker had to stop work for approximately one month while the mixer truck was repaired. This cost is the average monthly income for at least 12 months of the injured person.

TABLE 11.4: Accounting cost items for construction accidents based on Tang et al., 1997

Cost item	Separate total	Item total
1. Lost time of the injured person (job nature:____________________)		
1.1. Number of days lost	days	
1.2. Amount of compensation	$	
1.3. Percentage disability	%	
1.4. Disability compensation	$	$
2. Loss due to the injured person (after resuming work)		
2.1. Number of days lost (× 0.1 + % of disability × 100)	days	
2.2. Equivalent loss	$	$
3. Medical services and expenses		
3.1. Hospitalisation and medical expenses	$	
3.2. Others	$	$
4. Fines and legal expenses		
4.1. Court fines and solicitor fees	$	
4.2. Others	$	$
5. Lost time of other employees (time taken by other employees in assisting the injured person)		
5.1. Site agent (cost per day $ ____ × ____ days)	$	
5.2. Site engineer (cost per day $ ____ × ____ days)	$	
5.3. Site foreman (cost per day $ ____ × ____ days)	$	
5.4. Other labourers (cost per day $ ____ × ____ days)	$	$
6. Equipment or plant loss		
6.1. Damaged: replacement cost	$	
6.2. Repairing cost	$	
6.3. Others	$	$
7. Damaged materials or finished work		
9.1. Cost of damaged material	$	
9.2. Cost of damaged finished work	$	
9.3 Others	$	$
8. Idle machinery, plant, or equipment		$
9. Other costs		$
	Accident Cost Total	**$**

contractors to account for this. The following formula should be used to calculate such losses.

$$\text{Loss} = \text{Wage of injured worker} \times (\text{Days lost} \times 0.1 + \%\text{Disability})$$

For example, if a worker who earns HK$600 a day was absent from work for 7 days and was certified by a doctor to be 2% permanently disabled as a result of the accident, then the loss will be HK$600 × (7 × 0.1 + 2) = HK$1,620. For simplicity, the effects of different types of disability have been ignored in this equation. Since this factor only contributes approximately 10% of the total accident cost, this approximation in the calculation is not considered significant.

Medical services and expenses

The contractor has to pay all medical expenses, including the cost of transporting the injured worker to the hospital.

Fines and legal expenses

For serious or fatal accidents, the contractor will undoubtedly face prosecution and will, therefore, have to pay solicitor fees and any fines imposed by the courts in cases that involve breaches of safety laws or negligence.

Loss of time of other employees

When an accident occurs, safety personnel are responsible for assessing the injured person. Apart from the safety officer, the site agent, site engineer, and foreman may also be involved in assisting the injured worker. Even when these people do not directly help the injured, they may still be involved in carrying out work related to the accident, such as assisting in the accident investigation and writing the accident report. This scheme assumes that a site agent will lose approximately 0.005 day, a site engineer will lose about 0.05 day, and a foreman will lose 0.25 day for these processes. These assumptions, which are based on empirical research reported in the 1997 study, can then be used to calculate the total loss in this category. Apart from the time lost by the site agent, site engineer, and site foreman, the loss of time of others who work with the injured person must also be considered. When an accident occurs, one can assume that other workers nearby will immediately help the injured person. This scheme assumes that about four other workers are involved in a typical accident and that each worker has a time loss of 0.25 day. The above assumptions are made based on the experience of site safety staff who have been involved in numerous accident evaluations and costing. Although there may be variations from case to case, the assumed figures can be used to make an estimate that is typically close to the true cost.

Equipment or plant loss

Besides injury to the worker(s), an accident may cause damage to plant and equipment. While some accidents will involve significant damage to plant and equipment, and thus a significant financial cost, not every accident will result in such damage.

Damaged material or finished work

This cost category includes the replacement costs of any material damaged as a result of the accident and of any damaged finished work or products.

Idle machinery, plant, or equipment

In the aftermath of an accident, workers will often be required to temporarily stop all work. The time the machinery, plant, and equipment are idle can lead to a loss. The following formula can be used to calculate this loss.

Loss = (Construction sum × 20% × 2%) ÷ (No. of total working days)

This formula is based on the assumptions that 20% of the contract sum is attributed to plant and equipment and that 2% of the plant and equipment will be idle because of the accident. For example, if the contract sum of a project is HK$150 million and the number of working days of the contract is 700 days, the loss of an accident will be (HK$150 million × 20% × 2%) ÷ 700 = HK$857.

Other costs

Any other costs incurred that are not mentioned in the categories above can be included here.

WHY DO ACCIDENT ECONOMICS MATTER? THE LINKS BETWEEN COSTS AND SAFETY PERFORMANCE

The total cost of an accident on a construction worksite depends greatly on project safety performance. If the safety performance is good, the accident costs will likely be low, and vice versa. An optimised system involves two specific measures: the accident loss ratio and the safety investment ratio. Once optimised, it is then possible to quantify the overall safety performance as an accident ratio index. The following subsections explain each of these elements. Notably, while these elements can be calculated for accidents being audited with either of the schemes above, they were originally established in conjunction with the costing evaluation in Tang et al. (1997).

The accident loss ratio

To compare the accident costs of projects with different contract sums and carried out at different times (so that no inflation adjustment is necessary), a dimensionless quantity, the accident loss ratio (ALR), is employed. It is defined as follows:

$$\text{ALR} = \text{TC} \div \text{Contract sum} \times 100\%$$

where TC is the total costs of site accidents in a project

The general shape of an ALR versus safety performance curve is shown in Figure 11.1. The assumption of an exponential relationship seems to form a useful rule of thumb, but this is not based on any derivation from the theory.

FIGURE 11.1: Accident loss ratio (ALR) versus safety performance

(adopted from Tang et al., 1997)

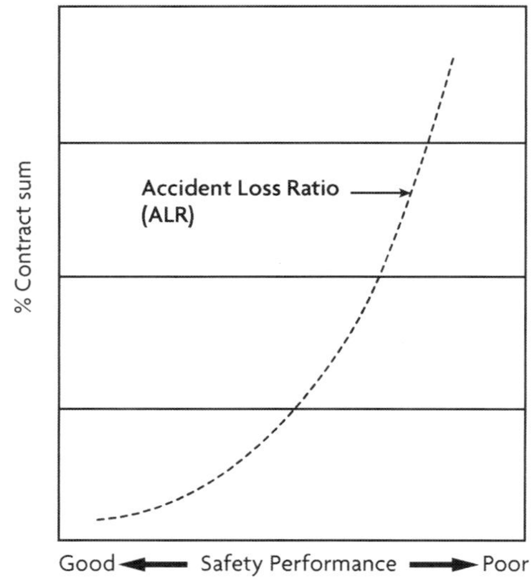

The safety investment ratio

Overall safety performance also varies with the amount of safety investment in a given project. In general, the higher the safety investment, the better the safety performance will be, and vice versa. Furthermore, safety investments on projects of different sizes and at different times can be compared only if they are a dimensionless quantity. Thus, like the ALR, a safety investment ratio (SIR) must be calculated. It is defined as follows:

$$\text{SIR} = \text{TSI} \div \text{Contract sum} \times 100\%$$

where TSI is the total safety investment in a project

The general shape of an SIR curve versus a safety performance curve is shown in Figure 11.2. Again, this is a rule of thumb relationship, rather than a theoretically derived curve.

Safety investment is generally aimed at protecting the safety and health of the workers and the material assets of the contractor. The TSI in the equation for SIR has four major investment components: (1) safety

FIGURE 11.2: Safety investment ratio (SIR) versus safety performance

(adopted from Tang et al., 1997)

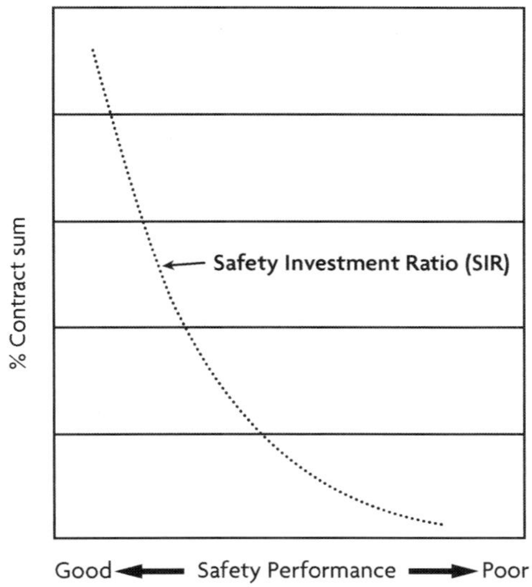

administration personnel; (2) safety equipment (such as personal protective equipment); (3) safety training, information, and instruction; and (4) safety promotion. These costs can be accounted for as shown in Table 11.5

Safety administration personnel comprise site staff and head office staff. According to Hong Kong law, a contractor has to employ registered safety officers and safety supervisors on-site to manage safety-related matters. Some large contractors also employ corporate safety managers or senior safety officers at their head offices to direct and coordinate site safety staff. The salaries of these personnel and their supporting staff, such as office administration staff, are also a part of safety investment and should be included in the accounting costs.

Safety equipment spending includes the cost of personal protective equipment, such as safety boots, goggles, helmets, and safety nets, as well as first-aid items and any other equipment related to the provision of safety on the worksite. Contractors are required by law to provide personal protective equipment to their workforce.

TABLE 11.5: Safety investment on one project

Investment item	Total
1. Investment on safety administration personnel 1.1. On-site module • Safety supervisor (No. personnel ____ × monthly wage $ ____) • Safety officer (No. personnel ____ × monthly wage $ ____) • Secretary/typist/clerk (No. personnel ____ × monthly wage $ ____) • Others (No. personnel ____ × monthly wage $ ____) 1.2. Head office module (Fill in monthly wages on pro rata according to no. of projects supervised in the same period) • Safety manager (No. personnel ____ × monthly wage $ ____) • Chief safety officer (No. personnel ____ × monthly wage $ ____) • Senior safety officer (No. personnel ____ × monthly wage $ ____) • Secretary/typist/clerk (No. personnel ____ × monthly wage $ ____) • Others (No. personnel ____ × monthly wage $ ____)	$
2. Safety equipment investment on the project	$
3. Safety training, instruction, etc. costs	$
4. Safety promotion costs	$
5. Other costs	$
Investment Total	**$**

Financial investments for safety training, information, and instruction as well as those for safety promotion are also included in the TSI metric. Contractors usually organise regular safety training courses for their employees, and such instruction is often mandated by law. Safety promotion includes the costs of designing and printing safety pamphlets and posters, the production expenses for safety advertising boards and banners, the costs of organising safety campaigns, and any monetary rewards for individual workers or sub-contractors who consistently achieve high safety standards.

Qualitative optimisation: Total cost ratio

If the ALR and SIR curves in Figures 11.1 and 11.2 are combined, a third curve of the total costs ratio (SIR + ALR) versus safety performance can be obtained. This curve will have a minimum point, as shown in Figure 11.3, which corresponds to the optimal safety investment for a construction project.

Accident occurrence index

In the ALR, SIR, and Total costs ratio, the safety performance metric is qualitative, being shown as a range from good to poor. It is possible to quantify the qualitative safety performance on a worksite using the accident occurrence index (AOI). However, before explaining this metric it is necessary to define the various terms involved in its calculation. The first of these is the Equivalent day loss of an accident (EDLoA), which is calculated based on the number of days lost, a multiplication factor (F), and the percentage disability for the worker(s) involved in the accident using the following equation:

$$\text{EDLoA} = \text{Real days lost} + (\text{F} \times \%\text{D})$$

The number of real days lost following an accident should be noted in the company's record of the accident. The %D of the worker(s) will need to be assessed by a medical professional. The multiplication factor (F) is based on the industry standards at the time for the average maximum payment for a fatal case ($Max) and the worker's average wage ($W), whereby

$$\text{F} = (\$\text{Max} \div \$\text{W}) \div \%\text{D}$$

At the time of writing, the average maximum compensation for a fatal case is HK$2.4 million. The %D for a fatal case is 100%. The average daily wage for a construction worker is HK$1,000 per day (notably, this is a bold assumption as there are well over 30 different trades in the construction industry that may be working on a single project, but this is an average used specifically for the purpose of calculating the multiplication factor). Thus, ($2.4 million ÷ $1,000) ÷ 100 = 24. Using this multiplication factor to calculate the EDLoA in 2022, the following equation can be used:

$$\text{EDLoA}_{(\text{in } 2022)} = \text{Real days lost} + (24 \times \%\text{D})$$

FIGURE 11.3: Total costs ratio (ALR + SIR) versus safety performance

(adopted from Tang et al., 1997)

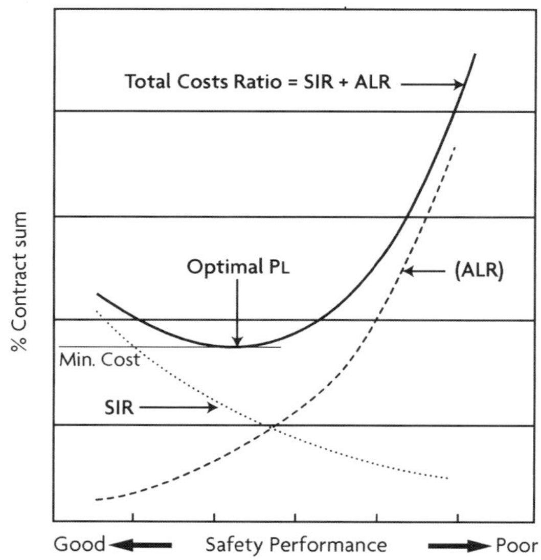

For example, say a worker is injured in an accident and has to be absent from work for 20 days and is certified by a doctor to be of 5% permanent disability as a result of the accident, then the EDLoA will be 140 days (i.e., 20 + 24 × 5). For accidents resulting in 100% disability (meaning they are unable to come back to work) or involving a fatality (equal to the maximum percentage of disability at 100), the EDLoA is 2,400 days (i.e., 24 × 100). It is therefore possible that cases of serious injury (but the worker will eventually return to work) can result in an EDLoA higher than that of a fatal case (e.g., if the days lost are above 2,400 and the % disability is still high). To calculate the compensation that should be granted to that worker, the EDLoA is multiplied by the worker's average earnings per day (in Hong Kong this is about HK$1,000 a day, as stated earlier). Thus, for the worker absent 20 days and 5% disability (with an EDLoA of 140 days, as calculated above), their compensation should be 140 × $1,000 = HK$140,000.

To calculate the total equivalent day loss (TEDL) for an entire project, the EDLoA for every accident should be summed. For example, say a contractor has recorded five accidents for a construction project, with the following EDLoAs:

Accident 1 (10 days lost, 1% disability): $10 + 24 \times 1 = 34$
Accident 2 (30 days lost, 5% disability): $30 + 24 \times 5 = 150$
Accident 3 (20 days lost, 3% disability): $20 + 24 \times 3 = 92$
Accident 4 (10 days lost, 0.5% disability): $10 + 24 \times 0.5 = 22$
Accident 5 (10 days lost, 0.5% disability): $10 + 24 \times 0.5 = 22$

The TEDL would, therefore, be 320 days (the sum of the five EDLoAs). Alternatively, the contractor can also sum each factor and apply the same equation used to calculate the individual EDLoAs (i.e., 80 days + $24 \times 10 = 320$). Alternatively, the mathematical equation for TEDL can be shown as

$$TEDL = \sum_{i=1}^{n} EDLoA$$

where n is the total number of accidents in the project

Using the TEDL, it is possible to calculate the AOI of the project. It is defined as follows:

AOI = TEDL ÷ TDR
where TDR is the total number of man-days required for the project

For the example project with five accidents outlined above, if a total of 7,000 man-days was recorded to complete the project and the TEDL is 320, then the AOI would be 0.046 (i.e., 320 ÷ 7,000). This measure can then be compared between projects as well as monitored for a company over time.

Table 11.6 can be used to assist contractors in collecting the data required for these calculations. While such information should certainly be collected at the end of each construction project, it is also important to keep up-to-date records across the duration of the project to keep track of any and all accidents. This is particularly important as it can help companies identify issues between projects as well as over time.

TABLE 11.6: Data required to calculate the accident occurrence index (AOI) of a project

1. **Contractor name:** ____________
2. **Contract title:** ____________
   ____
3. **Contract sum:** **$** ____________
4. **Contract period:** Start date: ____________
   Completion date: ____________
5. **Number of working days:** ____________
6. **Total man-days employed (include sub-contractors):** ____________
7. **Total number of accidents:** ____________
8. **No. of bodily injuries cases:** ____________
   No. of deaths: ____________
9. **Total number of days lost:** ____________
10. **Total percentage disability all:** ____________

In addition to the information above, contractors and safety officers should stay informed about any changes in the legal requirements for worker compensation (based on the Employees' Compensation Ordinance) as well as changes in the average maximum compensation for fatalities ($Max) and average worker wage ($W), as these figures will alter the multiplication factor which will, in turn, alter these calculations.

Quantitative optimisation: Total costs and extrapolation

If the ALR and SIR curves as well as the quantitative AOIs are considered together, then a quantitative total cost equation can be determined using a regression model. The data highlighted in Table 11.7 should be collected (items 1–9) and calculated (items 10–13) for each project.

The information for each project should be inserted into a spreadsheet. The SIR and ALR curves can then be plotted with the percentage contract sum on the y-axis and the AOI value for that project on the x-axis (Figure 11.4). Each project will have a single point on each curve. Using the regression method, the equations of the ALR and SIR curves can be calculated. Importantly, for a regression model to be useful and accurate, a company will need to have a substantial number

TABLE 11.7: Data for each project required to calculate the total costs

1. Contract title/nature: ______
2. Contract sum: $ ______
3. Total number of accidents (n): ______
4. Number of working days: ______
5. Total man-days employed (include sub-contractors) (TDR): ______
6. Total number of real days lost for all accidents: ______
7. Total percentage disability for all accidents (sum %D): ______
8. Total safety investment (TSI): ______
9. Total accident cost (TC): ______
10. Total equivalent day loss (TEDL): ______
11. Safety investment ratio (SIR) (calculated as item 8 ÷ item 2 × 100%): ______
12. Accident loss ratio (ALR) (calculated as item 9 ÷ item 2 × 100%): ______
13. Accident occurrence index (AOI) (calculated as item 10 ÷ item 5): ______

FIGURE 11.4: Total cost curve (ALR + SIR) versus accident occurrence index (AOI)

(adopted from Tang et al., 1997)

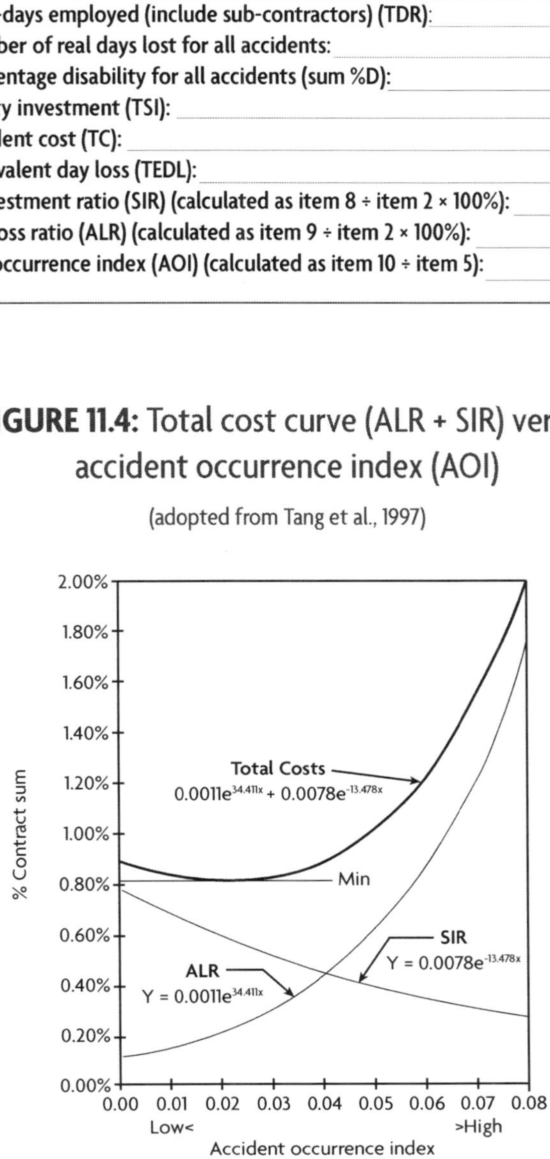

of projects (at least five) with at least one accident recorded for each. The equations for the ALR and SIR curves can then be used to determine the total cost curve (ALR equation + SIR equation). This equation can then be used to plot the total cost curve, from which it is possible to determine the minimum total cost and the associated AOI.

SUMMARY

Assessing the accident economics and costs for a construction project is essential to understanding a company's overall safety performance. This chapter describes two cost accounting methods for accidents arising from construction activities. Both schemes were first developed in Hong Kong and focus on practical and applicable items for local use. The first method, developed by H.K. Lee in 1991, is simple and can be easily applied to small construction companies without any additional resources. The second method, developed in 1997 by Tang et al., is more advanced and is more often applied to larger construction companies carrying out more complex construction work. To start, it may be best to use the first method as an initial assessment tool and then graduate to using the second scheme as the company gains experience and more data are compiled. It may also be beneficial for companies to establish spreadsheet algorithms to help calculate these metrics. However, caution should be used to ensure that the calculations are made correctly. It is, therefore, essential that safety officers be well versed in these methods, but it may be beneficial for companies to hire staff or consultants for the specific purpose of accident costing and assessment.

Both of the methods described in this chapter focus on items that can be accounted for in real dollar terms. They do not consider the impact of accidents on the company's reputation or other indirect costs. In the United Kingdom and the United States, costing studies have shown that these indirect costs can be 8 to 12 times those of the direct costs, meaning they must be considered at multiple levels of the business. Safety management is business management. Thus, in addition to assessing the financial costs of accidents and the relationship to safety performance, it is important to regularly audit safety procedures to ensure that accident prevention (being proactive rather than reactive) is the primary goal. The next chapter focuses on safety management systems audits and details two audit schemes.

FURTHER READING

Poon, S.W., Tang, S.L., and Wong, K.W. (2008) *Management and Economics of Construction Safety in Hong Kong*, Hong Kong University Press.

Tang, S.L. (2003) *Financial and Social Costs of Construction Accidents in Construction Safety Management Systems*, Chapter 28, Spon Press.

Tang, S.L., Lee, H.K., and Wong, K. (1997) "Safety cost optimization of building projects in Hong Kong", *Construction Management and Economics*, Vol. 15, No. 2, pp. 177–186.

Tang, S.L., Chan, S.K., De Saram, D.D., and Lee, H.K. (2006) "Costs of construction accidents in the social and humanity context: A case study in Hong Kong", *Journal of the Hong Kong Institution of Engineers*, Vol. 14, No. 2, pp. 35–42.

DISCUSSION QUESTIONS

1. Discuss the opening quotations to this chapter. Do you think these statements are still relevant in today's construction industry? Why or why not?
2. What is the role of a safety officer during accident costing? How can they help ensure transparency in the costing process?

"Safety management systems auditing—A tool for certainty"

"Safety management is business management"

– A common business saying

12 Safety Auditing

INTRODUCTION

The traditional approach to occupational safety and health tends to only focus on very specific controls and the requirements necessary to meet the legal minimums and avoid prosecution by regulatory bodies. Indeed, the safety inspection procedures adopted by most regulatory officers and safety officers primarily deal with compliance with safety legislation and the "hardware" aspects of accident prevention. They are mainly hazard spotting exercises emphasising the provision of safety devices and the identification of unsafe working conditions. A comprehensive audit of safety and health at work systems must, of course, evaluate these "hardware" aspects in order to comply with the law, but the audit should also consider the "software" aspects—administration; organisation monitoring; instruction, training, and supervision; and the general systems of work in the workplace. An audit should also involve assessing the "human factor" inherent in safety management.

This chapter describes two tailor-made safety management system audit schemes for construction activities: one in tabular form and one in the form of a checklist that consists of questions. It is first necessary to understand the parts and purpose of a safety management system audit within the context of construction safety.

PARTS AND PURPOSE OF A SAFETY MANAGEMENT SYSTEM AUDIT

The Occupational Health and Safety Assessment Series (OHSAS 18001:2007) Standard defines an audit as "a systematic examination to determine whether activities and related results conform to planned arrangements and whether these arrangements are implemented effectively and are suitable for achieving the organisation policy and objectives". Objectives, in this respect, are defined as occupational safety and health performance goals that an organisation sets and strives to achieve. Another standard, the ISO 45001:2018, has been introduced for certification purposes.

The Factories and Industrial Undertakings (Safety Management) Regulation (abbreviated as "FIU(SM)R"), enacted on 24 November 1999, defines a safety audit as "an arrangement for (a) collecting, assessing, and verifying information on the efficiency, effectiveness, and reliability of a safety management system (including the elements specified in Schedule 4 contained in the system); and (b) considering improvements to the system". Under this regulation, proprietors or contractors of certain industrial undertakings are required to develop, implement, and maintain a safe management system. Schedule 4 of this regulation prescribes a list of elements for a safety management system. There are 14 elements categorised into three parts, which are outlined in the following sections. If the contractor employs an aggregate of 100 or more workers, then they are required to develop, implement, and maintain all 14 elements of the safety management system, while those having an aggregate of 50 or more but less than 100 workers only need to focus on the 8 elements in Part 1.

Part 1

The FIU(SM)R requires that a contractor has:

1. A safety policy which states the commitment of the proprietor or contractor to safety and health at work.
2. A structure to assure implementation of the commitment to safety and health at work.

3. Training to equip personnel with knowledge to work safely and without risk to health.
4. In-house safety rules to provide instruction for achieving safety management objectives.
5. A programme to identify hazardous conditions and for the rectification of any such conditions at regular intervals or as appropriate.
6. A programme to identify exposure or the risk of such exposure to the workers and to provide suitable personal protective equipment as a last resort where engineering control methods are not feasible.
7. Investigation of accidents or incidents to find out the cause of any accident or incident and to develop prompt arrangements to prevent recurrence.
8. Emergency preparedness to develop, communicate, and execute plans prescribing the effective management of emergency situations.

Part 2

Contractors must also have in place:

1. Evaluation, selection, and control of sub-contractors to ensure that sub-contractors are fully aware of their safety obligations and are in fact meeting them.
2. Safety committees.

Part 3

Finally, the regulation specifies that contractors must have:

1. Evaluation measures of job-related hazards or potential hazards and means of developing safety procedures.
2. Processes in place for the promotion, development, and maintenance of safety and health awareness in the workplace.
3. A programme for accident control and elimination of hazards before exposing workers to any adverse work environments.
4. A programme to protect workers from occupational health hazards.

Purpose of a safety audit

There are different focuses between an audit under the OHSAS 18001 Standard or ISO 45001 Standard and those under the FIU(SM)R. The former focuses on the management loop of plan-do-check-act with a view to continually improve in its objectives towards better safety and health performance, while the latter stresses the prescribed and scheduled safety management elements highlighted in the sections above. The ISO 45001 is intended to be compatible with ISO 9001 (quality management) and ISO 14001 (environmental protection management), making it a total quality management concept. The FIU(SM)R is mandatory under the law. The mandatory safety elements only provide management controls against the general hazards encountered in all workplaces. As such, they reflect the minimum compliance with the safety legislation. Safety management is invariably based on good practices, not all of which are enshrined in legislation.

Audits are normally designed for one or more of the following purposes:

- To determine the conformity or non-conformity of the safety management elements with specific requirements.
- To determine the effectiveness of the implemented safety management systems in meeting specified safety and health objectives.
- To provide the auditee with an opportunity to improve their safety system.
- To meet regulatory requirements.
- To make a self-determination and declaration of conformance with international specifications, such as the OHSAS 18001 Standard (or the ISO 45001 Standard).

Regardless of the primary purpose, audits are carried out by auditors. Whether an audit is considered to be beneficial for the organisation depends very much on the competency of the auditors. In general, auditors should have a good education, preferably having a university degree and experience in the field of work being audited. Thus, if a management system audit is being conducted, then the auditor should ideally possess at least some managerial experience. In general, auditors should be carefully selected. Auditors should be observant, impartial, resilient, concise, self-disciplined, articulate, and patient. It is best to avoid employing auditors who are oblivious, biased, too sensitive, long-winded, disorganised, or uncommunicative. Under the FIU(SM)R, the auditor must be a registered safety auditor. In addition to being a registered safety auditor, the selected individual should also:

- show excellent time management skills;
- identify themselves while on the worksite;
- dress appropriately for the location;
- be experienced and knowledgeable;
- be a good listener and ask relevant questions;
- have good communication skills;
- be flexible; and
- add value to the organisation.

These skills will play a significant role in how the auditor can achieve the ultimate purpose of the audit. They should also be well versed in common audit schemes in their field.

AUDIT SCHEMES

There are proprietary audit schemes devised by international institutes and local organisations such as the International Safety Rating System (ISRS) and the Independent Safety Audit Scheme (ISAS) administered by the Occupational Safety and Health Council. This chapter introduces two safety audit schemes, both of which are tailor-made and applicable to the local construction industry in Hong Kong.

The Lee and Evans audit scheme

The first audit scheme discussed here originated from Lee and Evans in 1988 and has been extensively used to audit construction companies operating in Hong Kong. It has been continually refined since its initial development. The existing scheme now consists of a set of descriptions or statements in tabular form. The statements are divided into six major areas of managerial commitment and functions that are considered essential for improving safety and health at work. These are:

A. Management Leadership and Commitment
B. Planning, Administration, and Organisation
C. Supervisory Participation, Motivation, and Training
D. Accident Investigation, Statistics, and Reporting Procedure
E. Site Hazard Control
F. Audits or Reviews

Each of these areas includes some important safety activities. For example, within the area of administration and organisation, the audit asks about the company's stated emergency control plans. The questionnaire is designed to assess the degree to which these activities are carried out. This is accomplished by providing four statements that describe situations that vary in the degree to which the activity is implemented. Using the example of the company's stated emergency control plan, the first scenario may state that the company has no plans or procedures. In the second statement, it may have a written plan outlining the minimum requirements. In the third statement, it may have comprehensive written procedures that cover all types of emergencies as well as clearly defined personnel responsibilities as well as assigned backup personnel. In the fourth statement, all types of emergencies are covered by written procedures, and plans are regularly tested and practised. During the audit, the auditor will mark one of the four descriptions that most closely fits the situation at the company, requesting more evidence if necessary.

The selection of written descriptions is qualitative. The following values are then used to grade each description: 0 for scenario/column one; 1 for column two; 2 for column three; and 3 for column four. The marks are then summed to form a total score. Not all items in the full audit are applicable to the activities of an organisation. The higher the score, the better the safety performance is assumed to be. The scores also provide a step-wise recommendation for improvement. Subsequent audit scores can then be used to monitor improvement in the safety management systems. However, it is important to note that the scores can only be regarded as a guide because the choices will involve personal judgment and interpolation, and the scoring scheme is necessarily subjective. The audit scheme is reproduced in the following pages. The areas that directly comply with the FIU(SM)R are indicated with an asterisk (*).

A. Management Leadership and Commitment

The following activities can be used to assess and examine the degree of commitment from the top management of an organisation. An audit is one of the most important elements in the promotion of safety and health at work and the prevention of accidents on worksites. Not all activities are applicable to an organisation, and the audit should focus on the questions that apply to the business's size and activities.

Activity	Mark the description that most closely fits the organisation being audited			
A1 Safety and health policy statement*	☐ No safety and health policy	☐ A "standard" safety and health policy	☐ Safety and health policy written and communicated to all staff and concerned bodies	☐ Policy is reviewed periodically. A drugs and alcohol policy is also available. Total commitment is shown. Signed by top or senior executive(s)
A2 Management review of policy	☐ No review	☐ Limited management review (e.g., change in safety targets only)	☐ Management review with improvements (e.g., safety targets)	☐ Effective management review with achievable improvement over time
A3 Corporate safety organisation	☐ No corporate safety organisation	☐ Part-time engagement of corporate safety personnel	☐ Full-time corporate safety organisation exists	☐ Effective corporate safety organisation with appointed personnel charged with specific duties and responsibilities
A4 Objectives and targets	☐ Just xx per 1,000 workers worked per year and/or xx per 10,000 man-hours worked (i.e., reactive indicators)	☐ Objectives and targets are set but cannot be met (e.g., there are prosecutions by regulatory bodies or issues with key performance indicators)	☐ Both objectives and targets are set, with injury rates being met and no prosecutions or other issues with key performance indicators	☐ Objectives and targets are realistic, reasonable, and humanly achievable. Practical indicators are available, such as lower insurance premiums. Shown to be an industry leader in worksite safety
A5 External safety and health performance reporting	☐ No external reporting	☐ Occasional and informal release of external reporting	☐ External and independent safety and health reporting	☐ External reporting with independent verification. Safety and health performance are periodically reported to interested parties (e.g., publication of annual report in safety and health)

B. Planning, Administration, and Organisation

These elements assess and examine how safety and health at work are planned, managed, and organised. Technical excellence is not enough; the organisation and management must deliberately devise, implement, and maintain control. This is the "software" or the administrative side of an organisation.

Activity	Mark the description that most closely fits the organisation being audited			
B1 Appointment of safety personnel	☐ No appointment of safety personnel	☐ Appointment of safety personnel (e.g., part-time and contracted out), satisfying legal requirements only	☐ Appointment of full-time and resident safety personnel, satisfying legal requirements	☐ Appointment of full-time and resident safety personnel, exceeding legal requirements and complying with contractual requirements, if any
B2 Competence of safety personnel	☐ No competency required	☐ Competency requirements according to the law only	☐ Competency requirements above the law	☐ First-class safety personnel with adequate working experience, educational background, and qualifications are employed
B3 Roles and responsibilities of personnel (e.g., managers, safety officers, safety supervisors, etc.)	☐ Job descriptions do not include safety and health responsibilities	☐ No hierarchy is given for safety and health responsibilities (e.g., trainee safety officer, safety officer, senior safety officer, manager)	☐ Full descriptions of safety responsibilities are given for all levels of working personnel	☐ Full hierarchy descriptions are given and safety performance is viewed as necessary for career advancement
B4 Auditing/ inspection	☐ No auditing/ inspection	☐ Self-auditing/ inspection	☐ Cross-level auditing/ inspection with in-house staff	☐ External and independent auditing/inspection. Creative audit/ inspection demonstrated
B5 Safety committee(s)	☐ No safety committee	☐ Safety committee as per legal requirements only. Communication is not discernible	☐ Safety committee is formed with appropriate representatives	☐ Safety committee formed and shown to be effective and successful. Positive contribution by members is evident

B6 Hazard identification [a] and risk assessment [b]	☐ No risk assessment	☐ Ad hoc risk assessment	☐ Full risk assessment by a risk assessment team with established methodology	☐ Comprehensive risk assessment performed with an independent review by a third party. An in-house databank of risk assessments is available
B7 Line responsibility, safety responsibility, and accountability	☐ Line responsibility not defined	☐ Line responsibility concept present but no evidence is shown	☐ Line responsibility present but only partial evidence is shown	☐ Line responsibility concept demonstrated with sound evidence
B8 Management of sub-contractors (e.g., selection, evaluation, and control)*	☐ No management of sub-contractors in safety and health processes	☐ Fair management of sub-contractors in safety and health	☐ Good management of sub-contractors in safety and health	☐ Excellent management of sub-contractors in safety and health
B9 Safety budget for individual projects	☐ No safety budget	☐ Below 0.5% of the contract sum	☐ Above 0.5% but equal or below 1% of the contract sum	☐ Above 1% of the contract sum and sufficient
B10 Instruction of site safety procedure and in-house safety rules*	☐ No instruction	☐ Limited instruction	☐ Instruction given but not fully effective	☐ Site personnel are aware of and display obedience to instructions. Evidence of disciplinary procedure enforced for non-compliance
B11 Emergency control plans	☐ No emergency control plans in place	☐ A few emergency plans expressed or verbally understood	☐ Emergency plans identified with minimum requirements	☐ Emergency plans identified, practised, and reviewed with backups. Outside bodies, like government departments or other services, are involved
B12 Compliance with safety and health legislation	☐ Three or more prosecutions [c] by regulatory bodies in the past 12 months	☐ One or two prosecutions in the past 12 months	☐ One or two prosecutions in the past 5 years	☐ No prosecutions in the past 5 years

B13 Safety and health information	☐ No safety and health information sources	☐ Safety and health information only to comply with legal regulations	☐ Safety and health information covers wider scopes of safety and health	☐ Safety and health information from regional and international sources, in-house safety and health library in existence. Worldwide safety-at-work standards, literature, technical and journal papers are available
B14 Safety rules*	☐ Only few written rules (e.g., generic ten-point rule)	☐ Safety rules developed and posted	☐ Safety rules are incorporated into work activities	☐ Safety rules are established, firmly enforced to achieve management objectives, and reviewed at least annually

a "Hazard identification" is defined as process of recognising that a hazard exists and defining its characteristics (see OHSAS 18001:2007).

b "Risk assessment" is defined as process of evaluating the risk(s) arising from a hazard(s), taking into account the adequacy of any existing controls, and deciding whether or not the risk(s) is acceptable (see OHSAS 18001:2007).

c "One prosecution" is counted as "one summons" issued by a regulatory body under the Factories and Industrial Undertaking Ordinance, Chapter 59, and its subsidiary regulations or the Occupational Safety and Health Ordinance, Chapter 509, and its subsidiary regulations.

C. Supervisory Participation, Motivation, and Training*

The success of safety and health promotion depends on people, namely how they are motivated and how they communicate with each other. No one can do a good and safe job without being trained for it.

Activity	Mark the description that most closely fits the organisation being audited			
C1 Induction of new employees	☐ No induction of new employees (e.g., not all workers have green cards)	☐ Induction of company employees, but only those with green cards	☐ Induction of company employees for those with and without green cards	☐ Induction of all employees, visitors, and all contracted employees
C2 Line supervisor safety training	☐ None of the supervisors have received basic safety training	☐ Only some of the supervisors have received basic training	☐ All supervisors participate in regular safety training sessions	☐ All supervisors are trained and specialised sessions are conducted on specific safety problems

C3 Training for specialised operations in parallel with the result of risk assessment	☐ No training, instruction, or information provided to any specialised operators	☐ Some training, instruction, or information provided to some specialised operators	☐ Certification and appointment for all specialised operators	☐ Certification and appointment as well as refresher training instruction and information for all specialized operators in accordance with results of risk assessment (e.g., use of simulators for crane operations training)
C4 Internal self-inspection	☐ No written programme to identify and evaluate hazardous practices or conditions	☐ Internal inspection under Form 3A of the CS(S)Rs[a] only	☐ A written programme outlining inspection guidelines, responsibilities, frequency, and follow-up is in effect	☐ Inspection programme is measured by results (e.g., reduction in accidents and costs). Inspection results are followed up by senior management
C5 Safety promotion and publicity	☐ No internal promotion. Bulletin boards are the main means of safety promotion	☐ Limited to site promotion. Additional safety displays, signs, and posters are used, but demonstrations and films are used infrequently	☐ Site promotion and corporate promotion. Safety displays and demonstrations are used on a regular basis	☐ Themed site promotion accredited by outside bodies. Special display cabinets, windows, etc. are provided. Displays are used regularly and are keyed to special themes
C6 Unsafe act auditing	☐ No unsafe act auditing	☐ Limited to a few work activities	☐ Cover major identified high-risk work activities	☐ Effectiveness evident from regular unsafe act auditing
C7 Safety incentive scheme	☐ No incentive scheme	☐ Limited incentive scheme	☐ Incentive scheme available but effectiveness is not reviewed	☐ Effective incentive scheme established (e.g., safety fun day for employees' families)

a "CS(S)Rs" is the abbreviation for the Construction Sites (Safety) Regulations.

D. Accident Investigation, Statistics, and Reporting Procedures*

Why do we keep having the same accidents? Accidents are seen to be a manifestation of management failure.

Activity	Mark the description that most closely fits the organisation being audited			
D1 Accident definition	☐ No accident/ incident definition	☐ Use of accident definition under Employees' Compensation Ordinance	☐ Use of own accident/incident definition	☐ Company has its own "accident" definition (e.g., lost-time injury, medical treatment case, first-aid case, fatal case)
D2 Accident/incident investigation	☐ No accident investigation	☐ Ad hoc accident investigation by line management, completing an accident form	☐ Full and detailed accident investigation. Answers provided to questions like: (a) what went wrong? (b) who was responsible? (c) who can prevent it from happening again? and (d) how?	☐ Investigation with management lapses/ failures in mind, engaging external and independent investigation
D3 Accident causation, analysis with statistics	☐ No analysis or identification of causes of an accident	☐ Limited analysis. Analysis is not in depth. Only involves filling in the accident form	☐ Analysis with management lapses/failures in mind	☐ Analysis with management lapses/ failure in mind, engaging external and independent investigation. Management is kept informed on status. A databank of all accidents has been developed in-house. Costing of accidents is available
D4 Investigation of accidents involving property damage	☐ Not addressed	☐ Ad hoc inquiries about property damage accidents	☐ Investigation of property damage accidents with a set amount (e.g., over HK$5,000)	☐ Rigorous investigation of all property damage accidents. Cost of property damage accidents is available
D5 Investigation of dangerous occurrences[a]	☐ No investigation, non-reporting common	☐ Ad hoc investigation	☐ Full and detailed accident investigation	☐ Investigation with management lapses/ failures in mind, engaging external and independent investigation

D6 Potential accidents[b]	☐ No discussion	☐ Ad hoc discussion but superficial investigation	☐ Full and detailed investigation and analysis	☐ Investigation and analysis with possible management lapses/ failures in mind
D7 Accident costing	☐ No costing	☐ No definite plan for costing	☐ Cost method confirmed but only for limited items	☐ Accidents are costed in a wider perspective. Management is updated

a Dangerous occurrences are defined and prescribed under the Factories and Industrial Undertakings Ordinance, Chapter 59.

b A potential incident means any hazardous scenario which (a) is a credible possibility; (b) is relevant to the construction activities being carried out; (c) the consequences can be both foreseen and quantified; and (d) offers safety lessons that can be learned.

E. Site Hazard Control*

This element establishes a control programme that can be applied to all construction processes, such as the construction of buildings and structures, foundation engineering, highway engineering, bridge engineering, tunnelling, water engineering, diving operations, etc.

Activity	Mark the description that most closely fits the organisation being audited			
E1 Scaffolding (metal, bamboo, or mixed)	☐ No inspection	☐ Internal inspection under the CS(S)Rs only	☐ Internal inspection under the CS(S)Rs plus ad hoc inspection	☐ Internal inspection plus ad hoc plus external inspection

E2
Lifting appliances and lifting gear

- The activities audited should include erection, alteration, dismantling, and transportation. This is governed under the Factories and Industrial Undertakings (Lifting Appliances and Lifting Gear) Regulations, which are hereafter abbreviated as "FIU(LA&LG)Rs".
- "Lifting appliances" means a crab, winch, teagle, pulley block, or gin wheel used for raising or lowering, and a crane, sheerlegs, excavator, pile driver, pile extractor, dragline, aerial ropeway, aerial cableway transporter or overhead runway, and also any part of such appliances.
- "Lifting gear" means a chain sling, rope sling, ring, or similar gear, and a link, hook, plate clamp, shackle, swivel, or eyebolt.

E2.1 Material hoists	☐ No inspection	☐ Internal inspection under the CS(S)Rs and FIU(LA&LG)Rs only	☐ Internal inspection under the CS(S)Rs and FIU(LA&LG)Rs, plus ad hoc inspection. Operational manual available	☐ Internal inspection plus ad hoc and external inspection

E2.2 Tower cranes	☐ No inspection	☐ Internal inspection under the CS(S)Rs and FIU(LA&LG)Rs only	☐ Internal inspection under the CS(S)Rs and FIU(LA&LG)Rs plus ad hoc inspection. Operational and maintenance manual available	☐ Internal inspection plus ad hoc and external inspection as well as technical audits on a regular basis. Service life is specified
E2.3 Mobile cranes	☐ No inspection	☐ Internal inspection under the CS(S)Rs and FIU(LA&LG)Rs only	☐ Internal inspection under the CS(S)Rs and FIU(LA&LG)Rs plus ad hoc inspection. Operational and maintenance manual available	☐ Internal inspection plus ad hoc and external inspection as well as technical audits on a regular basis. Service life is specified
E2.4 Lorry-mounted cranes	☐ No inspection	☐ Internal inspection under the CS(S)Rs and FIU(LA&LG)Rs only	☐ Internal inspection under the CS(S)Rs and FIU(LA&LG)Rs plus ad hoc inspection. Operational manual available	☐ Internal inspection plus ad hoc and external inspection
E2.5 Chain blocks	☐ No inspection	☐ Internal inspection under the CS(S)Rs and FIU(LA&LG)Rs only	☐ Internal inspection under the CS(S)Rs and FIU(LA&LG)Rs plus ad hoc inspection	☐ Internal inspection plus ad hoc and external inspection
E2.6 Tripod lifting devices (e.g., roof or derrick cranes)	☐ No inspection	☐ Internal inspection under the CS(S)Rs and FIU(LA&LG)Rs only	☐ Internal inspection under the CS(S)Rs and FIU(LA&LG)Rs plus ad hoc inspection	☐ Internal inspection plus ad hoc and external inspection
E3 Electricity hazards	☐ No inspection	☐ Internal inspection under the CS(S)Rs and FIU(Electricity)Rs only	☐ Internal inspection under the CS(S)Rs and FIU(Electricity)Rs plus ad hoc inspection. Inspections carried out by a qualified electrician	☐ Evidence of installing a residual current circuit breaker (RCCB) or magnetic circuit breaker (MCB); reduction of voltage to 110 volts; injury record bears this out (i.e., no electrical accidents reported or recorded for many years)

E4

Personal protective equipment ("PPE") programme*

- This element includes the implementation of personal protective equipment as the result of a risk assessment. PPE provision should be considered to be a last resort prevention measure.
- Equipment provided should comply with high and well-understood standards or specifications. Use of safety equipment should be recognised as an employment requirement.

E4.1 Safety helmets	☐ No provision	☐ Partial provision (e.g., few workers seen not wearing safety helmets)	☐ Excellent (e.g., all workers were seen wearing safety helmets with chinstraps properly attached)	☐ Full provision with system for replenishment (e.g., safety helmets replaced after 1 year of use)
E4.2 Eye goggles	☐ No provision	☐ Partial provision and use	☐ Full provision and use	☐ Full provision with system for replenishment
E4.3 Earmuffs/ earplugs	☐ No provision	☐ Partial provision and use	☐ Full provision and use but only to comply with the law	☐ Full provision with system for replenishment
E4.4 Breathing apparatus	☐ No provision	☐ Partial provision and use	☐ Full provision and use but only to comply with the law	☐ Full provision with system for replenishment. Are of world-class specification
E4.5 Safety harness/belts	☐ No provision	☐ Partial provision and use	☐ Full provision and use but only to comply with the law	☐ Full provision with system for replenishment. Are of world-class specification
E4.6 Fall arrest system and safety nets	☐ No provision	☐ Partial provision and use	☐ Full provision and use but only to comply with the law	☐ Full provision with system for replenishment. Are of world-class specification
E4.7 Safety shoes	☐ No provision	☐ Partial provision and use	☐ Full provision and use	☐ Full provision with system for replenishment
E5 Machinery	☐ No guarding of dangerous parts of machinery	☐ Partial guarding and use	☐ Full guarding and use	☐ Full guarding with a system for effectiveness. Periodic checking and testing occur

E6 Fire control measures	☐ No control (e.g., cigarette ends found, flammable gases and liquids used with no control)	☐ Partial control	☐ Full control. Fire-fighting appliances such as extinguishers and fire pumps are provided	☐ Full control with fire safety inspection programme in place. A fire crew organised and fire audits are regularly conducted
E7 Housekeeping	☐ Poor housekeeping	☐ Fair housekeeping	☐ Good housekeeping with dedicated workforce 5S[a] practised	☐ Excellent housekeeping. Considered a leader in the construction industry
E8 Hazards from toxic or flammable substances/ chemicals	☐ No provision of Material Safety Data Sheets (MSDSs)	☐ Incomplete list of hazardous substances used, only some MSDSs	☐ List of hazardous substance available with appropriate MSDSs	☐ A databank of all flammables, toxic, or hazardous substances is available and regularly updated
E9 Fencing of dangerous places or workplaces liable to be dangerous	☐ No action; no one designated as responsible	☐ Limited action; fencing inadequate or incomplete	☐ Full fencing with specifications and standards established	☐ Planned fencing of dangerous places. Standards promulgated and reviewed with site employees
E10 Excavation (e.g., earthwork and caissons)	☐ No attempt to control	☐ Partial but inadequate control	☐ Controlled but only to comply with the CS(S)Rs	☐ Planned programme; soil conditions given; frequent reviews with site personnel
E11 Hearing conservation programme	☐ No control	☐ Control is minimal	☐ Full provision of ear protection only to comply with the law	☐ Programme devised to control noise at the source (e.g., purchasing machinery or equipment with lower noise level). Provide audiometric test
E12 Use of ladders, platform ladders, kung-fu stools	☐ No provision	☐ Partial provision	☐ Full provision	☐ Full provision with system for replenishment

a "5S" is a housekeeping method practised by the Japanese and commonly applied in Hong Kong. It refers to Seiri (categorising), Seiton (identifying), Seiso (cleaning), Seiketsu (hazard spotting), and Shitsuke (implementing).

F. Other Activities

This section is intentionally left blank for the inclusion of work activities undertaken by the organisation. Four levels should be pre-determined by the auditor.

Activity	Mark the description that most closely fits the organisation being audited			
Other work activities can be added, examples are: diving, pre-stressing, welding, woodworking, use of cartridge-operated fixing tool, use of mobile elevating working platform, etc.	☐ (lowest mark)	☐ (mid-level mark)	☐ (good mark)	☐ (excellent mark)

G. Audits

The term "audit" will extend to other type of audits that are relevant to accident prevention. These audits may include: housekeeping audit, fire prevention audit, mobile crane technical audit, tower crane technical audit, etc. These audits may involve third parties and should preferably be carried out independently and externally.

Activity	Mark the description that most closely fits the organisation being audited			
G1 Safety management systems audit	☐ No safety audit	☐ In-house audit/ review but only to comply with the FIU(SM)R	☐ Audit/review exceeds legal requirements, independent and external auditors are engaged	☐ Audit/review of various aspects such as fire, lifting appliances, housekeeping, etc.

The question checklist scheme

The second audit scheme discussed here was developed in the form of questions and complies with the 14 safety management elements prescribed under the FIU(SM)R. It is designed to supplement the Code of Practice on Safety Management issued by the Labour Department of the

Hong Kong SAR. The questions are relevant to all levels of management and all construction work activities. A proposed grading as a result of the audit is given at the end of the checklist.

1 A safety policy which states the commitment of the proprietor or contractor to safety and health at work

1.01 Is there a written safety and health policy?
1.02 Is there a drugs and alcohol policy?
1.03 Is there an auditing policy?
1.04 Does the safety policy commit the organisation to full compliance with all relevant safety and health legislation?
1.05 Does the safety policy set targets for safety and health performance, including a commitment to continual improvement?
1.06 Does the chief executive, managing director, or other top management sign the policy?
1.07 Is the latest safety policy prominently displayed on the worksite or in the office?
1.08 Is the date of issue shown on the safety policy?
1.09 Are there effective arrangements for reviewing the safety and health policy at least biannually?
1.10 Is the policy explained to new employees as part of their induction training within a reasonable time before their commencement of work (e.g., two days)?
1.11 Is the policy written in the appropriate languages for workers of different nationalities?
1.12 What are the company's long-term objectives in safety and health at work?

2 A structure to assure implementation of the commitment to safety and health at work

2.01 Is there an organisational chart showing the names and positions of those responsible for safety management?
2.02 Is the authority (e.g., the director or a senior executive) leading the safety and health procedures clearly shown on

the organisational chart? Are they ultimately responsible for safety and health matters?

2.03 Have the individual safety and health responsibilities of all "safety-sensitive positions" been clearly defined?

2.04 Has a sufficient number of competent safety officers been appointed and engaged for the site or in the organisation?

2.05 Has a sufficient number of competent safety supervisors been appointed and engaged for the site?

2.06 Is someone in charge of updating the safety and health information including changes to regulations, new codes of practice, newly identified hazards, and new work practices?

2.07 Do line managers at all levels demonstrate their commitment to safety by commending safe work, refusing to compromise on agreed standards, discussing safety with employees, putting safety first on the agenda of all business meeting, etc.?

2.08 Are adequate funds made available for safety needs?

2.09 Do all levels of management spend an adequate proportion of their time on safety matters?

2.10 Do managers hold their subordinates accountable for the safety performance of the people for whom they are responsible?

2.11 Do employees recognise that working safely is a condition of their employment?

3 Training to equip personnel with knowledge to work safely and without risks to health

3.01 Has an analysis of safety training needs been carried out to ensure all employees received appropriate safety training?

3.02 Is there a safety and health training programme? Is it reviewed regularly?

3.03 Are sufficient funds provided for safety and health training?

3.04 Have all workers received basic mandatory safety training?

3.05 Have all workers received site-specific safety training?

3.06 Have all workers received toolbox training related to their required tasks?

3.07 Have all managers received safety management training?

3.08 Have all supervisors received appropriate safety training?

3.09 Have all workers responsible for carrying out high-risk or specialised activities received relevant training?

3.10 Is the effectiveness of safety and health training monitored? Are behavioural-based observations made and reported?

3.11 Are suitable venues and facilities provided for training?

3.12 Are safety training records kept? Are these records for individual workers?

3.13 Are the trainers competent?

3.14 Are competent persons handling the technical problems of safety?

4 In-house safety rules to provide instruction for achieving safety management objectives

4.01 Are there written occupational safety and health rules?

4.02 Are there written specific safety and health rules?

4.03 Are these rules posted in the vicinity of the activities where they apply?

4.04 Are the general safety rules brought to the attention of all employees?

4.05 Is there an arrangement for monitoring compliance with these safety rules?

4.06 Are there disciplinary arrangements for ensuring compliance with safety rules?

4.07 Are all the rules documented and regularly reviewed?

4.08 What do employees think of the safety rules and standards?

5 A programme of inspection to identify hazardous conditions and for the rectification of any such conditions at regular intervals or as appropriate

5.01 Has a comprehensive inspection checklist and inspection programme been developed?

5.02 Are there appropriate arrangements to ensure that senior management actively participates in the safety inspection of their areas of responsibility at regular intervals?

5.03 Are there appropriate arrangements to ensure that the site inspections check the level of compliance with safety standards and procedures?

5.04 Do safety officers and safety supervisors carry out safety inspections at regular intervals?

5.05 Are external and independent safety inspections arranged?

5.06 Are there appropriate arrangements to ensure that action is taken based on the findings of the safety inspections?

5.07 Are safety inspection results collated and analysed?

6 A programme to identify hazardous exposure or the risk of such exposure to the workers and to provide suitable personal protective equipment as a last resort where engineering control methods are not feasible

6.01 Have the statutory requirements for the provision of protective clothing and equipment been identified?

6.02 Has the need for protective clothing and equipment been identified as part of a hazard identification and risk assessment exercise?

6.03 Is there an arrangement for selection and procurement of appropriate protective clothing and equipment?

6.04 Has a sufficient stock of carefully selected and appropriate protective clothing and equipment been ensured?

6.05 Are there adequate and secure facilities provided for employees to store their personal protective clothing and equipment?

6.06 Is there a procedure to monitor the personal protective equipment brought to the worksite by workers?

7 Investigation of accidents or incidents to find out the cause of each accident or incident and to develop prompt arrangements to prevent recurrence

7.01 Does the organisation have a written procedure established and maintained for accident or incident notification, investigation, and follow-up actions? Are the company's definitions of an accident or incident clearly explained? Do these definitions highlight first-aid cases, medical treatment cases, lost-time injury cases, permanent injury cases, fatal cases, etc.?

7.02 Is it clear that the main purpose of an accident investigation is to prevent future accidents?

7.03 Are all minor injuries and near misses reported and recorded?

7.04 Is a well-designed form used to report accidents?

7.05 Who is the investigation team leader and who are the team members in cases involving a fatality? A lost-time accident? A dangerous occurrence as defined under the law?

7.06 Are accident trees used? Is fault tree analysis used?

7.07 Who endorses the accident investigation report?

7.08 Is a schedule set to implement recommendations?

7.09 How are follow-up actions monitored?

7.10 What is the worst disaster that could happen in the workplace or on the site?

7.11 If the worst disaster happened, could the company cope?

8 Emergency preparedness to develop, communicate, and execute plans prescribing the effective management of emergency situations

8.01 Is there a list of emergency situations identified based on the company's work activities? The emergency situations may include fire, chemical spillage, medical evacuation, electricity stoppage, disease outbreak, etc.

8.02 Is there an emergency plan for an effective and prompt response to adverse weather conditions (e.g., thunderstorms and rainstorms) that may affect the safety of personnel working on the site?

8.03 Does the emergency plan include necessary arrangements to ensure safety, such as means of fire escape, designation of a central gathering point, emergency lighting and power sources, availability and locations of emergency equipment, emergency coordinators, emergency and rescue equipment, and contacts with emergency and medical services?

8.04 Are qualified first aiders as well as first-aid facilities and equipment adequately provided and maintained on the worksite?

8.05 Is there a programme of drills and exercises for all identified emergency situations? Are these drills and exercises practised regularly?

8.06 Are the personnel responsible for emergency situations properly trained?

8.07 Does the current workforce know how to react in an emergency?

9 Evaluation, selection, and control of sub-contractors to ensure that sub-contractors are fully aware of their safety obligations and are in fact meeting them

9.01 Is there a procedure established and maintained for the identification of suitable sub-contractors?

9.02 Do sub-contractors know their safety and health responsibilities? Are these well defined?

9.03 Is there a procedure used to evaluate the safety performance of sub-contractors?

9.04 Are such safety performances being referenced when selecting sub-contractors?

9.05 Is there a procedure established and maintained to perform a safety audit for the sub-contractors?

9.06 Are sub-contractors required to submit a safety plan showing their safe work procedures and methods?

9.07 Are sub-contractors involved in carrying out risk assessments?

9.08 Is there an arrangement to communicate and coordinate safety and health matters to sub-contractors while they are working on-site?

10 Safety committees

10.01 Is there a safety committee established as required under section 10(a) of the Factories and Industrial Undertakings (Safety Management) Regulation?

10.02 Are the terms of reference, membership, frequency, agenda, and distribution of minutes of the safety committee clearly defined?
10.03 Do the committee members consist of at least 50% representatives of workers in the organisation or project?
10.04 Does the committee meeting cover all the appropriate safety and health matters?
10.05 Does the committee discuss potential incidents?
10.06 Does the committee have the active participation of senior management of the organisation or project?
10.07 Does the committee identify weaknesses, plan improvements, set objectives, and monitor performance?
10.08 Does the committee have effective, two-way communication between management and sub-contractors or employees?
10.09 Does the committee meet regularly? At least once every three months as required by law?
10.10 Does the committee keep records of its meeting for not less than 5 years after the date of the meeting?

11 Evaluation of job-related hazards or potential hazards and development of safety procedures

11.01 Is there a procedure established and maintained for the ongoing identification of hazards, the assessment of risks, and the implementation of necessary control measures?
11.02 Does the procedure apply to (a) routine activities, (b) non-routine activities, (c) activities of all personnel having access to the workplace (including sub-contractors and visitors), and (d) all facilities at the workplace, whether provided by the organisation or others?
11.03 Are the results of these assessments and the effects of these controls documented and kept up to date?
11.04 Is the organisation's methodology for hazard identification and risk assessment defined with respect to its scope, nature, and timing to ensure it is proactive rather than reactive?
11.05 Is "what-if mode" used in the company's risk assessment?

11.06 Are questions asked like: what will go wrong before it goes wrong?

11.07 Are risk assessment results being vetted by outside and independent consultants?

12 Promotion, development, and maintenance of safety and health awareness in the workplace

12.01 Is there a safety and health promotion programme in the organisation?

12.02 Are there clearly defined focuses, themes, and objectives for the safety promotion programme?

12.03 Has a coordinator been appointed for the smooth implementation of the safety programme?

12.04 Are the safety promotion activities designed for all levels of staff?

12.05 Is there an in-house safety bulletin or newsletter?

12.06 Is there a safety notice board displayed?

12.07 How well can the promotion activities help develop and maintain awareness of workplace safety and health?

13 A programme for accident control and elimination of hazards before exposing workers to any adverse work environments

13.01 Has a programme for accident control been established and maintained?

13.02 What are the routine and non-routine activities that could be hazardous to workers? What are the safety precautionary measures? Have these been implemented?

14 A programme to protect workers from occupational health hazards

14.01 Is there a procedure established to identify the hazards that could affect the health of workers?

14.02 Have all hazardous substances and processes been identified?

14.03 Have Material Safety Data Sheets (MSDSs) been obtained from manufacturers or other sources on the hazardous nature of chemical substances used on the site?
14.04 Are health risk assessments conducted? Are these assessments reviewed and updated?
14.05 Are the health risk assessments carried out by a competent person? Are occupational health consultants, occupational hygienists, and/or safety officers employed for this purpose?
14.06 Have control measures against occupational health hazards been developed? Are these measures regularly reviewed and updated?
14.07 Are medical examinations required? Are these conducted pre-employment, periodically, and or post-employment?
14.08 Are occupational health training sessions conducted by occupational health consultants?

15 Audit Grading

An example of the grading system used in conjunction with the questions above is shown in Table 12.1. The higher the total score, the better the safety performance.

SUMMARY

This chapter describes the parts and purpose of a safety audit as well as the details of two auditing schemes used in the construction industry in Hong Kong. The first audit scheme contains four levels of description concerning a management element and is designed to detect the current state of each activity in the safety management system. It can be used to benchmark the existing status of a particular element. The audit shows where the management system stands now and where improvement is needed. The necessary changes to go from one level to the next is also clearly defined in this scheme. In carrying out the audit, the auditor has to secure on-site evidence and make personal judgements. This scheme is suitable for organisations whose existing safety management system is fragmented and not very sound. It is also good for those just beginning to formally introduce audits as a management tool.

TABLE 12.1: The question checklist audit grading scheme

Interpretation	Level
The contractor fully meets the requirements of the best safety management principles in every aspect and is leader in industry.	5
The contractor meets the requirements of the best safety management principles but with minor exceptions which can be rectified before the next audit.	4
The contractor meets the requirements of the safety management principles in accordance with the law and its code of practice. Remedial action is required before the next audit.	3
The contractor does not meet the requirements of the safety management principles in several important areas. There are significant areas that will require step-wise improvement before the next audit.	2
The contractor does not meet any of the requirements of the safety management. Immediate management intervention is required to avoid mishap or significant issues.	1

The second scheme is a questionnaire-type scheme without prepared answers or responses, though reference can be made to the Code of Practice on Safety Management published by the Labour Department. The arrangement of the 14 safety management elements in the scheme follows Schedule 4 of the safety management regulations. The questions posed are designed to trigger investigation into the improvement of the management system. The questions can be posed to staff at various levels of an organisation. This scheme can be used for comparative purposes between two or more worksites carrying out the same activities as well as between different timepoints for activities on a single worksite. In contrast to the first scheme, this second scheme does not present specific recommendations as a result of the audit. The auditors carrying out the audit using this scheme have to make judgements based on these questions to provide a roadmap for change. The recommendations can be varied and subjective. This is yet another reason why auditor selection is critical.

Both audit schemes use a checklist-type scoring but belong to different categories. It is important to note that these scores are qualitative in nature, not quantitative, and that a company should not focus on the score alone but on how the quality of their safety management practices can be improved. In practice, they are best used as an *aide-memoire* to highlight items that are conducive to safety. These two audit schemes have been widely implemented across the construction industry in Hong Kong and are used by companies considered to be leaders in terms of safety. While both types of schemes comply with the 14 safety management elements of the law, the first scheme is quite specific, while the second scheme is more flexible as additional questions can be added. Both schemes demand more than just complying with the legal requirements. They demand higher safety and health management performance and continued improvement.

It is recommended that a third-party auditor who has no direct working relationships with the audited organisation be employed for the purpose of the audit. This ensures that the auditor will provide more assurance and greater objectivity. Such an external and independent audit will avoid any temptations for the auditor or the company to ignore or cover up deficiencies while also adding significant value and ensuring a safe workplace for staff.

No matter which audit scheme a construction organisation decides to utilise, they should note that auditing is a management tool designed to promote continual improvement in their system. This is the main purpose of conducting an audit. The effectiveness of any audit scheme, therefore, depends on the management's attitude towards the results of the audit as well as the specific findings and recommendations of the auditor.

FURTHER READING

Bigelow, P.L., and Robson, L.S. (2005) *Occupational Health and Safety Management Audit Instruments—A Literature Review*, Institute for Work & Health, Toronto, Canada.

BS 8800:1996, *Guide to Occupational Health and Safety Management Systems.*

ISO 45001: *Occupational health and safety management systems – requirements with guidance for use* (2018-03)

Labour Department, Hong Kong SAR Government (May 2015) *Guidance Notes on Registration as a Safety Auditor, Training Scheme Operator under the Factories and Industrial Undertakings (Safety Management) Regulation*, Hong Kong Government Printer.

Labour Department, Hong Kong SAR Government (draft under circulation) *Code of Practice on Safety Management*, Hong Kong Government Printer.

McKinnon, R.C. (2017) *Risk-based, Management-led, Audit-driven Safety Management Systems*, CRC Press, Taylor & Francis Group.

Shell HSE Committee (October 1989) *Enhanced Safety Management Checklist.*

DISCUSSION QUESTIONS

1. List ten questions that you would ask the on-site project manager during a safety management system audit. The questions should relate to the compliance with the Factories and Industrial Undertakings (Safety Management) Regulation and its Code of Practice.
2. Prepare a safety management system audit scheme for a bamboo scaffolding contractor who is doing demolition work only.
3. Comment on the existing Code of Practice on Safety Management published by the Labour Department, Hong Kong SAR.
4. Discuss the value of the following sources of information in auditing the safety management system of an organisation: leadership and organisation commitment to safety, risk assessment intensity, and thorough accident and incident investigation.

Conclusion and Future Directions

This book has been written with a purpose: to save lives and prevent bodily injuries in the construction industry. It explores avenues related to three subjects — safety law, safety management, and safety technology — which are vital to the purpose of improving safety on worksites. My work in the construction industry puts me in a unique position to comment on changes in the system as well as on things that need to improve.

The early chapters of this book in Part I lay out a basic foundation, including a look at the history of the construction industry in Hong Kong, a description of general principles for safety management, and an outline of Hong Kong's safety regulations applicable to the construction industry. This allows for more in-depth discussion in Part II about the legal enforcement and repercussions of these principles and regulations. Parts III and IV dive into Hong Kong-focused examples and assessment tools, respectively. The concepts of safety law, management, and technology are found throughout.

SAFETY LAW

In terms of safety legislation, there are codes of practice, guidance notes, technical memorandum issued by concerned institutes, corporations, and authorities in addition to the local and regional ordinances in place. No doubt, these demand contractors and their workforce to comply with these safe working procedures. The practicalities of these safety procedures should be based on how workman actually work and not on how others would like to think that they work. Consultation and communication must be taken seriously by the workforce and management, allowing for multiple discussions and negotiations before its publication. It is time to examine the practicalities of these publications and see whether they are realistically achievable.

Looking ahead, we must ask questions such as: Does the regulatory body work effectively? How effective are these laws in promoting safety on worksites? Is prosecution always an effective way to influence conditions at construction worksites and will it achieve real change towards reducing the number of bodily injuries and deaths? Will the existing ordinances and regulations address advances in construction technology? What changes must be made? How do our mindsets about safety need to shift?

It is my hope that those who disagree with the effectiveness of Hong Kong's current prosecution policy or believe the policy needs to be re-shaped to effectively address issues will join the debate. It is essential to hear the voices of younger generations of safety practitioners as well as those of young construction workers and tradespeople in order to evolve as an industry. Construction safety is ultimately about the people involved in the work.

SAFETY MANAGEMENT

The focus on the human aspect of safety is largely dealt with under the umbrella of safety management. Unfortunately, safety management is often viewed solely in response to accidents, being reactive rather than proactive. Construction accidents are often caused by a fault in the safety procedures, lack of communication about the procedures, or by highly independent workers exercising their personal choice to not follow defined procedures. Thus, while legislation and associated repercussions for breaches are helpful, the key to ensuring safety is to modify behaviours towards safer options. This is not just for the workers themselves but also for top management.

Such safety changes can be mediated with the help of safety practitioners and registered safety officers. Work psychologists also have a part to play in assisting with the development of training packages in education institutes and training centres for various trades. It is, therefore, essential that additional emphasis be placed on the education and training of safety practitioners and those involved in safety management. It is my belief that the education and training of these individuals will only continue to get stronger and become more important over the next 10 to 20 years. This makes it essential for seasoned safety officers, workers, managers, and legislators to pass along their knowledge to the next generation.

Furthermore, one aspect of safety management that has been getting more and more attention is health—comprehensive mental and physical well-being. Notably, ill-health caused by construction activities, though only rarely mentioned in this book, must not be underestimated. Occupational health on construction sites is vital for addressing issues with chronic disease development as well as to avoid the spread of communicable diseases. While silicosis and musculoskeletal disorders are the most commonly encountered diseases in the construction industry, more research should be carried out in excessive stress, quality of work-life balance, and the need to provide more welfare on worksites.

SAFETY TECHNOLOGY

Technology is always changing, even in the construction industry. This includes updates and variations on existing equipment, like tower cranes and mobile cranes, as well as the development of new technology. At present, there is very little design and manufacturing of such construction equipment in Hong Kong. However, operators must understand the use and safety of these modern machines to avoid human errors. The division between "knowledge-in-the-world" and "knowledge-in-the-head" should be narrowed. Looking ahead, there is an urgent need to establish a local working platform to identify common human errors and communicate and coordinate with the designers and manufacturers located elsewhere. The emphasis must shift to changes in the design to avoid danger and to integrate competent safe designs.

As new generations of construction workers, management, and safety practitioners enter the workforce, it is only natural that they will likely be well versed in some of the newer technologies, particularly regarding the software aspects and automated processes. They have the advantage of learning these systems as they are going through their initial training, unlike older practitioners who must instead take supplemental or refresher courses. For Hong Kong's construction industry to thrive, we must make use of new technologies, particularly as many of them come with better safety options.

THE FUTURE OF THE CONSTRUCTION INDUSTRY

In today's business world in general, including the construction industry, the "trust me" approach and the "tell me" approach are not enough. Construction organisations have to adopt a "show me" approach to stakeholders and the public. They must show them that health, safety, and environmental protection is a priority and are being adequately controlled. External reporting on the management of these matters must be on the agenda.

This book is mainly for safety practitioners and students undertaking courses and pursuing a career in construction safety. Construction managers or senior members in construction organisations, who are accountable for safety duties and responsibilities, will also find the book useful to meet their safety war. It is my hope that as a collective industry we can address accidents and gaps in legislation to enhance worksite environments across Hong Kong and around the world.

Bibliography

BOOKS, CHAPTERS, ARTICLES, ETC.

Accident Prevention Advisory Unit of HM Factory Inspectorate (1976) "Managing safety: A review of the role of management in occupation health and safety", *HSE Occasional Paper Series: OP03*.

Bamber, L. (1986) *Principles of Accident Prevention*.

Barrett, B., and Howells, R. (1997) *Occupational Health and Safety Law* (Third Edition), Financial Times Pitman Publishing.

Beckingsale, A.A. "The cost of industrial accidents: The 1963 Alexander Redgrave Memorial Lecture", *British Journal of Industrial Safety*, Vol. 6, pp. 34–42.

Beckingsale, A.A. (1996) "Finding the true cost of accidents", *Proceedings of the National Industrial Safety Study Conference*.

Bigelow, P.L., and Robson, L.S. (2005) *Occupational Health and Safety Management Audit Instruments—A Literature Review*, Institute for Work & Health, Toronto, Canada.

Bingham, T. (2011) *The Rule of Law*, Penguin Books.

Booth, R.T. (1979) "Safety: Too important a matter to be left to the Engineers?" Inaugural Lecture at the University of Aston-in-Birmingham (22 February).

Booth, R.T., Hale, A.R., and Dawson, S. (1991) "Identifying and registering safety practitioners", *Safety Science*, Vol. 14, pp. 231–240.

Buildings Department, Hong Kong SAR Government (September 2019) *Code of Practice on Design for Safety – External Maintenance* (First issue).

Chang, C.C., and Yu, T.X. (2002) *An Engineering Study for Improving Safety and Reliability of Bamboo Scaffoldings (Final Report) Submitted to the Occupational Safety and Health Council 14 June 2002.*

Cheung, S.O., Cheung, K.K.W., and Suen, H.C.H. (2004) "CCSHM: Web-based safety and health monitoring system for construction management", *Journal of Safety Research*, Vol. 35, pp. 159–170.

Chief Factory Inspector, Labour Department, Hong Kong Government (1982/1983) *Annual Reports*.

Clarke, J. (2016) *Redgrave's Health and Safety* (Ninth edition), LexisNexis.

Commissioner of Labour, Labour Department, Hong Kong Government (1951–1952) *Annual Departmental Reports*.

Commissioner for Labour, Labour Department, Hong Kong SAR Government (2014) "Safety alerts on systematic safety problems at construction sites", *Letter to registered safety officers*, dated 14 July 2014.

Committee for European Construction Equipment (October 2009) *Tower Cranes with the new European standard EN 14439:2009*.

Conference papers from the *Singapore WSH Conference (2018)* 29–30 August 2018, Singapore.

Congress papers from the *XXI World Congress on Safety and Health at Work 2017*, 3–6 September 2017, Singapore.

Construction Industry Council (November 2016) *Guidelines on Work-Above-Ground Safety, Version 1, Hong Kong*.

Construction Industry Council (September 2017) *Guidelines on Planking Arrangement for Providing Working Platforms on Bamboo Scaffolds, version 2*.

Construction Industry Training Authority in collaboration with the Labour Department, Hong Kong SAR Government (February 2000) *Case studies of Construction Accidents in Hong Kong* (Third edition).

Consultation Paper on the *Review of Industrial Safety in Hong Kong Education and Manpower Branch*, Hong Kong Government (July 1995).

Cross, J. (2017) *Australia ISO 31010: Risk assessment techniques and open system*, Tokyo.

Development Bureau, Hong Kong SAR Government (2018) *Construction Site Safety Manual, Chapter 2, March version*.

Dickie, D.E. (1982) *Mobile Crane Manual*, Canadian Construction Safety Association of Ontario.

Drucker, P.F. (1980) *Managing in Turbulent Times*, Harper & Rea.

Environment, Transport, and Works Bureau, Hong Kong SAR Government (2003) *Technical Circular (Works) No. 2/2003: Regulation Action where a Serious Incident has or Site Safety or Environmental Offences have occurred on a Construction Site*, dated 2 April 2003.

European Union (EU) (June 2018) *Accidents at Work Statistics*.

Eves, D.C.T. (2015) *Disasters: Learning the Lessons for a Safer World*, Routledge.

Eves, D.C.T. (2018) *Two Steps Forward, One Step Back: A Brief History of the Origins, Development and Implementation of Health and Safety Law in the United Kingdom, 1802–2014*, available at: www.historyofosh,org.uk/brief/index.html, accessed 19 September 2021.

Eves, D.C.T. (2006) *Questioning Performance: The Director's Essential Guide to Health, Safety and the Environment*, Routledge.

Ferry, T.S. (1988) *Modern Accident Investigation and Analysis* (2nd edition), John Wiley & Sons.

Fletcher, J.A., and Douglas, H.M. (1971) *Total Loss Control within the Industrial Environment*, Associated Business Programmes.

Friedman, M., and Friedman, R. (1990) *Free to Choose* (First Harvest edition), Harcourt.

Goldsmith, D. (1987) *Safety Management in Construction and Industry*, McGraw-Hill.

Groeneweg, J. (2011) "Hazard analysis: The accident causation model", *Encyclopaedia of Occupational Health & Safety*, International Labour Organisation, available at: www.iloencyclopaedia.org/part-viii-12633/audits-inspections-and-investigations/item/914-hazard-analysis-the-accident-causation-model.

Hakkinen, K.K. (1985) *Characterization of Safety Criteria for Load-bearing Materials and Components, particularly in Lifting Tackle*, Helsinki University of Technology.

Hallinan, J.T. (2009) *Why We Make Mistakes*, Broadway Books.

Hammer, J.D.G. (1990) *Symposium on Safety and Health Management: The General Duties of Employers and Employees at Work*, Hong Kong, 10 January 1990.

Handy, C.B. (1988) *Understanding Organizations.*

Harris, F. (1981) *Construction Plant, Excavating and Materials Handling, Equipment and Method*, Granda.

Harris, F. (1989) *Modern Construction Equipment and Methods*, Longman Scientific & Technical.

Harris, F., and McCaffer, R. (1977) *Modern Construction Management*, Crosby Lockwood Staples.

Health and Safety Authority, Ireland (2018) *Code of Practice for Access and Working Scaffolds.*

Health and Safety Technology and Management Limited (1988) *HASTAM Chase II: The Complete Health and Safety Evaluation Manual for Larger Organization*, Birmingham, United Kingdom.

Hendrick, H., and Benner, L. Jr. (1987) *Investigating Accidents with STEP*, Marcel Dekker.

HM Inspectors of Factories (1984) *Essays to Commemorate 150 Years of Health and Safety Inspection, 1833–1983*, London: HMSO.

Hong Kong Housing Authority (2018) *Site Safety Handbook, Volume 2, Chapter 7*, Hong Kong Government Printer.

Hong Kong Institution of Engineers (1998) *Symposium on Bamboo and Metal Scaffolding*, 23 October.

Hong Kong Occupational Safety and Health Association (November 1987) *Safety Bulletin*, Vol. 4, No. 9.

Hong Kong Occupational Safety and Health Council (2017a) *Study on the Redesign of the I-shape Metal Bracket for Truss-out Bamboo Scaffoldings.*

Hong Kong Occupational Safety and Health Council (2017b) *Survey on Occupational Safety and Health of Mobile Crane Operators.*

Hong Kong Government, *Report of the Commission of Inquiry into the fire on the "Jumbo" floating restaurant 1972.*

Hong Kong SAR Government (2014) *Press Release*, 30 May 2014.

Hong Kong SAR Government (2017) *Press Release*, 15 May 2017.

Hong Kong Society of Registered Safety Officers (2001) *A Memoir of the 10th Anniversary Celebration.*

Janssen, J.J.A. (1981) *Bamboo in Building Structures*, PhD thesis, Enidhoven University of Techonlogy, Holland.

Jenkyn-Jones, T.R.W. (2016) *Skeleton Legal Argument on Section 13(1) of the F&IU0, Cap. 59, Summonses TWS 847-853/2012*, 16 May 2016.

Kletz, T.A. (1990) *Learning from Accidents in Industry*. Butterworths.

Kwok, A.K.Y. (ed) (2013) *The Qualification and Performance of Occupational Health and Safety Personnel: Ensuring Occupational Health and Safety for Workers. Venture Track Program Hong Kong*, Hong Kong Department of Civil and Environmental Engineering, The Hong Kong Polytechnic University.

Labour Department, Hong Kong Government (1951, 1954, 1956, 1958) *Annual Reports.*

Labour Department, Hong Kong SAR Government (1997) *The 50th Anniversary of the Labour Department 1946–1996*, Hong Kong Government Printer.

Labour Department, Hong Kong SAR Government (2004) *Safe Systems of Work*, Hong Kong Government Printer.

Labour Department, Hong Kong SAR Government (October 2011) *Code of Practice for Safe Use of Tower Cranes.*

Labour Department, Hong Kong SAR Government (2012) *Letter to the President of the Hong Kong Construction Association*, dated 27 June 2012.

Labour Department, Hong Kong SAR Government (2014) "Safety alerts on systemic safety problems at construction sites", *Letter to Registered Safety Officers/Registered Safety Auditors*, dated 14 July 2014.

Labour Department, Hong Kong SAR Government (May 2015) *Guidance Notes on Registration as a Safety Auditor, Training Scheme Operator under the Factories and Industrial Undertakings (Safety Management) Regulation*, Hong Kong Government Printer.

Labour Department, Hong Kong SAR Government (September 2017a) *A Guide to the Provision for Safe Places of Work under Part VA of the Construction Sites (Safety) Regulations*, Hong Kong Government Printer.

Labour Department, Hong Kong SAR Government (2017b) *Code of Practice for Safe Use of Mobile Cranes* (Second edition), Hong Kong Government Printer.

Labour Department, Hong Kong SAR Government (2017c) *Code of Practice for Bamboo Scaffolding Safety* (Fourth edition), Hong Kong Government printer.

Labour Department, Hong Kong SAR Government (2017d) *Concise Investigation Report for the Fatal Accident in Hong Kong-Zhuhai-Macao Bridge Project on 29 March 2017.*

Labour Department, Hong Kong SAR Government (March 2018) *Overview of Work-at-Height Safety*, Hong Kong Government Printer.

Labour Department, Hong Kong SAR Government (2019) *Consultation on the Proposed Amendments to Guidance Notes on Continuing Professional Development Programmes for Registered Safety Officers*, letter dated 19 June 2019.

Labour Department, Hong Kong SAR Government (n.d.) *Codes of Practices published by Labour Department made under section 7 of the Factories and Industrial Undertakings Ordinance, Chapter 59.*

Labour Department, Hong Kong SAR Government (draft under circulation) *Code of Practice on Safety Management*, Hong Kong Government Printer.

Labour Department and Occupational Safety and Health Council, Hong Kong SAR Government (2003) *Analysis on Occupational Fatalities Casebook Volumes 1–3.*

Lee, H.K. (1979) *Health and Safety on Construction Sites*, BSc Project, Department of Civil Engineering, Loughborough University of Technology, United Kingdom.

Lee, H.K. (1988) *Managing Safety and Health in Construction Companies*, MSc Dissertation, Department of Industrial Engineering, University of Hong Kong.

Lee, H.K. (1989a) "The professional development of safety officers", *Safety Officers Conference*, Macau, 10 and 11 March 1989.

Lee, H.K. (1989b) "Health and safety in factories and industrial undertakings in Hong Kong", *Journal of Health and Safety, British Health and Safety Society*, Vol. 3, pp. 33–44.

Lee, H.K. (1991) *Safety Management: Hong Kong Experience*, Lorrainelo Concept Design.

Lee, H.K. (1995) *Enhancing the Role of the Safety Practitioner in Hong Kong into the 21st Century*, The Society of Registered Safety Officers.

Lee, H.K. (1996) *Construction Safety in Hong Kong*, Lorrainelo Concept Design.

Lee, H.K. (1999–2000) "OHSAS 18001: 1999 Specifications", *Newsletter of the Society of Registered Safety Officers of Hong Kong*, Issues 9/99, 12/99, 3/00.

Lee, H.K. (2002a) *Bamboo Scaffolds: Past, Present and Future from a Safety Practitioner's View Proceedings of International Seminar on Bamboo Scaffolds in Building Construction*, INBAR, 101–104.

Lee, H.K. (2002b) "Safety and health management auditing in Hong Kong", *Journal of the Hong Kong Institution of Engineers.*

Lee, H.K. (2007) "Development of a safety training pack for personnel undertaking dismantling of tower cranes in Hong Kong", unpublished paper.

Lee, H.K. (2011) "Code of practice for safety management: Some observations", *Journal of the Hong Kong Institution of Engineers*, Vol. 39, pp. 14–15.

Lee, H.K. (2012) "Tower crane accidents: Can we prevent them?" *Journal of the Hong Kong Institution of Engineers*, Vol. 40, pp. 19–20.

Lee, H.K. (2013) "The court's word on the Construction Sites (Safety) Regulations", *Journal of the Hong Kong Institution of Engineers*, Vol. 41, pp. 25–26.

Lee, H.K. (2014) "The courts' view of safe systems of work in construction", *Journal of the Hong Kong Institution of Engineers*, Vol. 42, pp. 18–19.

Lee, H.K. (2015) "Bamboo scaffolding safety", *Journal of the Hong Kong Institution of Engineers*, Vol. 43, pp. 16–17.

Lee, H.K. (2019) *A 60-min safety management appraisal for project managers*, HK Lee & Associates Limited.

Lee, H.K., and Evans, W.A. (1991) "An evaluation of the role of management in construction safety in Hong Kong", *Journal of Health and Safety, British Health and Safety Society*, Vol. 7, pp. 41–54.

Lee, H.K., and Evans, W.A. (1993) "The role of construction foremen in safety on construction sites: Hong Kong experience", unpublished paper.

Lee, H.K., and Tang, S.L. (1994) *Optimal Safety Investment in Construction*, China Safety Science [In Chinese].

Lee, H.K., et al. (2002) *Safety Auditor Training Scheme*, Construction Industry Training Authority (now known as Hong Kong Institute of Construction) and Lloyd's Register Quality Assurance of Hong Kong.

Legislative Council, Hong Kong Government (1955) *Official Report of Proceedings*, 20 July 1955.

Legislative Council, Hong Kong Government (1973–1986, 1993) *LC Papers*.

Legislative Council, Hong Kong SAR Government (2019) *Occupational Safety Performance in Hong Kong, Panel on Manpower, LC Paper No. CB(2)563/18-19(4)*, 15 January 2019.

London Chemical Industrials Association (1973) *Safety Audits: A Guide for the Chemical Industry*.

MacCollum, D.V. (1993) *Crane Hazards and their Prevention*, American Society of Safety Engineers.

Maslow, A.H. (1968) *Towards a Psychology of Being*, Van Nostrand.

McKinnon, R.C. (2017) *Risk-based, Management-led, Audit-driven Safety Management Systems*, CRC Press, Taylor & Francis Group.

Ministry of Social Affairs and Health (2016) *Occupational Safety and Health in Finland*.

Occupational Safety and Health Branch, Labour Department, Hong Kong SAR Government (August 2016) *Occupational Safety and Health Statistics Bulletin, Issue No. 16*.

Occupational Safety and Health Branch, Labour Department, Hong Kong SAR Government (November 2017) *Concise Investigation Report for the Fatal Accident in Hong Kong-Zhuhai-Macao Bridge Project on 29 March 2017*.

Occupational Safety and Health Branch, Labour Department, and Occupational Safety and Health Council, Hong Kong SAR Government (2003–2008) *An Analysis on Occupational Fatalities Casebook, Volumes 1–4.*

Occupational Safety and Health Council, Hong Kong SAR Government (2002) *Independent Safety Audit Scheme, version 1.4.*

Occupational Safety and Health Council, Hong Kong SAR Government (January 2009) *Independent Safety Audit Scheme, HASAS version 1.4.*

Occupational Safety and Health Council (2017) *Survey on Occupational Health of Mobile Crane Operators, Hong Kong.*

Parker, J.E. (2011) "Respiratory diseases: Silicosis", *International Labour Organization Encyclopedia of Occupational Health and Safety* (Chapter 10).

Petersen, D. (1978) *Techniques of Safety Management*, McGraw Hill.

Poon, S.W., and Lee, H.K. (1992) *Mobile Crane Accident*, 3rd International Conference on Modern Techniques in Construction, Engineering & Project Management, 24–26 March 1992, Singapore.

Poon, S.W., Tang, S.L., and Wong, K.W. (2008) *Management and Economics of Construction Safety in Hong Kong*, Hong Kong University Press.

Potain (May 1993) *Erection-dismantling Manual: MD175-G10-H10.*

Potain (October 1999) *General Notes—Instruction for use: MR 220.*

Pugh, D.S. (1971) *Organization Theory.*

Reason, J. (1990) *Human Error*. Cambridge University Press.

Reason, J., and Parker, D. (1993) *Managing the Human Factor in Road Safety*, The Hague, Shell International Petroleum.

Reason, J., Shotton, R., Wagennar, W., Hudson, P., and Groeneweg, J. (January 1989) *Tripod: A Principled Basis for Safer Operations Prepared for Shell International.*

Report of the Commission of Inquiry (1972) *Fire on the "Jumbo": Floating Restaurant*, Hong Kong Government Printer.

Report of the Robens Committee on Safety and Health at Work 1971-1972 (July 1972 (Cmnd 5034).

Rowlinson, S. (1997) *Hong Kong Construction: Site Safety Management*, Sweet & Maxwell Asia.

Samelson, N.M. (June 1977) *The Effect of Foreman on Safety in Construction*, Stanford University Department of Civil Engineering, Technical Report No. 219.

Selwyn, N.M. (1982) *Law of Health and Safety at Work*, Butterworths.

Shapiro, H.I., et al. (1991) *Cranes and Derricks*, McGraw-Hill.

Shell Chemicals (January 1988) *A Guide to Risk Management.*

Shell Group Public Affairs Review (1994) *Reputation: A License to Operate.*

Shell Hong Kong Limited (January 2001) *Safety Data Sheet for Formula Shell Super Unleaded.*

Shell Health, Safety, and Environment Committee (1985) *Enhanced Safety Management.*

Shell Health, Safety, and Environment Committee (October 1989) *Enhanced Safety Management Checklist.*

Shell Health, Safety, and Environment Committee (1994) *HSE Management System: Integrating HSE into the Business.*

Shell Health, Safety, and Environment Panel (April 1999) *Risk Assessment Matrix.*

Shell International Petroleum Company (November 1999) *Effective Proactive HSE Culture.*

Simonds, R.H., and Grimaldi, J.V. (1963) *Safety Management: Accident Cost and Control* (2nd edition), RD Irwin.

Sinclair, T.C. *A Cost-effectiveness Approach to Industrial Safety Committee on Safety and Heath at Work*, Research Paper, London: HMSO.

Singapore WSH Council (2014) *Code of Practice on Safe Lifting Operations in the Workplaces* (First revision).

Singapore Standards Council (2014) *Specification for Lifting Gear; Part 1: Wire Rope Slings.*

So, F.Y.S. (1996) *Scaffold Development in Hong Kong: A Critical Review,* MSc in Engineering Business Management, University of Warwick.

So, F.Y.S. (2009) *Scaffolding Systems in Hong Kong: Current Practice and Development of MBMSS*, PhD thesis, City University of Hong Kong.

Standards Australia/Standards New Zealand (2004) *Risk Management Guidelines Companion to AS/NZS 4360: 2004.*

Stranks, J. (2001) *A Manager's Guide to Health and Safety at Work* (Sixth edition).

Surry, J. (1971) *Industrial Accident Research,* Labour Safety Council, Ontario, Canada.

Tam, C.M., and Fung, I.W.H. (1996) "Effectiveness of safety management strategies on safety performance in Hong Kong", *Construction Management and Economics*, Vol. 17, pp. 49–55.

Tang, S.L. (2003) *Financial and Social Costs of Construction Accidents in Construction Safety Management Systems*, Spon Press.

Tang, S.L., Lee, H.K., and Wong, K. (1997) "Safety cost optimization of building projects in Hong Kong", *Construction Management and Economics*, Vol. 15, No. 2, pp. 177–186.

Tang, S.L., Chan, S.K., De Saram, D.D., and Lee, H.K. (2006) "Cost of construction accidents in the social and humanity context: A case study in Hong Kong", *Journal of the Hong Kong Institution of Engineers*, Vol. 14, No. 2, pp. 35–42.

United Kingdom CIRIA (2006) *Publication C654: Tower Crane Stability.*

United Kingdom Construction Plant-Hire Association's Tower Crane Interest Group (TCIG) (2008) *Technical Information Notes: Maintenance, Inspection and Thorough Examination of Tower Cranes*, CPA Best Practice Guide.

United Kingdom Health and Safety Commission (1996) *Control of Substances Hazardous to Health.*

United Kingdom Health and Safety Executive (1976) *Success and Failure in Accident Prevention,* London: HMSO.

United Kingdom Health and Safety Executive (1980) *Management's Responsibilities in the Safe Operation of Mobile Cranes: Report on Three Crane Accidents,* London: HMSO.

United Kingdom Health and Safety Executive (June 1981) *Managing Safety: A Review of the Role of Management in Occupational Health and Safety by the Accident Prevention Advisory Unit of the HM Factory Inspectorate*, London: HMSO.

United Kingdom Health and Safety Executive (1983a) *A Guide to the HSW Act, Health and Safety Series Booklet*, HS(R)6, London: HMSO.

United Kingdom Health and Safety Executive (1983b) *Her Majesty's Inspectors of Factories 1833–1983: Essays to Commemorate 150 Years of Health and Safety Inspection*, London: HMSO.

United Kingdom Health and Safety Executive (1991) *Successful Health and Safety Management* (HSG 65).

United Kingdom Health and Safety Executive (1992) *Personal Protective Equipment at Work* (Second edition).

United Kingdom Health and Safety Executive (1993) *The Costs of Accidents at Work,* London: HMSO.

United Kingdom Health and Safety Executive (1997a) Safe *Work in Confined Spaces,* HSE Books.

United Kingdom Health and Safety Executive (1997b) *Successful Health and Safety Management* (HSG65) (Second edition), HSE Books.

United Kingdom Health and Safety Executive (2000) *A Report about the HSE Investigation into the Collapse of a Tower Crane in Canada Square London E14, on 21 May 2000.*

United Kingdom Health and Safety Executive (Reprinted 2003) *Safety in Working with Lift Trucks.*

United Kingdom Health and Safety Executive (2005a) *Investigating Accidents and Incidents: A Workbook for Employers, Unions, Safety Representatives and Safety Professionals* (HSG245).

United Kingdom Health and Safety Executive (Reprinted 2005b) *Safety in the Use of Abrasive Wheels.*

United Kingdom Health and Safety Executive (July 2008) *Report on the Technical Aspects of the HSE's Investigation into the Collapse of a Luffing Tower Crane at a Liverpool Construction Site on 15th January 2007.*

United Kingdom Health and Safety Executive (2014) *Safe Use of Lifting Equipment—Lifting Operations and Lifting Equipment Regulations (Approved Code of Practice and Guidance)* (Second edition), L113, HSE Books.

United Kingdom Health and Safety Executive (n.d.) *HSE Guidance Note PM3: Erection and Dismantling of Tower Cranes.*

United Kingdom Health and Safety Executive (n.d.) *HSE Guidance Note PM9: Access to Tower Cranes.*

United States Department of Labour, "Accident costs", In: *Safety Subjects Bulletin No. 67*, Chapter 4, United States Government Printing Office.

United States Department of Labour (1965) "Accident cost control", In: *Safety in Industry: Instructor Outline Bulletin No. 268*, United States Government Printing Office.

Vincoli, J.W. (1993) *Basic Guide to System Safety*, Van Nostrand Reinhold.

Wagenaar, W.A. (1986) *The Cause of Impossible Accidents*, The Sixth Duijker Lecture University of Amsterdam.

Wallach, M.B. (1962) "Accident costs: A new concept", *Journal of the American Society of Safety Engineers*, Vol. 7, pp. 25–26.

Westrum, R. (1988) *Organizational and Inter-organizational Thought,* Presentation to World Bank Conference on Systems Safety, The World Bank.

Westrum, R. (2016) *A Typology of Organizational Cultures*, Eastern Michigan University.

Wong, F.K.W. (April 1998) *Bamboo Scaffolding: Safety Management for the Building Industry in Hong Kong.*

Woo, K.H. (1997) *Final Report of the Inquiry into the Garley Building Fire on 20 November 1996*, Hong Kong, 26 August.

Workplace Health and Safety, Queensland, Australia (2017a) *Tower Crane Code of Practice.*

Workplace Health and Safety, Queensland, Australia (2017b) "Tower crane safety on construction sites: A complex sociotechnical system perspective", *Safety Science*, Vol. 109, pp. 95–108.

Works Bureau, Hong Kong Government (May 1995) *Construction Site Safety Manual.*

Yeung, K.Y. (1989) *Speech to the Conference on Safety and Health Management: A Japanese Experience*, Hong Kong, 20 November 1989.

Yiu, N.S.N., and Chan, D.W.M. (2018) "In-depth investigation of safety management system in the Hong Kong construction industry: Literature review and research agenda", *International Advances on Mechanical and Civil Engineering*, Vol. 5, Issue 1, pp. 6–10.

Zehui, Jiang [江澤慧] (2002) *Bamboo and Rattan in the World*, Liaoning Science and Technology Publishing House.

Zhou, W., Zhao, T., Liu, W., and Tang, J. (2018) "Tower crane safety on construction sites: A complex socio-technical system perspective", *Safety Science*, Vol. 109, pp. 95–108.

LEGISLATION

Hong Kong

Codes of Practice published by the Occupational Safety and Health Branch of the Labour Department, Hong Kong SAR Government

Factories and Industrial Undertakings Ordinance, Chapter 59 and its subsidiary regulations

Guidance Notes issued by the Labour Department, Hong Kong SAR Government

Occupational Safety and Health Ordinance, Chapter 509 and its subsidiary regulations

Singapore

Workplace Safety and Health Act, Chapter 354A

United Kingdom

Health and Safety at Work etc Act 1974

Lifting Operations and Lifting Equipment Regulations 1998

STANDARDS

British Standard. CP 3010:1972, Code of Practice for safe use of cranes (mobile cranes, tower cranes and derrick cranes).

BS 7121 Code of Practice for safe use of cranes

BS 7262 Code of Practice for automatic safe load indicators

BS 7121-5:1997 *Code of Practice for safe use of crane* (1997)

BS 8437:2005. *Code of practice for selection, use and maintenance of personal protection systems and equipment for use in the workplace.*

BS 8800:1996 *Guide to Occupational Health and Safety Management Systems.*

BS EN 13000:2010 Standard Cranes - Mobile Cranes (updated to BS EN 13000:2010 A1:2014)

British Standard Institution (2010) *Cranes—Mobile cranes BS EN 13000:2010.*

BSI Standards Publication. *Drilling and foundation equipment–Safety,* BS EN 16228-1:2014.

IEC/ISO 31010. *Risk Management - Risk Assessment Techniques.*

ISO 4310 Cranes- Test Code and Procedure (2009)

ISO 4306-1, Cranes—Vocabulary—Part 1: General.

ISO 7363, Cranes and lifting appliances—Technical characteristics and acceptance documents.

ISO 11629, Cranes—Measurement of the mass of a crane and its components.

ISO 13202, Cranes—Measurement of velocity and time parameters.

ISO 14518, Cranes—Requirements for test loads.

IEC/ISO 31010 *Risk Management—Risk Assessment Techniques* (2009)

ISO 45001: *Occupational health and safety management systems – requirements with guidance for use* (2018-03)

LEGAL CASES

Speed v Thomas Swift and Company Limited [1943] 1 KB 557

Schwalb v Fass and Son (1946) 90 Sol Jo 394, 175 LT 345

Carr v Mercantile Produce Co. Ltd (1949) 2 KB 601 at 608

Edwards v National Coal Board [1949] 1 KB 704

Winter v Cardiff Rural District Council [1950] 1 All ER 819 (HL)

Pease v British India Steam Navigation Co. Ltd (1953) 1 Lloyd's Rep 207

Marshall v Gotham Co. Ltd [1954] AC 360 (HL)

HSE v Spindle Select Limited (*The Times Reports*, 9 December 1966)

Tesco v Nattrass [1972] AC 153

Tom Kee Engineering & Construction Company Limited v R (Criminal Appeal No. 2 of 1978)

AG v Lee Yu Kee Ltd (Criminal Appeal No. 325 of 1981)

AG v China Light & Power Co. Ltd (CA No. 1112/1981)

The Queen v Lo Hing Tang trading as Lo'S Engineering Company (Criminal Appeal No. 1395 of 1983)

Gammon (Hong Kong) Limited v AG [1983] HKLR 93

AG v John Lok & Partners & George Wimpey International Limited (HCMA 62/1985)/ 1986] HKLR 325

The Queen v Otis Elevator Company (H.K.) Limited (MA 931/1985)

AG v Harbour Engineering Company Limited (MA 1098/1985)

AG v Liu Ching-sun trading as Sun Lee Air Condition Co. (HCMA 438/1986)

AG v Marples International Limited (HCMA 803/1987)

AG v Cheung Kee Fung Cheung Construction Company Limited (HCMA 874/1989)

R v Good Days Industries Co. Ltd (HCMA 1429/1989)

The Queen v Associated Coatings Limited (MA 864/1990)

The Queen v Manfield Building Contractors Limited (HCMA 499/1991)

Queen v Boldwin Construction Company Limited (HCMA 56/1992)

Queen v Sime Darby Property Services Limited (HCMA 239/1993)

R v Tsui Wai Ping [1993] 2 HKC 675 (HCMA 575/1993)/[1993] 2 HKC 675

AG v Hsin Chong Construction (Asia) Limited (HCMA 708/1993)

R v Tai Fong Textile Finishing Work Limited (HCMA 264/1994)/[1994] 3 HKC 285

The Queen v Chung Chen-hsin (HCCC 397/1995)

The Queen v Hip Hing Construction Co. Ltd (HCMA 440/1995)

R v Kone Elevator (HK) Limited (HCMA 452/1995)

Queen v Ping On Foundation (Piling) Co. Limited (HCMA 879/1995)

The Queen v SOGEA/CAMPENON BERNARD SGE/FRANKI JOINT VENTURE (HCMA 890/1995)

The Queen v Kai Tai Construction Engineering Company Limited (HCMA 1123/1995)/[1996] 1 HKC 645

AG v Fong Chin-yue & Others [1995] 1 HKCLR 193

Ta Xuong v The Incorporated Owners of Sun Hing Building (HCPI 496/1995)

R v Nishimatsu Construction Company Limited (HCMA 1441/1996)

HKSAR v China State Construction Engineering Corporation (HCMA 347/1997)

HKSAR v Paul Y-ITC Construction Limited (HCMA 476/1997)/[1998] 2 HKLRD 35

Cheung Ping v Pak Kee Transportation Company Limited, & Another B+B (HCPI 963/1997)

HKSAR v Shun Shing Construction & Engineering Company (HCMA 322/1998)

HKSAR v Hanison Construction Company Limited (HCMA 687/1998)

HKSAR v Hip Hing Construction Company Limited (HCMA 858/1998)

HKSAR v Lau Ping Sun (HCMA 725/1999)

HKSAR v Chun Wo Building Construction Limited (HCMA 749/1999)

Leung Lai Yin v Yeung Kei Chi and others (HCPI 317/1999)

R v Nelson Group Services (Maintenance) Limited [1999] WLR 1526

HKSAR v Eastime Engineering Limited (HCMA 82/2000) [2000] HKCFI 798

HKSAR v Leighton Contractors (Asia) Limited (HCMA 1029/2000)

HKSAR v Kwan On Construction Company Limited (HCMA 1109/2000)

HKSAR v Hip Hing Construction Company Limited (HCMA 1253/2000)

HKSAR v Ken On Concrete Company Limited (HCMA 1304/2000)

HKSAR v China Merchants Container Services Limited (HCMA 597/2001)

HKSAR v Gold Ram Engineering & Development Limited (HCMA 912/2001)/[2002] 2 HKC 600

HKSAR v China Civil Engineering Construction Corporation (HCMA 1020/2001)

HKSAR v China State Construction Engineering Corporation (HCMA 1188/2001)

HKSAR v Hip Hing Construction Co. Ltd (HCMA 376/2002)

HKSAR v Hip Hing Construction Co. Ltd (HCMA 399/2002)

HKSAR v Ngo Kee Construction Co. Ltd (HCMA 404/2002)

HKSAR v Leighton-China State JV (HCMA 430/2002)

HKSAR v Hyundai Engineering Construction Co. Ltd (HCMA 815/2002)

HKSAR v China Civil Eng - Express Builders JV (HCMA 1212/2002)

HKSAR v Michael M. Nkasu (HCMA 479/2002) [2002] HKCFI 715

HKSAR v Chun Wo Construction and Engineering Co. Ltd and Others (HCMA 134/2003)

HKSAR v Paul Y-ITC General Contractors Limited (HCMA 347/2003)

香港特別行政區政府 *v* 中國土木工程集團公司 (HCMA 568/2003)

HKSAR v Kum Shing (K.F.) Construction Company Limited (HCMA 645/2003)

HKSAR v Teemway Engineering Limited (HCMA 1081/2003)

HKSAR v Dickson Construction Company Limited (HCMA 92/2004)

HKSAR v Takasago Thermal Engineering Company Limited (HCMA 398/2004)

HKSAR v Sunley Foundation Engineering Company Limited (HCMA 615/2004)

HKSAR v China Overseas Engineering Company Limited (HCMA 781/2004)/[2005] 2 HKLRD 771

HKSAR v Chong Kei Shue (莊紀樹) (HCMA 928/2004)

HKSAR v Chun Fai Construction Company Limited (HCMA 161/2005)

HKSAR v China Overseas Building Construction Limited (HCMA 434/2005)

HKSAR v Freight Transportation Co. Ltd (HCMA 914/2009)/[2014] 3 HKLRD 570

HKSAR v Chuen Kee Construction Company Limited (HCMA 986/2005)

HKSAR v Lee Fung Construction Company Limited (HCMA 1062/2005)

HKSAR v Fai Lung Exploitation Limited (HCMA 1189/2005)

HKSAR v Poon Wing Lam, Chee Cheung Hing & Co. Ltd (HCMA 520/2006)

HKSAR v Shun Tak Properties Limited (HCMA 1014/2006)/[2009] 3 HKLRD 299

HKSAR v Alliance Engineering Co. Ltd (HCMA 1154/2006)

HKSAR v Chun Wo Construction & Engineering Co. Ltd and Another (HCMA 1190/2006)/[2007] HKCLRT 711

HKSAR v Sun Kam Sing Stephen (HCMA 27/2007)

HKSAR v Paul Y Construction & Engineering Co. Ltd and Paul Y Plant Hire Co. Ltd (HCMA 161/2007)

HKSAR v Adrian Engineering Limited and Another (HCMA 561/2007)/[2007] HKCLRT 597

HKSAR v Southa Technical Limited (HCMA 566/2007)

HKSAR v Otis Elevators Company (H.K.) Limited (HCMA 154/2008)/[2008] 2 HKCLRT 73

HKSAR v Juh Wang Engineering Co. Ltd (築泓工程有限公司) (HCMA 625/2008)

R v Chargot Limited and others [2008] UKHL 73

HIN LIN YEE & LO SIU KUEN v HKSAR (FACC No. 7 of 2009)/[2010] 2 HKLRD 826/(2010) 13 HKCFAR 142

HKSAR v Sun Fook Kong Construction Limited and Worldstar Engineering Limited (HCMA 298/2009)

HKSAR v Woo Hing Holding Limited trading as Woo Hing Company (HCMA 590/2009)

HKSAR v Otis (Hong Kong) Co. Ltd (HCMA 1018/2009)
HKSAR v Kaden Construction Limited (HCMA 757/2010)
Tangerine Confectionary Limited & Veolia ES (UK) Limited v The Queen [2011] EWCA 2015
HKSAR v Aggressive Construction Company Limited (HCMA 190/2011)
HKSAR v Cheung Kee Fung Cheung Construction Company Limited (HCMA 600/2011)
Baker v Quantum Clothing Group Limited and Others [2011] UKSC 17/[2011] 1 WLR 1003
HKSAR v Paul Y General Contractors Limited & Lucky Engineering Company Limited (FACC Nos. 4 and 5 of 2012)/(2013) 16 HKCFAR 487
HKSAR v Yau Hop Scaffolding Engineering Company Limited (HCMA 219/2012)
HKSAR v Optimum Engineering Limited (HCMA 423/2012)
HKSAR v Cheung Kee Fung Cheung Company Limited and Another (HCMA 813/2012)
HKSAR v China Geo-Engineering Corporation (TWS 847-9/2012)
HKSAR v Freight Transportation Co. Ltd (HCMA 399/2013)
HKSAR v Goldenwall Engineering Limited (HCMA 731/2013)
HKSAR v VW-VES (HK) Limited & Others (HCMA 742/2013)/(FAMC 69/2014)/(2015) 18 HKCFAR 84
HKSAR v Skyfield Construction Limited (HCMA 747/2013)
香港特別行政區 *v* 中輝工程有限公司 [2013] CHKEC 327
HKSAR v Gammon Construction Limited (FACC No. 10 of 2014)
HKSAR v Dragages Hong Kong Limited (HCMA 238/2014)
HKSAR v Projexasia Limited (HCMA 345/2014)/[2015] 5 HKLRD 501
HKSAR v 增力服務有限公司 *(Tsang Lik Services Limited)* (HCMA 199/2015)
HKSAR v Leighton Contractors (Asia) Limited (HCMA 508/2015)
HKSAR v Hip Hing Construction Co. Ltd [2015] 2 HKLRD 831
香港特別行政區 *v* 何振威 [2016] CHKEC 315/(HCMA 634/2015)
HKSAR v Golden Field Glass Company Limited (HCMA 358/2016)
HKSAR v Modern Concrete Drill Cut Co. Ltd (HCMA 362/2016)/[2017] HKEC 676
HKSAR v Modern Terminals Limited (HCMA 680/2016)/[2018] HKCFI 1003
Lee Yam Kan v Ng Pui Kuen [2016] HKEC 611
HKSAR v Leighton Contractors (Asia) Ltd [2016] HKEC 781
香港特別行政區 *v* 祥記馮祥建築有限公司 [2017] CHKEC 37
HKSAR v Kwan On Construction Company Limited (HCMA 11/2017)/[2018] HKCFI 1640/[2019] HKCFI 474
HKSAR v Hong Dau Construction Company Limited and Two Others (HCMA 186/2017)/[2018] HKCFI 1462

HKSAR v Union Contractors Limited (HCMA 227/2017)

HKSAR v K H Foundations Limited (HCMA 243/2017)

Secretary for Justice v Hong Dau Construction Co. Ltd & Another (HCMA 499/2017)

HKSAR v Gammon Construction Ltd [2017] 1 HKLRD 1291

HKSAR v FEWA Chinat Construction Limited (HCMA 439/2018)/[2019] HKCFI 1736

Secretary for Justice v Hong Dau Construction Company Limited (FAMC No. 7 of 2019)

Secretary for Justice v Expand Scaffolding Limited (FAMC No. 8 of 2019)

Baiada Poultry Pty Ltd v The Queen HCA 14 (High Court of Australia)

Summonses nos. FLS 7993/2012 and KCS 10929/2013 in magistracy courts

AUTHOR COMMUNICATION

The following people have communicated with the author at various times over his career regarding construction safety and specific concepts outlined in this book.

C.W. Chan (2008–2020)

Mandy S.W. Chan (2018)

S.Y. Chan (Former Occupational Health Consultant of the Labour Department, 2016)

W.K. Chan, Winky (Former Superintendent of Factory Inspectors of the Labour Department, 1992–1993 and 2000–2003)

T.P. Choy (Former Divisional Occupational Safety Officer of the Labour Department, 2018)

J.K. Ho (Former Divisional Occupational Safety Officer of the Labour Department, 2016).

Henry T. Lam (2008–2009)

C.Y. Law, (Liebherr (HKG) Limited, 2016–2019)

K.B. Lee (Singapore, 2017–2019)

Michael C.M. Leung (Past President of the Hong Kong Society of Registered Safety Officers, 2016–2019)

L.M. Leung (Former Senior Divisional Occupational Safety Officer of the Labour Department, 2016–2019)

Kelvin K.M. Lo (LLB, Solicitor HKSAR, 2018–2019)

Johnny Shing (Past President of Society of Registered Safety Officers, 2016)

So Yu-shing, Francis (Managing Director of Wui Loong Scaffolding Works Limited, 2016–2019)

Tang Siu-lam (Former Professor of Civil Engineering, Polytechnic University of Hong Kong, 2016)

About the Author

Mr LEE Hung-kwong (李鴻光) was educated at Loughborough University in the United Kingdom (B.Sc. Hon), The University of Hong Kong (M.Sc. Eng.), and Aston-in-Birmingham University in the United Kingdom (P-Cert). He served as a Factory Inspector in the Labour Department of the Hong Kong Government; a Chief Health, Safety, and Environment Adviser for Shell Companies in North East Asia; and an Assessor for Lloyds Register. He is now the managing director of HK Lee & Associates Limited. Mr LEE was the founding president of the Hong Kong Society of Registered Safety Officers. The society was formed in 1991.

He is a part-time lecturer at the Hong Kong Institute of Construction (formerly known as the Construction Industry Training Authority). He has lectured on safety and health at work subjects since 1985 and was an adjunct associate professor at the University of Hong Kong in the Department of Real Estate and Construction. He is also the author of *Safety Management—Hong Kong Experience* (1991) and *Construction Safety in Hong Kong* (1996), as well as various other articles and papers, the citations of which can be found in the references section of this book. This is his third book on construction safety.

FSC
www.fsc.org
MIX
Papier | Fördert gute Waldnutzung
FSC® C083411

Kolibri 360 GmbH
Ferdinand-Jühlke-Straße 7
99095 Erfurt, Deutschland
produktsicherheit@kolibri360.de